Social History of Canada

H.V. Nelles, general editor

Witness against War
Pacifism in Canada, 1900–1945

Rallying today to the call for nuclear disarmament, the peace movement in Canada is strong and growing. But it is by no means new.
In this study of pacifism during the first half of the twentieth century,
Thomas Socknat explores a critical chapter in the Canadian peace
movement's history. Canada's pacifist heritage, he argues, is rooted
in two distinct but complementary traditions, the historic non-
resistance of religious sects such as the Mennonites and the liberal
Protestant and humanitarian tradition associated with the social
reform movement.

The First World War radicalized pacifists, and the interwar era saw
a resurgent peace movement shaped by a socially radical pacifism.
During the Depression a pacifist-socialist alliance appeared to be in
the vanguard of Canadian social action. But by the mid-thirties, pacifists found their pursuit of social justice in direct conflict with their
commitment to non-violence. As social radicals began to abandon
pacifism for the fight against fascism, the Canadian peace movement
was severely weakened. Nevertheless, during the Second World War
sectarian and non-sectarian pacifists joined in the defence of civil
liberties and the individual conscience.

Socknat concludes that Canadian pacifists were a small but forceful
minority who exercised a dual function in Canada: prophecy of an
ideal of peace and reconciliation of social tensions. Above all, in its
uncompromising emphasis on questions of conscience, the pacifist
witness against war helped preserve those moral principles underlying Canadian culture and laid a solid foundation for the politicized
peace movement of the nuclear era.

THOMAS P. SOCKNAT teaches history at the University of Toronto.

THOMAS P. SOCKNAT

Witness against War

PACIFISM IN CANADA, 1900–1945

UNIVERSITY OF TORONTO PRESS
Toronto   Buffalo   London

© University of Toronto Press 1987
Toronto   Buffalo   London
Printed in Canada

ISBN 0-8020-5704-7 (cloth)
ISBN 0-8020-6632-1 (paper)

JX
1961
C3
S62
1987

Socknat, Thomas
Paul.

Witness against war

59,439

Canadian Cataloguing in Publication Data

Socknat, Thomas Paul
    Witness against war
    (The Social history of Canada, ISSN 0085-6007;
    40) Includes bibliographical references and index.
    ISBN 0-8020-5704-7 (bound) ISBN 0-8020-6632-1 (pbk.)
    1. Peace – History – 20th century.   2. Pacificsm –
    History – 20th century.   I. Title.   II. Series.
    JX1961.C3S62 1987   327.1'72   C87-093090-7

Social History of Canada 40

PICTURE CREDITS

Archives of the United Church of Canada: A.C. Courtice, W.B. Creighton, R. Roberts, J.L. Smith, J. Finlay, Carlton Street Church; Courtesy of Albert Dorland: A.G. Dorland; Manitoba Archives: F. Dixon, W. Ivens, V. Thomas, F.M. Beynon; Courtesy of Sydney Mary Barnett: R.E. Fairbairn; Public Archives of Canada: A. Macphail (C21557), the Woodsworths (C57368), Conscientious objectors in camp (RG 27, vol. 137, File 601-3-12, vol. 1 – C129020), Alternative service workers in Jasper (RG 84, vol. III, File V165-2 vol. 3), Canadian Peace Congress meeting 1950 (PA93777); Provincial Archives of British Columbia: L. Jamieson (A-8543); Toronto Jewish Congress/Canada Jewish Congress, Ontario Region Archives: M. Eisendrath; Courtesy of Kay Morris: WIL group photo 1931; Courtesy of Virginia MacLeod: A.A. MacLeod; Trinity College Archives: G. Grube; City of Toronto Archives, Globe and Mail Collection: WIL march 1935 (38447), Peace vigil 1935 (38445), WIL protest march 1938 (53041), Torchlight parade 1938 (53040); Courtesy of Carlyle King: C. King; Courtesy of Ken Muma: F. Haslam; Courtesy of Fritz Hertzberg: Friends Meeting House; Courtesy of George Wright: Friends Ambulance Unit in China

FOR CARMEN

Contents

Preface

Public pressure for world peace and disarmament has become a major social movement of the late twentieth century. To a large extent its attraction of mass popular support as an anti-nuclear campaign is a fairly recent phenomenon, but as an expression of pacifism and the rejection of violence and war it is only the latest stage in a long historical development. That evolution of the pacifist tradition in Canada during the first half of the century, those optimistic years before the frightening onset of the nuclear era, is the focus of this book.

Some readers will wish that this study extended beyond the dawn of the atomic age in 1945. It ends there, however, for a good reason. The new threat of mass nuclear destruction completely changed the tenor and tone of pacifism, resulting in a much more radical, politicized peace movement. Of necessity, therefore, the anti-nuclear phase requires a separate volume.

This book began as a PHD dissertation in the department of history of McMaster University under the direction of Richard Allen. Since then it has undergone several revisions, but its general contours have remained the same. Research for the study has spanned more than a decade, from 1975 to the present, and is based upon documentary sources scattered across the country and personal interviews. I am grateful to all those individuals who welcomed me into their homes to share their memories and to the archivists and librarians of the various institutions cited who made my research tasks easier.

Financial assistance for the final preparation of the manuscript came from the Queen's University Advisory Research Council and the Humanities and Social Sciences Committee of the University of Toronto Research Board.

This book has been published with the help of a grant from the Social Science Federation of Canada, using funds provided by the Social Sciences and Humanities Research Council of Canada, and a grant from the Andrew W. Mellon Foundation to the University of Toronto Press.

Like most historians who have prepared a manuscript for publication, I am indebted to numerous individuals. My friends and colleagues at Concordia University, Queen's University, and the University of Toronto have lent much support and encouragement over the last few years. Sylvia Van Kirk, in particular, offered important, sensitive suggestions as well as enthusiastic encouragement. My editor at the University of Toronto Press, Gerald Hallowell, and the editor of the social history series, H.V. Nelles, never wavered in their support of the project. They and Kathy Johnson, my copy-editor, made constructive criticisms and recommendations. The manuscript benefited from the suggestions of all readers, and as changes were incorporated the revised manuscript was typed and retyped with speed and accuracy by Karen Donnelly.

The above acknowledgments notwithstanding, I am most thankful for the help, understanding, and constant encouragement of my wife Carmen. As friend, critic, indexer, and proof-reader, she has earned the dedication of this book.

Andrew Cory Courtice

Arthur G. Dorland

Fred Dixon

William Ivens

Vernon Thomas

Francis Marion Beynon

W.B. Creighton

R. Edis Fairbairn

Agnes Macphail

Laura Jamieson

J.S. and Lucy Woodsworth

Richard Roberts   Maurice Eisendrath

Members of the Women's International League for Peace and Freedom attending the summer school held in Toronto, 29 May to 1 June 1931. Front and centre is Jane Addams (arrow), honorary president of the international section; on her left is Agnes Macphail, honorary president of the Canadian sec-

A.A. MacLeod

George Grube

tion; on Addams's right is Lucy Woodsworth, secretary-treasurer of the Canadian section, and Anna Sissons, president of the Toronto chapter. Directly behind Addams is Alice Loeb.

Toronto peace march to the cenotaph organized by the Women's International League for Peace and Freedom, Armistice Day 1935

Armistice Day peace vigil organized by the Women's International League for Peace and Freedom, Toronto, 1935. Maud Robinson, planning co-ordinator, with megaphone. Anna Sissons, national president, standing next to floral wreath with dove on bed of palms and oak leaves. The inscription reads: 'To the brave of all lands who died believing their sacrifice would save the world from war. Only co-operation, truth and love can insure lasting peace.'

Protest march staged by the Women's International League for Peace and Freedom, Toronto, 1938

Torchlight parade organized by the Canadian League for Peace and Democracy, Toronto, 1938

Carlyle King

J. Lavell Smith

James Finlay

Fred Haslam

Carlton Street United Church, Toronto

Conscientious objectors in alternative service work camp Hill 60 (c-1) in British Columbia

Society of Friends Meeting House on Maitland Street, Toronto

Canadian medical supplies for the Friends Ambulance Unit
arrive in Chengtu, China

Alternative service workers improving road in Jasper National Park

James Endicott addressing founding conference of the Canadian Peace Congress, Bathurst Street United Church, Toronto, 1950. The dawn of a new era.

WITNESS AGAINST WAR

Introduction

This book is a study of the manifestation of pacifism in Canada within the context of the Canadian reaction to war and social change during the first half of the twentieth century. It does not attempt to analyse the larger philosophical aspects of pacifism or to develop specific biographical studies of individual pacifists. It proposes only to trace the changing role of the pacifist idea in Canada in the recent past. In the course of the book, numerous individuals, groups, and organizations come to the fore, but their true significance lies in their interaction – the composite picture – and in their collective and distinctive contribution to the Canadian response to the social violence and wars of this century. By necessity, therefore, rather than adopting a narrow theoretical or analytical framework, I undertook to write a broad, inclusive study in the hope of laying the groundwork for an important new dimension of Canadian social history.

I

Most historians are agreed that pacifism is basically a Christian phenomenon with roots in the early Church. War has always been an inescapable social reality and ethical problem for Christians, causing pacifists and anti-pacifists alike to search the New Testament for support. The most relevant passages are the Sermon on the Mount (Matt. 5:38–48) and the Beatitudes (Matt. 5:5–9), but C.J. Cadoux, probably the leading scholar on the early Christian attitude to war, has emphasized that the pacifism of Jesus is expressed more in the spirit of his teachings than in his words.[1]

Pacifists have formed a minority in the Church since about the fourth century, although the early Christians universally had been pacifists for almost two centuries.[2] Early Christian pacifism was expressed by a withdrawal from both political and military affairs. The Church's pacifist period terminated with the accession of Constantine and the appearance of the theory of the 'just war' as formulated by St Ambrose and amplified by St Augustine. According to this doctrine, the Church approved of war as long as the end was just and the intention the restoration of peace.[3] In time, this conception of 'just war', combined with the Church's promoting of peace, was joined by the idea of the Crusades, a holy war in which the Church actually promoted war for religious ends. Medieval reactions to the Crusades appeared in the pacifism of Anabaptism during the radical reformation and in the humanist pacifism of Thomas More and Erasmus.

Christian pacifism, therefore, survived primarily among the sectarian pacifist enclaves scattered across Europe and later North America, while generally disappearing from the mainstream of Christian society. Although these peace sects promoted a conservative, withdrawn, quiet lifestyle, they offered at times what seemed a radical challenge to the established order. The subsequent growth of liberal rationalism, however, also promoted the idea of humanitarian pacifism and war-prevention, primarily through organized peace societies, and by the late nineteenth century the liberal ideals of peace and progress merged with the optimistic faith of evangelical Christianity in the liberal peace movement. Both traditions, the sectarian and the liberal, found expression in Canada.

As a phenomenon of the twentieth century, pacifist resistance to war has been largely confined to the English-speaking world. Its dimensions coincided with a North Atlantic culture based upon a similar religious, philosophical, and political heritage. Both the non-conformist conscience and a radical political individualism were common in the Anglo-American past but absent in most of Europe.[4] Great Britain, the United States, and Canada became important outposts in the struggle of the individual conscience against war and violence. It is no surprise, therefore, that most historical literature on the topic has concerned pacifist movements in Britain and the United States. Some of this work resembles hagiography more than historiography, since it was written by committed pacifists intent on expressing their particular faith or canonizing their own heroes. But there are also sound scholarly studies. For the most part, British scholars have tended to concentrate on the First World War and interwar periods, while the American pacifist experience has been more evenly explored.[5] Indeed, bursts of American scholarship appear to be related to periods of actual u.s. involvement in war.[6] In any case, historians generally agree that the peace movements in both Britain and the United States became linked with social radicalism and faced a serious internal crisis as pacifists confronted the reality of fascist aggression in the mid-1930s. That is the opinion, for instance, of Peter Brock, probably the most important historian of pacifism in Europe and the United States, and one mentioned often in the course of this book.

In contrast to British and American historiography, the historical study of Canadian pacifism has been largely ignored. Although some historians, such as Ramsay Cook and James Eayrs, have shown an appreciation of the pacifist phenomenon, most of those in the mainstream of Canadian historiography have made no more than passing references to pacifists in Canada.[7] This is so partly because the pacifist movement was not large, and partly because historians in both the liberal nationalist and Laurentian traditions, and certain social historians as well, were committed to more political, collective solutions to international disputes and finally to war itself as the least of evils. As Arthur Lower and Donald Creighton have demonstrated, these historians were not unaware of the pacifist tradition in Canada's past, although pacifists, like women and native peoples, were seen as largely irrelevant in the flow of history.

By the end of his career, however, even Creighton appears to have recognized the importance of pacifism during the interwar years, a time of bitter disillusionment in which a number of Canadians rejected the idea of war. 'It was a long drawn-out and painful experience,' he wrote, 'which ensured that English Canadian churchmen would look at the Second World War in a fashion very different from that in which they viewed the First.'[8] Still, Creighton failed to explore the depth of those feelings, and neither he nor other historians examined pacifism as an intellectual force in society. The continuing experience of war and the questionable state of international order, however, gives significance once more to the pacifist ideal and its role in the preservation of the moral basis of Canada's cultural identity, which includes the right of dissent, the right to freedom of conscience, respect for the non-violent resolution of conflict, and a commitment to achieving racial and religious harmony, gender equality, and social and economic justice for all.

Despite the limitations of Canadian historiography, important observations have been made concerning pacifism in Canada. Some of the best sources are the various monographs on specific pacifist groups, such as Frank Epp's two-volume history of Canadian Mennonites and

M. James Penton's *Jehovah's Witnesses in Canada*.[9] Still another view of pacifism can be found in church histories, such as the well-known theses by E.A. Christie and M.V. Royce, which contrast the Presbyterian and Methodist attitudes to war, J.M. Bliss's article 'The Methodist Church and World War I,' and David Marshall's recent revisionist work on that same topic.[10] The relationship between liberal pacifists and internationalists is explored in the thesis by Donald Page in 'Canadians and the League of Nations before the Manchurian Crisis.' Although Page tends to view the peace movement from the perspective of the internationalists, he provides a good introduction to the Canadian peace movement, particularly on the prairies. More recently, Joan Sangster has examined the relationship between pacifism and feminism in her study of women in the Canadian left.[11]

The most important basis for the further study of Canadian pacifism, however, was laid by Richard Allen in *The Social Passion*.[12] Allen claims that the resurgence of pacifism in the 1920s sublimated the crisis of social gospel reform and actually inhibited the development of a more profound Christian ethic of war or of peace, thereby leaving the whole question unresolved for a later generation. In contrast to this evasion of social reality, Allen argues, some social gospellers had already begun to reflect an international realism that ultimately helped give birth to a new radical Christianity in the following decade.

Roger Hutchinson examined some of these radical Christians in his study of the Fellowship for a Christian Social Order.[13] In his view, those radical Christians were realistic in their clear vision of the world as it was, and yet were idealistic in their determination to improve the social order. The same could be said of most socially radical pacifists in the 1930s. Hutchinson recognizes pacifism as an important part of social thought in the Fellowship for a Christian Social Order, but he does not adequately analyse that pacifism. He fails to subject the Fellowship's pacifism to the same scrutiny as its social radicalism. Likewise, Michiel Horn emphasizes the mixture of pacifism and socialism in the League for Social Reconstruction, but he largely ignores the concomitant role of LSR radicals in the peace movement and too easily identifies pacifism with isolationism. This mixture of pacifism and socialism is also recognized by Kenneth McNaught in his biography of J.S. Woodsworth,[14] but in the end McNaught tends to stress the socialist influence at the expense of the Christian basis of Woodsworth's pacifism.

The pacifist if not the socialist ethic of many social radicals was rooted in Christianity, but, as Thomas Sinclair-Faulkner argues in his study of the response of Canada's churches to the Second World War, the churches themselves had no trouble supporting the war because, despite pressure from a vocal pacifist minority, they had never endorsed outright pacifism.[15] Faulkner, however, fails to examine the pacifist churchmen in conjunction with the wider interwar peace movement. Neither does he adequately explain the fate of United Church pacifists after 1939. In fact, his claim that United Church pacifists ceased to act as a pacifist front after 1939 is a gross overstatement, if not entirely misleading. Nevertheless, Faulkner, as well as Allen, Hutchinson, Horn, and a few others, has begun the process of examining pacifism in the context of Canadian social history, which this study develops further.

II

This book begins with a discussion of the two distinct but complementary traditions that formed the basis of pacifism in Canada: the historic, absolute non-resistance and non-participation in the worldly state which Peter Brock has called 'separational pacifism,' characteristic of sectarian pacifist groups such as the Mennonites and Hutterites, and the liberal pacifism or 'integrational pacifism' associated first with the Quakers, later with the Protestant social gospel and the progressive reform movement, and ultimately with social radicalism.[16]

Pacifists in both traditions underwent a far-reaching transition and adjustment to social reality during the first half of the twentieth century. Two world wars, the social and economic upheaval of the depression years, and the popularization of socialism and the fear of fascism and communism all left their mark on the entire Canadian community, including pacifists. Even the meaning of the word 'pacifism' changed accordingly.

Since its initial appearance shortly before the Great War, 'pacifism' has often referred both to the belief that war is absolutely and always wrong and to the belief that war, though sometimes necessary, is always inhumane and irrational and should be prevented. The former belief was held mainly by the sectarians; the latter was representative of the liberal-progressive pacifists at the turn of the century who still reflected Victorian social attitudes – forcefulness of character, a militaristic patriotism, and hero worship. Their advocacy of international harmony as the route to peace was quite different from pacifist non-resistance or opposition to all wars. The subsequent growth of violence, death, and destruction between and within nations, however, gave birth to a specific twentieth-century pacifism defined by Brock as an ideology of 'personal non-participation in wars ... or in violent revolution with an endeavor to find non-violent means of resolving conflict.'[17] In effect, pacifism was adjusting to the challenges of a new age of mass international warfare and social revolution.

As a result of this etymological evolution, the exact meaning of pacifism in the twentieth century has often been vague. In terms of contemporary historical usage the definition of 'pacifist' usually narrowed during times of war to mean only those opposed to all wars; during times of peace it broadened again to include all those who worked on behalf of peace and therefore viewed pacifism as an instrumental value. In this book the term is often used in its broadest sense to reflect its common usage and meaning in Canada's past. Distinctions are drawn, however, between sectarian pacifism and the expressions of pacifism in the liberal tradition: first, that of the liberal-progressive reformers at the turn of the century who advocated international arbitration as the rational solution to international conflicts; second, that of the liberal internationalists of the interwar era who, while displaying a new awareness of the social and economic roots of war, reaffirmed their faith in the perfectability of man and the possibility of world peace through support for the League of Nations and disarmament, but stopped short of endorsing total pacifism; and third, that of the post-war breed of socially radical pacifists who blended liberal pacifist ideals with the socialist attack on the economic and political superstructure, thereby demanding both peace and radical social change. Since pacifist as well as social thought was in a state of transition, and since individual adherents held varying degrees of pacifist sympathies, differences between liberal internationalists and pacifists proper were often blurred, with the result that it is difficult, and historically somewhat inaccurate, to separate completely those two strands of the Canadian peace movement.

For the most part, the sectarian pacifists remained the constant factor in the survival of the pacifist idea in Canada, particularly in times of war, and their communal societies served as models for Canadians seeking new methods of social organization. Because they attempted to remain withdrawn from society, and hence from the larger peace movement, the peace sects were probably less noticeably affected by world events. Nevertheless, their experience during the two world wars ultimately resulted in a degree of accommodation with the state and a tendency towards assimilation into society.

Therefore, while this study does not minimize the role of sectarian groups, it focuses upon the radicalization of liberal pacifist thought and in doing so centres attention on the largely Protestant anglophone leadership. The anti-conscription movement in Quebec during both world wars does not figure prominently because it was neither pacifist in nature nor part of the peace movement; the Roman Catholic Church in Canada, both French and English, steered clear of the pacifist issue, and few Canadian Catholics were committed pacifists before 1945. There was, however, a small but important element of Jewish support for the peace movement, especially during the 1930s.

Regardless of their religious backgrounds, however, the majority of Canada's 'integrational' liberal pacifists underwent a leftward political transition in the course of their search for peace. As they examined the social and economic roots of war during and after the Great War, committed pacifists abandoned liberal reformism for a socially radical outlook. The merger of the pacifist means of non-violence and the radical ends of social justice into one broad movement, however, also posed a dilemma. In contrast to traditional non-resistance, socially radical pacifists increasingly sanctioned forms of social coercion, such as strikes, which threatened to compromise their pacifist rejection of the use of force. Sectarian pacifists had recognized the danger, and it was one of the reasons they avoided all contact with the peace movement. The crisis finally came to a head during the late 1930s when, under the pressure of increasing international tensions, liberals and social radicals rallied to the armed defence of Western democracies, thereby abandoning the pacifist idea. Their defection left the peace movement much weakened and resulted in the gradual retreat of committed pacifists behind the confines of a strictly Christian ideal not entirely unlike that of their sectarian brothers.

Although socially radical pacifists were forced by renewed warfare to shed their utopian vision and offer their pacifist witness in the context of the world as they found it, they did not entirely abandon a radical social criticism or cease to labour for social change. They attempted to combine a pacifist witness with a meaningful confrontation with social reality, and in doing so they too experienced a measure of accommodation with the state and were assimilated into the nation's war effort. Nonetheless, the assimilation was substantially on their own terms, and the war and post-war years found them opposing the state in a notable campaign in defence of civil liberties.

The end of the Second World War also signalled the beginning of the nuclear dilemma and a new stage in the history of twentieth-century pacifism. Before 1945 pacifists believed they would achieve world peace by means of the continued perfection of society through the spread of social and economic justice. After Hiroshima, however, that optimistic faith in the unfolding of human history was replaced by a sense of urgency that altered completely the character of pacifism and moved pacifists from the individual witness to the mass protest. This book ends at that critical point of change.

In a larger sense this study reveals that pacifism had become an important element in Canadian social activism and social criticism. The peace movement encompassed a broad campaign for disarmament, international harmony, and social and economic reorganization. Furthermore, pacifists were not typical men and women. As a prophetic minority, they were influential beyond their numbers. Canadian pacifists, for instance, exercised leading roles in the development of radical Christian social ethics, in the building of a social-democratic political alternative, and in the struggle for economic justice and civil liberties. Above all, pacifists lobbied against all types of militarism in Canadian society from conscription and cadet training in the schools to armament increases and nuclear weaponry. During the interwar years pacifists tried to create an anti-war public; but while they succeeded in broadening the public to which they appealed, they failed to increase substantially the number of adherents of pacifism. Thus, as in the case of most social movements, their efforts did not always yield the desired results, but in the end the peace movement and the pacifist witness of sectarian groups had important consequences for the changing nature of Canadian society. By mid-century much of their opposition to social violence had been absorbed by the wider community, and the foundation had been laid for the highly politicized peace movement of the nuclear era.

1

Early pacifist traditions in Canada

The historical roots of pacifism in Canada can be traced to its nineteenth-century manifestation within the two distinct but complementary traditions of radical religious dissent and liberal reform. The gradual immigration into Canada of pacifist religious groups strengthened the principle of passive non-resistance in Canadian society, thereby laying a firm foundation for broader pacifist activity. Although the non-conformism of peace sects ensured that they occupied a marginal position on the fringes of Canadian society, the simultaneous growth of the progressive peace movement in the established liberal reform tradition popularized the cause of world peace and order. The liberal peace advocates were broadly labelled pacifists, but not because they all adhered to genuinely pacifist, non-violent principles; most simply favoured arbitration and the peaceful, rational settlement of international disputes, while others viewed pacifism in an instrumental way. Nevertheless, whether held as a normative or an instrumental value, early Canadian pacifism was based primarily upon a Christian heritage reflecting the combined influences of the radical reformation and liberal Protestantism, and, until the First World War, was closely related to the activities of various Christian communities and small liberal peace organizations.

I

By far the largest element in the Canadian pacifist tradition has been the sectarian pacifism of the Anabaptists, the Society of Friends, and some other more recent Christian sects. The Anabaptists belonged to the radical wing of the reformation, since they rejected the ethic of the Old Testament as having been superseded by that of Christ. The Anabaptist belief in the complete separation of church and state and the condemnation of war and killing as contrary to Christ's ethic of love and respect for human life were exemplified in their pacifistic lifestyle. One group of Anabaptists in Moravia organized their communities along communistic economic lines under the leadership of Jacob Hutter, and thereafter became known as Hutterites; this group espoused adult baptism and non-violence.[1] Another wing came under the influence of Menno Simmons, who emphasized passivity and non-resistance as a basic tenet of faith. 'The regenerated do not go to war,' wrote Simmons, 'nor engage in strife. They are the children of peace who have beaten their swords into plowshares and their spears into pruning hooks, and know of no war.' His followers became known as Mennonites, and, together with Hutterites, they began to challenge accepted religious, social, and political norms.

From the very outset, therefore, the pacifist sects represented a radical revolutionary threat of unknown potential. Once the authorities reacted, large-scale persecution of Anabaptists occurred.[2] Consequently, they began their search for a new home, a place where they could live according to their consciences – a search that ultimately brought them to Canada.

It has been argued that Anabaptism was the parent of Quakerism.[3] Certainly, Quaker beliefs resembled the Anabaptist protest against the un-Christian state, but whereas sects like the Mennonites were, in Peter Brock's words, 'separational pacifists' who urged withdrawal from the world, Quakers were 'integrational pacifists' who sought to transform the world. They were part of the large non-conformist tradition in the seventeenth century. Founded by George Fox in the early 1650s, the Society of Friends based their spiritual life on a belief in the presence of the 'Inner Light' of Christ in all people. They were also apocalyptically minded, and supported Cromwell's war as a sign of the coming of the Kingdom. The persecution of Friends under the Commonwealth shattered their millenarian hopes, however, and after their early hesitation Quakers concluded that war and violence were against their beliefs and incorporated non-resistance into their basic creed.[4]

Through the centuries that followed, Mennonites and Quakers remained true to their pacifist beliefs, although individual Mennonites in Holland and Germany abandoned the principle of non-resistance as they integrated into society. But in Switzerland and Russia, and later in North America, 'separational' sects such as the Mennonites remained withdrawn from contemporary society and faithful to the doctrine of non-resistance. The 'integrational' Quakers, on the other hand, regarded politics as compatible with the pacifist stance. But they largely maintained a quietistic mood until the nineteenth century, when, under evangelical influences, Quaker pacifism became 'an outreaching creed and sought to find expression in both domestic politics and international relations.'[5]

Both these groups entered Canada as early as the eighteenth century, and their pacifist beliefs were officially recognized in militia acts and immigration guarantees. Although some Mennonites had settled in the Maritimes by mid-century, the first significant migration of pacifist sects coincided with the coming of the United Empire Loyalists during and after the American Revolution. While their doctrine of non-resistance forbade participation in British wars or political revolution, many felt a certain loyalty to the British, who had given official recognition to their religious freedom. The Militia Bill of 1757, for instance, had exempted Quakers, Mennonites, and Moravians from the bearing of arms. Upper Canada's adoption of English provisions respecting non-conformity and religious dissent, as well as the availability of land, attracted pacifists from the United States.[6] The emigrating sects included the Pennsylvania-centred Quakers, Mennonites, Dunkards (German Baptists), and Tunkers (later known as Brethren in Christ), a revivalistic group partly of Mennonite origin.

The principles of the radical pacifist Christian conscience and military exemption recognized in British legal precedents were extended to Canada with the migration of these sects. Upper Canada's first lieutenant-governor, John Graves Simcoe, personally invited Mennonites, Quakers, and Tunkers to settle in Upper Canada with the promise of the customary exemptions from militia duties. This promise was officially recognized by the first Parliament of Upper Canada in the Militia Act of 1793, which provided for exemption of Quakers, Mennonites, or Tunkers on condition of the payment of annual fines: 'the sum of 20 shillings per annum in time of peace, and five pounds per annum in time of actual invasion or insurrection.'[7]

The pacifist sects, however, were dissatisfied with the thought of paying fines. The Mennonites objected more on financial than moral grounds, but usually paid the levy as they had in Pennsylvania and Prussia. The Quakers usually refused to pay the fines, reasoning that the proceeds would go to support the militia. Those who did pay the fines were disciplined by their brethren as if they had joined the militia. The Quaker non-compliance resulted in some retaliatory incidents, such as the confiscation of a thousand dollars' worth of goods from the Yonge Street Monthly Meeting in 1810 and the jailing of eight members for one month.[8]

There followed what Frank Epp has called 'one of the most active lobbies in the half-century of Upper Canada' on behalf of Quakers and Mennonites to change the law.[9] This movement was briefly interrupted by the war of 1812–14, which saw the impressment of pacifists' horses and carriages. The Mennonites agreed to render material assistance, with 'extreme reluctance,' while the Quakers remained adamant and accepted additional fines and imprisonment rather than assist the military. Actually to enrol in the militia was a serious offence for a Friend, and could result in his being disowned by the meeting, as happened in the 1813 case of Peter Hunter, a Quaker who participated in military training in order to save his fine.[10] Following the war, the pacifist groups again petitioned the government until a new militia law passed under a reform administration in 1849 removed the principle of fining.

Another effect of the war in 1812 was a schism within the Society of Friends in Canada. The separation occurred when David Willson, a member of the Queen Street group of Friends near York, led a protest against the quietism that appeared to prevent Quakers from converting society to their ideal of brotherhood and peace. Willson believed Friends were too negative in their attitudes and 'too much passively aloof from the affairs of the world to have any real influence upon it.'[11] Instead, he proposed a broad, inclusive faith combining Quaker mysticism and Jewish ceremonialism.

Although Willson was disowned by the Yonge Street Meeting for abandoning traditional Quaker thought, he successfully attracted the majority of Queen Street Friends to his side. The new sect, known as the Children of Peace or 'Davidites,' congregated in the district around Sharon where they built a grand temple, a lofty wooden structure in imitation of Solomon's Temple, as a monument to their vision of society. Music was incorporated into their worship service, and the white-robed Children of Peace and their silver band often carried their message of brotherhood and peace directly to the citizens of York. Utopian in nature, the Children of Peace had little lasting influence upon the wider Canadian community. Following Willson's death in 1866, their numbers gradually declined, and by the late nineteeth century they ceased to have any organized existence. None the less, the Children of Peace were an early example of the eventual movement of Quakers to a more active role in the pursuit of peace and social justice.

A tradition of Christian pacifism, therefore, was firmly rooted in the early settlement of British North America, and its practical protection through military exemption was reconfirmed in the first military service act of the new Canadian confederation in 1868. The act provided for the exemption of Quakers, Mennonites, Tunkers, and persons of any religious denomination if their religious doctrine forbade the bearing of arms and personal military service.[12] With this important step Canada officially recognized the principle of religious pacifist dissent and military exemption characteristic of British law, and continued to make similar legal provisions for newly immigrating groups in the late-nineteenth century through a series of orders in council.

In 1793, at the time when the first Mennonites migrated to Canada from the United States, European Mennonites were moving into Russia. Nearly a century later, when the tsar began to withdraw the *privilegium* protecting Mennonite rights, a mass migration to North America resulted. The majority of these Russian Mennonites chose the United States as their new home, probably because of the prospect of better land. Those who chose Canada held their German culture and conscientious non-resistance to be of paramount importance. Only after a Mennonite delegation visited Canada in 1873 and received a Canadian version of the *privilegium*, including an order in council containing an entire exemption from military service, was the Mennonite exodus ensured.

The order of 1873 was the first of the special orders in council based on the earlier statutes exempting Quakers, Mennonites, and Tunkers. There followed an order in council in 1898 granting exemption to Doukhobors and one in 1899 exempting Hutterites, the two other pacifist groups immigrating into western Canada. In addition to their pacifism, all three groups shared a common Russian background and a type of communal organization. Thus, by the beginning of the twentieth century the old 'pacifist trinity' of eastern Canada – Quakers, Tunkers and Mennonites – was joined by a strange new grouping of Mennonites, Doukhobors, and Hutterites in western Canada. The non-conformist pacifist traditions of all were protected by Canadian law.[13]

In the 1870s the Hutterites had emigrated from Russia to the Dakotas, but by 1898, with the threat of the Spanish-American War, they looked northward to Manitoba. The Canadian government, eager to encourage settlement of the West, granted them permission to establish their communal colonies and exempted them from military service.[14] In 1899 a Hutterite colony was established on the Rosean River east of Dominion City, Manitoba, but, after only a five-year stay, the members of the colony returned to South Dakota. They had suffered hardships in their settling of the land, including flood damage, and in the meantime the Spanish-American war had ended. Although it was not until 1918 that large numbers of American Hutterites, fleeing from the threats of another war, migrated to western Canada, the legal precedent recognizing both their pacifism and the communal ownership of property had already been set.[15]

By far the most contentious of the new immigrant pacifist groups to arrive in Canada were the Doukhobors. Because of the persecutions of tsarist Russia, influential supporters, from Leo Tolstoy to British Quakers, encouraged the exodus of these Russian peasants to a new homeland in Canada. The Doukhobors injected a host of unorthodox social, political, and religious views into Canadian society, adding yet another variant to the pacifist tradition building within Canada.

The Doukhobor movement originated in south central and southern Russia during the eighteenth century, but did not crystallize until the early 1800s. Theirs was an undogmatic faith that abandoned traditional Christianity and rejected all outward rites and forms such as sacraments, icons, liturgy, and a separate priesthood. Love and brotherhood were the central principles of the sect; the Bible was of secondary importance. The Doukhobors were living examples of a messianic and millenarian Christianity that was dying out elsewhere in the world.[16] In their rejection of baptism they were more radical than Anabaptists, and in their rejection of the doctrine of redemption and denial of the authority of the scriptures they were more radical than the Quakers.[17]

Like that of Quakers, the Doukhobors' faith is based upon a radical belief in the presence of Christ's spirit in each person – a voice within that directs individual actions. This presence was supreme in the man Jesus.[18] 'Since the direction of their behaviour must come from within, they naturally deny the right of the state or other external authority to dictate their actions. And, since all men are vessels for the divine essence, they regard it as sinful to kill other men, even in war: hence springs the pacifism that is the most durable and widespread of Doukhobor attitudes.'[19] From the very beginning, Doukhobor faith has been 'a strange blend of religious anarchism and theocratic autocracy.'[20] While denying the need for government, they revered a semi-divine leader as head of their community.

The Doukhobor philosophy present in the twentieth century, however, did not appear until their old traditions were fused with Tolstoyan ideas in the late nineteenth century. When Tolstoy first heard of the

Doukhobors he thought he had found the natural peasant anarchists of his dreams, 'the germinating of that seed sown by Christ eighteen hundred years ago: the resurrection of Christ himself.'[21] Though he failed to understand their mystical and prophetic side with its support of theocratic authority, he found their philosophy generally in line with his own.

Tolstoy's conversion to pacifism occurred during the Russo-Turkish War of 1877–8. In *A Confession* (1879) he first expressed the concept of 'non-resistance to evil' that formed an important part of his broader program of social ethics.[22] His philosophy was one of individual ethics; it stressed personal responsibility for one's actions and the importance of taking a moral stand, and was similar to the Kantian absolute moral imperative. According to Tolstoy, non-violence was an ethical imperative evident in the moral rules laid down by Christ in the Sermon on the Mount.[23] Tolstoy's goal was Christian perfection. Since the realization of the law of brotherly love and sacredness of human life, however, was blocked by the existence of the state and its law of violence, Tolstoy advocated the total transformation of society. Thus, anarchism was an essential element of Tolstoy's Christian pacifism.[24] His complete opposition to authoritarian forms, including the state, clearly classifies his thought as anarchistic even though he preferred to call himself a literal Christian.[25] His attitude is best expressed in his words of advice to the Doukhobors: 'The Christian teaching cannot be taken piecemeal: it is all or nothing. It is inseparably united into one whole. If a man acknowledges himself to be a son of God, from that acknowledgement flows the love of his neighbour; and from love of his neighbour flow, equally, the repudiation of violence, of oaths, of state service, and of property.'[26]

In a display of civil disobedience in 1895, members of the Doukhobor community endured imprisonment and punishment under the tsar rather than submit to conscription. Tolstoy thought of them as Christian martyrs and appealed to British Quakers and other pacifists on their behalf. The Quakers responded with a special assistance fund to help resettle the Doukhobors in a new land, and Tolstoy donated the royalties from his last work, *Resurrection* (1899), to the same cause.[27] If the Doukhobor emigration to Canada in 1899 meant survival for their particular way of life, it also meant the addition of a peculiar, anarchistic type of Christian pacifism to the Canadian scene.[28] By an order in council in 1898, Doukhobor pacifism was sanctioned by Canadian law.

Quite apart from his link with the Doukhobor influx, Tolstoy's considerable influence upon the development of pacifism and social criticism in the twentieth century would make itself felt in Canada in its own right as the century passed. Tolstoy's thought was among the topics discussed at the annual Queen's Theological Alumni Conference in the 1890s where Christian ministers and laymen advocated broad goals of Christian social action, though few if any were persuaded pacifists.[29] It was Tolstoy who criticized the liberal peace societies of his day for concentrating on secondary issues while avoiding the fundamental issue of individual witness against war.[30] Another of his contributions was his influence on Mahatma Gandhi and the Gandhi's doctrine of non-violent resistance. Tolstoy, therefore, was instrumental in the formulation of a new pacifist idea built upon individual moral responsibility with a universal application to all mankind rather than just a sectarian Christian approach – a pacifism concerned with the extent to which war and violence are rooted in the social environment. Few pacifists in the twentieth century followed Tolstoy to the final repudiation of the state, but he made a powerful contribution to the socially radical pacifism that emerged, in Canada as elsewhere, in the century of the world wars.

In addition to groups now designated as 'Historic Peace Churches,' various fundamentalist and millennial sects holding radical objections to war entered Canada during the late nineteenth century from Britain and the United States.[31] The Plymouth Brethren, one of the most significant of the British groups, was organized around 1820–30. Their objection to war was based upon the well-known passage on non-resistance to evil in the Sermon on the Mount. The Brethren were strict literalists and initially remained aloof from politics and secular activities.[32] Together with several other sects, including Christadelphians, Seventh-Day Adventists, and Jehovah's Witnesses, they advocated an apocalyptic non-combatancy conditional upon the coming of the millennium. Thus, to use Brock's classification, they were 'eschatological pacifists' who professed a kind of interim ethic. While non-combatant in the present world, they foresaw the possibility of fighting under Christ's banner at Armageddon.[33]

The most important of these 'eschatological pacifists' in Canada were the Jehovah's Witnesses (also known as International Bible Students, Millennial Dawnites, and Russellites), founded by Charles Taze Russell, a Pittsburgh businessman, in the 1870s. Within a decade Pastor Russell had founded the Watch Tower Bible and Tract Society and written numerous books and articles espousing his beliefs.[34] According to Russell, human history is a struggle between Jehovah and Satan's forces of evil. Although Satan rules the world, including religious, political, and economic institutions, Christ eventually will come again to destroy the world's wicked system. Therefore, Russell urged Bible students to 'honour all men and be obedient to earthly authorities in matters not contrary to divine Law.' They should also 'refrain from participating in politics, voting, and killing their fellow men in the wars of the nations.'[35] Witnesses are strict biblicists, but they continually reassess the Bible in order to move from spiritual darkness to spiritual light. They also believe that every member in good standing should be a preacher.

Jehovah's Witnesses began to penetrate Canada soon after Pastor Russell began his activities. Watch Tower literature reached Ontario as early as 1881, and Pastor Russell's first visit to Toronto in 1891 was followed by frequent appearances in Canada before his death in 1916. At that time there were eighteen congregations in Ontario alone as well as individual Bible students in all the Maritime provinces and throughout the West.[36]

The absolute refusal of Jehovah's Witnesses and other recently organized 'eschatological' sects to participate in the wars of the state further enlarged the religious minority in support of pacifist non-violence. Indeed, Jehovah's Witnesses, Doukhobors, and the more traditional peace sects – Mennonites, Hutterites, and Quakers – formed the backbone of pacifist dissent in Canadian society and would provide the major resistance to compulsory military service in the course of the twentieth century.

II

Outside the religious sects there was little pacifist activity in Canada's early past, although the liberal, non-sectarian peace societies that appeared in the United States after 1812 also began to move into British North America; by 1826 there were twelve such societies in Upper Canada, and several in the Maritimes and one in Montreal by 1849. These non-sectarian groups were inspired by the enlightenment's emphasis on rationalism and humanism; biblical teachings were used as further support for establishing the ideal of peace.[37] Though Canadian peace societies were short-lived – they disappeared by mid-century – the same philosophical approach appeared again in the late nineteenth century in conjunction with the reform spirit.

Besides this movement, there were a few early examples of Canadian pacifists, such as the rather eccentric Henry Wentworth Monk, a self-proclaimed peace prophet. Monk, a descendant of a distinguished family from the Ottawa area, turned into a Christian mystic in reaction to industrialism and the 'barrenness of ecclesiastical Christianity.'[38] During the second half of the nineteenth century he travelled regularly to Britain to publicize various schemes for world peace, including the cause of Zionism. He predicted a series of world wars, which could be avoided by the creation of an international council, centred in Jerusalem, with power to enforce world peace. But the absence of enthusiasm for his plans and his failure to become a successful mediator for peace in the American Civil War discouraged him and damaged his credibility among supporters in Britain. By the 1880s Monk returned to the Ottawa area and spent the last twelve years of his life writing a barrage of peace propaganda, in pamphlet and letter form, urging the codification of international law, permanent international arbitration, establishment of a sort of League of Nations, and Anglo-American leadership in the movement towards peace.[39] Thus, although he started his career as a mystical peace prophet, he ended it by taking the rational approach common to nineteenth-century peace organizations.

The major growth of non-sectarian pacifism in late nineteenth-century Canada occurred within the framework of the North American liberal reform movement. The participants in this peace movement, both pacifists and non-pacifists, were affected by religious inspiration as well as philanthropic and reform impulses. For most active supporters, peace activities were just one of their reform concerns. This peace movement, therefore, was inextricably tied to other causes such as the movement towards Anglo-American rapprochement, the campaign for woman suffrage, and the social gospel. Since most social reformers shared the belief that their individual domestic concerns were affected by the international climate, the peace movement was elevated to a position of key importance and common interest.[40]

Although the non-sectarian North American peace movement eventually produced a socially radical wing, the pre-war peace movement was predominantly a conservative and moderate attempt to achieve order and stability within the world through the practical goals of international arbitration and the establishment of an international court. 'Peace,' writes Robert Wiebe, 'connoted order and stability, the absence of violence, the supremacy of reason and law. It suggested the disappearance of militarism and all other vestiges of a barbaric past.'[41] The liberal progressive rhetoric expressed a faith in the ability of progress to carry civilization beyond war.

The North American liberal reform tradition, including the non-sectarian peace movement, reflected the pragmatic institutional approach, but was greatly indebted to religious inspiration, particularly to Quaker and social gospel influences. While the impact on Canadian society of sectarian pacifism was extremely limited, liberal Quakerism emerged to bridge the gap between historic Christian pacifism and liberal progressive ideology. Quakers went beyond negative anti-militarism, and in conjunction with social gospellers began to relate war to socio-economic conditions and to encourage interest in international affairs. This was a gradual development, however, and the full impact of Quaker leadership was not felt in Canada until after the First World War when the three separate branches of the Society of Friends in Canada began to co-operate with one another.[42] But as early as the 1880s, the Canada Yearly Meeting of Friends established contact with Canadian evangelical churches in foreign mission work, and it was the influence of evangelical Methodism among orthodox Quakers that resulted in the separation and organization of the progressive branch of the Canadian Society of Friends in 1891.[43] In that same year Canadian Quakers also became involved in North American peace activities when all three Canadian yearly meetings became affiliated with The Peace Association of Friends in America.[44] And Canadian Friends were shortly involved in the Lake Mohonk Conference on International Arbitration, an annual affair initiated by a Quaker in New York State in 1895, which provided links with the turn-of-the-century spirit of liberal pacifistic internationalism and which attracted a wide range of adherents from politicians to businessmen and journalists. It was symptomatic of broadening Quaker concerns that in 1896 the Hicksite branch of Canadian Friends sent a deputation to Ottawa to present the Quaker position on 'The Responsibilities of Public Men, Militarism, Temperance, Judicial Oaths, and Capital Punishment.' During the course of their meeting with Sir Wilfrid Laurier, the prime minister praised Canadian Quakers for their advocacy of reforms.[45]

In the meantime, the evangelical spirit credited with broadening Quaker activities in society also affected the larger Protestant world, resulting, in one of its phases, in the liberal social gospel movement of the late nineteenth and early twentieth centuries. The social gospel was a social-religious outlook concerned with the realization of the Kingdom of God on earth. It represented liberal Protestantism's optimistic faith in an evolutionary progression towards the perfect Christian society. The evangelical creed of personal perfection was planted in Canada by the Baptists, Congregationalists, and Methodists, and later by the Free Kirk movement within Presbyterianism. Their belief in an immanent God, free will, and restrictive personal and social morality had become a dominant feature of Canadian Protestantism in the nineteenth century.[46] Canadian national expansion and the hope of establishing a Christian society in the northern half of the continent, the growing awareness of social problems, and the spread of liberal and social conceptions after 1867 pressed evangelicals to reinterpret their gospel in terms of a social as well as a personal creed. The need to Christianize the world blossomed into a program of social salvation, in the course of which the Christian doctrine of peace became inextricably linked with the hope of attaining the Christian social order.

One of the first Canadians to relate the social gospel to international affairs was C.S. Eby, who served as a Methodist missionary to Japan in the 1870s and 1880s. While in Japan, Eby edited the mission's *Chrysanthemum Magazine*, and in 1883 he delivered a series of lectures on 'Christianity and Civilization' to foreign and Japanese scholars at the Meiji Kuaido in Tokyo. His experience as a missionary had made him aware of the inability of the Christian church, 'entombed in institutions and anachronistic forms of thought,' to compete with secular forces shaping the destiny of the world.[47] His message, therefore, called for a Christianity that could lead towards the triumph of the Kingdom of God on earth. Once back in Canada, Eby founded the People's Institute, a socialist church in Toronto, in 1909; in the same year he became secretary of the Canadian Peace and Arbitration Society.[48] He also wrote a series of pamphlets on 'The Word of the Kingdom' that were later incorporated into his book *The World Problem and the Divine Solution*.

The world problem, according to Eby, was that the 'so-called Christian nations' were rotten within and world plunderers without, 'a travesty of the thing for which the Bible stands.'[49] But Canada, being part of the new world, had a choice and the opportunity to set an example for the rest of the world. 'Is Canada to be carried into this destructive flood,' he asked, 'under which all old nations have perished? Must we keep up the dance of death with all mature nations now heading in the same direction of moral failure? Or is it possible that we may find a better way and influence other nations for the common good?'[50]

Eby claimed that beneath war and the exploitation of man by man was a universal desire for peace and social justice, but he warned that the solution to the world problem did not lie in practical socialist planning; socialism by itself was a 'modern paganism' lacking intellectual and spiritual strength. The only solution was a world renaissance of Christianity, a revival of the spiritual and practical rules laid down by

Christ in the Sermon on the Mount, which would, in turn, ensure 'universal peace and a new earth.'[51]

The social gospel concern for peace and human justice, as voiced by Eby and others, became enmeshed in the liberal reform movement and the peace movement in particular. The altruistic spirit of most Canadian reformers, whether they were journalists, ministers, politicians, or trade unionists, was based upon social gospel principles. Their faith in the messianic quality of a peaceful Kingdom of God on earth, however, diverted their attention away from the consideration of the possibility and consequences of actual warfare. Only when the First World War broke out did social gospellers face squarely the issue of absolute pacifism. Until that time early social gospel rhetoric reflected the general faith that world peace and social justice would be the ultimate rewards for following the word of Christ, especially the Sermon on the Mount.

III

The first direct challenge to Canadian pacifists and peace advocates came with the outbreak of the Boer War in 1899. A Canadian contingent left for South Africa soon after the beginning of hostilities, and by Christmas of that year Protestant churches in Toronto offered special prayer services for the success of the British cause in bringing the blessings of civilization to South Africa.[52] Some isolated opposition to the war did exist among certain segments of Canadian society, such as the Protestant clergy, radical labour, farmers, and anglophobic minority groups, but the peace movement itself was more or less paralysed, causing the superintendent of the Dominion Women's Christian Temperance Union to lament that 'it seemed useless' to carry on peace work in an atmosphere charged with talk of 'imperialism, patriotism, heroism and loyalty.' Voicing what would become a familiar pacifist complaint, she claimed that 'the military craze has been carried to such an extent that those who did not bow down as hero-worshippers were looked upon as disloyal.'[53] Indeed, the pacifist stand remained far from popular in the tide of emotional imperialism that swept the country.[54] Recalling his father's pacifism, Roland Bainton remarked that it was more difficult to criticize the Boer War in Canada than in Britain itself.[55]

The Reverend James Herbert Bainton, newly arrived from Ilkeston, England, no sooner took charge of the Congregational church in Vancouver than a controversy erupted concerning his pacifism. He sometimes referred to the Boer War in his public prayers and asked God to look with compassion on the British and Boers alike. Such prayers incensed the 'super-patriots' of the congregation, and they demanded a forthright statement on the war from their new minister. The elder Bainton answered this request in a sermon in which he confided that he thought the war was deplorable and hoped his parishioners agreed. 'War blunts the moral feeling of the nation because it slays sympathy. We grow insensitive to human feeling and we hear of the slaughter of hundreds, perhaps thousands with less sorrow than we do of the death of a single friend.Compassion is in danger of dying when a nation is at war.'[56]

Reaction to the sermon split the congregation, and while the majority continued to support Bainton, the 'super-patriotic' faction seceded. Such a small congregation (about 125 persons) could not long afford such a division, so when the war was over Bainton decided to leave, hoping the dissidents would then return. The experience proved to be a sobering ordeal for the Bainton family, and it was decided that since all of Canada had been involved in the war it was best to emigrate to the United States. The Bainton experience was one example of a Christian minister's pacifist conscience in conflict with the position held by a significant part of his congregation. Similar scenes would be repeated in Canada again and again during the course of the century.

Denunciations of the Boer War came from the ranks of each major Protestant denomination in Canada. The Reverend Dr William Wright, the Anglican priest of St John the Evangelist parish in Montreal, preached that war was inconsistent with Christianity on the very Sunday designated by Anglicans as a day of support for the war.[57] The sermons of the Reverend J.C. Herdman, pastor of Knox Presbyterian Church in Calgary, expressed pro-Boer sentiments and condemned the wickedness of war. While Herdman's anti-war statements received wide press coverage, the widest public notice was won by the Reverend Morgan Woods, the minister of Bond Street Congregational Church, Toronto, whose pacifist protests appeared in the *Globe*, a dozen Ontario weeklies, and some out-of-province papers. His proposed peace movement, however, never got off the ground. There were also isolated cases of anti-war pronouncements by Methodist clergymen, although the majority were ambivalent.[58] The hierarchy of the Methodist church and other Protestant churches openly supported the war.

If not the pulpit then perhaps the pen would prove mightier than the sword; at least, that is what a few Canadians hoped as some pacifist sympathies emerged in the liberal, labour, and farm press. One of the most influential newspapers in that regard was the Toronto *Star*, whose editor, J.E. Atkinson, was a self-styled pacifist. Although his pacifism was founded upon social gospel principles and reflected the contemporary reform spirit, it is doubtful that he was an absolute pacifist. Nevertheless, according to his biographer, Atkinson believed that Canada was stampeded into participating in the war by British newspapers and the Montreal *Star*, and he sought to moderate the war's coverage, which was no small accomplishment at the time. 'As a newspaper man,' claims Harkness, 'Mr Atkinson had to report the war; as a pacifist, he was determined not to glorify it.'[59] When Atkinson actually advocated a negotiated peace with honour, he was buried in an 'avalanche of vituperation' and was thereafter confined to less controversial topics.

While the Toronto *Star* remained at best neutral, an unequivocal anti-war position was expressed by the occasional radical labour and farm journal. The *Voice*, a weekly publication endorsed by the Winnipeg Trades and Labor Council, at first adopted the radical critique of war as a capitalist creation and urged men to refuse to fight. Within a month, however, it changed its course and supported the British cause in order to bolster the political aspirations of one of its editors, Arthur W. Puttee, who went on to become the first labour member elected to the Canadian House of Commons in the wartime by-election.[60]

A more faithful anti-war position was expressed by the Toronto weekly *Citizen and Country*, the official journal of the Toronto Trades and Labor Council under the editorship of George Wrigley. From its inception in 1898 *Citizen and Country* advocated the Christian socialist position against war and in favour of social, moral, and economic reform common to the more radical element within the Canadian social gospel movement. The journal's content ranged from discussions of the benefits of Christian socialism and the single tax to the curse of militarism and the question of peace. It also reprinted British anti-war articles, since the editor shared the attitudes representative of Keir Hardie's Independent Labour party and the British pro-Boer faction.

George Wrigley had made a career of editing labour and reform journals,[61] and as secretary of the Direct Legislation League of Canada he actively promoted the Social Progress League, a citizen's discussion group in Toronto, and the Canadian Socialist League, which advocated a wide variety of reforms, including public ownership.[62] His pacifist position, based upon the Christian socialist conception of the brotherhood of man, was evident in his relentless denunciations of the Spanish-American War and the South African War. War not only was a setback for social progress, said Wrigley, but also led to a moral degeneration within Canada affecting the government, the press, and the Church. He believed that the Canadian people would have condemned England's policy in South Africa were it not for a 'purchased metropolitan press' that distorted the truth and misled the public.[63] 'We regret exceedingly,' wrote Wrigley, 'that Canada has a jingo press and jingo politicians. We fear, too, that her pulpits are jingoistic. Mammon is King, and War is her Minister.'[64] In one editorial he asked if clergymen were voiceless on the matter. On another occasion he warned that 'the clergyman who prays for his country when he knows it to be wrong is standing on the brink of hell.'[65] Above all, Wrigley feared that war unleashed a violent attitude that could brutalize Canadian society and create a dangerous cultural cleavage in the country.

During the course of the war Wrigley expressed the pro-Boer viewpoint and ran articles such as a biography of Paul Kruger. In October 1899 he noted with pride that 'Citizen and Country has a large constituency of thoughtful readers, and we are glad that no one has complained because we have championed the cause of the Boer. Canadians are not all jingoes.'[66] But Wrigley was not complacent, and the paper consistently carried warnings on the danger of militarism in Canada; typical of these was the alarm sounded by a contributor from Brandon, Manitoba: 'Canadians, wake up! or the Maple Leaf will wither. Almost every newspaper, especially the subsidized press ... are howling for militarism. Why is this? Even in the schools they are preparing for the same thing, they preach patriotism and invite the military spirit.'[67]

Such contributions added fuel to Wrigley's personal anti-war campaign. In another instance, working-class opposition to war was expressed in an article on 'Anglo-Saxon Jingoism' by Phillips Thompson of Toronto, a left-wing intellectual and the author of the book *Politics of Labor* (1888), the first Canadian radical critique of North American capitalism. Thompson echoed the classic British labour argument that workers gained nothing from war but a further setback in the realization of social progress.[68]

Wrigley never faltered as a war critic, even when the Reverend Elliot S. Rowe, the popular president of the Social Progress Company, *Citizen and Country's* publisher, threatened to resign. Rowe was the only one of the five directors to complain, however, and Wrigley argued that the journal actually was gaining in popularity.[69] *Citizen and Country* held capitalist and imperialist exploitation responsible for the Boer War, and concluded that there were 'few Canadians better able to correctly state the motives governing the Parliament of Great Britain in the South African question than Professor Goldwin Smith.'[70]

Goldwin Smith, arch-supporter of Anglo-American unity and anti-imperialist, was the best-known English Canadian to oppose the Boer War, and a good example of one who viewed pacifism as a progressive reform. His version of world peace was based upon the Manchester Liberal idea of order and stability rooted in laissez-faire economics. His arguments against the war reflected those of the British anti-imperialist Liberals. Of all Canadian anti-war spokesmen, he alone 'deplored British atrocities, the concentration camps, and the use of dum-dum bullets.'[71] In his two small Toronto weeklies Smith carried on a steady campaign against the war, and especially against Canadian enthusiasm for it. 'Most repulsive,' he lamented, 'is the sight of volunteers going ... to slaughter people who have done them no wrong in a cause about which they know nothing.'[72]

Smith's paper, the *Farmers' Weekly Sun*, was one of four Canadian rural weeklies firmly to oppose the war. The others were the *Bobcaygeon Independent*, the *Canadian Gleaner*, and the *Standard*. They all sympathized with the poor Boer farmers and appealed to the anti-militarism and strong moral sense of Canadian farmers. In contrast to Goldwin Smith, Robert Sellar, the editor of the *Canadian Gleaner* of Huntingdon, Quebec, appealed to farmers' isolationist sentiments. The *Gleaner* also posed as the last bulwark of Quebec's English Protestant farmers and expressed fear that Quebec nationalists would press for greater provincial autonomy owing to the English-Canadian zeal for war.[73]

Threats of internal cultural divisions were evident in the anglophobic/ anti-imperialist sentiments expressed by German Canadians, Irish Canadians, and particularly French Canadians. Anti-war sentiment ran rampant in Quebec, culminating in student riots in Montreal in March 1900.[74] The press in Quebec interpreted the war as imperial aggression, and French Canadian nationalists demanded the Canada prove her independent nationhood by refusing to fight in an imperialist war. Their leading spokesman was Henri Bourassa, the father of modern French-Canadian nationalism, who resigned his seat in Parliament to emphasize his convictions.

In 1900 Bourassa suggested to Goldwin Smith the creation of an anti-imperialist party. But no coalition of French-English dissidents was formed, and no peace party was created. As Carman Miller has stated, the anti-war factions failed to move from 'verbal protests to concerted action.'[75] Not only did they lack the numbers necessary for political force, they were divided in their motives and on the issues. Nevertheless, the protests of farm, labour, and French-Canadian spokesmen, though hardly pacifist in the strict sense, might have provided important support for a nascent peace movement if there had been a serious attempt to reconcile anti-imperialist opposition to war with the religious and liberal tenets of pacifism. That lesson of the Boer War would not easily be learned, and that failure would haunt pacifists in the years that followed.

IV

Although the Boer War had interrupted the growth of a Canadian peace movement, it did not seem to have a detrimental effect upon its subsequent development. In fact, there was a great upsurge in the progressive peace movement following the war, perhaps even in reaction to it, since liberal reformers came to believe that an important lesson of the South African conflict was the urgent need for some kind of international machinery to mediate disputes and prevent barbarian warfare.

The North American forum dedicated to the peaceful settlement of international conflict, and the breeding ground of support for the idea of arbitration in particular, was the Lake Mohonk Conference on International Arbitration. The annual conferences were attended by a wide variety of individuals interested in international affairs, from politicians to business and church leaders. The Lake Mohonk Conferences, however, concerned arbitration and the practical side of the peace movement, not pacifism. Indeed, the conference actually practised selectivity of membership and prescribed rules prohibiting references to the horrors of war, absolute pacifism, or specific alarming realities in order to maintain a genteel demeanour.[76] What was characteristic of the Lake Mohonk Conference was also true of the larger peace movement. The support of businessmen and other non-pacifists was believed to add prestige, but in reality it weakened the movement and made it unlikely that peace organizations would take a controversial stand.

Direct Canadian involvement in the Lake Mohonk scene began when Oliver A. Howland, a member of the legislative assembly of Ontario, was invited to attend the conference in 1904. As president of the International Deep Waterways Association, Howland had advocated the creation of a permanent International Court of Appeal to settle all disputes between Canada and the United States, thus capturing the attention of the American arbitration sympathizers.[77] Canadians were invited to each succeeding conference thereafter, and by 1915, when the conferences ended, thirty-one prominent Canadians – businessmen, politicians, justices, lawyers, clergymen, and journalists – had visited Lake Mohonk. These Canadian participants assured the conferences that Canada definitely supported their movement for peace and, on one occasion, cited an endorsement by Prime Minister Wilfrid Laurier.[78] Reflecting the overriding theme of most speeches, three-fourths of the Canadian addresses were devoted to praising the idea of arbitration as promoted by the Lake Mohonk Conference.[79]

Indeed, arbitration was hailed as the sure-fire remedy for all international ills. It was not only 'practically infallible' in preventing war, but also effective in removing a desire for war. This was the reasoning used by the organizers of the Lake Mohonk Conferences in their circulars entitled 'Why Business Men Should Promote International Arbitration' and 'How Business Men Should Promote International Arbitration.'[80] Support for this idea among the Canadian business community was encouraged by Elias Rogers of the Toronto Board of Trade, a frequent delegate to Lake Mohonk. By 1907 the principle of arbitration was endorsed by the Retail Merchants' Association of Canada, the Canadian Manufacturers' Association, and the Winnipeg, Hamilton, Toronto, and Montreal boards of trade.[81]

Other Canadian participants included John Murray Clark, a Toronto lawyer; John Lewis, the editor of the Toronto *Star*; William Lyon Mackenzie King; and Senator Raoul Dandurand. In his address to the 1909 conference, Clark drew attention to the uses of arbitration and conciliation by the Canadian government in settling labour disputes. The following year Mackenzie King, Canada's minister of labour, was present at Lake Mohonk to share his experience in the practical application of arbitration in domestic quarrels. 'The greatest contribution to the cause of international peace,' he said, 'will be the furtherance of industrial peace.'[82] If working men accept the appeal to reason in settling disputes, why not nations? The successful application of arbitration in the industrial world, he concluded, was a preview of its possibilities on the international scene.

On their return home the Canadians eagerly spread the faith in international arbitration and the hope for peaceful international relations. Although they failed to organize many Canadian branches of American peace organizations, they were successful in arousing interest in arbitration, especially with the founding in 1905 of the Canadian Peace and Arbitration Society, the first national secular peace organization in Canada. The creation of a non-denominational peace society had been initiated in 1904 by the Friends' Association of Toronto, a small group of Hicksite Friends under the leadership of William Greenwood Brown.[83] The major task of organizing the society and enlisting broader pacifist support was undertaken by Brown's brother-in-law, Andrew Cory Courtice, a former editor of the *Christian Guardian* and a Methodist minister in Toronto.

Courtice successfully secured endorsements from the Farmers' Convention of Ontario and several churches and attracted the active support of notable civic and religious leaders, including at least four university professors (Adam Shortt of Queen's, J.E. McCurdy of Toronto, Charles Zavitz of Guelph, and Lewis E. Horning of Victoria College), six ministers, and several politicians. Within a year the provisional executive of eighteen was expanded to twenty-nine, with a thirteen-member board of directors headed by Sir William Mulock, the chief justice of the Ontario High Court of Justice and a former member of the Laurier cabinet, as president; Courtice as secretary; Brown as treasurer; and J.W. Bengough, the well-known caricaturist, as auditor.[84] Other prominent directors and vice-presidents included W.D. LeSueur, Nathanael Burwash, Rabbi S. Jacobs, Dr Margaret Gordon, and W.C. Good. The support of the business community was also enlisted, largely through the efforts of Elias Rogers, the prominent Quaker businessman and Liberal politician who was a Toronto alderman and an unsuccessful reform candidate for mayor of Toronto in 1888. Although the centre of the society's activities always remained in Toronto where the directors held periodic meetings, usually monthly, in Mulock's home, eventually there were over a thousand members scattered across the country from Nova Scotia to British Columbia.

The breadth of the society's membership largely reflected the broad, liberal nature of its stated aims, which read: 'This society, being founded on the principle that war is contrary to true religion, sound morality and the best interests of humanity, shall have for its object the promotion of universal and permanent peace by means of arbitration and by cultivating the spirit of peace and goodwill among men.'[85] Rather than radical or strictly pacifist solutions, therefore, the primary goal of the Canadian Peace and Arbitration Society was international arbitration as that concept was articulated at Lake Mohonk. Moreover, when a number of the society's members, such as Shortt, became successful mediators in industrial disputes, they became convinced that similar principles of negotiation could be applied to international conflicts.[86]

Clearly, in formulating goals and planning an agenda the Canadians owed much to the Lake Mohonk Conference, which, Courtice claimed, had identified the three most pressing steps of world organization 'in their proper order of importance':

- A plan by which the Hague Conference may become a permanent and recognized Congress of Nations with advisory powers.
- A general arbitration treaty for the acceptance of all nations.
- A plan for the restrictions of armaments by concurrent international action.[87]

That first goal of strengthening the Hague Conference, hailed by Courtice as 'the most intensely interesting and significant sign of the times,' became the focus of pacifist praise and publicity, and through the spring of 1907 the society lobbied for official Canadian support of the idea. On the provincial level they succeeded; as the Ontario legislative assembly endorsed a resolution to turn the Hague Conference into a permanent international congress with powers of arbitration.[88]

A similar but less satisfying attempt to win federal approval was Senator Raoul Dandurand's effort to secure Canadian membership in the Interparliamentary Union for Peace, an international endorsement of arbitration at the Hague. Again the society campaigned to strengthen the Hague's authority. Although Prime Minister Laurier rejected the idea because 'Canada was not a sovereign state' and therefore was not concerned, Dandurand did manage to persuade over one hundred Canadian parliamentarians to subscribe to the principle of arbitration in settling international disputes, only to discover in the end that he could not obtain official membership for colonials until 1913. In the meantime interest waned and the exercise never generated much more than enthusiasm for the general idea of arbitration.[89]

In its effort to build a national peace movement, the Canadian Peace and Arbitration Society was encouraged by the response from Canada's Protestant churches. In particular, the endorsement of the Presbyterian church was quite a change from its previous statements during the nineteenth century in support of British wars and the use of armed force.[90] Canadian Presbyterianism had never questioned the morality of warfare from a Christian viewpoint until the popularization of peace rhetoric by the Peace and Arbitration Society; thereafter the Church moved towards an increasingly pacifist position.

Meeting in Ottawa in 1911, the Presbyterian Assembly officially condemned war as contrary to Christian morals; endorsed 'every wise effort' to restrain and abolish war, including the use of conciliation and arbitration; and affirmed that 'the great Commandment: Thou shalt love is binding upon nations as well as individuals.'[91] As a spokesman later explained, this change of heart was based as much upon memories of the Boer War experience as upon scripture. 'Canadians can do nothing better for the Peace Movement,' declared the Reverend R.W. Dickie of Montreal, 'than to do some hard thinking about the fruit of past wars and the present burden of armaments ... as Christians it is our duty to stand against the war idea.'[92] The *Presbyterian*, an unofficial church weekly in Toronto, also endorsed the movement for disarmament and peace, arguing that the most significant consequence of the international arms rivalry was moral rather than economic. 'The effect of all this military preparation and enthusiasm,' wrote the editor, 'is to enthrone force rather than justice as arbiter of international disputes.'[93] The ideals of Christ were being replaced by those of paganism.

Similar arguments were raised by Methodists, especially those participating in the Canadian Peace and Arbitration Society. The official organ of the Methodist church, The *Christian Guardian*, expanded its pacifist-oriented approach to include specific proposals for the prevention of war through direct strike action by unions and occupational groups. Dr W.W. Andrews, an ordained Methodist minister and an unorthodox evolutionist working in scientific research at the University of Saskatchewan, suggested that various groups within society could take individual actions to prevent war: banks could refuse to make loans; labour declare an international strike; worldwide press services could help publicize a commercial boycott. Never, he concluded, had the promise of peace been stronger.[94]

A more traditional approach to peace, shared by most Methodists, was presented to the Lake Mohonk Conference in 1911 by the Reverend William Sparling, the pastor of St James' Methodist Church in Montreal. Sparling had social gospel leanings, but his speech also showed how the older evangelism of the heart persisted, even in peace rhetoric. He claimed that what was needed in Canada was a strong public opinion on the moral question of peace, since 'the forces that make for peace are moral forces, and those moral forces reside in the heart of the individual.' The war spirit was the arch-enemy of Jesus Christ; war and Christianity were mutually destructive forces. Sparling proposed that the Christian church preach 'that love is the all-conquering force in the world' and thereby help create the national opinion that 'will bring about the day of peace.' 'If we could only get the Thirteenth Chapter of First

Corinthians written upon the hearts of people,' he argued, 'we would have no war.'[95] Sparling concluded by warning the conference that there were people 'who profess to point out some good things of war in history but I do not think war can possibly bring Canada anything but what is bad.'

Despite the highly visible efforts of a Sparling or a Courtice, only a small proportion of the Canadian clergy was actively involved in the peace movement; and although most Canadian churches adopted resolutions endorsing the Hague principles of arbitration, overall they gave little serious attention to the real problems of war and peace.[96] Canadian churchmen continued to hold divergent views on the role of the church in promoting peace, and they were as uncertain as the general public about how best to maintain peace. Even the Methodists, the most vocal advocates of peace, had their supporters of armed preparedness. Rather than advocate radical changes, therefore, Canada's churches concentrated on such innocuous activities as celebrating Peace Sunday, an annual commemoration of the first Hague Conference. In this they attracted the support of the entire peace movement, especially such women's groups as the Women's Christian Temperance Union (WCTU).

One of the first attempts to involve Canadians in the peace movement had been made in the early 1890s when the Dominion WCTU established a Peace and Arbitration Department with the avowed purpose of moulding public opinion 'to believe that arbitration and reconciliation are better for a nation than war and conquest.'[97] After the Boer War the department accelerated its work and, although it was later active in Nova Scotia, its main support remained in central Canada.[98]

By 1904 a similar peace and arbitration committee was created by the Canadian National Council of Women. Ada Mary Courtice, a WCTU peace activist and the Quaker wife of the founder of the Canadian Peace and Arbitration Society, was named convenor. Like her husband, Courtice believed that peace through arbitration was 'the greatest movement of the age,' and that the Hague Conference represented a model example of international co-operation.[99] Echoing the maternal feminist argument that women should take the lead in peace work since they suffered most from the effects of war on family life, Courtice at once set out to establish subcommittees within the local councils across Canada. It proved to be difficult, frustrating work and, although she persevered for eight years, the response of Canadian women was disappointing. By 1905 only eight of the twenty-five councils had appointed representatives to the national peace committee; that number finally reached thirteen by 1912. There was a limited sense of achievement in persuading some libraries to carry peace literature and in collecting over two thousand signatures for a world peace petition endorsing the Hague, but for the most part, as Veronica Strong-Boag has argued, the Canadian National Council of Women was ambivalent about if not actually hostile to pacifism.[100]

In theory, however, it and all other women's organizations in Canada were supposed to be pacifist, since most feminists still accepted the nineteenth-century stereotype of women as the morally superior sex. The central assumption was that women, as nurturers of life, were free from aggressive instincts and thus were men's moral superiors at all times. If they received political rights, it was argued, 'society would be cleansed of conflict and nation states would no longer go to war.'[101] The special interest of Canadian women in peace, therefore, was closely allied to the wider middle-class movement for universal suffrage and temperance. According to this reformist solution, once women received the vote they could prevent war and prohibit drink, resulting in international and domestic peace and in Christian progress.

It was the view of war as an instrument of the patriarchal state, however, that most clearly influenced radical feminists such as Flora Macdonald Denison, a columnist for the Toronto *World*. In a biennial presidential address to the Canadian Suffrage Association she claimed that 'the male through centuries upon centuries has been combative and war has resulted.' Only with political freedom and equality could women effectively combat militarism and foster peace.[102]

A similar message was echoed by the suffragist and social reformer Nellie McClung when she condemned Canada's national policies of unjust taxation, legalized liquor traffic, and militarism as the result of 'male statecraft.' She insisted that war was not inevitable. 'War is a crime committed by men, and, therefore, when enough people say it shall not be, it cannot be.'[103] At the core of McClung's feminism, a product of the social gospel, was the faith in women as redeeming agents in a militaristic civilization. Peace would not arrive until women were allowed to say what they thought of war. 'Up to the present time,' she claimed, 'women have had nothing to say about war, except pay the price of war – this privilege has been theirs always.'

A close friend and associate of Nellie McClung and a leading figure in the Canadian women's movement was Judge Emily Murphy of Edmonton. Among her various civil and feminist endeavours, Murphy headed the Canadian National Council of Women's Peace and Arbitration Committee in 1914, the year its membership more than doubled.[104]

She too praised the work of the Hague Court and predicted 'a world without war' in the twentieth century.[105]

Despite the rather high profile of peace in the women's movement, it became painfully obvious to Ada Courtice and other feminists that Canadian women were not inherently pacifists. Neither the National Council of Women nor the WCTU was able to penetrate the general apathy of Canadian women concerning war and peace, even though they avoided specific commitments to disarmament. Instead, like the Canadian Peace and Arbitration Society and the churches, the women's groups concentrated on praising the principle of arbitration while attacking militarism. Of the two, as the WCTU discovered, it was easier to voice platitudes about international arbitration than actually to enlist support against cadet training or the sale of war toys.[106] It was popular to pray for peace, explained Nellie McClung, but 'the next day we show God that he need not take us too literally, for we go on with the military training, and the building of the battleships.'[107]

V

Although they were relatively successful in arousing public support for the idea of peace through arbitration, the progressive peace reformers faced a harder task in challenging the militaristic values of Canadian society. As McClung noted, it was one thing to praise arbitration or pray for peace, but it was quite another actually to take some positive steps in halting the militaristic spiral towards war. Pacifists like the Courtices recognized that the ultimate objective of their educative campaign was to 'alter public opinion by replacing the negative forces of nationalism and militarism with the positive virtues of patriotism and humanitarianism.'[108] Such sweeping changes in societal attitudes would not be accomplished easily or quickly, but as a start in that direction pacifists launched attacks upon the two glaring examples of Canadian militarism – increasing armament expenditures and the practice of cadet training in public schools.

Although the cadet movement in Canada dated back a half-century, it had blossomed only since the Boer War as English-speaking Canadians came increasingly to equate Canadian patriotism with British imperialism. As this imperial fervour continued to build, a huge cadet parade became an annual event in Toronto on Empire Day.[109] In fact, the injection of the martial spirit into Empire Day celebrations actually increased public support for the day. Nevertheless, nearly all pacifist groups, especially the WCTU and the Society of Friends, opposed such militia training and claimed it fostered militarism on the local level. As an alternative to military drill, the reformers advocated true physical education, which would contribute to the general physical and mental health of children and therefore help prevent disease. Pacifist pressure and escalating costs eventually restrained the spread of military training into several school districts and excluded it entirely in others, particularly in Nova Scotia and the West.[110]

If pacifists believed that cadet training in the schools corrupted the moral fibre of the nation's young men and perverted the goal of a liberal education, they were equally convinced that increasing armament expenditures would endanger rather than protect the peace and security of Canada. The question of military spending was of particular interest in the West, where farmers were reminded not to squander their heritage 'in aggravating Old World ills.'[111] The Regina temperance crusader C.B. Keenleyside, later a Methodist chaplain during the war, proposed that spending thirty million dollars to spread the gospel would give greater national protection than spending the same amount on defence.

On the whole, such pacifist warnings found a sympathetic audience in the farm community, but, as John H. Thompson suggests, the most common reaction of Westerners tended to be 'pacifism of the pocketbook as much as of principle.'[112] Although the National Grange had earlier endorsed the idea of disarmament and international peace, it was not until the Canadian naval debate in 1910, when the prospect of increased military expenditures arose, that Canadian farmers joined in the discussion of foreign affairs and the call for peace. The *Grain Grower's Guide*, the leading voice of Canadian farmers, always considered the question of international affairs and armaments in economic terms.[113] Free trade and lower taxes, claimed the *Guide*, would lead to international co-operation, disarmament, and peace; protectionism would lead to higher taxes, increased defence expenditures, and war. It was obvious, therefore, that farmers would benefit from free trade and international peace. A poll conducted by the *Guide* in 1913 revealed that a majority of those who replied agreed that Canada should divert defence funds earmarked for naval armaments towards the realization of disarmament and arbitration.

Leading Canadian farm journals, including the *Guide*, the *Weekly Sun*, and the *Farmer's Advocate and Home Magazine*, consistently denounced militarism and increased defence spending throughout the pre-war years.[114] Some farm leaders, such as W.C. Good of Ontario, also addressed these problems, but, overall, most Canadian farmers resembled the rest of Canadian society. They shared the illusion of a peaceful and secure North American continent and were generally apathetic to international affairs. It was difficult, in the isolation of rural life, to think about the horrors of war.

Labour also opposed the trend towards militarism and war, and the Trades and Labor Congress of Canada (TLC) passed numerous resolutions condemning war as a capitalist ploy. As early as 1911 the TLC convention in Calgary resolved to support a general strike to help prevent the outbreak of war, and for the next three years the TLC reiterated its opposition to international conflicts with the argument that wars resulted in the degradation of the working class. In May 1914 James Simpson, vice-president of the TLC, warned a labour meeting in St Thomas, Ontario, that workers would not be faithful to both their unions and the militia at the same time, an idea that would pose a real dilemma later that year.[115] But in pre-war Canada, the TLC and Canadian labour, like farmers, were not deeply concerned with world issues and were content to follow the progressive path to peace through resolutions praising international arbitration and condemning the various facets of militarism. Nevertheless, the fact that they did anything at all reflected some anxiety about world affairs in farm and labour circles.

The attacks on militarism that surfaced in the peace movement among such groups as the National Grange and the WCTU were directly challenged by the Canadian Defence League, a rival organization founded in 1909 that mounted a public campaign to increase military expenditures and encourage military training in the nation's schools with the future aim of compulsory militia service. One of the strongest reactions to this renewed defence of militarism came from the Quakers. In an article in the *Canadian Friend* entitled 'Militarism in Canada,' Arthur G. Dorland, a young Quaker destined to become the leading spokesman for the Canadian Friends, claimed the military propagandist was attempting to recover ground recently lost to the 'phenomenal progress of the Peace Movement.' He warned Canadian pacifists not to lapse into a 'condition of self-congratulatory inaction' since their success had 'aroused just as determined an effort on the part of the militarists to recapture public opinion.'[116] He accused the militarists of using war-scare talk to prepare people for universal military training and compulsory military service. 'If the militarists can win over the younger generation to their propaganda,' he warned, 'they will have set back the cause of peace for over a century and have won Canada for militarism.'

Dorland proceeded to point out that military conscription had recently become law in Australia and New Zealand. If the minister of militia, Colonel Sam Hughes, and the Canadian Defence League could have their way, this would happen in Canada too. Consequently, Dorland warned, the most immediate danger stemmed from military training at collegiate institutes and high schools in which attendance was already virtually compulsory. He explained that for several years it had been the policy of the government to subsidize schools that provided military training, thus discriminating against those where it was not available. 'And all this with a definite purpose,' he argued. To pretend that the training was meant to further the physical development of the students would not do. 'Uniforms and guns have a definite significance. They minister to the war passion. They signify War.'[117]

Although the Canada Yearly Meeting of Friends sent the usual cable to Ottawa condemning increased military expenditures and the entire war system, by 1913 the Friends were moving beyond mere resolutions. As a form of affirmative action, therefore, Quakers also proposed the creation of a National Peace Commission, or Department of Peace, which would help eliminate distrust between nations, promote the feeling of brotherhood and understanding among all peoples, and help stem the tide of militarism within Canada.[118] Although nothing came of this novel suggestion, the Friends were still thankful for what they considered an advance in the peace movement. At the same time, however, they were saddened at the prospect of peaceful peoples 'being sucked into the vortex of military preparations,' and, despite their hope for peace, by 1913 they were candidly warning their membership that the time might not be distant when they would be called upon to defend their pacifist principles 'at heavy cost.'[119]

Another such warning came from Lewis G. Horning, a professor of classics and Teutonic philology at Victoria College and Mulock's successor as president of the Canadian Peace and Arbitration Society. On the eve of the Great War Horning undertook a speaking tour to alert the nation to the growing menace of militarism and the escalating trend towards war. Horning declared that the hope for world peace lay not with commercial, educational, or religious forces but with the common man and personal interaction and friendship between England and Germany.[120] Horning's emphasis on the survival of Teutonic ideals made war between Germans and Anglo-Saxons unthinkable. He concluded that peace among Teutonic peoples was of special concern to Canadians since Canada was destined to produce 'a new race combining the political sagacity of the Anglo-Saxon, imagination of the German, the polish and tact of the French ... an unequalled and unbeatable combination.' The realization of that goal, however, required 'the fostering of peace and amity between the great sisters, England and Germany.'

Although Horning exhibited some faith in biological evolution, unlike the social Darwinists he assaulted those 'upholders of war' who claimed war trained men in heroic conduct and led to the survival of the fittest. 'How can war result in survival of the fittest,' he asked, 'when the flower of our young men are led away to death?' He concluded that rivalry among nations, rather than finding expression in war and armaments, should be expressed in work towards the 'uplifing of humanity and ... in the increasing of opportunity for each individual to round out his life in the highest and noblest service ... If we believe these things, then we must work for peace and goodwill upon the earth.'[121] What better way to begin this work than by reiterating the popular call for Anglo-American unity? 'We in Canada and the United States,' he boasted, 'have a mission in this world. We have no entanglements in our alliances. We have the chance to show the best of all civilization.'[122]

The idea of North American unity as a basis for peace found its most vocal exponent in James Alexander Macdonald, the managing editor of the Toronto *Globe* and a representative of various u.s.-based peace organizations in pre-war Canada.[123] As one of the directors of the World Peace Foundation, the philanthropic research organization endowed by the American publisher Edwin Ginn, Macdonald travelled, lectured, and wrote not only on peace but on one of his favourite topics – the 'North American Idea.' This idea, which Macdonald viewed as almost a prerequisite for world peace, drew upon the North American example of peaceful relations and the eventual spread of 'liberty, democracy and fraternity to a world community of free nations.'[124]

As the world situation began to worsen, the *Globe* urged Britain, Germany, and America to lift themselves above the barbarism that disfigured international relations. 'The new and critical world situation which this decade faces,' ran one editorial, 'is a challenge to Christendom to Christianize the ideals and motives of all the world and to do it in this generation.'[125] There was no better example to follow, Macdonald thought, than that of Canada and the United States, the trustees of hope for all humanity.

Macdonald's note of optimism struck a common chord in Edwardian

Canada. Progressive reformers and the public in general were little inclined to recognize the dangers of militarism in their own society; on the contrary, they were anxious to prove the opposite by commemorating the North American ideal – one hundred years of peace between Canada and the United States. It was this single event, the crowning achievement of friendly negotiation and disarmament, that fired the imagination and enthusiasm of the Canadian public, joined the forces of all Canadians interested in peace, and diverted attention from the more serious and controversial questions of war and peace.

The idea of celebrating the Anglo-American Peace Centenary was first suggested by Mackenzie King. He was successful in persuading both the Americans and the British to establish committees to organize the celebrations, but he found the Canadian government reluctant to act until the British government indicated its final support of the idea in 1912. Prime Minister Robert Laird Borden then proceeded, with the assistance of Sir George Perley and Sir Joseph Pope, to organize an 'unofficial' Canadian Peace Centenary Association.[126] An international conference in 1913 co-ordinated the efforts of the committees and decided that the public festivities would be held in 1915. The object of the celebrations was to instil in the public mind 'the value of international goodwill.'[127]

Since the Canadian government wished to avoid any broad international commitments, the association confined its activities to the usual praise of Anglo-American harmony and internationalism. The association also co-ordinated the centenary projects of its local affiliates across Canada. Most communities confined their plans to classroom studies of Canadian-American relations, thanksgiving services, and the erection of memorials. The more ambitious international proposals included a centenary monument in each of the three capitals; archways over international highways at the British Columbia-Washington State border and at Rouses Point on the Quebec-New York border; a bridge across the Niagara River; and water-gates between Detroit and Windsor.[128]

As the time for the celebration approached, however, the carefully laid plans for commemorating peace in North America were interrupted by the stark reality of war in Europe. The executive committee of the Canadian Peace Centenary Association decided that although the association should be kept alive to carry on some quiet work, the public festivities in Canada should be postponed.[129] So ended the momentum of the much-heralded peace celebrations, as well as that of the progressive peace movement and its campaign against militarism in Canada.

VI

By the early twentieth century strong pacifist traditions had evolved in Canada. A legacy of Christian pacifism was inherited from an assortment of immigrant religious sects with radical roots. For some time, however, their religious radicalism had socially conservative cast deriving from the separatism of the Mennonites, Hutterites, and Doukhobors and the early quietism of the Quakers. Although these and the later fundamentalist groups developed their own peculiar beliefs and ways of life, they all shared in principle the millennial ideal of a perfect society. 'In the Judaeo-Christian tradition,' writes J.W. Bennett, 'the millennial ideal has played an important role as a revolutionary force and as an impetus for renewal and reform. It has led some men towards a utopian vision, and others toward the active reform of contemporary institutions.'[130] The majority of the sectarian pacifists did not follow the latter course; they remained 'separational' pacifists aloof from politics and society. Their religious tradition of non-resistance, confined as it was to their own communities, resulted only in isolated pockets of pacifist practice across the country.

The 'integrational' Quakers, on the other hand, exerted an increasing influence in the liberal reform movement and in the adaptation of Christian pacifism to the realities of a new age.[131] Together with liberal Protestants preaching a social gospel they hoped to realize the practical application of the Sermon on the Mount. The non-sectarian peace movement, however, was not pacifist in the strict sense. It was an example of the liberal, rational approach to international affairs – the belief that reason and arbitration could prevent war. Liberal pacifists in the Canadian Peace and Arbitration Society and the WCTU were pragmatic and promoted a generally inoffensive campaign for peace through arbitration and international goodwill. They were also largely 'fair-weather' pacifists, and when war became a reality they, like the majority of Canadians, eagerly or sorrowfully supported the new cause.

This dilemma of the progressive peace movement was clearly defined a year before the war by Arthur Dorland when he warned that the position adopted by many of the liberal converts to pacifism differed fundamentally from that of Quakers. Although the former condemned the disastrous results of war, they still believed that 'many wars are under certain circumstances justifiable and right,' while true pacifists like the Friends believed that since war was inherently immoral it could never be right.[132] In other words, the liberal pacifists were not truly representative of the radical Christian tradition since, as Dorland noted, they were preoccupied with the futility of war. Largely avoiding moral issues, the progressive peace reformers concentrated on the benefits of arbitration and the generalized threat of militarism, the two concerns upon which they could all agree. Little or no thought was given to the preparation of pacifists for the reality of war or to the formulation of some contingency plan of action for pacifists in time of war. No system or international machinery existed to allow Christian goodwill to be expressed in action. Instead, pacifism was viewed by many as negative and passive. As J.M. Bliss has concluded, 'Ripples from the world tide of peace sentiment increased the volume of pacifist rhetoric in Edwardian Canada. They did not produce a serious re-examination of the ethics of war.'[133]

The absence of an ethical stand weakened the effectiveness of the progressive peace movement throughout the pre-war years and ultimately led to its collapse during the Great War. But liberal pacifism did not wither completely; rather it began to show signs of an important transition towards a socially radical pacifism that combined the progressive optimism of the liberal creed and the moral radicalism, millennialism, and non-conformism of the historic peace sects. It was this regenerated pacifist idea that would capture the imagination of a notable minority of Canadians during and after the Great War and that would become the hallmark of Canadian pacifism throughout the first half of the twentieth century.

2

The collapse of liberal pacifism

On the eve of the Great War, Canadians were relatively comfortable and confident about what the future would bring. As historians have noted, it was a time of optimism, and perhaps no Canadians were more enthusiastic and optimistic than the large numbers who vaguely thought of themselves as pacifists. The popular commitment to peace was visible across Canada in churches influenced by the social gospel, in women's clubs, and in business, farm, and labour organizations concerned with international affairs. Although its adherents were often associated with various reform causes, the peace movement had become a particularly attractive outlet for the middle-class reform impulse. Respectable and uncontroversial, it associated pacifism with order, stability, and the status quo. 'Peace, prosperity, and progress' was the watchword of the day.

On the whole, however, the generalities and moving platitudes characteristic of peace rhetoric were ambiguous, causing that perennial observer of Canadian affairs, J. Castell Hopkins, to comment that pacifism was 'difficult to oppose and hard to discuss,' but 'easy of presentment and popular acceptance.'[1] 'Peace,' said Hopkins, 'had become a habit of thought with many minds in Canada and, in some cases, was almost a religion.' Hopkins, himself an ardent imperialist, claimed that the 'peace school of thought' had always been a strong factor in tempering Canadian responses to imperial obligations, national responsibilities, and support of the militia. The degree of pacifist influence is questionable, but certainly the antagonism of the nation's farmers towards increased military expenditures and the French Canadian 'passive' and 'instinctive' opposition to imperial entanglements were well known.

The threatening climate of world events increased the pacifist calls for the peaceful settlement of international disputes through arbitration and international courts of justice. Canadians poured into crowded meeting-halls to listen to such prominent liberal pacifists as J.A. Macdonald, Lewis E. Horning, and Goldwin Smith and such international figures as Andrew Carnegie and Norman Angell. Riding the crest of his popular book, *The Great Illusion*, Angell advised the Canadian Club of Toronto that the best service Canadians could render for British ideals was to push for the rule of international law over force, but not to supply aid to the British navy.[2] Indeed, all types of military preparedness were condemned by pacifists as 'militarism.'

It was in this charged atmosphere that Principal Maurice Hutton of University College warned a Toronto audience that 'the air is so full of pacifism that it is necessary to urge upon the country the duty of national defence.' Another critic predicted that 'the debauch of pacifism now sweeping over the country will be followed by a rude awakening.'[3] And pacifists, even more than the nation at large, did suffer a 'rude awakening' with the outbreak of war in August 1914.

Like most Canadians, they were surprised by and totally unprepared for war. Just as they were about to celebrate one hundred years of peace with the United States, peace advocates found themselves in an unthinkable position. To them war was an atavism contrary to their faith in Christian progress. In fact, the whole basis of Christian civilization seemed to be crumbling before their eyes. In their shock and dismay they attempted to gather up the pieces and keep their pacifist goals intact, but few succeeded. The progressive peace movement was shattered, and would never be the same again.

Canada's liberal pacifists responded to the war in various ways. Some attempted to maintain a moderate stance, recognizing the necessity to support the war effort while at the same time attempting to uphold pacifist ideals. This was perhaps the most difficult position to maintain. Others gradually came to think that Christianity and the ideal of Christian peace were in danger of extinction at the hands of enemy forces, and joined in a crusade against German 'barbarism.' At the opposite extreme were radical pacifists irrevocably opposed to any involvement in war and militarism. Although some, like the historic pacifist sects, rejected the worldly social order and attempted to remain relatively withdrawn from society and its wars, other radical pacifists began to broaden their attack to include the whole social and economic system they believed produced war in the first place. These socially conscious pacifists represented new groups of woman suffragists, social workers, labour organizers, and social gospellers who found war and militarism antithetical to the Christian basis of their social philosophy and threatening to their particular reform concerns. Unlike earlier peace advocates, they came to view radical social change as essential to world peace, and thereby began a far-reaching transition that ultimately changed the intrinsic nature of pacifism from that of an ideal liberal reform into a new form of social radicalism. Liberal peace advocates re-emerged in the post-war era, but the synthesis of pacifism and radical social change, even if not fully articulated, was forged during the first war.

I

While the pre-war peace movement more or less disintegrated with the shock of war, the immediate reaction of most peace advocates was temperate. On the whole they agreed with the majority of their fellow Canadians that the war was unfortunate but necessary to rid the world of European militarism, and they supported the British cause. As this initial critical acquiescence to the war gradually developed into a militant crusade, some pacifists attempted to maintain a moderately realistic position by combining support for the war with a continuing struggle against militarism and its brutalization of society. Consequently, their outright pacifist remarks were carefully aimed at future post-war society rather than at the current conflict.

As noted in the previous chapter, the editors of two of Toronto's leading newspapers, J.E. Atkinson of the *Star* and J.A. Macdonald of the *Globe* were influential liberal pacifists before the war, and both exemplified the ultimate wartime transition of those who attempted to remain pacifist in spirit if not in action. Macdonald in particular had been one of the leading spokesmen of the progressive peace movement in Canada, and from the outbreak of war he combined support for Canada's war effort with his familiar peace rhetoric, claiming that a time of war was also a time to prepare for peace and disarmament.[4] He asked Canadians to look to the future and choose either militarism and war or disarmament and peace. 'Either the New World idea of reason and international faith must be pushed to the limit of disarmament,' he wrote, 'or the old world idea of brute force and international distrust must be accepted by all countries.'[5] He concluded that Canadians had to make a choice: 'Either we must all stand with Christ or all stand with Caesar.' None the less, Macdonald tried to stand with both.

At first, the *Globe* exercised a moderating influence on the public as its editorials protested against creating anti-German sympathies among Canadian youth and argued that 'no Canadian cadet should be allowed to think of a German or any other man as a target for his marksmanship.'[6] In the circumstances, however, the two lines of thought were impossible to maintain for long, and in 1915 Macdonald resigned as editor, thus freeing the *Globe* to assume a more ardent patriotic position. Macdonald himself began a series of patriotic addresses in which he urged young men to enlist, and in 1917 he called upon Canadians to stand, to fight, and if need be to die in the defence of 'the North American idea, the inalienable and priceless right of a free people to govern themselves.'[7] In the end he joined those liberals who accepted the war as a means of creating a new democratic world order, but he still denounced the idea of armed peace or preparedness as 'doomed to the rubbish heap of the world's barbarism.' 'Another idea must be set free,' he said, 'a world idea, the idea not of international strife, but of international partnership.' Macdonald's final sanction of war as a means to an end was indicative of his nineteenth-century liberal thought, which stressed the progressive search for world order.

A more extreme transformation occurred when J.E. Atkinson declared his all-out support for the war effort. Atkinson reasoned that war was the ultimate and logical conclusion of the worship of materialism, especially in Germany. He accepted the war, therefore, as an attempt to secure the liberal goal – that of protecting the liberties and rights of all peoples. In an address to the Canadian Club of Toronto he even claimed that the war was a crusade 'to secure the possession to mankind of Christianity itself.'[8] That remark was indicative of the growing support for the war effort among former peace advocates.

The underlying conflict within the liberal conscience was most clearly reflected by the Canadian Peace and Arbitration Society as it adjusted to the reality of war. The society's wartime president, Lewis E. Horning, spearheaded an effort to convince a dwindling audience to think 'soberly, righteously and fairly' about the events occurring around them and thereby to resist the growing war frenzy. The aim of the society was to combine support for Canada's war effort with some type of constructive action in line with pacifist principles. As a start in that direction, members of the society made financial contributions, through the Canadian Society of Friends, to the Friends' Ambulance Unit organized by British Quakers.[9]

Although Horning accepted the war as a just struggle between democracy and militarism, his most perplexing problem was to reconcile it with Christianity. One solution, he suggested, was for peace-loving Christians to waste no time in building a new Christian spirit to supplant war. He warned that the peace movement had failed to prevent war, not because it encouraged unpreparedness but because it was very young in an old world accustomed to the tradition of war.[10] What was needed was a 'New Christianity' that would replace the 'ideas of the past' with the 'Law of Love.'[11] Horning hoped that the Canadian Peace and Arbitration Society, like the League for Democratic Control in Britain, would preserve clarity of thought during the war while working towards the post-war emergence of a new international system in accordance with liberal ideals.

Shortly after the outbreak of war, this position was articulated clearly by Horning in a letter to Dr T. Albert Moore, secretary of the General Conference of the Methodist Church of Canada. He explained that although it was not an 'opportune time' to talk of pacifism, the members of his small society wished to ensure that coming generations would think 'more sanely and soundly than the past and present generations.' He appealed to the Methodist church for support in this endeavour. 'A great many of us are saying "never again," ' he wrote, 'but to make sure of this, we ask for your sympathy, wholehearted co-operation and active support.'[12]

As a course of action, Horning suggested combating the martial spirit that had infiltrated daily life and language by building a new vision of patriotism free from the taint of militarism and war. He argued that 'the old Patriotism is altogether too often associated with the soldiers life. The language of our everyday life and of our past literature smacks very much of the martial, that is, it is a language based upon old ideals and old habits. 'Patriotic Fund' … Why not *Soldiers* fund?'[13] The word 'patriotism' was to be reserved for references to peace, self-sacrifice, and brave service for one's fellow man. 'The New Patriotism,' claimed Horning, 'calls for life and opportunity for life, not death and destruction and vandalism and horrors.' By this definition, pacifists could be viewed as patriots, contrary to the 'fallacious arguments' of militarists.

The Canadian Peace and Arbitration Society also maintained that its members and sympathetic friends had a special duty to perform regarding Canada's own peculiar problems, such as French-English relations, which had been further complicated by the war, and the question of state ownership and control of the nation's productive wealth. 'On all sides,' Horning warned, 'we need new light, new thought, a new spirit … we should believe in another destiny, that of the saving of the nations.' In conclusion, Horning made a final appeal to the Church: 'Preachers of Peace and believers in Goodwill, help us ... by your heartfelt sympathy, cordial co-operation and willing openmindedness ... we can be of great service to each other.'[14]

Although the Church ignored Horning's appeal for a 'New Patriotism,' the Canadian Peace and Arbitration Society and other moderates continued to sponsor peace meetings and addresses, at least as long as the United States remained neutral. In October 1915, for instance, Chrystal MacMillan, a British pacifist, addressed a meeting of the Canadian National Council of Women in Toronto with Horning and other members of the Peace Society in attendance. The lecture was organized by two Toronto pacifists, Mrs Hector Prenter of the Political Equality League and Mrs Wesley Barker, past president of the Business Women's Club, who had resigned in protest against the club's war work.[15]

Gradually, however, most pacifists grew passive and silent. Even Horning ceased his attempt to organize a pacifist program of action and retreated to safer pursuits. In keeping with his personal desire to educate the public, for instance, he delivered a nationwide series of lectures during the summer of 1918 concerning problems of war and Canadian citizenship.[16] Members of the Peace Society and other frustrated liberals had tried in vain to prevent the development of an over-zealous war mentality; in the end, moderation in defence of the war or of pacifism succumbed to more extreme and vocal positions as the war continued and a deeper commitment was made by Canadians. While some moderates were converted to one extreme or the other, most were simply silenced by the rising tide of militant Christian patriotism.

II

Almost all groups of liberal reformers came to reflect this militant patriotism in one way or another. Women's groups, for instance, quickly redirected their energies towards more respectable pursuits in Red Cross work and patriotic activities. Indeed, it is ironic that the women who helped popularize the idea that women would react to war differently from men because of their moral superiority were the very ones who contributed substantially to the disintegration of this myth through their various wartime endeavours. Initially, Canadian women agreed with Flora Macdonald Denison, a columnist for the Toronto *World*, that 'the women of England have no quarrel with the women of Germany.'[17] In a matter of months, however, most women were actively involved in some type of war support activity. Even Denison changed her mind and supported the war after her son Merrill enlisted.

The most enthusiastic response of women's groups came from the staunchly patriotic Imperial Order of the Daughters of the Empire and the Women's Institutes. In fact, the effectiveness of the latter's co-ordinated war effort led to the federation of Women's Institutes in Canada under the guidance of Judge Emily Murphy, an idea that spread ultimately to Britain and the United States.[18] The National Council of Women, on the other hand, organized a Khaki League in Montreal to operate a convalescent home for sick and wounded officers and a number of recreation centres near army barracks. Other patriotic women's groups included the Queen Mary's Needlework Guild, which provided garments for incapacitated soldiers and sailors of the empire and their dependants; the National Ladies' Guild for British sailors in Canada; and the Lady Jellicoe's Sailors' Fund, a Toronto-based committee.[19] It was through such groups that war work became a great organizational aid to the women's movement.[20] Certainly, long before women voted for a Union government and supported conscription they shared responsibility in the war, even though they did so for gender-specific reasons, as wives and mothers, and in gender-specific ways, through traditional female support activities.

The most vocal expression of this moral transformation, however, was provided by the nation's churches. Overall, the response of Protestant forces representative of pre-war social gospel pacifism reflected the dilemma of the patriotic Christian in time of war.[21] The war became the supreme challenge to the idea of the partnership of church and state in developing the national culture. Anxious to 'prove' themselves, Christians gradually identified almost totally with national policy. As a result, the religious press championed the war as a righteous cause.

From the beginning of the war this was the unqualified position of the *Canadian Baptist* and the Anglican *Canadian Churchman*, as well as of the official periodicals of the Presbyterian church, the *Presbyterian Record* and the *Presbyterian Witness*.[22] The *Presbyterian*, an unofficial Toronto weekly, was more cautious and maintained its pacifist tendencies for some months before finally succumbing to the pressure for an 'all-out war effort.' The *Presbyterian* cited European militarism rather than Germany as the cause of hostilities and condemned war for sowing seeds of hatred among men. 'We Canadians and Britons everywhere,' wrote the editor, 'should guard against unchristian and unreasoning feelings of hatred.'[23] Another editorial urged that the 'irrational blasphemy of war' be replaced by arbitration and 'tribunals of peace and justice.' The Manitoba Presbyterian Synod adopted a resolution deploring war (while absolving Britain of any responsibility for the calamity) and reaffirmed the righteousness of the empire's cause. But the resolution concluded that the war might never have begun if European Christian churches 'had been more under the sway of the Prince of Peace.'[24]

This attitude was also expressed by the Methodist church's *Christian Guardian*, previously a leading peace organ. Its editor, Dr W.B. Creighton, was well known as a pioneer in social reconstruction, promoter of missions, and a crusader for world peace. Shortly after the outbreak of war Creighton warned that God must be asked not for victory but only for forgiveness and guidance. Creighton condemned the war as foolish, costly, and unchristian: 'There is nothing like war to demonstrate the inexcusable folly of war.'[25] Although Creighton reaffirmed his faith that Christian pacifism, that new 'vision of brotherhood,' was still attainable, the *Christian Guardian* supported the war because it was 'not a war of conquest, but a struggle which has been forced upon us by a military autocracy.'[26]

By autumn the *Guardian* began to promote the war effort with increasing zeal. The general superintendent of the Methodist church, Samuel Dwight Chown, for instance, urged Methodists to enlist in the Canadian army and 'go to the front bravely as one who hears the call of God.'[27] The passionate call to arms soon became a familiar plea, and within a year the war Chown had originally described as 'just, honourable and necessary' was transformed into an apocalyptic crusade, an eschatological confrontation between good and evil, between Christianity and the Antichrist epitomized by Germany. The traditional concept of the 'just war,' prescribing justice and moderation in warfare, gave way under various wartime pressures to the crusading spirit characterized by the dangerous qualities of self-righteousness and fanaticism. 'The conflict that began as a necessary, if somewhat idealized campaign to safeguard national interests and rid the world of a military despotism was transformed under the pressure of events into a holy war, ending as a frenzied crusade against the Devil incarnate.'[28] Albert Marrin's description of British war fever applies equally to Canada. Stories of German atrocities in Belgium and government-controlled war propaganda triggered an emotional response and helped reinforce fears for the future of Christendom itself. The crusading war effort became in effect a new attempt to attain the old nineteenth-century illusion of eternal peace, progress, and prosperity by casting out the German devil.

The conversion of liberal pacifists to a passionate desire for victory required much rationalization and a good deal of serious soul-searching. It was a complex internal struggle in which individual tensions were resolved in a variety of responses. For instance, the western feminist Nellie McClung successfully combined feminist demands with the war effort without abandoning her earlier faith in Christian peace and progress. In 1915 she could still condemn war as the antithesis of all her teaching. On the one hand, war proved nothing and twisted the whole moral fabric by hardening society to human grief and misery, taking the fit and leaving the unfit to perpetuate the race, and – the greatest inequity of all – setting aside the arbitrament of right and justice in favour of brute force.[29] On the other hand, she could support the war as a purgative that would assist in the redemption of the world.

In retrospect McClung described her new perception of the world shared by like-minded Christians:

In the first days of panic, pessimism broke out among us, and we cried in our despair that our civilization had failed, that Christianity had broken down, and that God had forgotten the world. It seemed like it at first. But now a wiser and better vision has come to us, and we know that Christianity has not failed, for it is not fair to impute failure to something which has never been tried. Civilization has failed … we know now that underneath the thin veneer of civilization, unregenerate man is still a savage; and we see now … that unless a civilization is built upon love, and mutual trust, it must always end in disaster, such as this. Up to August fourth, we often said that war was impossible between Christian nations. We still say so, but … we know now that there are no Christian nations.[30]

It was in this frame of mind that liberal reformers came to think of participation in the war as an act of 'national regeneration.'[31] The apocalyptic war hysteria demanded an all-out fight against all evil in society. The devil Hun, the demon rum, the scourge of venereal disease, and other vices and evils affecting humanity became the prime targets of this crusading zeal. As the temperance movement joined forces with the war effort, the *Christian Guardian* maintained that 'theoretically the church knows no peace – she is always at war with evil.'[32] The same line of argument was used by the *Record*'s editor, who equated war against Germany with the war against the liquor traffic and reflected that 'war is never wrong when it is war against wrong.'[33]

Given this radical redefinition of war, some peace advocates went full circle and labelled pacifism itself as evil. The shifting perspective could be observed in November 1916, when W.B. Creighton, while still praising pacifism as 'one of the most hopeful signs of our time,' claimed that pacifists were guilty of 'dull obstinacy,' 'bitter prejudice,' and 'plain stupidity' in the manner in which they attempted to apply pacifism to the war with Germany.[34] If pacifists were disappointed to read such words from a former sympathizer, they were assuredly shocked to read the conclusion to that line of thinking in the *Guardian* of 3 April 1918. In the cover page editorial entitled 'The Vice of Pacifism,' Creighton argued that, far from being a virtue, pacifism was 'a vice revealing the terrible fact that the conscience has lost its sensitiveness and the soul has lost its courage.'[35]

As if this rejection of pacifism as a legitimate Christian doctrine was not harsh enough, the following month Creighton developed his assault further and declared in no uncertain terms that there was no room in the Methodist church for ministers with a pacifist conscience, even though the church had been pacifist in the past. 'As a Church we have opposed war, and our preachers have denounced it most vehemently,' he wrote; but now the situation should be viewed in a 'fresh light,' especially when it was 'clear beyond dispute' that the country was forced into war. As the state 'rightly refused to allow a peace propaganda to be carried on in its midst,' so the church must prevent 'unpatriotic sermons in her pulpits.' Both the country and the church had a right to insist on the 'truest patriotic utterances.' 'If a man cannot conscientiously declare himself a patriot,' warned the editor, 'he has no business in any Church which prides itself upon its patriotism.'[36] Creighton concluded that the church had no choice but to silence pacifists, since 'the sin of unpatriotic speech and act is one which the church cannot afford to condone.' The same sentiments were echoed by the official Presbyterian press: 'To be at peace with evil-doing is to share in that evil-doing ... to cease fighting the German wrong, while that wrong remains, is to be a partner in the wrong. In 'pacifism' we become sharers with Germany in her guilt. Such pacifism is a crime against humanity and against God.'[37] This wholesale condemnation of pacifism and denial of the right of conscience either silenced pacifists or drove them from the church entirely. It was after the publication of Creighton's remarks, for instance, that J.S. Woodsworth resigned from the Methodist ministry.

Most pre-war pacifists, such as Creighton, had not abandoned the nineteenth-century concept of peace and Christendom as a fragile world order that bound men and nations to conduct themselves in accordance with Christian principles and understanding.[38] The pacifist ideal, therefore, was viewed more as an end than a means. Their concept of peace remained one of pure idealism with no room for compromise; but now it was peace at any price, even if that price was war. The result, as J.M. Bliss states, was a paradox: idealized Christian pacifism produced an extreme zeal for a holy war.[39] The former peace advocates who could not rationalize support of a just war with their dedicated faith in the Christian gospel more easily accepted the idea of a holy crusade to save Christianity and peace from the diabolical German menace. In 1918 the editor of the *Presbyterian Record* concluded: 'The world's real crusade is now on, and men in millions are thronging across the seas as did European legions to Asia a millennium gone, but with a more intelligent purpose and a higher, holier aim.'[40]

Although, by the end of the war, the crusading zeal of these former peace advocates resulted in ardent support of the military, it would be unfair to classify them as militarists per se. While they absorbed and reflected the martial spirit, their principal concern was not the development of militarism but the attainment of a world safe for the realization of the Kingdom of God. Thus, some of them combined support for 'the war to end war' with their commitment to social reform.

III

A small minority of Canadians maintained their radical opposition to the war and its accompanying infringements on individual rights and freedoms. One variety of this radicalism was the religious non-resistance expressed by the historic peace sects and fundamentalist groups. As we have seen, the right to live according to religious principles of non-violence was protected by several orders in council and by 1914 had become a tradition entrenched firmly in Canadian law and custom. Most of the pacifist religious communities, such as the Mennonites and the Hutterites, lived apart from the larger Canadian society and therefore remained more or less silent on the war until they were threatened directly with conscription.

The other committed pacifists were the pre-war reformers who began to link pacifism with social radicalism. They included confirmed social radicals who adopted pacifism during the war as part of their overall struggle against the existing social and economic system, and staunch pre-war pacifists such as the Quakers. From the very beginning of the war the Quakers attempted to maintain a program of pacifist activity.

The Canadian Peace and Arbitration Society counted several Quakers, including W. Greenwood Brown and Elias Rogers, among its membership. Quaker concern, however, was largely expressed through the Society of Friends' own peace and arbitration committees, which urged individual Friends to continue their public pacifist witness and to waste no opportunity to 'testify that all war is contrary to Christ's teaching.' Friends condemned the moral effect of the war in creating an indifference to the destruction of human life and suggested that pacifists assume the role of reconcilers. All peace groups, proclaimed the Genesee Yearly Meeting, should 'check and mitigate as far as possible the disastrous feeling of bitterness and hatred that is being intensified between the warring peoples, and thus prepare them sooner for the new regime of universal brotherhood.'[41]

Canadian Friends began searching for some type of positive service to be undertaken by pacifists in time of war, and in this way they bridged the gap between historic non-resistants and the non-violent activists of the twentieth century. Their general position was expressed by Arthur Dorland, the chairman of the peace committee, in his report to the Canada Yearly Meeting in 1917. The report urged Friends to extend 'moral support to those who, though not members of our Society, nevertheless hold genuine religious objection against war.'[42] Dorland also reminded Quakers of their special duty to 'render to our country and to those who have suffered because of the war some equivalent service and even sacrifice.'[43] As an example of a practical pacifist service he cited the loan of Pickering College, a Quaker school, to the government as a convalescent hospital for returned soldiers. Other Quaker activities included a 1916 petition for physical training for boys and girls in schools in lieu of military training, and support of the English Friends Ambulance Unit and the English War Victims Relief Committee.[44] Through these various fields of service Quakers demonstrated that social action was entirely consistent with their peace testimony.

They pressed even further, however, extending their association of pacifism with social reform by insistently examining both the conditions that made for war and their own complicity in them. 'Have we,' they asked, 'either as Christians or as responsible citizens of our respective countries, done all that we might or should to remove these conditions?'[45] Clearly, Friends were moving towards a synthesis of their historic radical Christian pacifism with a radical political outlook. Once they discovered the seeds of war sown within the existing social order, modern Quakers replaced their older emphasis upon mercy in a static society with a radical commitment to change that society.[46] Canadian Friends began to endorse government control and possible ownership of all industries manufacturing war-related articles. Furthermore, anticipating the post-war years as early as 1917, they began to discuss the implications of their social philosophy in such national and international matters as the future role of the state and the relationship between capitalism and war.[47]

Another example of socially radical pacifism was a small group of radical feminists. Largely centred in Toronto, they worked through the Women's Social Democratic League and the Toronto Suffrage Association until the summer of 1915, when Miss Alice Chown, Miss Laura Hughes, and Miss Elsie Charlton founded the Canadian Women's Peace Party, a branch of the International Committee for Permanent Peace.[48] Charlton and Hughes, aware that the women of England and Australia were organized in this regard, expressed concern that Canada should not lag behind. The conspicuous involvement of Alice Chown and Laura Hughes in wartime pacifism proved to be a matter of some embarrassment to Chown's cousin, the Reverend S.D. Chown, the general superintendent of the Methodist church, and Hughes's uncle, Colonel Sam Hughes, the Canadian minister of militia, but the two women remained undeterred. Although Colonel Hughes tried to bribe his niece to cease her activities in return for a half-section of prairie land, Laura Hughes's parents appear to have at least tolerated her peace work and allowed her to distribute pacifist literature from their home address.[49]

The original Women's Peace Party was formed in the United States in January 1915 by Jane Addams and her feminist associates; the idea spread to other nations after the International Congress of Women first met at the Hague in the spring of 1915. Hughes, and possibly Chown, unofficially represented Canada at the congress, which was billed as a women's peace conference. The majority of Canadian women's clubs rebuffed the invitation from the congress as 'untimely peace propaganda' and endorsed the public reply drafted by the National Committee of Patriotic Services of Canada, a federation of nationally organized women's societies. This letter, sent to Jane Addams, the president of the congress, explained that Canadian women felt they could not send delegates since they believed that 'the time for peace has not yet arrived.' The presence of delegates would imply acquiescence in, for example, the devastation of Belgium.[50] The Hamilton chapter of the National Council of Women agreed, and condemned those women calling for a halt to the war as 'guilty in the eyes of God.'[51]

Supplanting a planned meeting of the International Suffrage Alliance, the International Congress of Women provided a forum in which women from around the world discussed plans for ending the war. Besides the suggestion that women's peace societies be formed at home, the congress's most important achievement was a proposal for continuous mediation between the belligerent powers by a group of neutral experts. Although the plan was presented to the congress by Jane Addams, it was the work of Julia Grace Wales, a Canadian from Quebec who was teaching at the University of Wisconsin. Miss Wales conceived her plan for 'Continuous Mediation without Armistice' (or the Wisconsin Peace Plan, as it became known after being endorsed by the Wisconsin Peace Society) in the hope of averting a 'prolonged, irrational and un-Christian war.' The plan was unanimously accepted by the congress and a scheme was devised for putting it into operation, but the worsening events of the war precluded any chance of its success.[52]

Meanwhile, the Canadian Women's Peace Party, later renamed the Women's International League for Peace and Freedom, based its program for a new international order on the reforms outlined at the Hague, including compulsory arbitration, universal disarmament, and the establishment of a league of democratic nations.[53] Upon closer examination, however, the Women's International League appeared to be a 'stop the war' movement, and Laura Hughes actually admitted as much privately. She favoured an immediate unilateral Canadian withdrawal from the war, but she had to be discreet in public in order to avoid the charge of treason.

Generally, Hughes moved towards an increasingly radical outlook. With the Women's International League she directed her wrath at the military-capitalist complex behind the war effort and joined with the labour socialists in their attack on the war profiteering of financial trusts and armament makers. Hughes was converted to the labour cause after touring armament factories as an inspector; she concluded that an independent labour party was the only solution to the disgraceful working conditions she found.[54] At the 1916 TLC convention Hughes electrified the delegates with a stirring radical speech supporting an independent labour party. When the Ontario Independent Labor Party was formed in 1917 she served on its executive committee. In addition, as the leading organizer of a budding pacifist women's network, Hughes corresponded with a few kindred souls across the country, such as Zoe Haight and Violet McNaughton in Saskatchewan. By the end of the war, however,

Hughes had married a radical conscientious objector and moved to Chicago.[55]

Alice Chown, the other founding member of the Women's Peace Party, was also no newcomer to radical activities. A free spirit who usually appeared barefoot to emphasize her independence, Chown was committed to furthering the cause of women's suffrage and women's trade unions. Her early interest in socialism stemmed from the social gospel influence and from a religious hope for a new social order. She tried living in a social settlement for a time, taking particular interest in the British utopian community, Garden City, where emphasis was placed on non-resistance and co-operation.[56] In 1910 she marched through the streets of London with the Women's Social and Political Union carrying a Canadian banner. The following year she wrote a series of articles for a Toronto newspaper on the life of an average working girl, and, horrified by the conditions she discovered, entered into trade union activities. The evolution of her social outlook appeared to reach its final form when, after hearing an address by Emma Goldman, Chown became obsessed with the assault against special privilege, and, although rejecting the anarchist approach, she recognized Goldman's ultimate goal as her own. Faith in laws, institutions, and customs enforced by the state, the church, or some other external authority, she argued, must be replaced by faith in the life force present within all people.

By 1915 Chown turned her attention to the war, and, calling herself a 'strenuous pacifist,' condemned all violent methods of settling disputes, whether strikes, anarchistic actions, or wars, as too costly and only partially successful. She asserted that non-violent action was the best alternative and 'the only right path for a nation to follow.'[57]

Arguing that Christ was a better psychologist than any human being, Chown proposed that Germany be conquered through a new conception of brotherhood, which included the elimination of injustice and selfishness in Canadian society. Her public declaration that 'to conquer your enemy is to love him' received a hostile reception from a country at war, resulting in public abuse and demands that Chown be confined in an asylum or a jail. Undaunted, Chown continued to work towards 'the brotherhood of nations' and 'the abolition of special privileges for individuals and states.' 'But for the people around me,' she recalled, 'the most heroic thing that they could do was to throw themselves disinterestedly into the war.'[58]

Alice Chown also feared the war would have a brutal effect on Canadian society in general. 'I am positive that the evils we go out to fight with violence we shall graft upon our own nation's life,' she wrote. 'Starting with hatred of our enemy's cruelty, we shall end by being cruel ourselves; detesting the subservience of the German people to their state, we shall become indifferent to the subservience of our people to our state. We shall lose our free institutions, free speech, free press, free assemblage, and have to struggle to regain them.'[59]

Shortly after the armistice she explained to her cousin, S.D. Chown, how she had fought all through the war for a knowledge of facts, for justice to the enemy, and for an end to 'acts of unrighteousness' in Russia on the part of the Allies, while he and his associates in the Methodist church hierarchy had allowed themselves to become 'dupes' of the militarists. 'I kept my faith in the sermon on the mount,' she exclaimed, 'and you have put your faith in force and have acquiesced in the lies of the censored press.'[60]

The experience of the Women's International League and the Quakers during the first few years of the war, therefore, reveals that committed pacifists had moved a long way from the progressive call for peace, order, and stability characteristic of the pre-war peace movement. Their blending of pacifism and social radicalism signified the beginning of an important transition in the Canadian pacifist tradition: the pacifist initiative had passed from the old coalition of progressive reformers to a developing realignment of pacifists with the political left. The liberal peace movement itself disintegrated as the majority of its adherents deserted pacifism in favour of a new means of achieving peace – a holy war. Even those who attempted to maintain a moderately realistic position were smothered in the process. The ease and enthusiasm with which this reversal was made betrayed the superficial nature of pre-war liberal pacifism.

But the death of the progressive peace movement early in the war was not the end of liberal pacifism in Canada. It would re-emerge in the post-war years among such groups as the League of Nations Society, and once again would attempt to ensure world peace without directly challenging the state. Amid the pressures of the escalating wartime crusade, however, liberal pacifism proved to be utterly untenable. Those who wished to maintain a pacifist protest found it necessary to adopt a radical critique of the social and economic roots of war, and in doing so to abandon their liberal reformism for some variant of the socialist creed. For some, that too would become a type of eschatological warfare against the existing social order not entirely unlike that of their erstwhile colleagues, no less committed to social change, who sought the reign of peace via 'the war to end war.' Furthermore, just as the democratic socialist movement in the English-speaking world built upon and incorporated the historic tenets of liberalism, the socially radical pacifism forged during the war would retain a glimmer of its liberal past.

The Quakers and radical feminists were among the first to make this shift, but it was not until individual liberties were directly threatened by conscription and other repressive measures that the new socially radical pacifism was fully expressed. Conscription became the catalyst in a radical pacifist response. Nevertheless, even before 1917 Canadian pacifism showed signs of survival as a moral and social alternative.

3

Conscription and conscience

By the time of the Great War pacifism and anti-militarism had become an important dimension of the Canadian radical movement, reflecting the increased influence of Marxist internationalism, Christian social ethics, and the British labour tradition.[1] Indeed, a number of liberal pacifists from religious, farm, labour, and feminist backgrounds moved towards the radical left as their wartime expression of pacifism blended with a socialist critique. The Society of Friends had become one of the leading exponents of this socialized pacifism, thereby bridging the gap between social radicalism and historic religious non-resistance. But Quakers and other sectarian pacifists, who had a long and recognized history of dissenting from the established social order whenever it intruded upon their religious beliefs and way of life, could capitalize upon their history and secure a grudging and even respectful tolerance, while the new social radicals who came more from the mainstream of society, were viewed as dissenters in a more directly political sense. Their pacifism may have been based on Christian ethics, but it was also an expression of their general discontent with the whole social and economic system, and led to suspicions of subversion and treason in the minds of militant patriots. Nevertheless, the socially radical pacifists, as well as the traditional religious pacifists, faithfully exercised their witness against the war, particularly in response to conscription, and thereby set important precedents for minority dissent within Canadian society in wartime.

I

Although a pacifist social critique began to take shape prior to 1917, the conscription issue proved to be a catalyst in mounting opposition to the war. Following a prelude of national registration, conscription was established by the Military Service Act (MSA) in August 1917. The MSA provided for compulsory military service for all male inhabitants in Canada between the ages of eighteen and sixty unless otherwise exempted. The concripts were divided into six classes and called up in order, beginning with the young and single. Apart from cases of hardship, ill health, and conscience, most exemptions applied to men working in occupations considered to be in the national interest.[2]

Although these provisions were readily acceptable to the vast majority of the English-speaking population, they irritated some Canadians and posed a direct challenge to pacifists. Young male pacifists especially were confronted with a traumatic decision of conscience. Consequently, a relatively silent pacifist minority was provoked to speak out against the war and the restrictions of individual liberties. In addition to its well-known effect upon other sectors of society, therefore, conscription triggered pacifist protests and resistance.

For most Canadians, however, the real crisis of conscription in 1917 concerned Quebec's nationalist and anti-imperialist opposition to war rather than pacifist stirrings or radical discontent. The introduction of conscription, further complicated by threats to the linguistic rights of Franco-Ontarians, caused an explosive reaction among French Canadians that resulted in violent anti-conscription riots. The most serious disturbance occurred in Quebec City during the Easter weekend of 1918 over the government's rigid enforcement of the MSA and Quebec's frustrating, powerless position after the 1917 election. When the violence finally subsided on Easter Monday, four civilians were dead and more than fifty civilians and five soldiers injured.[3]

Although government authorities feared a nationwide movement of resistance to conscription because anti-conscription disturbances had occurred elsewhere in Canada, Quebec represented the most serious challenge to the MSA. The majority of Quebec registrants wished to be exempted, mainly for occupational reasons, however, rather than as conscientious objectors. When exemption attempts failed, French-Canadian draft resisters fled either to the mountainous Laurentian countryside or to the United States.[4] The effect of this resistance was that French Canada, accounting for 40 per cent of the total Canadian population, made up only about 5 per cent of the Canadian Expeditionary Forces during the war.[5]

In English Canada conscription also triggered an emotional response, which, on the whole, intensified support for the war effort. The major churches, for instance, enthusiastically endorsed the MSA. In fact, at times the churches resembled auxiliary recruiting units for the government.[6] A number of patriotic clergymen were appointed recruiting directors, and the churches themselves seemed to be in competition for the most recruits. The Methodist emphasis on recruiting, for instance, was partly a response to government recruitment figures, which revealed that the Methodist church had produced the lowest percentage of recruits of any Protestant denomination. Although those figures were later supported by the Methodists' own tabulations, the general superintendent, Dr Chown, publicly refused to accept the government's figures and maintained that Canadian Methodism was willing to do its share.[7]

The war effort of the Methodist church was directed by the Department of Social Service and Evangelism until the creation of a special Army and Navy Board during the winter of 1915. Besides being responsible for Methodist enlistment and employment of chaplains, the board became the official voice of the Methodist church in consultation with military and government departments. Similar boards were established by the Presbyterian, Baptist, and Congregationalist churches.[8]

Once voluntary enlistment was officially recognized as insufficient, the churches quickly supported conscription as the necessary step 'to enrol the man-power of the country in a final and decisive effort to secure a permanent peace.' The *Christian Guardian* reminded its readers that service to God and Country were closely allied, and argued that the church had a right to demand conscription since ministers and their sons were in uniform. 'Yes,' remarked the editor, 'the Church has a right to inculate patriotism and to rally her sons to the defence of the flag in the great world-war.'[9] The *Presbyterian and Westminster* also came out for conscription, even though its editor suggested the bill might have been defeated in a national referendum.[10]

Given the patriotic attitude of the churches and their lack of concern for pacifists, conscientious objection was clearly inconceivable to most Canadians. The average young man was under almost irresistible pressure to enlist. In Canada as in Britain, women and children were encouraged to shame men into uniform. Not to be in uniform labelled one a slacker or shirker, words not reserved for men of the pacifist sects. The *Presbyterian Record* broadly defined the 'slacker' as 'the self indulgent of either sex, and of every age and station, who does not lend every energy to help win the war.'[11] Likewise, the *Christian Guardian* claimed that, although 'slacker' 'had something of a nondescript quality' in the past the war had given it a new connotation of contempt.[12] Although the incriminating term was directed most frequently against French Canadians, it was clearly intended to include all those opposed to the MSA and generally critical of the war effort.

Outside Quebec, opposition to the national registration scheme came from farm and labour critics. Although alarmed, the national executive of the Trades and Labor Congress eventually recommended that trade unionists comply with the registration plan. Their recommendation met with general approval in the eastern trades councils, but the leadership of the western labour movement bolted. The trades council and socialists in Winnipeg established an Anti-registration League, and across the West trades and labour councils emphatically opposed the scheme as a prelude to conscription and urged workers not to fill out the registration cards.[13]

Conscription met with even stronger disapproval. Mass protest meetings organized by the national TLC and the Socialist Party of Canada aroused talk of a general strike. At first the TLC executive favoured a national general strike to force the government to conscript wealth before manpower, but later decided that once conscription became law they should yield to the increased clamour for political action rather than take the direct action of a general strike or passive resistance.[14] Some historians have argued that the entry of organized labour into independent politics in opposition to the Union government was the culmination of labour's strong resistance to war regimentation, but, as John H. Thompson has shown, the opposition of some labour leaders to the registration and conscription of manpower was not shared by the rank and file of the Canadian labour movement.[15] On the contrary, most workers and farmers, including those in the West, wholeheartedly supported the war effort. Nevertheless, some militant workers viewed the military draft as anti-democratic, especially since radical leaders complained that workers' applications for exemptions were routinely rejected.

The most notable labour opposition to the war effort occurred in the West. For instance, the British Columbia Federation of Labour assumed the function of a political party and issued a manifesto calling for the repeal of the MSA and the abolition of the capitalist system, which it believed to be at the root of all wars.[18] The Winnipeg Trades and Labor Council took the lead in opposing both registration and conscription and continued to press for a general strike even after its national congress had decided otherwise. When the 1917 TLC convention endorsed the executive recommendation that the congress not oppose the implementation of conscription, the western delegates remained openly defiant.[17]

At times western radicals protested violently,[18] and, as in Quebec, some workers fled into the woods to avoid induction, thus giving birth to 'rag-tag colonies' of draft resisters on Indian reservations in southeastern Manitoba, on British Columbia's lower mainland, and on Vancouver Island. In August 1918 the western radical movement became outraged when one of these resisters, Ginger Goodwin, the socialist leader of the miners' union, was killed by a dominion police officer.[19]

Overall, labour opposition to conscription was based on the fear that it would result in industrial conscription, government control of workers in specific industries, and thereby the destruction of collective bargaining and trade unionism. Despite these larger concerns, however, the radical labour anti-war position 'certainly had a doctrinal dimension' and remained sympathetic to pacifism.[20]

Labour's insistent demand for the conscription of wealth before men was echoed by farmers and was officially endorsed by the United Farmers of Ontario. In effect, conscription became the focus for agricultural grievances over urbanization, rural depopulation, and the shortage of farm labourers. Confronted with the MSA, farmers demanded exemptions for their sons in order to keep them on the farms, especially since farm work was considered essential to the war effort. With the 1917 election on the horizon, the government temporarily agreed to their request, but in April 1918 cancelled all special exemptions except for conscientious objectors. About five thousand Ontario farmers, feeling angry and betrayed, marched on Ottawa on 15 May 1918 to show their displeasure.[21]

Despite their opposition to conscription, however, most farmers strongly supported the war effort and denounced suggestions that they were in any way unpatriotic. This sensitiveness was clearly reflected in the following message sponsored by the Citizens Union Committee prior to the 1917 election:

The Man is a slanderer who says that
the Farmers of Ontario
will vote with
Bourassa, Pro-Germans,
Suppressors of Free Speech
and Slackers.
Never
They will support Union Government.[22]

Western farmers were no less committed, and, unlike their eastern counterparts, they quietly accepted the cancellation of exemptions as 'inevitable.'[23] Those who did protest usually did so on the ground that 'conscription of farmers would reduce the Canadian contribution to the allied cause.' It appears that initial western opposition to the MSA was not so much a reflection of anti-war sentiment as it was an expression of resentment of the uneven enforcement of conscription. Eventually the farmers' overall support for the war effort overcame their reluctance to accept conscription as a military necessity.

II

Despite some initial anti-conscription sentiment, the mainstream of Canada's church, labour, and farm communities accepted conscription, as well as the whole war effort, as compatible with their broad goals of social reform. Within their ranks, however, there remained a small minority of radical pacifists critical of the war. The introduction of conscription further intensified their pacifist inclinations. As with radical labour, the centre of this pacifist activity was Winnipeg, a city where notable reformers such as J.S. Woodsworth, William Ivens, F.J. Dixon, A. Vernon Thomas, and Francis Marion Beynon, some of whom were already known for their social radicalism, had begun to express radical pacifist sentiments.

F.J. Dixon, a single-taxer and an organizer of the Direct Legislation League of Manitoba, was committed to gradual peaceful change. Dixon was a pacifist during the war. As early as the 1912 naval debate, for instance, Dixon wrote Prime Minister Borden protesting strenuously against the growing spirit of militarism in Canada. He asked Borden to pause and consider whether it was wise to 'in any way assist in drawing Canada into the maelstrom of militarism which is the curse of Europe at the present time.' 'You may ignore this letter or you may not,' he concluded, 'but I do hope that you will receive a large number of letters from the peace advocates in Canada.'[24]

During the war years many forums were closed to Dixon, and he became a prime target of public abuse when he aired his anti-war views. An independent member of the Manitoba legislature since 1914, Dixon was almost the only member of the House to speak out strongly against the war. In one particularly stormy session Dixon denounced the proposed national registration scheme as the first step towards conscription and declared he would not sign the card. When Premier T.C. Norris proposed that those who opposed the scheme be put in jail, Dixon responded: 'Any tyrant would allow the expression of opinion with which he agreed. But freedom demanded the right of expression for minorities. The way to meet a weak argument was to refute it, not to imprison the upholders of it.'[25] Dixon's remarks were interrupted with cries of 'traitor' and 'throw him in jail,' and a movement to impeach him began. But the effort failed, as did a recall campaign, and Dixon continued to blast away at conscription, maintaining that it was absurd and morally wrong to force a man to place his life at the disposal of the state.

Once the Winnipeg Trades and Labor Council declared its unyielding opposition to conscription and called for a national referendum on the issue, Dixon, prominent socialists, and labour leaders organized the Anti-conscription League. Its purpose was to circulate petitions, publicize the league's views, and hold meetings to rally anti-war support. Sometimes these league meetings were broken up by members of the Returned Soldiers' Association and their supporters, and at one gathering Dixon and other speakers were mobbed.[26] Nevertheless, Winnipeg's labour paper, the *Voice*, aired the views of Dixon and other pacifists throughout the war and, while rejecting the principle of non-violence, urged tolerance for Canadians conscientiously opposed to the war for either socialist or religious reasons.[27]

One of the casualties of the anti-war campaign was the Winnipeg reformer and journalist A. Vernon Thomas. Thomas was attracted to the *Free Press* from the *Manchester Guardian* and became involved in Winnipeg reform circles soon after his arrival. In time he became friends with J.S. Woodsworth, and was one of Woodsworth's main allies in the establishment of the People's Forum. Thomas's wife, Lillian Beynon, a leading Winnipeg reformer and suffragist, was also a journalist, like her sister Francis Marion Beynon. All three were radical pacifists.[28] For a journalist to demonstrate such views publicly was dangerous, and Thomas was quickly fired from his job at the *Free Press* after he walked onto the floor of the legislature to congratulate F.J. Dixon on one of his anti-war speeches. Shortly afterward the Thomases, bitterly disappointed, left the country and spent the duration of the war in New York.

Writing to Woodsworth from his self-imposed exile, Thomas confessed that the sacrifice involved in their 'little attempt at freedom' seemed contemptible compared to the personal vigil of Woodsworth and other pacifists in Canada. 'So far we have been comfortable,' he reported, 'and I have in fact had a larger salary than I had in Winnipeg. But we have felt very much being cut off from our friends and then our position has been and still is one of uncertainty.'[29] Thomas found most of his office colleagues fairly tolerant of his pacifist views, but because of the continual pressure of liberty loan campaigns he never felt secure in his new job. 'I may get it put up to me very unpleasantly before the campaign is over,' he wrote; 'however, I shall stand to my guns and take whatever comes along.'[30] Although Thomas continued to contribute anti-war articles to the *Voice*, he often wondered if he could not make a greater protest. 'I don't think the pacifist note of my articles can be mistaken,' he wrote. 'But it ends there and my position is simply that I am not extolling the war in my daily work, which is a great satisfaction.'[31]

Thomas maintained that there would be plenty to do once the war was over and 'immediate fear is removed from the hearts of the people.' He looked forward to the day when he could return to Canada and join Woodsworth in the work 'of absolutely challenging the present constitution of society and its ideals.' Confident that the future would be with them, he cautioned: 'Frankly, until then I do not see what we can do. The only thing, as I see it, would be to ensure ourselves a speedy removal to prison, and we may get there anyway before this horror is over.'[32] Thomas had considered the prospect of imprisonment seriously, and decided he would certainly go to prison rather than enlist if called up; this was a distinct possibility, since he was in the last class but one in Canada. But to do more active propaganda work would also mean prison, and he felt he did not have the reserve of physical strength necessary for such an ordeal.[33]

Despite his attempt to remain optimistic about the post-war era, Thomas became depressed over the increasing toll the war was taking on Canadian society. The evil fruits of war, he warned, were growing every day: 'We cannot think the war out of existence. People are not what they were. Their minds have become militarized and we shall have to deal with people of that kind. The workers have not been spared. A good deal of the labor movement is now war. It is all a tragedy and we can only make the best of it.'[34]

Thomas's sister-in-law, Francis Marion Beynon, stayed behind for a time in Winnipeg as the editor of the women's page of the *Grain Growers' Guide* and carried on the anti-war struggle. Social discontent was on the rise in wartime Winnipeg, and Francis Beynon exemplifies the transition of a pre-war liberal into a radical. Like most liberals before 1914, Beynon subscribed to the usual anti-militarist, pacifist sentiments. But as Ramsay Cook has explained, the war raised serious questions about fundamental liberal intellectual assumptions, exposing a naïve faith in moral progress.[35] Although she believed women had a greater interest in social and ethical questions than men, Beynon questioned the validity of the pacifist influence of women.[36] In a short time her growing scepticism seemed justified by the thorough involvement of women in various war activities and the intolerant, conformist attitude associated with their patriotism. Consequently, Beynon became convinced that there was something radically wrong with the whole social order.[37] Patriotism and nationalism merely defended the established order, she argued, while its intolerant, militarist spirit was the same spirit that crucified Christ and continued to threaten those preaching his pacifist doctrine.[38]

The super-patriotic atmosphere of the country strengthened Beynon's resolve and her radical commitment to pacifism and social reconstruction. Initially, however, the popular association of dissent with subversion cautioned Beynon to restrain her pacifist sentiments in favour of safer demands – for example, the conscription of wealth as well as men. But unlike those who associated this proposal with some form of graduated income tax, Beynon made it clear she favoured the actual 'taking over by government of all real property.'[39] As she became more outspoken she also echoed the familiar charge that the most fervent patriots were those getting rich from 'sweated labor and war profiteering.'[40] Her anti-war statements and the radical tone of her column, she suspected, had aroused the wrath of the press censor and ultimately placed her at odds with her editor, George F. Chipman, who had moved towards support of conscription and Union government. Consequently, rather than restrain her pacifist and radical beliefs, Beynon resigned in the summer of 1917 and joined the Thomases in exile.[41]

Francis Beynon became convinced that the war was the result of capitalist economic conflicts and a militant mentality, and that it would create more problems than it would solve. Like other radical pacifists, for example, she feared that wartime mobilization was causing Canadian society to become increasingly insensitive to social injustice, as its treatment of enemy aliens testified.[42] The only way to solve world problems and to prevent future military conflicts was through a social and intellectual revolution, the fear of which, she asserted, haunted Canadian capitalists by 1918.[43]

Before the war, social reformers like Beynon had depended upon the theology of liberal Protestantism, but it now appeared that the progressive social gospel lacked the intellectual depth required to support a major movement of social and moral reconstruction.[44] What was necessary, according to the radicals, was a synthesis of the moral and ethical aspects of Christianity with an intelligent, dynamic philosophy for radical change. The radicalized social gospel was an attempt to move in that direction.

According to Richard Allen, by 1914 the social gospel began to crystallize into three wings, conservative, progressive, and radical, each conflicting with the other throughout the following decade. At the same time, however, there was a general leftward movement of the social gospellers as a whole, a movement reflected in increased radicalism during the war years.[45] The majority of social gospellers found reform – and some amount of radical reform – quite in harmony with the war effort. Nevertheless, a committed minority, including some leading radicals, separated from the mainstream of the social gospel over the issue of pacifism. By taking the pacifist stand they believed they were remaining faithful to pre-war social gospel pronouncements on the necessity of attaining world peace before the Kingdom of God could be realized.

Among these dissidents was C.S. Eby, one of the earliest proponents of the social gospel. He continued to voice anti-war sentiments while calling for a 'great spiritual revolution' based upon the Sermon on the Mount or the 'Charter of the Kingdom.' Unless such a change occurred, the war would be but a prelude to still greater struggles. 'The obscene vermin of vice, degeneracy and more war, that will rise out of this war, as they always rise out of every war,' warned Eby, 'can be met ... only by the positive creative spirit of Christ.'[46]

The newer breed of radicals in the churches generally agreed with Eby's diagnosis, but when they sought to put their pacifist preaching into practice some lost their parishes and some left the ministry entirely. J.S. Woodsworth, a radical Methodist reformer who ultimately became Canada's most famous pacifist, was one of the latter group.

Woodsworth favoured the practical extension of the gospel of love during wartime, both as an ideal and as a method of reform. His pacifism was an integral part of a larger concern for social justice based upon the ethical demands of Christianity. According to his biographer, Kenneth McNaught, Woodsworth represented a complex mixture of the moral doctrine of religious pacifism and the pragmatic tenets of socialism.[47] He and other radicals suspected that the established social order was based on the same ethic of force that produced war; consequently, they united their opposition to the war with a call for social reconstruction.

Woodsworth's pacifist convictions evolved slowly. His student life at Oxford and the events of the Boer War started him thinking along new lines, but he still accepted 'the existing order of things.'[48] Gradually, as he examined the cruelty of war and its disastrous effect upon private and public morality, his pacifist sympathies grew stronger. As chairman of the Canadian Welfare League in 1914, Woodsworth compiled *Studies in Rural Citizenship*, a book authorized as the basis for adult study courses by the Canadian Council of Agriculture. In it he suggested a number of controversial resolutions for debate; for example, 'Resolved that commercial interests are at bottom of modern wars,' and 'Is war justified by the teachings of Jesus?' The book also contained a pacifist statement by Nellie McClung and Salem Bland's proposal for the moral transformation of Canadian politics.[49]

The outbreak of war began a time of 'heart searching' for Woodsworth. He later recalled attending a Sunday night service in St James' Methodist Church, Montreal, in which a military man reviewed the atrocities in Belgium while the president of McGill University made a patriotic appeal to youth; 'then the pastor of the Church in approved evangelistic style appealed for recruits, urging that the young men give their name to sergeants in uniform stationed at the door. This in the name of Jesus! The whole performance seemed to me absolute sacrilege. I walked the streets all night.'[50]

Throughout the following year Woodsworth corresponded with numerous pacifists and became increasingly adamant in his own pacifist convictions. In June 1916 he was labelled a pacifist by the Manitoba press following an address to the Young Men's Club of Winnipeg's Grace Church in which he expressed doubt that moral issues could be settled by military force.[51] It was not until conscription became the issue of the day, however, that Woodsworth spoke out publicly. In the meantime he was deeply absorbed in social welfare work.

His pioneering work with Winnipeg's All Peoples' Mission and his work with the Canadian Welfare League earned Woodsworth the reputation of a Canadian authority in the field of social welfare. In 1916 he was appointed director of the Bureau of Social Research, an agency established by the three prairie provinces. It promised to be an eventful enterprise, but within a year the bureau was closed following Woodsworth's protest against the introduction by the federal government of a national registration scheme. Woodsworth decided the time had come to take a public stand. In a letter to the *Manitoba Free Press* he condemned national registration as a prelude to conscription: 'This registration is no mere census. It seems to look in the direction of a measure of conscription. As some of us cannot conscientiously engage in military service, we are bound to resist what – if the war continues – will inevitably lead to forced service.[52] He also raised the labour-socialist argument that 'conscription of material possessions should in all justice precede an attempt to force men to risk their lives and the welfare of their families.' Woodsworth later recalled that, following the closing of the bureau, he was denounced as a fool, even by his closest associates.[53]

Although Woodsworth's action coincided with the protests of organized labour, it appears evident, as Richard Allen maintains, that Woodsworth's dismissal was due to his pacifism rather than to his social and economic radicalism. The three provincial governments were aware of his radical political outlook before appointing him, but his pacifism represented a threat of 'unknown potential' in the context of talk in labour circles of passive resistance to the registration scheme.[54] At any rate, considering the patriotic feeling in the country, the prairie provinces were in no mood openly to endorse a pacifist.

After his dismissal Woodsworth for a time contemplated joining a Doukhobor community and even made inquiries in that direction. The Doukhobors were sympathetic, but wondered if Woodsworth could adapt to their ways. Perhaps Woodsworth shared their doubts, for he finally accepted another charge in Gibson's Landing, British Columbia, a small coastal mission. His outspoken pacifist views, however, were no more welcome in British Columbia than in Manitoba, and the following year the British Columbia Stationing Committee complied with the congregation's request that he be removed. In response, and chagrined by Creighton's anti-pacifist editorial in the *Guardian*, Woodsworth resigned from the ministry, and for the remainder of the war he worked as a longshoreman on the west coast while his wife Lucy organized the Vancouver chapter of the Women's International League for Peace and Freedom.

In citing the reasons for his resignation, Woodsworth emphasized that the war policy of the church and the issue of pacifism were of central importance. Although there was little opportunity to protest against participation in the war at first, 'as the war progressed, I have protested against the curtailment of our liberties which is going on under the pressure of military necessity and the passions of war.'[55]

Woodsworth's letter of resignation, even more than Beynon's protest, revealed a new socially radical pacifism – a synthesis of absolute Christian social ethics with a radical political critique – that was to become more common in the twentieth century. For instance, Woodsworth asserted that war was the 'inevitable outcome of the existing social organization with its undemocratic form of government and competitive system of industry.' A murder in Serbia or the invasion of Belgium was not the cause of the war, he argued, and to claim that they were was a product of 'ignorance or a closed mind, or camouflage, or hypocrisy.'[56] Woodsworth warned that, rather than solve any problems, the war would have a brutalizing effect upon society. 'The devil of militarism cannot be driven out by the power of militarism,' he wrote, 'without successful nations themselves becoming militarized. Permanent peace can only come through the development of good-will.'

Above all, however, Woodsworth emphasized that the spirit and teachings of Jesus were 'absolutely irreconcilable with the advocacy of war.' 'Christianity may be an impossible idealism,' he declared, 'but so long as I hold to it, ever so unworthily, I must refuse, as far as may be, to participate in or to influence others to participate in war ... When the policy of the State – whether that state be nominally Christian or not – conflicts with my conception of right and wrong, then I must obey God rather than man. As a minister I must proclaim the truth as it is revealed to me. I am not a pro-German; I am not lacking, I think in patriotism; I trust that I am not a slacker or a coward. I had thought that as a Christian minister I was a messenger of the Prince of Peace.[57]

In closing his letter, Woodsworth criticized church leaders for their intolerant and militaristic attitude; they denounced pacifism as a vice, replaced love with hatred, and turned churches into recruiting agencies. 'A minister's success seems to be judged by the number of recruits in his church rather than the number of converts.' To support his accusations, Woodsworth quoted the *Christian Guardian's* editorial advocating the silencing of all pacifists in the church. 'Apparently the Church feels that I do not belong,' he lamented, 'and reluctantly I have been forced to the same conclusion.'[58]

Woodsworth's brand of pacifism was shared by William Ivens, the pastor of McDougall Methodist Church in Winnipeg. A British immigrant and a former student of Salem Bland at Wesley College, Ivens was already a radical social gospeller in 1914, but had shown no sign of pacifist conviction. He had come to McDougall in the hope of establishing a labour-oriented church.[59] His increased radicalism after the introduction of conscription paralleled that of organized labour, with whom he sympathized. But it was his pacifism, not his radicalism, that led to a crisis in his church.

Although he refrained from voicing pacifist views from the pulpit, Ivens felt free to express himself on the outside. He contributed several anti-war articles to the *Voice* and became involved in trade union activities. Ivens's actions split his congregation, and in the spring of 1918 church officials made an urgent appeal to the Manitoba Stationing Committee for his removal. Unintimidated, Ivens immediately embarked on a speaking tour of the prairies. Vernon Thomas told Woodsworth that Ivens's tour of western Canada demonstrated that it was possible for one with his reputation to speak publicly.[60] Thomas praised Ivens for fighting a tremendous fight and 'winning his way into the hearts of people.'[61] 'I am sure a great many must admire him in their hearts who dare not speak out. We must not forget that there is a tremendous intimidating force at work now in all countries to crucify any opinions except those of the powers that be.'[62]

Despite numerous letters and petitions supporting Ivens, the Methodist Stationing Committee removed him from McDougall and offered him a different station in Winnipeg. Ivens declined the offer, claiming that his pacifist views would only cause more difficulties, and assumed the editorship of the *Western Labor News*, the official organ of the Winnipeg Trades and Labor Council.[63] His old friend Vernon Thomas was quick to wish him luck in the new undertaking, which, unlike the Methodist church, might allow him to interpret Christ in his own way – as a pacifist.[64] But Ivens was soon under attack again when the chief press censor, Ernest Chambers, threatened to outlaw the paper unless Ivens purged the publication of revolutionary and pacifist articles.[65]

The most visible example of Ivens's radicalism, however, was the Labor Church he founded in July 1918 as a creedless church aimed at the 'establishment of justice and righteousness on earth, among all men and nations.' Linking ethical Christianity and social radicalism, the church was also a protest against war, as J.S. Woodsworth, shortly to be associated with Ivens's new enterprise, later commented: 'We believe that physical force settles nothing ... what is won by physical force must be maintained by physical force. Physical force is a deceptive shortcut. Moral ends can be attained only by moral means ... education, then, not the sword, is to be the instrument of our emancipation.'[66]

A new pacifist ethic clearly emerged as Woodsworth, Ivens, and other social radicals voiced their opposition to conscription and to the war. By linking war and capitalism, they combined a socialist anti-war critique with the radical Christian belief in the moral necessity of pacifism in any meaningful social revolution. Thus, they staunchly opposed the existing social order, the state's war effort in particular; as a result, pacifist ministers lost their churches and others were forced from their jobs.[67] In the end, however, the war resistance of a small number of social radicals strengthened not only the principle of minority dissent but the idea of a socially radical pacifism.

III

Despite the protests of social gospel radicals, the most ardent pacifist opposition to conscription was exhibited by the historic peace sects, especially the Society of Friends, which by this time had come to represent radical social change as well as traditional religious non-resistance. As early as May 1917 a joint committee representing all three branches of Canadian Friends met in Toronto to outline Quaker resistance to an anticipated conscription bill. An executive subcommittee composed of Albert S. Rogers, Charles A. Zavitz, and George Clark, representing the three branches, forwarded a resolution to Prime Minister Borden in which they reaffirmed the 250-year-old opposition of Friends to the bearing of arms and requested that the exemptions allowed under the old Militia Act be carried over in any new measure. Furthermore, reflecting a radical concern with individual rights of conscience, the Quakers urged that the new exemption clause should be broadened to include not only recognized pacifist sects but all those 'whose conscience forbade them to carry arms regardless of their membership in any particular church or society.'[68]

Once the conscription bill became law, Albert S. Rogers interpreted the Military Service Act to the members of the peace committee, explaining the division of classes and the list of possible exemptions. Friends of military age were advised to report to the proper authority in plenty of time to process their applications for exemption and to be prepared to appear before the local tribunal to explain their claims and present the certificates of membership issued by the clerk of their Monthly Meeting.[69] The certificate forms were devised by the peace committee and distributed to the clerks of the various Monthly Meetings in order to help organize Friends along uniform lines.[70]

As the defenders of their faith the young men in question received enthusiastic support from their fellow Quakers.[71] It was expected, however, that young Friends would claim exemption as absolute pacifists, and when a few enlisted or, like LeRoy Cody, joined the non-combatant military corps, they were severely criticized. One of Elias Rogers's sons actually joined the Royal Flying Corps and was killed in action in June

1916.[72] A few other Canadians, including Albert Rogers's nephew David and Edwin Zavitz, joined the Friends Ambulance Unit in Italy and France respectively, an acceptable though still unfamiliar alternative version of active pacifist service.[73]

Just as most young Quakers conscientiously refused to bear arms, many older Friends were conscientiously unable to subscribe to war loans since they believed such money was used solely for the destructive purposes of war. They contributed instead to the Friends' Ambulance Unit fund in order to support conscientious objectors in constructive service.[74]

At first, the majority of Quakers, as well as Mennonites and Hutterites, found it less complicated to receive exemptions from military service as farmers rather than as pacifists, especially since the Military Service Act was somewhat ambiguous on the question of religious objectors. Unlike the Militia Act or the order in council that provided for pacifist exemptions, the MSA failed to name the pacifist sects specifically; rather, it included them in general either under an exemption clause, offering exemption from combatant service only, or under an exception schedule, excepting some from the provisions of the act altogether. The requirements for exemption were that the applicants 'conscientiously [object] to the undertaking of combatant service and [be] prohibited from so doing by the tenets and articles of faith, in effect on the sixth day of July, 1917, of an organized religious denomination existing and well recognized in Canada at such date, and to which he in good faith belongs.'[75] The exception schedule applied to those men holding a certificate of exemption, on grounds other than conscientious objection, and to 'those persons exempted from Military Service by Order-in-Council of August 13th, 1873 and by Order-in-Council of December 6th, 1898.'

It appeared that, except for the Mennonites and Doukhobors referred to in the above-mentioned orders in council, Canadian religious pacifists were to be exempted only from combatant service unless they could receive exemption on one of the other possible grounds: work in the national interest, completion of education, serious personal hardship, and ill health or infirmity.[76] It was possible, therefore, for religious pacifists who were also farmers to receive exemptions from all service, even non-combatant work. Other pacifists undoubtedly were aware of that 'loophole.' As an escape from military service, however, it was by no means used exclusively by pacifists, for 95 per cent of all those called up across Canada in October 1917 claimed exemption for one reason or another.[77] Faced with such wholesale avoidance, the government, in April 1918, cancelled all exemptions except those for conscientious objectors.

Various religious groups remained uneasy over the lack of any specific guarantees, and some, such as the Seventh-Day Adventists and the Christadelphians, petitioned the House of Commons to recognize officially their opposition to military service.[78] Their worst fears were realized when the Ontario registrar wrongly ruled that Tunkers, fellow religious pacifists, were not exempted, thereby exposing Tunker men to military discipline for remaining faithful to their beliefs. One such case involved Ernest J. Swalm, later a Canadian Tunker bishop. After being denied exemption both as a Tunker and as a farmer, Swalm refused military duty and was sentenced to two years' hard labour. Within a month he was released, and the Tunker church was recognized; nevertheless, other pacifist groups feared similar experiences. Finally, the central appeal judge, in an effort to help clarify a confusing situation, ruled that Mennonites, Dunkards or Tunkers, Christadelphians, Seventh-Day Adventists, and the Society of Friends all qualified as bona fide pacifist sects eligible for exemptions.[79]

As far as the Mennonites were concerned, however, their legal status under the MSA remained uncertain until the end of the war. At first a temporary problem arose concerning the proper identification of young men as Mennonites, since they were not baptized until they reached the age of twenty-one. The issue was settled when government authorities accepted the argument of the Mennonite church that unbaptized children were as much Mennonites as baptized adults and that their earlier petitions for exemption from military service had always assumed and intended that to be the case.[80]

The main point of contention for Mennonites was the interpretation of the exemption and exception provisions. All the Mennonites of western Canada, those who immigrated in 1873 as well as those who migrated from Ontario, were excepted from the MSA, while the Mennonites of Ontario were exempted from combatant service only. At times it appeared that all Canadian Mennonites would be excepted; at least, this was the attitude the Justice Department conveyed to a Mennonite delegation headed by Bishop S.F. Coffman in November 1917. Yet in Ontario the district registrars continued to insist that eastern Mennonites were exempt only from combatant service. Their judgment was upheld by the central appeal judge five weeks before the war ended. In practice, however, Ontario Mennonites escaped all service when granted a 'leave of absence,' a special procedure arranged by Bishop Coffman in conjunction with friends in the House of Commons. The 'leave of absence' became automatic under presentation of proper Mennonite identification, and allowed the tribunals to avoid the question of exemption and exception.

One of the reasons for the reluctance of administrators to grant a blanket exception to Mennonites was the public concern over the influx into Canada of Mennonite and Hutterite conscientious objectors from the United States. Once the United States entered the war and enacted compulsory military service, war hysteria swept that country, creating an oppressive, intolerant atmosphere for pacifists, especially those of German ancestry. In contrast to the situation in Canada, religious objectors in the United States faced the real possibility of military induction, maltreatment, and prison terms. Added to this, the Germanophobia of the Midwest and the vicious harrassment of Hutterite communities in South Dakota produced a crisis for Mennonites and Hutterites in the United States. Glowing reports from their Canadian brethren of the tolerance and freedom of religious practice extended by the Canadian government resulted in a mass emigration to Canada that increased as the war progressed.[82] While some Hutterite communities resettled en masse,most Mennonite youths emigrated alone. With the encouragement of their families, they slipped across the border in underground fashion throughout the war years. In 1918 alone, approximately 600 Mennonites and 1,000 Hutterites entered Canada, according to the Honourable J.A. Calder, minister of immigration.[83]

The exaggerated figures of 30,000 to 60,000 quoted in the press and the House of Commons, however, reflected a growing nativist reaction against Germans, shirkers, and 'slackerism' in the Canadian West. Westerners in particular resented the ease with which pacifists received exemptions from military service. They argued that while their own sons were away in the military, the new settlers or 'dirty shirkers' were acquiring the most desirable farm land. Singled out as 'one-man exemption tribunals,' Mennonite ministers such as Bishop David Toews were accused of signing exemption certificates indiscriminately regardless of the bearer's citizenship.[84] Political organizations, major Protestant denominations, and veterans' groups such as the Great War Veterans Association, all denounced the Mennonites. The Great War Next-of-Kin Association even suggested that they be drafted and anglicized. During the autumn of 1918 the mounting public hostility erupted in demonstrations against the new Mennonites at Swift Current, Moose Jaw, and

Regina. In October 1918, shortly before the end of the war, the governor-general in council ruled that immigrant Mennonites and their descendants not covered by the 1873 order in council would not be exempted or excepted from military service.[85]

Although Canadian Mennonites were at first ill-prepared in organization and structure to cope with government bureaucracy and adverse public opinion, they began to pull together during the war in order to secure their common pacifist goal. The various groups of Mennonites also began to unite in an attempt to undertake some active, constructive, humanitarian service during wartime. Early in 1917 the western Mennonites made financial contributions to the Canadian Patriotic Fund for the support of war victims, invalids, widows, and orphans. The next year the various factions of Ontario Mennonites and Tunkers joined together to form the 'Non-resistant Relief Organization' through which funds were collected for relief and charitable purposes.[86] The crises of war and imperilled liberties produced among Canadian Mennonites a new awareness of themselves, their unique position within Canadian society, and their possible future role in non-violent constructive action in this world. The lessons they learned in the first war eased considerably their adjustment to the second.

From Mennonites to Quakers, regardless of their perceived roles within society, the historic peace sects were largely responsible for exercising the ultimate in pacifist dissent – the steadfast refusal on the part of individuals to undertake military service for reasons of conscience. The question of pacifism in twentieth-century Canada was purely academic until young men were directly challenged by conscription; thereafter it was in the personal response of pacifists to conscription that pacifism left its mark upon Canada.

IV

The actual process of applying for conscientious objector (CO) status was relatively simple, even though the climate of public opinion hindered the applicant's chances of success. The religious pacifist reported to the authorities, claimed exemption as a conscientious objector, and then reported to his local tribunal to present his case and prove his membership in a recognized pacifist denomination. The Military Service Act provided for three levels of tribunals: local tribunals, appeal tribunals, and a central appeal judge. Each local tribunal was composed of two members, one appointed by a board of selection and the other a country court or district court judge. The chief justice of the court of last resort in each province acted as the appeal tribunal, while the central appeal judge was one of the justices of the Supreme Court of Canada.[87] The local tribunals, of course, were the most important in determining a young man's status as a conscientious objector.

The attitude of local tribunals varied from one locality to the next, but overall, in Canada as in Britain, they represented the patriotic elements of society and tended to look askance at claims for exemption for reasons of conscience. They and the majority of Canadians were not well acquainted with religious pacifism, and neither understood nor trusted the variety of claimants. It was much easier for a young man to receive an exemption for occupational reasons such as farm work. Whatever the reasons, however, ultimately half the men registered under the MSA were granted exemptions.[88]

An exemption for a religious pacifist depended largely upon the religious denomination to which he belonged. If he did not claim membership in a denomination recognized by authorities as a legitimate pacifist sect, and if he persisted in his pacifist stand, the claimant faced military discipline and possible imprisonment. At first the government did not know quite what to do with conscientious objectors. Since the religious groups qualifying for exemptions were not specifically named in the MSA, registrars depended on rulings by the central appeal judge to determine the legitimacy of certain claims.

Initially, those individuals who did not belong to one of the required religious affiliations and those whose exemptions were refused were tried by district courts martial and punished by imprisonment for up to two years.[89] While some military districts reported that a short period of detention produced a 'complete cure' and discouraged further conscientious objections, the military district headquarters in Toronto argued that such sentences failed to provide a sufficient deterrent to conscientious objections and claimed that many men preferred 'a short sentence of imprisonment at the Burwash Industrial Farm to military duty.' Consequently, commanding officers of units receiving COS were ordered to determine the sincerity of a man's conscientious objections. Under this system, if a pacifist's objections were recognized as bona fide, he was transferred to a non-combatant unit; if it was decided that he was insincere or if he refused non-combatant duty he faced a general court martial and a sentence ranging from five years' imprisonment to life.[90] According to a memorandum issued by the office of the judge advocate general in October 1918, the imposition of longer sentences proved 'very effective' in discouraging the claims of cos. Of approximately 130 imprisoned cos, only about 25 cases involved a general court martial.

Following a clumsy beginning, the Justice Department and the Department of Militia and Defence settled in with their task of enforcing the MSA and handling the problem of conscientious objectors refusing non-combatant service. Although their prime concern was to discourage conscientious objection, military and government authorities began to take a more tolerant and imaginative attitude. By the summer of 1918 the chief of the general staff suggested several possible courses of action regarding the absolute pacifists. The first option, to continue sending them to ordinary jails and penitentiaries, raised the most serious objections, since it was recognized that the men were not, 'properly speaking, criminals, and to punish them adequately in this way may arouse public criticism.'[91] The benefits of congregating the cos in one place of detention were offset by the loss of their possible services to the community. Finally, serious consideration was given to the idea of organizing a forestry unit in British Columbia, especially since men were needed to get out the white spruce timber for airplane manufacturing. Also, this seemed to offer the possibility of constructive service for cos who 'would otherwise spend their time uselessly in the penitentiary.'[92] Another suggestion involved the use of cos in non-combatant duty as cooks in the Naval Service. The deputy minister of militia and defence had no objections to this idea, but he doubted that any imprisoned cos would agree.[93] Although the war ended before any of these plans were formalized, the idea of a forestry unit was reintroduced during the Second World War.

Government and military authorities were besieged with requests and petitions regarding specific problem cases from a wide variety of religious groups, including Quakers, Doukhobors, and Moravians, and some unusual sects such as the 'Holiness Movement Church' and the 'Community of the Son of God.' The Unitas Fratum, or United Brethren, in Alberta claimed that they were excepted from all military service by virtue of 22 Geo. II, c. 30,[94] but the director of military service disagreed; he maintained that a man's status in regard to military service was determined by the legislation of the dominion only and not by 'ancient Imperial Statutes.' A different sort of problem arose concerning non-combatant service. Canadian Seventh-Day Adventists argued that, although they were willing to serve in any non-combatant capacity, that outlet might be closed if they were forced to perform drills and unnecessary labour on their sabbath.[95] It was a difficulty the authorities had not foreseen, but it was remedied quickly when the adjutant-general ordered all military districts to relieve all Seventh-Day Adventists of duty on Saturdays.[96]

A different and more difficult question of the status of young pacifist members from churches supporting the war was raised by the Reverend Fred F. Prior, pastor of the Free Methodist Church, St Boswells, Saskatchewan. He claimed that one conscientious objector in his church was 'an intelligent, consistent-living young man, objecting a hundred times more intelligently, and with far more conscience in the matter, than many members of exempted Churches.' It was a tragedy, the pastor concluded, that this young man and others like him were forced either into the 'category of criminals' or into what was to them 'Treason against Jeasus Christ.'[97] This dilemma could have been avoided if the Quakers' radical suggestion that individual conscience rather than religious affiliation had been adopted as the basis of exemption. But as it stood, the MSA made no provision for conscientious objectors within the established churches or for individual belief. The central appeal judge further limited the possibilities of conscientious objection when he ruled in 1918 that the Church of Christ, or Disciples, Pentecostal Assemblies, Plymouth Brethren, and the International Bible Students' Association failed to meet the necessary qualifications for conscientious objection.[98]

Restricting the number of exemptions was clearly in harmony with the mood of the country. While some Canadians even complained about Quakers being exempted or let out of prison,[99] most private citizens directed their venom against all 'slackers.' On the part of a few people the issue became an obsession, as an excerpt from a letter to the commanding officer of the military district of Montreal illustrates: 'I have reason to say I am positive that many young men which are fit for service to the Country will try to elude undercover of night from Military Service, as the majority of them are called Night Birds. They are never seen in the day-time, but if you will take my advice and give me a special commission I will do everything to bring these slackers to serve the country.'[100] This reference to 'Night Birds' undoubtedly included French-Canadian resisters, since very few men claimed CO status in Quebec. Most religious exemptions were granted by tribunals in the districts of London and Toronto and in western Canada. Of 636 such exemptions granted between February and March 1918, 278 were from Regina alone, but few, if any, were from Quebec or the Maritimes.[101] In a confidential report prepared in December 1918, the military district of Montreal estimated that it encountered no more than twelve conscientious objectors during the war, and of these the majority were International Bible Students or Jehovah's Witnesses.[102] As early as 1916 several International Bible Students applied for conscientious exemptions by submitting prepared affidavit forms in which they claimed that they were obligated by conscience to 'follow peace with all men and to do violence or injury to none.'[103] The commanding officer of the district, at first perplexed by the sudden appearance of form letters all properly notarized by a justice of the peace, remarked angrily that he would like to 'take damn good care that everyone of these fellows would be enlisted.'[104] Following a brief inquiry he discovered the men were advised by J.F. Rutherford, editor of the *Watch Tower* magazine, to complete the forms, legal proof of their status and beliefs as Bible Students, as protection from conscription.[105]

Rutherford must have been unaware that the central appeal judge supported the government's contention that the International Bible Students' Association was not an 'organized religious denomination' within the meaning of the MSA. If Bible Students could not obtain a different form of exemption, therefore, they had to serve when conscripted or suffer the consequences. Although there were members of other denominations in the same position, as a group the Jehovah's Witnesses proved to be the most radical and stubborn in their passive resistance, and accordingly they experienced the worst treatment accorded Canadian conscientious objectors in the First World War and later in the Second World War.

The most scandalous mistreatment of conscientious objectors occurred during the winter of 1917–18 at the Minto Street Barracks, Winnipeg, where, it was alleged, conscientious objectors were tortured into accepting authority. While serving a sentence of three days' confinement in the barracks for refusing to obey a lawful command, two Bible Students, Robert Clegg and Frank Naish, and a Pentecostal, Charles Matheson, were forcibly undressed and held under ice-cold showers until they either accepted military authority or collapsed.[106] Matheson broke down after several hours' resistance and agreed to obey orders. Later, testifying before a court of inquiry, he described his encounter with Provost-Sergeant Simpson:

[The water] was very cold, and as I stood under it, it got colder, till it became icy cold. My whole body began to heave ... when I would stand with my back to it, he would make me turn around and face it, and make me turn my face up to it. I was shading my face with my hand ... he made me take my hand down ... I was beginning to get dazed, and I was tumbling around ... He asked me, 'Will you give in now?' I said no. He put me in again ... this went on three or four times ... He said 'we will either break you or break your heart' ... I was put into my undershirt and things, and I was dragged away. My body was wet, my hair was wet, I was taken up to the guard room and put in there.[107]

The firm resistance of Clegg and Naish to such punishment ended with Naish in a state of nervous collapse and Clegg, reportedly unconscious, being admitted to hospital. In a sworn affidavit published in Winnipeg newspapers, Clegg charged that he was stripped of his clothes and 'subjected to a violent treatment of ice-cold water, which was from time to time directed at my neck, shoulders, spine, kidneys, forehead, chest.' Clegg then stated that he was violently lashed dry before being subjected to a second cold-shower treatment.

I was in a semi-conscious state during the greater period of the second treatment, and when taken out, I was seated upon a cold stone slab, which caused me to lose control of myself and became absolutely incapable of any control of my limbs or muscles ... while still wet and in a condition of complete nervous prostration, and helplessness, I was dressed ... dragged on the concrete floor, upstairs, through the drill hall, to the place of detention ... Subsequently, while unconscious, I was removed to St Boniface hospital.[108]

Although the military authorities claimed the affair was greatly exaggerated, the objectors' allegations were supported by several witnesses, including Pte Paul E. Case, a member of the depot battalion. Writing on behalf of fellow soldiers, Case substantiated the report of cold showers and harsh treatment and reported that the soldiers of the barracks were 'highly incensed over such cruel treatment and have questioned if even Germany can beat it ... We, as men, regret there are those so debased who would tolerate such treatment on human beings when it would be unlawful to mete out such treatment even to a dog.'[109]

F.J. Dixon, the voice of radical anti-war protest, raised the matter in the Manitoba legislature and demanded an immediate investigation by authorities. In a letter to T.A. Crerar, the federal minister of agriculture, Dixon maintained that there was no doubt about the facts of the case and suggested the minister of militia and defence, Maj.-Gen. S.C. Mewburn, issue a general order regarding the treatment of conscientious objectors. 'The day of torture should be past,' argued Dixon. 'If there is no other way of dealing with these men, it would be more humane to shoot them at once than to submit them to torture which endangers their reason.'[110]

The *Manitoba Free Press* was also aroused by the incident and, in an editorial entitled 'Stop It!', declared that the Canadian people would 'simply not stand this sort of thing.' Convinced that there was conclusive evidence of 'hazing' and 'physical coercion' similar to the British experience, the *Free Press* warned against the repetition in Canada of the 'very serious mistakes made across the water.' 'It is idle to pretend,' the editor concluded, 'that, in cases like this, the hazing is the result of spontaneous indignation by the companions of the recalcitrant; these things happen because some one in authority is desirous that they shall happen.'[111]

Joining in the protest, the Roaring River Branch of the Manitoba Grain Growers' Association drafted a resolution condemning the mistreatment of conscientious objectors at the Minto Street Barracks as 'German Frightfulness methods.'[112] The public outcry reached all leading government officials, including Prime Minister Borden, who favoured an immediate investigation.[113]

The court of inquiry, which has been described as 'little more than a judicial farce,' took no action regarding the future treatment of conscientious objectors.[114] Neither did government or military authorities. In his report to the prime minister, Major-General Mewburn supported his subordinates in Winnipeg and concluded that the affair had been blown out of proportion.[115] The Militia Council merely ordered that future cos who refused military orders face courts martial and be sent to civil prisons. Consequently, Clegg, Naish, and another Jehovah's Witness, Frank Wainwright, were convicted by district courts martial of wilful disobedience of a military order and sentenced to two years' imprisonment. Their sentences were soon interrupted by an overseas draft, and they were shipped to England.[116]

Meanwhile, within a month of the Minto Street incident, public attention was focused again on the treatment of conscientious objectors in Manitoba with the death in February 1918 of David Wells, a Pentecostal co. A month earlier Wells had been sentenced by Sir Hugh John Macdonald to two years' imprisonment in the Stony Mountain Penitentiary for refusing military service. Within two weeks, however, Wells was declared 'violently insane' and was moved to Selkirk Asylum, where he died approximately a week later.[117] The public outcry was led by the radical pacifist clergymen William Ivens, who told T.A. Crerar that 'the time had come for protest on the part of the people and effective action on the part of authorities.' Ivens reiterated the radical pacifist demand that individual conscience be given full and proper respect rather than the type of maltreatment that led to Wells's death. 'It may be that his death was necessary,' Ivens remarked, 'to convince the Government that there are Conscientious Objectors in the Dominion outside of Pacifist Churches and Organizations who are prepared to die for their convictions rather than submit to perform military service.' Although the Justice Department reported that Wells was a manic-depressive who had been overcome with shame, Crerar evidently agreed with Ivens and submitted the matter to Borden for consideration.[118]

The prime minister also received a petition from the Winnipeg Trades and Labor Council requesting an immediate investigation into the treatment and death of Wells and the treatment of cos generally. Their resolution criticized the MSA's unequal application of CO status, and concluded: 'We request that the Act be so amended as to apply equally to all bonafide Conscientious Objectors and that those Conscientious Objectors now suffering incarceration under the Act be immediately released by being placed in the same category as those belonging to the recognized sects.'[119]

Such protests did not seem to have much of an effect on the government, however, and in March 1918 the Military Council ordered that conscientious objectors sentenced to civil prison were to be sent overseas. In the first group shipped to England in April were Clegg, Naish, and Wainwright, all of whom had been released from penitentiary for the draft.[120] The remainder of the first group included two more Bible Students from Winnipeg, John Gillespie and Claude Brown; a Baptist, N.S. Shuttleworth; and two Plymouth Brethren, W. Bagnall and E.W. McAulay. All had appealed to tribunals for conscientious exemptions, and all had been rejected on the ground that they did not belong to recognized sects.[121] The second group, which sailed from Halifax on 20 June 1918, was composed of four cos from Fort Henry in Kingston, Ontario: J.L. Adams, J. Running, O.K. Pimlott, and Syndey Ralph Thomas. Pimlott, from Belleville, and Thomas, from Haliburton, were Bible Students.[122]

Once in England the cos were sent to Seaford Camp, Sussex, where they were subjected to brutal punishment in an attempt to force them to obey military commands. Pimlott reported that he was dragged over knolls and dales by the feet, beaten over the head, kicked with heavy boots until he became unconscious, and finally taken to Eastbourne

Hospital for an x-ray examination. The other cos reported similar experiences. Thomas claimed that he was 'dragged, shoved and kicked several miles into the country to the edge of a 150 foot precipice and threatened to be thrown over.' He also charged that 'ten officers took turns in beating him, threatened to bayonet him ... shoved him against a target and fired at him from the other end of the range, tried to shoot him at close range and cursed because the gun would not go off.'[123] Finally, he was pounded with the butt of a gun until he became unconscious. In one of his beatings Clegg received a broken rib.

While at Seaford Camp, Shuttleworth abandoned his Baptist faith to become a Bible Student convert. He then joined the other Jehovah's Witnesses from Manitoba, Clegg, Naish, Wainwright, Gillespie, and Brown, in their transfer to Wandsworth Prison, where they received the usual harsh treatment.[124]

Meanwhile, as protests mounted in Canada against sending conscientious objectors overseas, both Canadian and British authorities began to recognize that the action was a mistake, especially since the cos were considered a 'constant menace to other soldiers undergoing detention with them.'[125] Consequently, on 22 April 1918, the Military Council issued a new order to the effect that conscientious objectors would no longer be sent overseas; instead they would be obliged to serve in Canada in the Canadian Engineers, Army Service Corps, Army Medical Corps, Canadian Ordnance Corps, or in clerical capacities.[126] Evidently, the second group of cos had been sent overseas in error.[127] In August the government began to arrange for the return of all Canadian cos except for three who agreed to perform non-combatant service in England. The young absolutists arrived back in Canada on Armistice Day, 11 November 1918, and shortly thereafter were released from the army with dishonourable discharges.[128]

The end of the war, however, did not necessarily mean the automatic release of the radical pacifists imprisoned in Canada, and by January 1919 there were still 117 conscientious objectors in custody.[129] In an attempt to alleviate this situation, the government appointed a special committee composed of the solicitor-general, the judge advocate-general, and the deputy minister of justice to consider the sentences being served by cos and military defaulters on a case-by-case basis. The committee decided that regardless of religious affiliation, conscientious objectors who were found to be bona fide objectors would be released after serving a six-month term.[130]

Meanwhile, private citizens protested the continued punishment of religious pacifists, and in the spring of 1919 the issue was raised in the House of Commons.[131] On 24 March the Honourable Rodolphe Lemieux introduced a motion for amnesty: 'That, in the opinion of this House, amnesty should now be granted to religious conscientious objectors to military service.'[132] Lemieux reminded the House that Great Britain had always led the world in the protection of religious and civil freedom and urged the government to be 'merciful to these honest and sincere young men, lawabiding citizens in every other respect, who did not default but presented themselves boldly before the tribunals and stated their objections ... I have received many letters on this subject from different parts of the country, and I say that the least we can do, now that the war is over ... is to act generously.'[133] Lemieux withdrew his motion, however, following Solicitor-General Hugh Guthrie's explanation that a general amnesty was unnecessary since all conscientious objectors would be released before summer. In his closing statement Lemieux praised the active, non-violent service undertaken by Quakers in France and Belgium and suggested strongly that the Military Service Act be amended to contain more liberal provisions for conscientious objectors in the future. Above all, the amnesty motion reminded the House of the staunch resistance to military service of young pacifists in Canada.

In addition to imposing conscription, the War Measures Act empowered the government to censor, control, and suppress free speech and to arrest, detain, exclude, and deport individuals. Any public statements that could weaken the country's spirit were specifically prohibited. The result was a list of banned organizations and publications and the harassment of those citizens opposed to the war, all in the name of patriotism.[134] A further infringement on individual liberties occurred when the Wartime Elections Act disfranchised conscientious objectors, persons of German speech and all enemy aliens, including those naturalized since 1902. Such actions were clearly in harmony with the mounting anti-German sentiment abroad in the land, especially since some Canadians actually viewed pacifists as part of a vast German espionage system.[135] In their eyes, German-speaking Mennonite and Hutterite communities were guilty on two counts, and there was little pacifists could do to change that impression.

In a letter to Woodsworth, for instance, Vernon Thomas predicted that the government's 'vicious' attempts to prohibit public criticism of the war effort would ultimately silence pacifists altogether.[136] Another radical pacifist and well-known labour spokesman, Phillips Thompson, came out of retirement to attack the denial of the right of free speech:

'To ostracize and hound down every man who opposes Canada's participation in the war is a practical demonstration of the fact that our boasted self-government is a sham.'[137] Just as Woodsworth and other pacifists had warned, the war hysteria that swept the country had a brutalizing effect upon Canadian society; it increased the nation's insensitivity to the rights and problems of individuals, as evidenced by the treatment of conscientious objectors and the internment of enemy aliens.[138] But Thomas was also correct. Given the War Measures Act and the temper of the time, there was little pacifists could do to halt the growth of prejudice and the erosion of civil liberties.

v

The Great War and the conscription issue in particular had confronted Canadian pacifists with a crisis. The majority of pre-war pacifists responded by supporting the war, but others, such as Quakers and some feminists and social gospellers, remained stalwart pacifists and began to formulate a new pacifist ethic as they united their opposition to war and violence with a leftist critique of the capitalist social and economic system as the breeding ground for international and domestic violence. In addition, a complementary though more traditional pacifist witness was exhibited by Canada's sectarian pacifists. Except for the Society of Friends, the historic peace sects and the more recent pacifist groups, such as the Jehovah's Witnesses, maintained a staunch isolation from war and society alike, and their resistance to compulsory military service reinforced the principle of conscientious objection and pacifist dissent in general within Canadian society and encouraged individual resistance to warfare.

It would be too much to suggest that the radical pacifism of the historic peace groups was cross-fertilized by a radicalized liberal reformist pacifism in the war years. But in the pacifist front that extended from the Quakers to Woodsworth there was an ideological configuration that reflected elements of both traditions: the radical sectarian adherence to the principle of non-resistance to evil while awaiting the millennium, and the liberal faith in man's ability to bring about this millennial ideal of a perfect society. At best it was an unstable alliance, but the tension could help propel the activism of social dissent.

For the most part, however, the synthesis of radical pacifism with radical social change was still in its infancy in Canada. In Britain the Union for Democratic Control and the No-Conscription Fellowship organized a socialist-pacifist base; in Canada there was no practical coalition of pacifist forces, nor was there an active peace party. In fact, at the war's end there was little understanding of the pacifist ethic in Canada and little evidence of inquiry into the ethics of war or Christian pacifism in the centres of theological training.[139] Also, in both Britain and the United States, a newly formed Christian pacifist organization, the Fellowship of Reconciliation, was engaged in activities on behalf of aliens and conscientious objectors and in the promotion of a radical vision of social and moral reconstruction. The fellowship did not enter Canada until after the war. Nevertheless, Canadian pacifists were already expressing a radicalized pacifism born of the wartime experience.

Although the new pacifist ethic was not fully articulated at the close of the war, radical pacifists such as Woodsworth, Beynon, and Thomas clearly recognized the necessity for far-reaching social and economic reconstruction in order to prevent the occurrence of another war. The Society of Friends had also come to the conclusion that the real cause of war lay in the realm of economics. No permanent peace could be secured, they warned, without ending economic injustice first.

Woodsworth was among the first to notice that Quakers were 'beginning to abandon their old rather negative and abstract position with regard to war and to attack the evils which are responsible for modern wars.'[140] Although somewhat surprised to find Quakers advocating 'scientific socialism,' he was encouraged by their new line of thinking. In 1919, for example, Friends warned that 'the crime, the wickedness, the deceit, the hypocrisy that stood at the back of the conditions that produced the first war' still existed, resulting in the post-war unrest that threatened to erupt in a violent social revolt, equal in horror to the war, unless there was a radical reconstruction of Canadian society. What was needed was a 'revolution, not necessarily violent, and an edifice of new design' that would guarantee labour 'shorter hours, more of the product it produces, larger opportunities, [and] a different interpretation of justice.'[141] In effect, Quakers had merged their traditional religious opposition to war with the struggle for social justice, something that was central to the new socially radical pacifism engendered by the Great War. Despite their prophetic warnings of future violence unless social and economic justice was realized, however, socially radical pacifists failed to foresee a serious dilemma awaiting them beyond the horizon: their momentum towards radical reform and social change to secure peace and justice was on a long-term collision course with their pacifist rejection of the use of violence in any cause.

4

A resurgent peace movement

The years following the Great War were filled with discontent in Canada as elsewhere in the Western world. Physical and spiritual exhaustion and the economic strains associated with post-war readjustment were aggravated by the fact that despite the terrible scale of wartime sacrifices, the war had failed to purge the world of evil and to produce a more just social and economic order. Many Canadians had shared this expectation. Liberal social gospellers and conservative imperialists alike had convinced themselves that the post-war years would be a new era. When the desired changes did not materialize, initial disappointment turned to disillusionment, frustration, and protest. In Britain and the United States strikes were endemic. In Canada the mounting wave of labour and farm unrest evident during the war began to be felt on a new scale.

Within a year of the cessation of hostilities in Europe, the largest labour demonstration in Canadian history, the Winnipeg General Strike, ended in violence as strikers and returned war veterans battled special police forces while the military stood by at the ready. At the time, few Canadians connected such domestic violence with international warfare, but pacifists had earlier warned their countrymen that their support of the war would ultimately unleash the same type of violence upon the domestic scene. Militarism and war, they had argued, legitimized violence, a condition that would be reflected in the future values and responses of Canadian society. By 1919 Canadian Quakers viewed the Winnipeg Strike as the possible beginning of a violent social revolt equivalent to warfare unless there was a radical reconstruction of the social and economic structures of Canadian society.[1] That analysis, as well as the active support for the labour cause displayed in Winnipeg by F.J.

Dixon, J.S. Woodsworth, and William Ivens, was indicative of the socially radical pacifism the war had bred.

Canada's committed non-sectarian pacifist minority emerged from the
war convinced of the urgent need for radical social and economic change
in order to eliminate war and violence from the world. But like their
counterparts in Britain and the United States, they remained suspicious
of a socialist workers' state and preferred the idea of a decentralized co-
operative commonwealth similar to the tradition of guild socialism in
Britain and based upon the moral conscience stressed in the social gospel.[2] Woodsworth and Ivens, for instance, had become leading spokesmen for democratic socialism and had popularized the cause in the
political arena. As a pacifist, Woodsworth also emphasized that the
people's enemy was not just capitalism but capitalism in league with
militarism and imperialism – a deadly mixture that caused war.[3]

Canada's socially radical pacifists agreed that without a more equitable
distribution of wealth neither domestic nor international tranquillity could
be maintained for long. The cultivation of public awareness of this fact,
however, was not easily accomplished in the post-war era. In fact, as
Richard Allen has suggested, support for social reform and pacifism
developed somewhat inversely in the 1920s.[4] The initial resurgence of
pacifism appeared to be not a commitment to radical social action, but
rather an act of national repentance built upon both disillusionment with
war and hope that international peace would be secured by the League
of Nations. Once again Canadians began to rally to the peace movement,
and by the late 1920s there was a great upsurge in pacifist feeling. But
the abhorrence of war and the desire for a peaceful world were not the
equivalent of pacifism, especially a socially radical pacifism. The relationship between war and social injustice, although recognized during
the 1920s, was not profoundly explored in Canada until the Great
Depression and the international crises of the 1930s. In the meantime,
Canadian peace advocates felt free to fight militarism without directly
challenging the state.

I

Post-war pacifism first surfaced in Britain. In 1921 a central pacifist organization, the No More War Movement, was formed around a core of
left-wing intellectuals and members of the labour movement. Socialism
as well as pacifism was part of its program.[5] But the No More War
Movement never attracted widespread labour support, nor did it succeed

in mobilizing the various forms of anti-war sentiment that were manifested near the end of the decade. During most of the 1920s, therefore, the British peace movement remained a loose coalition of religious and non-religious pacifists, socialists, and anti-militarists.

In contrast to the pragmatic and largely secular bias of the British pacifists, the peace movement in the United States was closely associated with the social gospellers' pursuit of a new social order. By the late 1920s, for instance, the American movement was dominated by the Fellowship of Reconciliation, the radical Christian organization that united both Christian pacifists and Christian socialists in a struggle against capitalism and war.

As in the United States, the resurgence of pacifism in Canada did not gain momentum until mid-decade, after the energies of early post-war protests had begun to wane. The principal protest, although less dramatic than the Winnipeg Strike, was the political revolt of farmers in Nova Scotia, New Brunswick, Ontario, Manitoba, Saskatchewan, and Alberta. In provincial elections from 1919 to 1922 and in the federal election of 1921, agrarian progressives were swept to the threshold of national political power.[6] Although largely a political revolt against the financial establishment, the farmers' action also reflected long standing anti-war sentiment and social grievances. Farmers had become especially critical of war owing to the conscription of their sons and in reaction to the related problem of rural depopulation and reports of war profiteering and graft.[7] As a result, discontented farmers strongly supported the anti-militarist and anti-imperialist designs of a broadly based peace movement.

Anti-imperialism was an important factor in generating support for a Canadian peace movement. One of the lessons of the Great War appeared to be that the British imperial connection had propelled Canada into the European war, and might do so again unless counteraction was taken. Consequently, the liberal nationalist argument for Canadian autonomy found eager converts throughout Canada, especially among peace advocates.

Regardless of their particular motivation, most Canadians appeared to be interested in Canadian autonomy. At the Imperial Conference of 1921, for instance, the Canadian prime minister, Arthur Meighen, warned British delegates that Canada would not support imperial policy unless the Anglo-Japanese Alliance was abrogated. Popular sentiment across Canada was heavily against any international agreement that might involve Canada in another war or strain relations with the United States.[8]

Again, in 1922 the Liberal government of Prime Minister Mackenzie King refused to support Great Britain against the Turks in the Chanak affair, and repudiated any responsibility for the resulting Treaty of Lausanne. In such a manner official government policy continued to reflect anti-military and anti-imperial sentiment throughout the 1920s, attitudes pacifists could in some measure exploit.

Canadian nationalists and pacifists, however, did not intend autonomy to mean isolation on the North American continent. They had tasted international power as part of the British empire, and they now desired to remain a constructive force within the international order – but without imperial military obligations. The League of Nations captured the imagination of most Canadians interested in international affairs during the 1920s.[9] Pacifists rallied to its support, and as early as 1919 Canadian Quakers were encouraged to work hard for the 'education and enlightenment of public opinion' on the subject of the league. 'We have stood together through the war for the service of peace, under all sorts of limiting and restrictive conditions,' reported the *Canadian Friend*; 'let us now stand together for the international practice of peace, even though it be circumscribed by many limiting human circumstances and conditions.'[10] The problem for pacifists was how this was to be done.

Despite their general approval of the League of Nations, former wartime pacifists in 1919 'had neither the respectability nor the energy' to launch a major pro-league movement, in part because their move towards social radicalism had further tarnished their public image. The churches, while sympathetic, became engrossed in more immediate social problems.[11] In the end it was a new grouping of like-minded internationalists, both pacifist and non-pacifist, who established the Canadian League of Nations Society in 1921. One of the major problems faced by the new society was the struggle between those who favoured armed preparedness and those who were outright pacifists. At first the society tried to present a respectable façade by excluding wartime pacifists from membership, but when that practice did not prove feasible the imperialists indiscriminately branded all pro-leaguers as pacifists.[12]

Although the leadership of the League of Nations Society carefully emphasized the distinction between themselves and pacifists, in reality they shared a common desire for disarmament and world peace. Through their separate experiences, however, both groups ultimately discovered that the post-war Canadian public was largely unwilling 'to accept any responsibility for the creation of a peace mentality throughout the world.'[13]

Pacifists could take comfort, however, in the fact that on the international scene itself the question of disarmament had become a major issue of the decade. The League of Nations endorsed the idea, and several international conferences wrestled with the problem. The Washington Naval Conference of 1921–2, the Geneva Conference of the mid-1920s, and later the London Disarmament Conference all took an urgent view of the problem and expressed confident hope for its solution. Nowhere was the concern more evident than in the Protestant press, even though the churches themselves were embroiled in the domestic issues of progressive politics, evangelism, and church union. Presbyterian publications, for example, gave lengthy coverage to the League of Nations and the related issues of the cancellation of war debts and the Allied punishment of war criminals.[14] Moreover, following the example of the 1920 Lambeth Conference in Britain, the Anglican Church of Canada praised the League of Nations, while its Council for Social Service, confident that the church could help create and mobilize public opinion, distributed a pamphlet containing a detailed examination of the League as an embodiment of Christian principles. Together Anglicans, Presbyterians, and Methodists led the nation in prayer for the success of the International Disarmament Conference in Washington and similar attempts at international co-operation. In effect, this postwar support for disarmament and the rational approach to peace associated with the League of Nations, as displayed by the church press, had begun to revive the remnants of the progressive peace movement, and by the mid-1920s these liberal internationalists joined with pacifists in a broad interwar peace movement.

II

The initial resurgence of pacifism in Canada was primarily a reassertion of social gospel concern for the international order, and through the 1920s Canadian churchmen were instrumental in widening the debate. Social gospellers, having led the churches into new areas of social concern, were by mid-decade increasingly disillusioned with the prospects of social reconstruction; they therefore diverted their crusading spirit to a new outlet – the peace movement.[15] It was not a complete diversion for the more socially radical pacifists who believed that social inequities and war were caused by the same competitive economic system, but, by concentrating on the cause of peace, social gospellers avoided and therefore failed to absorb the meaning of the crisis confronting their other programs of social reform.[16] Nevertheless, they set the stage for renewed pacifist activity.

Many of the Canadian churchmen who lent support to a nascent peace movement had travelled full circle from their pre-war pacifist rhetoric through enthusiastic support of the war and back again to an anti-war, pro-peace position. Of those exhibiting this reversal, the most prominent were some of the leading social gospellers of the Methodist church, particularly the Reverend S.D. Chown, since 1914 the general superintendent of his church, and William B. Creighton, editor of the *Christian Guardian*. In his quadrennial address to the general conference of the Methodist Church in October 1922, Chown called upon all nations 'to cease their moral insanity' and to settle all future difficulties 'on terms of Christian equity.'[17] The following summer Chown sent a manifesto to all Methodist ministers in Canada asking them to set aside 29 July as 'Anti-War Sunday' in order to emphasize the 'folly of war as a means of settling international disputes' and to create a 'no more war' sentiment in the church.[18] Chown became a staunch supporter of the League of Nations, and after his retirement as general superintendent in 1925 he devoted himself to the campaign for peaceful settlement of international disputes.[19]

The most dramatic change of heart was exhibited by Creighton, whose earlier editorials in the *Guardian* had driven some pacifist ministers out of the church. By the time of the so-called Chanak crisis, however, Creighton was condemning the spectacle of 'Christian and enlightened men' in Canada urging vehemently that Canadians 'pledge themselves without reserve to stand back of the Motherland should she decide that war was inevitable.' 'God forgive us,' wrote Creighton, 'that our first reaction was not of such a character that there would go up from a united people one thunderous, mighty NO.'[20] He insisted that Canadians must learn to feel and think in different terms, and must remember 'how cruel and wicked and unchristian and inhumane war is ... We must learn to think peace, to talk peace, to insist on peace, because anything else is a horrible anachronism.' Those who had missed the meaning of these words could not fail to notice Creighton's dramatic announcement on the cover of the *Guardian* of 20 February 1924.[21] As if to cancel his wartime editorial on the 'Vice of Pacifism,' Creighton now declared that there was no 'virtue or goodness or saving grace in war ... And most of us have been driven far beyond that negative position to the very positive and inescapable belief that war is, for our day and time, a hideous, utterly unchristian, unforgivable crime.'

In reference to the church's pro-war position a few years before, Creighton confessed that 'many of us are ready to acknowledge our fault in truest humility, and seek pardon for our ignorance and our lack of the Spirit of our Master.' But 'never again, under any condition,' would war have Creighton's sanction or blessing. 'We have made up our minds,' he concluded, 'that in this matter we must try to be Christians' and 'set our face forever against war.'

Creighton's testimony to peace initiated a serious discussion in the pages of the *Guardian* and its successor, the *New Outlook*. One of the first responses questioned the basis of Creighton's new sympathy with 'the once despised brotherhood of pacifists.' The correspondent was Douglas Hemmeon, a pacifist minister from Wolfville, Nova Scotia, who described himself as one who had 'paid a bitter penalty in suffering and loss which will never be regained.'[22] Hemmeon suggested that Creighton's announcement was plainly pacifism 'without reservation and without qualification,' and he demanded to know 'by what processes, intellectual and emotional, and by what methods, historical, scientific, philosophical, religious ... ' Creighton had arrived at such a 'radical and significant conclusion.' The question was a valid one, since Creighton had reversed his position without offering his readers any type of reasoned explanation. In reply to Hemmeon, Creighton confessed that his 'changed viewpoint and conviction' had been the result of 'a slow disillusioning process that has been going on ever since the close of the war,' rather than a study of 'Jesus' attitude and teaching as to non-resistance.' Furthermore, the sad experience of the war had underlined the conflict of the 'whole issue of war' with Christian teaching, particularly with the coming of the Kingdom of God. The principle of brotherhood, he argued, left no 'place in the world for war among nations.'[23]

Although Creighton's explanation left much to be desired, it was an honest attempt to come to grips with the issue of Christian responsibility and war. In the years that followed, Creighton refined his thinking, but he continued to steer away from the question of passive resistance. In fact, neither Creighton nor Chown ever embraced outright pacifism, even in the 1920s; they continued to recognize the possibility of 'just war': 'Just and inevitable wars have come into the world,' wrote Creighton; 'it is even conceivable that they may still come.'[24] In order to help Christians make such wars impossible, Creighton concentrated his thinking on education and international co-operation. He thought of war as a 'state of mind' resulting from preparedness and traditional ways of thinking, and therefore concluded that the task of the church was 'to educate the public mind for peace.'[25]

The return to pacifist thinking by Canadian churchmen such as

Creighton and Chown reflected in part the strong influence of an out-spoken pacifist minority in American Protestantism. Although a few Canadians attended peace rallies in the United States, American pacifist thought reached most Canadian ministers through such avenues as the *Christian Century*, an American religious journal that aligned the social gospel with pacifism. Its editor, Clayton C. Morrison, became well known among his Canadian readers, and addressed the first General Council of the United Church of Canada in June 1925. The previous year the Social Service Council of Canada had invited the famous American pac-ifist, Kirby Page, to speak at its annual meeting.[26] Page was the editor of *The World Tomorrow*, which had some Canadian readers. By and large, the American peace movement provided the major inspiration for Ca-nadian pacifism in the early 1920s.

Following the American lead, Canadian churches recognized that peace had become a vital issue that had to be considered at their conferences. The Methodist church, for example, adopted several anti-war resolutions supporting the League of Nations and the peaceful settlement of inter-national disputes, but stopped short of taking a truly pacifist position.[27] Although the Department of Evangelism and Social Service was in-structed to arouse public opinion on the issue, the most important dis-cussion of pacifism took place in the *Christian Guardian* with the encouragement of its editor. The 1924 May and June issues of the *Guard-ian* carried a series of feature articles on 'The Struggle for Peace' by Archibald F. Key. Following a survey of past peace movements and international conferences, Key concluded that the best hope for future peace lay in educating people about international affairs.[28] 'It is only when the people of the world begin to take an active interest in inter-national affairs,' he wrote, 'that war will cease to exist.'[29] He endorsed the peace movement as a means of accomplishing this end, but lamented that, according to the Peace Year Book of 1923, only one peace organi-zation in Canada had survived the war – the Women's International League for Peace and Freedom.

In the months that followed, a controversy on the issue of pacifism developed in the 'Readers' Forum' section of the *Guardian*. W.R. McWilliams of Grafton, Ontario, suggested that if the church really wanted to do away with war it would announce its position to the world just as the Society of Friends had done.[30] J.A. Hart of Truro, Nova Scotia, doubted that Canadians possessed the 'spiritual control' of the state necessary to prevent a reversion to war.[31] When Herbert S. Cobb wrote from Griffin, Saskatchewan, that there were 'more logical, as well as

Christian ways' than pacifism to accomplish peace, he was challenged by the editor to explain himself. Creighton also criticized an article by Alfred E. Lavell that presented the case for preparedness. It was a faulty argument: 'It leaves us just where we were before the last war broke out and as a scheme it will work just as ineffectively the next time as it did the last time.'[32]

Throughout the 1920s Creighton remained determined to encourage full discussion of the peace issue, even though he was aware that some of his readers had grown tired of his campaign against war. 'While in some ways it might be more comfortable if we were all to decide that we would leave this whole perplexing problem in the lap of the gods,' he confessed, ' ... we cannot get away from the conviction that as intelligent Christian men and women it still remains our problem,' a problem that demanded 'the most careful and honest investigation at this very hour.'[33] The editor heard from several unsympathetic correspondents who 'appeared to think that they settled the whole thing by a few strong sentences.' Creighton declared that there was more to be said and some decisions to be reached. 'As Christian men and women,' he wrote, 'the time has fully come when we must do some very hard and very honest thinking.' Creighton surely helped create an atmosphere and provide a forum in which the peace issue could be explored, but he left to others the major task of developing pacifist thought and strategy. Accordingly, the *Guardian* welcomed the entry of R. Edis Fairbairn into the fray, and with Creighton's enthusiastic endorsement Fairbairn began a long series of provocative articles that marked him as 'one of the most able and certainly the most contentious pacifist writer in the church.'[34]

Edis Fairbairn was one of several prominent Canadian churchmen who began to articulate a radical pacifist argument during the early and mid-1920s. He originally hailed from England, where he had entered the Wesleyan ministry in 1904; never completely satisfied with the Wesleyan Methodists, particularly because of what he considered their increasing dogmatism, he left England for Canada in 1914. During the First World War the Army and Navy Board of the Methodist church assigned Fairbairn to Bermuda where he acted as a chaplain under the British admiralty. It was this wartime experience in Bermuda, especially his firsthand exposure to the reaction of young men in bayonet drill, that launched Fairbairn on the road towards pacifism.[35]

It was also in Bermuda that Fairbairn first demonstrated his impetuous and outspoken manner over a matter of principle. The controversy, or so-called Bermuda scandal, concerned Fairbairn's decision to criticize publicly the moral conditions at the Sailor's Home on Ireland Island without first reporting to the commandant of the dockyard.[36] The British admiralty and the Wesleyan Methodist church 'took a very strong line' and demanded Fairbairn's removal or, at the very least, an apology, but left the final decision up to the Army and Navy Board in Canada.[37] Fairbairn adamantly refused to render an apology 'except on the explicit instructions of the Board, and even then most unwillingly.'[38] In the end the board decided that rather than apologize, Fairbairn should offer nothing more than an 'expression of regret at having made public statement before making official complaint,' thereby taking issue with only the method and not the content of Fairbairn's remarks.[39] Fairbairn complied and the matter was closed, but the incident served as a preview of his stormy career in the ministry.

By the time Fairbairn began his examination of 'Christianity and War' in the *Christian Guardian*, he had become a committed pacifist and a radical. His pacifist argument incorporated a socialist analysis of Western capitalism as the 'war system,' a system that compelled 'otherwise honourable' men to behave unscrupulously and made future wars inevitable.[40] The root cause of modern wars, he argued, was the monopolistic expansion of international commerce with the support of military force. It was the same war mentality that still characterized domestic industrial relations and posed 'possibilities of civil war within the nation, and of a class war extending over all the nations.'[41] Furthermore, militarism and imperialism were natural allies with capitalism, since all three 'isms' promoted the selfish belief 'that it is your duty to yourself to assert your power over others to your advantage.'[42] The alternative to this whole unchristian 'war system' was for the world to organize for peace 'as in the past it has been organized for war.'[43] Pacifism and a campaign for the institutionalization of pacifistic relations in social life, therefore, were man's best hope of averting future war.

Fairbairn rejected the argument that Jesus had never condemned war, since the whole message of Jesus, not just his references to non-resistance to evil, was an indirect rejection of war. 'It is literally true,' wrote Fairbairn, 'that for Jesus there were but two alternatives – a Messianic war, or the Cross. That He chose the Cross is demonstration of what He thought of war.'[44] At the heart of Fairbairn's pacifism was the social gospel belief in the imminence of the Kingdom of God on earth. Consequently, war, as the greatest sin, had to be stopped in order to pave the way for that kingdom.[45]

Unlike some other social gospellers who were attracted to pacifism, Fairbairn became a dedicated and radical pacifist and remained so for the rest of his life. He was a prolific writer of articles in church journals, and earned a reputation as the most vocal if not the most radical pacifist in the United Church of Canada.[46] As long as he felt something needed to be said on the war issue, Fairbairn refused to remain silent, and at times he enraged his readers and provoked a host of critics. But in the end, although Fairbairn developed a careful analysis of the past war and how it should have been avoided, he devoted little imaginative thought to the application of pacifism to the international problems of the 1920s. None the less, Fairbairn and other churchmen helped greatly to revitalize Canadian interest in pacifism.

The regenerated peace campaign was stimulated further with the immigration to Canada of one of the leading pacifists of the day. Richard Roberts, a pacifist Presbyterian minister and a co-founder of the Fellowship of Reconciliation, came to Canada from England via the United States. From the time Roberts assumed the pulpit of the American Presbyterian Church in Montreal in 1922, he exerted a gentle but important influence upon young Canadians in the United Church and the Student Christian Movement in particular. Although it probably went unnoticed at the time, Roberts's arrival provided an awakening Christian pacifist consciousness with important intellectual depth and a direct link to the Anglo-American pacifist experience.

Shortly after the outbreak of the Great War, Roberts and the British Quaker Henry Hodgkin agreed upon the necessity of forming an organized body that would maintain a Christian pacifist front during the war. Through their efforts the Fellowship of Reconciliation (FOR) was born at Trinity College, Cambridge, in the last four days of 1914.[47] According to original members of the FOR it was Roberts who chose the word 'Reconciliation' for the fellowship's name. Roberts thought peace was more than just the absence of war; it was something to be waged, as war was waged. 'Peace is not a passivity ... a lull between wars,' he wrote. 'It must be conceived as an activity; and the name of that activity is *Reconciliation* ... the act and practice of turning enemies into friends.'[48]

By the spring of 1915 Roberts's pacifist stand necessitated his resignation from Crouch Hill Presbyterian Church; in July he accepted the secretaryship of the new FOR and became the first editor of its monthly periodical, *The Venturer*. In 1917, after Hodgkin had planted the roots of the FOR in the United States, Roberts accepted a call to the Congregational Church of the Pilgrims in Brooklyn, New York, where he remained for the duration of the war.

In New York Roberts maintained close connections with the FOR and served on the editorial board of the *World Tomorrow*, a radical Christian journal that was at the time banned in Canada.[49] It appears that his radical pacifist activities were of some concern to United States government authorities, and on at least one occasion Roberts was questioned by the U.S. attorney-general's office about his communications with anti-war radicals such as Floyd Dell, Max Eastman, and the Masses Publishing Company.[50] Despite his apparently important reputation in New York as a leading Christian pacifist, it is not known if Roberts had any contact with Vernon and Lillian Thomas of Winnipeg, who had exiled themselves to New York at that time.

Roberts did continue his correspondence with British pacifists such as Hodgkin and Fenner Brockway and to some extent strengthened their liaison with such American pacifist figures as Rufus Jones. Hodgkin kept Roberts informed on the development of the FOR in Britain and in return solicited his advice, particularly on the role of pacifists in the post-war world. 'Very often do I wish that you were here again,' wrote Hodgkin, 'in order that we might think out together some of these questions, and ... to prepare for the situation which we can, in some measure, foresee.'[51]

Roberts's major concern during these years, however, was the 'problem of conscience' and the personal dilemma faced by conscientious objectors. In a letter to Fenner Brockway he confessed his sympathy for the absolutist position but warned that absolutists must be exceedingly careful not to allow their own position to dominate their thinking and cause them to believe that 'what is right for us might be right for everybody.' The only safe and right course, he argued, was to 'go so far – neither more nor less – as your conscience compels you.'[52] Shortly after the war, in an article in the *International Journal of Ethics*, Roberts praised conscientious objection as a healthy exercise of the individual conscience and therefore invaluable to the stability and growth of democracy. 'The ultimate battleground of democracy is in men's hearts,' he wrote, 'and its appeal must at last ever be to men's consciences.'[53] Even in time of war, it is safer for democracy to let a hundred shirkers go scot-free rather than run the risk of penalizing an honest conscience.'[53] Roberts hoped that the pacifist witness in the last war might have begun a new reign of personal idealism and individual conscience in the Western world.

Indeed, he believed it was 'only by a frank recognition of the moral autonomy of the individual that we can establish any kind of moral order in the world. There are, of course, other ways of securing a quiet world – for a time; but in any case a quiet world is not necessarily a moral world.'[54]

In 1920 it appeared as if Roberts would assume the presidency of the Pacific School of Religion in Berkeley, California, but when opposition arose to his pacifism and his labour sympathies he withdrew his name from consideration.[55] In 1922 he left the United States for Canada and the prestigious American Presbyterian Church in Montreal. There in 1926 Roberts joined with other members of the Protestant Ministerial Association of Montreal to produce *The Christian and War*, the definitive Canadian pacifist statement of the interwar period.

Although *The Christian and War* represented the consensus of several Montreal clergymen, including Roberts, M.F. McCutcheon, T.W. Jones, W.D. Reid, and Canon A.P. Shatford, its major author was W.A. Gifford, a professor of ecclesiastical history at United Theological College in Montreal. The signatories, all Canadians by birth or adoption, contributed little original thought to the question of the church and war, but they recognized the vital necessity for a new Christian ethic of war and, through Gifford's hand, made a sweeping appeal for a pacifist state of mind. 'Our object,' wrote Gifford, 'is to present the Christian view of society, to judge war in the light of that view, to indicate ways of making the Christian view effective against war.'[56] In language becoming a pacifist, Gifford talked of armed preparedness, secret diplomacy, and national fears as immediate causes of war; the ultimate causes were economic imperialism and militarism, especially 'the education of childhood for war.'

Unlike absolute pacifists such as Fairbairn, Gifford distinguished between the question of war and the more general question of the admissibility of force, as in international police actions. 'We conceive that there are circumstances in which force can be made to serve the ends of love, reverence and service.' The use of force was admissible as long as it was kept subsidiary to, controlled by, and exercised in accordance with moral ends. This could not apply to war, he argued, since war 'obscures all moral ends, and never can be a Christian weapon, even when waged in a righteous cause.'[57] The Christian alternative to war, therefore, was the active promotion of peace. The conscience of the Christian Church was awakened, reported Gifford, and many Christians were ready to stand with the Quakers for pacifism and strive towards a warless world.

He endorsed the League of Nations, treaties of arbitration and disarmament, and the whole concept of international co-operation as practical means to that end. Particular emphasis was placed upon the promising roles of such associations as the World Alliance for International Friendship through the Churches, the War-Resisters International, and the Fellowship of Reconciliation.

The book did not completely ignore the question of what Christian men should do in the event of a future war. In fact, Gifford's most important message concerned the heavy responsibility of the individual Christian conscience when confronted with the 'immediate presence of war.' Although the authors had left the door open for the use of force in certain situations, Gifford asserted: 'We who make this appeal cannot conceive any future war in which Christian men can participate.' Regardless of this belief, Gifford recognized that the final decision was up to each individual and gave strong words of encouragement to the principle of individual conscientious objection to war: 'If some men and women should have to stand alone in their resistance to war, let them remember that the City of Man-soul has but one citizen ... Let them remember too that by suffering for their cause they will accredit it. Those who think out the great human issues in advance of mankind, and endure the reproach of dissent, help to clarify the thoughts of others and thus become creative factors in progress. Being lifted up from the earth, they draw others unto them.'[58]

On the one hand, Gifford elevated conscientious objectors almost to the level of sainthood; on the other hand, he failed to give serious consideration to alternative decisions of conscience in the event of a future conflict. The omission was understandable, since the underlying premise of *The Christian and War* was the social gospel faith in the 'coming of the ultimate order of history' in which there was no room for war.[59] If Gifford and his associates ever really considered war a future possibility, they found it difficult to follow to its end a train of thought contrary to their whole frame of mind; consequently, they missed the opportunity to develop a viable Christian response to war and left the matter unresolved for a later generation of Canadians.

The authors of *The Christian and War* also failed to recognize an important new dimension of liberal pacifism. Their qualified approval of force for moral ends and controlled by moral means ruled out complete non-resistance, but they did not go so far as to develop this qualified use of moral force into a method of pacifist social action. In other words, they failed to bridge the gap from liberal pacifism to the idea of non-violent force or resistance then taking root within the pacifist outlook of the Quakers and the more radical Anglo-American Protestants. Nevertheless, *The Christian and War* was welcomed by pacifists in Canada and helped justify a fledging Canadian peace movement.[60]

To a certain extent the pacifist spokesmen in the church were responding to the increasing international awareness and pacifist commitment of Canadian university students. In *The Christian and War*, for instance, Gifford recognized students as one of the groups most supportive of the new internationalism,[61] and W.B. Creighton claimed that his conversations with war veterans and students were decisive in his return to the pacifist fold.[62] The leading force in developing this internationalism and peace sentiment among students was the Student Christian Movement (SCM). Its organization in 1921 was initiated by those veterans (to whom Creighton referred) who had returned from the war profoundly dissatisfied with the existing world order and determined to eliminate the social and economic injustices that caused wars.[63] These men emphasized the need for a new moral force to prevent war, and for intellectual guidance they called upon Richard Roberts, who, from his arrival in 1922, figured prominently in the student movement and became a frequent speaker at SCM gatherings.

After a few years the SCM members who had had direct contact with the war began to be succeeded by a new generation of students,[64] but the general interest in the peace question continued to gain momentum. In 1923 the SCM concluded that 'the way of peace can only be discovered if ordinary people have a reasoned and passionate belief in the creative possibilities of peace and give themselves in a conscious effort to establish international solidarity.'[65] Later that year pacifism became the focal point of debate at the Student Volunteer Convention in Indianapolis. While pacifism was not the predominant view to emerge from the conference, it made a profound impression upon the Canadian delegates.[66] Norman A. Mackenzie, Maritime secretary of the SCM, regarded the pacifists as 'by far the most aggressive, determined, convincing group' present, and he returned to Canada hopeful that the 'war cursed world' could be transformed if a sufficient number of young people were convinced of the 'invariable futility of war' and would refuse to fight.[67] The pacifist debate itself received full coverage in a special supplement to the University of Toronto student newspaper, the *Varsity*.[68] For the balance of the decade it was primarily through student newspapers and its own journal, the *Canadian Student*, that the SCM focused student attention on issues such as war and disarmament and campaigned against the Officers' Training Corps in universities.[69]

By the mid-1920s university students were joined by an increasing number of Canadians attracted to the pacifist idea. The resurgence of pacifism was particularly evident within the nation's Protestant churches, and was articulated by several spokesmen, including Fairbairn, Roberts, and Gifford. But it was also reflected in the rediscovery of pacifist groups such as the Women's International League for Peace and Freedom, which dated back to the war years. Together, this wide range of individuals and groups, from liberal internationalists and social gospellers to students and feminists, began to forge a popular movement.

III

Although Gifford and other churchmen provided intellectual and moral support for pacifism, the active organization of a more rigorous peace campaign was undertaken by new and enthusiastic converts such as those students in the scm and, even more important, by the small group of radical pacifists who had survived the war. The wartime pacifists had kept alive the ongoing tradition of pacifism in Canada; now their contribution would be central to a much expanded peace movement. Except for the historic peace sects, however, the only organized peace group still functioning in Canada after the war was the Women's International League for Peace and Freedom, popularly known as the WIL. During the war the WIL assumed the pacifist role discarded by other women's groups, and although the WCTU and the National Council of Women later revived their respective peace and arbitration committees, the WIL remained dominant in post-war women's peace activities and a major presence in the Canadian peace movement in general.

Although the WIL was not formally organized on a national scale until the late 1920s, several branches and affiliated groups sprang up across the country, including major chapters in Toronto and Vancouver. The original women's peace organization in Toronto had been the sole representative of the WIL in Canada until the Vancouver branch was established in 1921. At the war's end, however, the Toronto section appeared to be a 'factious' group of women who devoted their energies to negative attacks on the military and the celebrations of Empire and Armistice Days.[70] The Vancouver branch, in contrast, took a fresh post-war approach which involved educating the public about peace.

The organization of the Vancouver section was largely the work of its first president, Lucy Woodsworth, and its secretary, Laura Jamieson.[71] Mrs Woodsworth, the wife of Canada's most renowned pacifist, was active in the WIL in the early Vancouver days and later in Winnipeg. Mrs Jamieson succeeded Mrs Woodsworth as president of the Vancouver branch and became one of the most prominent and influential pacifists in Western Canada. Through her initiative the Vancouver branch co-operated with other civic groups in sponsoring public lectures on peace, a peace library, peace pageants, and an annual international fair during Armistice Week.[72] Jamieson, like Fairbairn, thought of peace not merely as the absence of war but as 'a way of life built on co-operative human relationships which provided for the interchange of ideas and emotions.'[73] In her opinion, this pacific spirit was already visible in the international friendship and co-operation of women in the WIL. Peace would be assured, she maintained, when the co-operative spirit of peace-loving people replaced the aggressive, competitive spirit of the capitalist economic system. When she spoke of peace as the extension of the co-operative idea to international affairs, farm women on the prairies, already attuned to internationalism through the progressive movement, were attracted to the peace campaign, and by the mid-1920s several local chapters of the United Farm Women of Alberta had become affiliated with the Vancouver branch of the WIL.[74]

One of Jamieson's earliest and most important disciples was Mrs Violet McNaughton, the women's editor of the *Western Producer* in Saskatoon. McNaughton was well known in Saskatchewan for her role in the founding of the Women's Section of the Canadian Council of Agriculture and the Saskatchewan Women's Grain Growers Association. She was first attracted to pacifism and the Women's International League for Peace and Freedom as a suffragette during the war.[75] Subsequently, she began to combine the WIL's pacifist principles with the co-operative ideology then popular in the Prairie provinces; ultimately she arrived at a peace philosophy similar to that of Jamieson. Indeed, she was indebted to Jamieson for major concepts and inspiration. The two women became close friends and remained regular correspondents throughout the interwar period.

As the editor of the women's page of one of western Canada's most widely read farm newspapers, McNaughton popularized Jamieson's brand of pacifism and became a regular propagandist for the WIL and the peace issue.[76] The pacifist slant of the women's page actually reflected the official policy of the newspaper. The publisher of the *Western Producer*,

Harris Turner, was a disabled war veteran who was intent upon educating the public about the causes of war and the necessity for an effective peace campaign. He encouraged McNaughton in her pacifist views, and hoped that her message would help create a broad movement for world peace among western farmers.[77]

McNaughton presented her readers with the usual pacifist and labour view of international diplomacy and the causes of the last war, but she assigned major importance to the co-operative spirit of pacifism. Considerable space was also devoted to reviews of books with a pacifist message and to those issues dear to the WIL, such as the struggle against cadet training in schools and militarism in school textbooks. McNaughton's commitment to the WIL and the peace issue was a personal one, not just that of a journalist and feminist. In Saskatoon, for instance, she organized a peace group and sponsored 'peace evenings' that consisted of debates, addresses, discussions, and plays. Readings featuring such pacifist works as Siegfried Sassoon's war poetry proved popular.[78] Gradually, through the 1920s, McNaughton raised the consciousness of her readers on the issues surrounding world peace, and introduced prairie women to the WIL.

The growth of Canadian interest in the Women's International League for Peace and Freedom did not really gain momentum until after the fourth International Congress of the WIL met in Washington in 1924. This was partly because previous WIL conclaves had been largely inaccessible to most Canadian members. For instance, there was no Canadian representative at the 1921 Vienna conference, and when the WIL met at the Hague in 1922 Dr Rose Henderson, a member of the Toronto Board of Education and the Toronto branch of the WIL, was the sole Canadian delegate.[79] When the international body convened in North America, however, it drew a larger response from Canadians.

The theme of the Washington conference was 'A New International Order.' The gathering was attended by representatives of twenty-two national sections of the WIL, including large delegations from the United States and Canada. Among the most notable Canadian delegates were Lucy Woodsworth from Winnipeg and Agnes Macphail, a federal member of Parliament from Ontario. One of the first female politicians in Canada, Macphail provided important encouragement and inspiration to the organization of a strong Canadian section of the WIL and was a key spokeswoman for peace advocates in Ottawa. It was Macphail who invited the European delegates at the Washington conference to include Canada in their tour of North America.[80]

In June the 'much heralded' train dubbed the 'Pax Special' pulled into Toronto carrying a distinguished delegation of twenty-five women, including the German pacifist, Lida Gustava Heymann; Marcelle Capy, the feminist editor of the radical French magazine *La Vague*; and Lady Claire Annesley, the British pacifist and member of the No-Conscription Fellowship.[81] Following advance publicity in the *Christian Guardian* and Toronto newspapers, the WIL delegation received an enthusiastic reception in Massey Hall with Toronto's religious and labour leaders were in attendance. The delegates also addressed a large gathering at Parliament House in Toronto under the auspices of the prime minister.[82] Despite a generally favourable reception, there was some noisy opposition to the presence of the WIL women, particularly those from Austria and Germany. The Toronto *Evening Telegram* attacked the visit and persuaded the Toronto Board of Education to denounce the gesture of goodwill as a 'sinister attempt to undermine British patriotism.' The *Telegram* was accused of creating the 'vicious vehemence' that earlier had blocked an appearance at the University of Toronto by Jane Addams, the noted American social reformer and president of the International WIL.[83]

Despite the occasionally hostile atmosphere, the Canadian women tried to build a broad coalition for peace. The previous summer, for instance, the 'No More War' campaign staged a mass demonstration at Queen's Park in Toronto, complete with a parade, banners, and a series of speakers that featured the WIL representative Agnes Macphail. Other participants included religious figures such as the Reverend Father L. Minehan and the Reverend Dr George Pidgeon, and labour leaders such as Rollin Brickner and James Simpson. A special appearance was made by G. Stanley Russell, the representative of the British council of the No More War Society, who shortly was to take up residence in Toronto as a cleric of note.[84] The next year a World Peace Rally held in London, Ontario, attracted a similar variety of civic representatives.[85] The Society of Friends was so impressed by this new surge of peace activity, which seemed to indicate the growing popularity of pacifism, that it suggested the slogan for the year 1924 in Canada should be 'Stop War! Co-operate!'[86] The Friends added to the impetus by joining with the WIL in the formation of a Toronto branch of the Fellowship of Canadian Youth for Peace, a body first organized in Montreal, which included a wide diversity of religious and ethnic groups.[87] Such actions on the part of Quakers and the WIL, especially the visit to Toronto of the international women's delegation from Washington, brought the whole issue of peace much closer to Canadians and heightened public interest in the movement.

For the WIL specifically, the second half of the decade was a time of growth and expansion. By the late 1920s there were WIL branches in Toronto, Winnipeg, and Vancouver, and several affiliated groups in Saskatchewan and Alberta. Since at the time there was no single national organization with elected officers, Laura Jamieson took it upon herself to serve as the Canadian secretary of the WIL and designated the Vancouver branch the office of the Canadian section.[88] In the fall of 1927 she further publicized the WIL peace program during a speaking tour she made through western Canada under the auspices of the Canadian Club, a sign that pacifists were no longer persona non grata to the Establishment.[89]

The following year, with the aid of several women's organizations and the League of Nations Society, Jamieson co-ordinated a one-day peace conference in Vancouver during Armistice Week. The idea spread, and in April 1929 a similar conference was held in Winnipeg in which thirty-seven different societies co-operated.[90] Saskatoon followed with a peace conference in June. The program featured talks by Jamieson on 'How to make the Kellogg Pact a Reality,' J.B. McGeachy on 'Economic Aspects of War and Peace,' G.W. Simpson on 'Arbitration and International Law,' Claude Lewis on 'Practical Educational Steps towards Peace,' and J.S. Woodsworth on 'Armaments.' At the same time, the Saskatoon Farm Women's University Week concluded with the passage of various resolutions concerning peace. It was suggested, for example, that the Saskatchewan Peace Conference Committee hold an annual peace conference and work towards a national conference. It was also recommended that every women's local lodge and women's section of the United Farmers of Saskatchewan take out membership in the Women's International League for Peace and Freedom through the Vancouver branch, a suggestion that was later adopted by the Regina peace society. Furthermore, the Saskatchewan women endorsed the WIL proposition that 'for every hundred dollars now devoted to preparations for a possible war, one dollar should be given to establish a fund ... to provide in each university in Canada a chair and Scholarships for the study and development of better International relationships.'[91] This was one of the WIL's favourite projects; a similar proposition was introduced in the House of Commons by Agnes Macphail in 1930.

The popularity of the peace conferences reflected the commanding influence of Laura Jamieson and the Vancouver branch of the WIL in western Canada. Vancouver's second annual peace conference was staged in November 1929, with over thirty societies co-operating. The theme of the conference was 'Education and Peace.' According to Jamieson, the whole tone of the conference was 'practical and realistic' rather than visionary. 'Peace was spoken of, not as a pious hope,' she wrote, 'but as an objective which must have some assurance of attainment if any other form of social service is to be worth while.' It was useless to work for human betterment, she added, if another war was to wipe out civilization.[92] Even though most of those in attendance were already converted to the cause of peace, the conference was considered a huge success. It was a notable advance in mobilization and for many it led to the crystallization of thought and the revitalization of commitment. The one-day peace conferences, usually held during Armistice Week, became popular events as the peace movement continued to build momentum across Canada.

One of the high points of WIL activities occurred in 1929 when Agnes Macphail, Violet McNaughton, and Laura Jamieson represented Canada at the International Congress of the WIL in Prague. The presence of a Canadian delegation representing three regions of the country was symbolic of both the growing influence of the WIL in Canada and the desire for closer co-operation between the various Canadian branches. While in Europe the Canadian delegates discussed future plans for peace work at home and agreed that the time had come to co-operate on a national basis. Jamieson and McNaughton noted that the United Farm Women of Saskatchewan already favoured such a move.[93] The three women returned inspired by their international experience and hopeful that a stronger WIL could be built in Canada. As acting Canadian secretary, Jamieson began to circulate monthly WIL newsletters in which she reiterated the plea for unity.

Within a year the move for nationwide co-ordination of the WIL was completed. A Canadian section was formally organized with official branches in Toronto, Winnipeg, and Vancouver and affiliated groups in the Prairies. In Alberta, for instance, seventeen locals of the United Farm Women of Alberta and the Alberta WCTU joined the WIL. But neither the WIL nor the peace movement in general was successful in organizing a base east of Montreal.[94] Vancouver remained the national headquarters, probably because Jamieson was retained as the Canadian secretary. Other national officers included Agnes Macphail as president, Lucy Woodsworth as treasurer, and vice-presidents from each of the five provinces with WIL representation – Ontario, Manitoba, Saskatchewan, Alberta, and British Columbia. McNaughton headed a publicity committee, Alice E. Loeb of Toronto a committee on militarism, and Beatrice Brigden of Brandon, Manitoba, a committee on education.[95]

In their publicity brochure the Canadian women described the WIL as an active organization in touch with reality. The aim of the WIL, was to 'unite women of all countries, and of all parties and classes, who are opposed to war, exploitation and oppression.'[96] Their overall peace philosphy was revealed in the stated 'plan of work' for the Canadian section. Although the program included the usual support for the League of Nations and arbitration and conciliation, its major aspect concerned the education of Canada's youth. Without being specific, the WIL hoped to ensure that teachers were properly instructed about the League of Nations 'so that our youths may learn to solve international problems by peaceful and constructive methods.' They also reiterated their well-known demand that a university course in international relations be offered in each province, along with the creation of appropriate libraries and international scholarships. This could easily be accomplished if the Canadian government would show its good faith in the Kellogg Peace Pact by financing preparation for peace as it did preparation for war. Central to the Canadian program was the abolition of cadet training in the schools and the substitution of physical education courses. Another suggestion called for the development of peace activities that would catch the imagination of young people, 'thereby making Peace as interesting as War.' The practice of holding one-day peace conferences across Canada was also endorsed, as was the desire for a stronger emphasis on peace and 'less military display' during Armistice Day observances.

Overall, the WIL concentrated on what it considered practical steps for world peace, emphasizing the futility of war rather than religious or moral non-resistance. Most WIL members were not pacifists in the true sense of the word, but they eagerly accepted the label, and by doing so tended to blur any real distinctions in the general make-up of the interwar peace movement. Their broad pacifist sympathies were reflected in their suggested reading list, which recommended leading pacifist publications such as *The Christian and War*, the Canadian pacifist statement by Gifford and his Montreal associates, and the radical Christian journal the *World Tomorrow*. The Canadian section also recommended two new publications of their own entitled 'Military Training in Canadian Schools' and 'World Federation Takes a Stand on Military Training.'[97]

IV

The primary objective of the Women's International League for Peace and Freedom and other Canadian pacifist groups and individuals during the 1920s was the elimination of militarism in education. The issue was the catalyst that united pacifists and built a stronger and more cohesive peace movement in general. As is evident from their pamphlets on the subject, the WIL provided the initial impetus in the campaign. The central object of their attack was the glorification of war and the military in Canadian school textbooks. The WIL and their pacifist supporters favoured a complete revision of textbooks in Canada in order to replace a militaristic bias with lessons on the prevention of war, international goodwill, and the economic and spiritual unity of mankind. J.S. Woodsworth was one of the first to join in the attack on textbooks. 'Unless our children are taught the futility and suicidal tendency of modern war,' he wrote, 'they will as adults find themselves engaged in another war which experts tell us will almost certainly wipe out western civilization.'[98] Woodsworth reported 'a good deal of interest' in the issue across central and western Canada as early as 1924. In Toronto the Society of Friends waged a successful campaign with the support of the Toronto *Globe* against the use of the textbook entitled *Flag and Fleet* in Ontario schools.[99] The whole issue came to a head at the end of the decade when the Toronto branch of the WIL sponsored an independent survey of all history textbooks used in Canadian schools. Although the report of the survey committee concluded that between 17 and 30 per cent of the content of most texts was devoted to military history, it provided no evidence that a militaristic bias prevailed in the books.[100] The percentage of text devoted to military history was certainly excessive, however, and the WIL remained convinced that a revision of history books was necessary in order to curb the growth of militarism.[101]

The other major target of pacifist derision, and the one that aroused the most interest and debate, was cadet training in the schools. The widespread practice of military training in Canadian schools began with the creation of a special trust fund for that purpose by Lord Strathcona in 1907. From that time its growth accelerated, particularly during the war.[102] Ironically, the greatest increase in the number of cadets occurred in the 1920s when opposition to military training was stirring. For instance, the number of cadets in Canada jumped from 47,000 in 1913 to 112,000 in 1926 while the national expenditure on cadet training rose from $74,000 in 1920 to $412,000 in 1926.[103] Alarmed pacifist groups cited the statistics as further evidence of the trend towards a militaristic society. When the annual grant to cadet services was debated in the House of Commons, opposition was voiced repeatedly by J.S. Woodsworth and Agnes Macphail. Farm organizations in particular passed numerous resolutions condemning the cadet program, while farm journals such as the *Western Producer* publicized the Woodsworth-Macphail speeches against military training in schools. Macphail painted such a lurid picture of schoolboys being sent to a bloody slaughter that there was a general outcry from the public. In 1924 she made the first of many ill-fated motions in the House protesting cadet training. 'Why should we take our boys,' she asked, 'dress them in uniforms and teach them to strut along to martial strains with their foolish little guns and swords at their sides?'[104] The same line of argument was used by Macphail's colleagues in the WIL. For instance, the Toronto branch, through the efforts of its post-war presidents, Alice Loeb and Berta Hamilton, continually raised the issue in public meetings and lectures, and by mid-decade was effective in placing an anti-cadet resolution before every trade union in Toronto, with satisfying results.[105]

Officially, cadet training consisted of military drill, rifle-shooting, and physical training, but its opponents maintained that it also included psychological conditioning in the desirability of war as a means of settling disputes and the glorification of war as an ideal.[106] As an alternative they proposed proper instruction in physical education. According to a 1927 report of the educational committee of the Toronto WIL, however, even physical training programs had come under military influence. The committee found that three-fourths of all instructors in physical training courses at teacher-training institutions were officers of the permanent militia. In Ontario, only men with a cadet instructor's certificate issued by the Department of Militia and Defence could be granted certificates as specialists in physical culture by the Ontario Department of Education.[107] Furthermore, although military training was not compulsory in Canadian schools and colleges, the report maintained that strong pressure was exerted upon boys to join the cadets, 'sometimes taking the form of an indication that preference will be given to cadets in the choice of boys to place on the sport teams.' The report concluded that Canada was 'in great danger of *becoming* a militaristic country' with schools as the culture-medium for 'an embryo army.'[108]

The WIL pamphlet on military training received a hearty endorsement from the Society of Friends for use in their study groups.[109] The Quakers were major critics of military drill in Canada before the Great War, and in the 1920s they renewed their attack by criticizing the post-war cadet program as antagonistic to the progressive reconstruction of the world and arguing in favour of alternative physical training courses in schools. They recognized the value of physical exercise in the educational system, but they insisted that 'any instruction that inculcates in a boy at such a time in his life the ideals of militarism' not only was contrary to the spirit of love and brotherhood but would inevitably cause Canadian youth 'to forget or miss the lessons of the horror and futility of war.'[110] In resolutions and individual actions Quakers struggled to support the campaign against the cadet program and militarism in education. In 1924, for example, Edgar Zavitz of the Genesee Yearly Meeting tried to organize a letter-writing campaign in support of Agnes Macphail's stand in Parliament against increased cadet expenditures.[111] A few years later Raymond Booth, secretary of the Toronto monthly meeting, suggested an oratorical contest – that favourite device of all causes – to help combat the spirit of militarism in Toronto schools.[112] *The Canadian Friend* followed the issue closely and excited its readers with rhetorical questions: 'Are we as a people being militarized? Are our sons and daughters being trained for war? Are we taking any steps to check the insidious propaganda of those interested in shackling the youth of this land with the blight of the war-mind?'[113]

Despite the determination of the Society of Friends, the Women's International League, and other pacifists, the campaign against cadet training was largely ineffective during the 1920s. The cadet corps in Canadian schools continued to grow, and by 1927 the government expenditure on military training had risen to a half million dollars.[114] In the opinion of Arthur Dorland, a leading Quaker spokesman, it was convenient for school officials and boards of education to continue militia training because of the strong incentive of the government grants.[115] Indeed, the average cadet instructor had a vested interest in the program, since he received at least an additional $140 per year for every ninety cadets he taught.[116] Local school boards were also reluctant to abolish the cadet corps because 'they liked the cheap means of providing for physical education.'[117] Finally, the WIL appealed to the United Church to condemn the cadet corps as unchristian.

The first general council of the United Church in 1925 had considered a resolution favouring the abolition of cadet training, but had postponed a final decision.[118] William Creighton, now the editor of the *New Outlook*, took up the WIL cause, arguing that 'if it can be shown that military training in our schools tends to foster the military spirit among our youth, and lends itself to a sympathetic attitude towards war as an established institution of our world order, the church cannot consistently give it her approval.'[119] Although they were sympathetic, the United Churchmen remained noncommittal on the issue until the 1927 general council appointed a special commission on the cadet corps and officers' training corps. The investigation revealed that church membership was divided over the issue, but more than 90 per cent of those answering a questionnaire reported that they found no evidence of militarism in the schools and that they approved of the cadet corps. Ernest Thomas, perhaps a little too facilely, declared that the commission narrowed the issue down to one question: 'Is the presence within the school life of the national government in the person of an inspecting officer on one day in the year such an infringement of Christian obligation that the Church should call for its abolition?'[120] The commission thought not, and ultimately the church agreed that cadet training was not contrary to the Christian conscience. The decision, while a severe blow to pacifists, far from settled the issue, and the anti-cadet campaign persisted into the 1930s, at which time it met with limited success.

v

The co-operation of the Society of Friends in the campaign against cadet training was indicative of both the broad makeup of the interwar peace movement and the general transition in Quaker thought. By the end of the war Friends around the world had revised their definition of 'pacifism' to give it an active rather than a passive meaning. In keeping with their belief in the perfectibility of the world, Friends adopted a more dynamic approach to removing the evils that obstructed the achievement of the Kingdom of God on earth. They opposed not only the violence of war but all forms of social oppression. Thus, the new goal of twentieth-century Quakers was not merely a peaceful way of life but a complete radical reconstruction of the political and economic order within and among nations. Furthermore, their acceptance of the state and the use of force, such as a police force, to sustain it allowed Friends to broaden their historic tradition of passive non-resistance into an active but non-violent resistance as a means with which to achieve the new social order.[121] Twentieth-century Quaker pacifism became synonymous with non-violent resistance. Quaker acceptance of non-violent compulsion to bring about social change challenged traditional religious pacifism, and, even though it was rejected by the other historic peace sects, the idea received considerable support from liberal Protestants in the peace movement. For Friends, however, their new creed posed a special dilemma: once pacifism became an instrument of radical social change and their concern centred on the achievement of a new social order, they faced the constant temptation to sacrifice the purity of their non-violent means in order to reach their goals. Nevertheless, the Quaker transition from passive non-resistance to a more active pacifism, although gradual, was an important factor in the growth of the peace campaign in Canada. Canadian Friends were kept abreast of the changing interpretations of Quakerism largely through the efforts of Albert S. Rogers, chairman of the Canada Yearly Meeting, Professor Arthur G. Dorland, chairman of the peace committee, and Fred Haslam, treasurer of the finance committee and later the leading figure in the service committee. In August 1920 Dorland and Rogers were among the Canadian delegates to the first World Conference of All Friends in London. The purpose of the conference was to clarify and deepen the peace testimony of the Society as well as to 'bind together its scattered branches in common work for the coming of the Kingdom of God.'[122] The conference produced various pamphlets for publication, including 'The Fight against War,' a new statement of the Quaker position. Upon his return Rogers reported that the London discussions were primarily concerned with the implications of pacifism in 'civic and international relations ... in personal and social relations ... ' and in the 'life of the society.' He also noted that the general tone of the conference emphasized individual responsibility in the building of 'a new world order through practical application of the Teachings and Spirit of Jesus.' The Canadian delegates returned from England with a host of mental and spiritual impressions concerning their peace testimony. 'We must have much quiet time at home,' reported Rogers, 'to sort them, to make them more fully our own and to show as much of them to our friends as we can.'[123] Canadian Friends had always thrived on Anglo-American inspiration, but it appears to have been the post-war influx of ideas and people that propelled them on the road to social activism.

The post-war attitude of the Society of Friends in Canada came to reflect the dependence of the cause of peace on the successful quest for social and economic justice. The *Canadian Friend* publicized the correlation between the two ideals and reprinted numerous articles on the subject by internationally known pacifists. The November 1926 issue, for instance, carried an article by Mahatma Gandhi, the famous Indian pacifist and social activist, which originally had been printed in the *World Tomorrow*. Gandhi praised non-violence as the greatest force available to man in the struggle against evil. Then, following an endorsement of the peace movement, he confessed: 'I cannot help the growing fear that the movement will fail if it does not touch the root of all evil – man's greed.'[124] A similar note was struck when Arthur Dorland described the wider implications of the Quaker peace testimony: 'It means a peaceable and loving spirit in our home circle, in our neighbourhood, a proper sense of economic and social justice, a consideration for the rights of others in all the manifold relations of life.'[125]

The most important expression of this philosophy by Canadian Friends in the early 1920s was their support for post-war relief work in Europe. In the two years from 1919 to 1921 Canadian Quakers contributed almost five thousand dollars to the American Friends Service Committee for famine relief in Poland, France, Germany, and Austria.[126] Apparently, they agreed with Dorland that European relief work presented the opportunity 'to send our Quaker message of goodwill to those who have so recently been called our enemies, and so help to heal the wounds of war.'[127] Some young Canadians who had served with the Friends Ambulance Unit in Europe during the war remained to assist in the relief program. The tragedy of the Russian famine in 1922 prompted Albert Rogers to organize a drive for emergency aid to Russia. With the support of John Lewis, editor of the Toronto *Globe*, and Charles D. Gordon, manager of the head office of the Dominion Bank, over sixty thousand dollars in public donations was collected in Toronto alone. As treasurer of the Canada Yearly Meeting finance committee, Fred Haslam administered the national appeal. Initially, the Canadian funds were sent to the American Friends Service Committee for use in relief work in Russia, but later, 'in the interest of wider appeal,' the Friends directed their funds for Russian famine relief through the Canadian Save the Children Fund.[128]

The direct co-operation of Canadian Quakers with other religious groups in furthering the cause of peace was accelerated when the Canada Yearly Meeting authorized Arthur Dorland to approach 'other churches in order to organize some form of peace association in Canada.'[129] The association Dorland had in mind was the World Alliance for International Friendship through the Churches, a group founded by Joseph Allen Baker, a Canadian-born Quaker residing in Britain and a personal friend of the Dorland family.[130] The World Alliance was the reorganized post-war version of the Associated Councils of Churches in the British and German Empires for Fostering Friendly Relations between the Two Peoples. Prior to the war the Associated Councils of Churches had enlisted the support of over one thousand Canadians; the Canadian Peace and Arbitration Society acted as the official Canadian section.[131] Since the

Peace and Arbitration Society had disintegrated during the war, however, Canadians had no contact with the new World Alliance until Dorland took steps to restore the connection.

After meeting with the American council of the World Alliance in 1921, Dorland was convinced that the first step was to get Canadians into the World Alliance and then to organize a separate Canadian section. Subsequently, with assistance from the British council, over three hundred Canadian clergymen were persuaded to join the American council.[132] At first the World Alliance had little impact in Canada, primarily because Canadian members were merely part of an American organization. Dorland's efforts to organize a Canadian council were rejected by the other denominations, who were suspicious of Quaker pacifism. The reluctance on the part of Canadian clergymen to co-operate with the Quakers was overcome only when the Archbishop of Canterbury, as president of the International World Alliance, endorsed the idea of a Canadian section.[133] Quakers, Anglicans, and other major Protestant denominations finally joined together to form the Canadian council of the World Alliance in November 1926. The most active members where those already prominent in the peace debate. They included Dorland, Albert Rogers, and Fred Haslam, all Quakers; Archbishop Samuel P. Matheson, primate of the Anglican church in Canada; S.D. Chown, the former general superintendent of the Methodist church; and Professor P.V. Pilcher of Trinity College, Toronto. Pilcher became particularly active in the Canadian council and on several occasions had to assure his Anglican colleagues that the World Alliance was not strictly a pacifist organization, 'but a means of promoting world peace by both pacifists and non-pacifists who hoped to discover mutually acceptable means of furthering Christian goodwill and friendship.'[134]

The effectiveness of the World Alliance in Canada was hampered by the fact that its staunchest supporters, the Quakers and Anglicans, represented the two extremes of pacifism and armed preparedness. Consequently, the World Alliance avoided the controversial topics of the day, such as cadet training, and became involved instead in more mundane issues – for example, the promotion of the League of Nations or the celebration of Peace Sunday.[135] By 1930 the primary Canadian role in the World Alliance appeared to be the promotion of Anglo-American co-operation, an objective reminiscent of pre-war Canadian peace societies. Regardless of its particular activities, however, the creation of a Canadian council of the World Alliance further broadened the base of a Canadian peace movement and focused attention on the moral ne-

cessity of international co-operation. Its chief purpose, according to Dorland, was to arouse the church 'to create that enlightened, Christian,
public opinion in which the peace of the world and the success of any
machinery designed to secure it, ultimately rest.'[136]

One of the most important contributions of Friends to the peace movement was their attempt to create an 'intelligent public sentiment' and a
sense of public responsibility for domestic and international peace.[137]
Friends also promoted Canadian membership in various pacifist or peace-
oriented associations, including the League of Nations Society, the World
Alliance, the Women's International League, and the Fellowship of Reconciliation. The peace committee of the Canadian and Genesee Yearly
Meetings maintained a peace library of pacifist publications and encouraged their membership to read important new books.[138] The Canadian pacifist publication *The Christian and War*, for instance, was
recommended highly by Dorland to readers of the *Canadian Friend*.[139]
Although Canadian Friends had begun to radicalize their thinking in
terms of the real social and economic prerequisites for world peace, they
also maintained their faith in the power of a public peace mentality and
therefore welcomed the Kellogg Peace Pact as a great step in that
direction.[140]

Unlike the Quakers, the other historic peace sects in Canada were
relatively silent on the public issue of international conflict and the popular movement for world peace. The Mennonites, Hutterites, and Doukhobors remained faithful to the principle of non-resistance and tried
to maintain the separation of their communities from the mainstream
of Canadian society. Although Mennonites in the United States actively
opposed the Quaker 'heresy' of non-violent resistance, Canadian Mennonites were too preoccupied with the immediate problems confronting
their communities, such as the immigration of more Mennonites from
Russia, to mount any opposition to new Quaker ways even if they had
been disposed to do so. Indeed, there was an unintended collaboration
between the two groups when the humanitarian work of the Friends in
Russian famine relief in 1922 coincided with the efforts of Canadian
Mennonites to resettle Russian Mennonite refugees in Canada.

Ever since the Bolshevik Revolution large numbers of Russian Mennonites had wished to join their North American brethren, but the immigration into Canada of Mennonites, Hutterites, and Doukhobors had
been specifically banned by a 1919 order in council. The discriminatory
measure was passed in response to widespread public reaction against
the Hutterian communal lifestyle, the Mennonite resistance to learning

the English language, and their common German background and conscientious objection to military service. Following the war, Mennonites lobbied to get the order in council rescinded and solicited the support of William Lyon Mackenzie King, who had been raised in Ontario's Mennonite country. Finally, in 1922, after King and the Liberal party were returned to power, the order in council was repealed and the door was open for Russian Mennonites to enter Canada once more. In conjunction with the colonization program of the Canadian Pacific Railway, waves of Mennonites reached Canada in the 1920s. The largest movements occurred between 1923 and 1927. By the time immigration was again restricted in 1929, over twenty thousand new Russian Mennonites had flocked to the Canadian prairies. The newcomers who arrived from Russia after 1920 became known as *Russlaender*; the Canadian Mennonites who had left Russia in the 1870s identified themselves as *Kanadier*.[141] Although the influx of Mennonite immigrants increased the number of those in Canada opposed to military service and warfare, the Mennonites themselves recoiled from the pacifist debate until they were again directly threatened by conscription during the Second World War. Hutterites also remained withdrawn from Canadian society and concentrated on protecting the integrity of their communal colonies from local prejudice and discriminatory legislation designed to prevent their further expansion.

The resentment of western Canadians of the idea of conscientious objectors profiting at the expense of those in uniform also plagued the Doukhobors in British Columbia. Although they had been relatively unmolested during the war, they were the victims of post-war discontent and suspicion. In 1919 British Columbia deprived the Doukhobors of their right to vote in provincial elections, while the citizens of Nelson and Grand Forks passed resolutions demanding the deportation of Doukhobors to Russia and the expropriation of their lands for redistribution to returned soldiers.[142] Dissatisfaction and uneasiness mounted among the Doukhobors, and in 1922 a new confrontation with the state was triggered when they began to withdraw their children from the schools. Attempts by authorities to seize property in payment of fines levied against the parents were followed by a wave of school-burnings. From 1923 to 1925 nine schools were destroyed by arson, along with the house of Peter Verigin, the Doukhobor leader, and other Doukhobor property in Brilliant, British Columbia. 'Peter the Lordly' himself was killed in October 1924 when the railway coach in which he was riding exploded.[143] The mysterious series of violent acts notwithstanding, most Doukhobors remained adamantly opposed to military force and war. Their pacifist beliefs, however, permitted the exercise of physical protests such as the boycott of schools and nude marches, tactics in keeping with non-violent resistance. Contrary to most liberal pacifist practices, however, Doukhobor protests were tied to their anarchistic rejection of the authority of the state. Above all, Doukhobor concern centred on the maintenance of their freedom and peculiar way of life; they were largely unaffected by the general clamour for world peace during the interwar years. An exception was Peter Makaroff, a Doukhobor lawyer who played an important role as a pacifist and socialist in Saskatchewan before and during the Second World War.

VI

As the 1920s came to a close, the Canadian peace movement reached an important stage in its growth and development. Although most of the historic peace sects remained aloof, the movement had become a 'broad front of groups and activities' made up of absolute pacifists, who were adamantly opposed to all wars and violent revolutions, and liberal internationalists and other peace activists who believed war, though sometimes necessary, was always irrational and inhumane and therefore should be prevented. This interwar coalition was made possible when, in the absence of an immediate threat of war, 'the social hope of the social gospel fused with the world hope of pacifists and a broad range of internationalists.'[144] Once this merger of social gospel and pacifist groups began, a wide variety of social and political activities were brought under the banner of the peace movement, with the result that the larger social and political outlook of people such as W.B. Creighton, Edis Fairbairn, Richard Roberts, Laura Jamieson, Violet McNaughton, Agnes Macphail, and J.S. Woodsworth became inseparable from their pacifism. But that is not to say that the broad range of individuals associated with the movement agreed on one philosophical approach. Not all, for instance, shared the pacifist belief in the total renunciation of war or a radical commitment to social change. Indeed, the pacifist alignment with socialism that had begun during the war evolved slowly during the 1920s. Socially radical pacifists such as Woodsworth and Fairbairn continually emphasized the relationship between war and capitalism, but most of the liberal internationalists and social reformers who rallied to the peace movement felt free to display both their revulsion against war and militarism and their generally progressive reformism without engaging in a radical challenge to the political and economic order. Consequently, the socially radical dimension of pacifism was not fully demonstrated in the 1920s; it would become more apparent in both declaration and action under the social and economic pressures of the depression years.

In the meantime, socially radical pacifists united with the rest of the peace movement in a campaign to redirect the thinking of Canadian society towards peace and international co-operation. Although they could 'hardly hope to exercise any very great influence in the international field,' as Woodsworth told the British pacifist E.D. Morel, Canadian pacifists were doing 'whatever is possible in the interests of peace.'[145] Given the broad nature of the pacifist coalition, its members evaded questions that might have provoked disagreement in their ranks, and instead joined forces in endorsing the League of Nations and disarmament and in combating the various manifestations of militarism in society, from the sale of military toys to military appropriations and cadet training in the schools.[146] The expansion of the Women's International League into a national organization and the effort of the SCM to keep Canadian university students interested in both pacifism and social action were accomplishments that contributed to an upsurge of pacifist feeling in Canada by the end of the 1920s.[147]

Indeed, no event better characterized the Canadian peace movement than its reaction to the signing of the Kellogg Peace Pact in 1928. Climaxing a decade of pacifist activity dedicated to the condemnation of war, the pact was heralded as proof that the pacifist idea had taken root. The enthusiastic response of Canadians ranged from endorsements by numerous organizations and churches to displays of copies of the pact in schools across the country.[148] The importance of the pact in Canada was underlined by the fact that Prime Minister Mackenzie King had been the Canadian representative in Paris. The Kellogg Pact was not a concrete plan to guarantee the peaceful settlement of international disputes; rather, it was a mere statement of intention not much different from any other peace resolution. Nevertheless, to pacifist forces the spirit of the peace pact seemed to promise 'a new and better day.'

As peace advocates looked to the future, however, they were painfully aware of the existence of conditions in the world that contributed to the threat of war. In his report to a United Church sessional committee on war and peace, Newton W. Rowell, the father of the League of Nations Society in Canada, warned that 'the presence of immense standing armies, the development of great navies and the creation of mighty air-fleets cannot but be an occasion of unrest and constitute an ever present reminder that we have not yet passed from the menace of war.' As a course of action, Rowell urged the church to enter a new crusade in order 'to lead and to develop the peace purpose of the nations,' especially the creation of 'a Christian public opinion and the obliteration from the national life of such continuing evils as racial antipathies, selfish nationalism and international jealousies.'[149] The United Church, Rowell concluded confidently, had declared her desire for peace and consecrated herself to its attainment. The same determination characterized the entire peace movement as it accelerated its campaign for peace and social justice amid the crises of the 1930s.

5

In search of peace and social justice

An interwar peace coalition gained momentum after the mid-1920s, and Canadians enjoyed a period of economic prosperity. As the 1920s drew to a close, however, the short-lived boom collapsed and Canada, along with the United States, Great Britain, and most other industrial nations, found herself in the Great Depression, the social and economic upheaval that characterized Canadian life for the next decade. After the Wall Street crash of 1929 the Canadian situation grew steadily worse. The price of wheat tumbled and unsold grain surpluses increased each year. Years of crop failure spelled economic disaster for Canada, a crisis aggravated by severe drought on the prairies. Meanwhile, unemployment mounted in urban areas, and by 1933, with approximately one of every two wage-earners out of work, Canada faced a challenge to its very social and economic structure.

Canada was not alone in its despair, however, and Canadians were becoming increasingly aware of the international ramifications of the depression. Industrial capitalism was face to face with the deepest crisis of its history, and liberal democratic regimes and ideology were thrown on the defensive before collectivist and racist solutions. In partial reaction to its economic plight, for instance, Japan was the first to defy the post-war ideal of collective security by moving into Manchuria in 1931, and by 1933 Hitler's Third Reich had replaced the Weimar Republic in Germany by promising simple solutions to colossal economic confusion and unemployment. The international situation gradually deteriorated, and by mid-decade the optimism of the peace movement was severely shaken by increased fascist aggression.

In the meantime, in the depression years of the early 1930s, Canadian pacifists strengthened their alliance with League of Nations internationalists and the political left in the quest for both peace and social justice at home and abroad. Pacifists continued to place their faith in disarmament as a means of reducing international tension, but on the domestic scene, as new groups promoting radical solutions to the economic crisis proliferated, pacifist sentiment became closely linked with social radicalism. In the period after the Great War pacifists had come to appreciate the positive uses of the state to secure greater social welfare and, they believed, the institutionalization of pacifistic thought in society. That did not, of course, run counter to their belief that human nature was essentially good – it was just that new social and economic circumstances required a more collective response to social needs. Consequently, pacifists were influential in the various socially radical groups organized in response to the depression; during the first half of the 1930s, the peace movement became unequivocally allied with the movement for radical social change.

I

The new decade of peace activities began with the organization of socially concerned Toronto pacifists around a small nucleus of activists. One of these activists was Richard Roberts. Since his arrival at Toronto's Sherbourne United Church in 1927, Roberts had become an influential force in both the Student Christian Movement and the wider peace movement. By the spring of 1930 Roberts and Dr W.P. Firth, a Quaker, succeeded in organizing the first chapter of the Fellowship of Reconciliation (FOR) in Canada, and within a year the Toronto organization attracted approximately three hundred members of diverse religious, political, and social backgrounds.[1] Later, various peace groups across the country adopted the name of the fellowship, but Canadian pacifists did not attempt to affiliate with the international parent organization until the late 1930s.

A leading activist in the Toronto FOR, and its first president, was Maurice N. Eisendrath, rabbi of Holy Blossom Temple. Newly arrived from the United States in 1930, Eisendrath professed not only Reform Judaism but a strong admiration for the Protestant social gospel and its belief in human progress and the ideal of universal peace. Throughout the 1930s, therefore, he was instrumental in building bridges between Canada's Jewish and Christian communities through such forums as the first Canadian Jewish-Gentile seminar organized in conjunction with the United Church. He also became well known for his regular Sunday

All Day Peace Conference

Auspices of

FELLOWSHIP OF RECONCILIATION

and Affiliated Peace Groups in Toronto

MONDAY, NOVEMBER 10th, 1930

PROGRAMME FOR THE DAY

Chairman: RABBI M. N. EISENDRATH, Pres., F.O.R.

---

9 A.M.—at Mt. Pleasant Cemetery, Yonge Street Entrance.

DECORATION OF GRAVES OF HEROES OF PEACE

Participants in flower-strewing ceremonies:

ARCHIBISHOP NEIL McNEIL   RABBI SAMUEL SACHS
REV. E. CROSSLEY HUNTER   MR. JAMES SIMPSON
VEN. ARCH. J. C. DAVIDSON   MR. WILSON MACDONALD

DR. GEO. T. WEBB, presiding.

---

10 A.M.—at Alhambra Theatre, Bloor, near Bathurst Street.

YOUNG PEOPLE'S PROGRAMME

Special showing of **"High Treason"** a British moving picture

with a Peace lesson. Discussion of picture will be led by

MR. EARL LAUTENSLAGER, of Victoria College.

---

3 - 5 P.M.—at Lecture Hall, Yorkminster Church, Yonge and Heath Streets.

Peace Conference - Discussion Groups

Conference will be opened by   Chairman: REV. G. R. BOOTH,
MR. J. S. WOODSWORTH, M.P.   Exec.-Sec. F.O.R.

8.00 P.M.—at Lecture Hall, Yorkminster Church, Yonge and Heath Street.

Public Meeting on Disarmament

under auspices of Women's International League for Peace and Freedom.

Speaker: MR. J. S. WOODSWORTH, M.P.   Chairman: DR. S. G. BLAND.
MR. WILSON MACDONALD will read his poetry.

Music   Book Exhibit

EVERYBODY WELCOME!

COME!

morning sermons at Holy Blossom Temple, which attracted a sizeable non-Jewish audience, as well as the 'Forum of the Air,' a Sunday afternoon radio show broadcast by station CFRB that continued for six years.

From the pulpit of his synagogue and over the airwaves, Eisendrath always spoke as a pacifist. Although his pacifism was not derived solely from Judaism, neither was it entirely alien to Jewish teaching. Micah's famous prophecy of swords beaten into ploughshares was one example cited by Eisendrath. Certainly, he argued, pacifism was not exclusively Christian, and to espouse it did not mean that one became 'unconsciously assimilated to the Christian gospel'.[2] His wife Rosa became active in the Women's International League for Peace and Freedom, and Eisendrath assumed the presidency of the Toronto FOR. In that capacity he represented Canada at the World Assembly of the Fellowship of Reconciliation at Lunteren, Holland, in 1931.

Meanwhile, under Eisendrath's direction, one of the first activities of the new FOR was its co-operation with affiliated Toronto peace groups, such as the WIL, in sponsoring an 'All Day Peace Conference' on Armistice Day 1930. Built around the issue of international disarmament, the event was organized by Eisendrath and G. Raymond Booth, FOR executive secretary and chairman of the Toronto Monthly Meeting of Friends. The conference began with the decoration of graves of 'Heroes of Peace' at Mount Pleasant Cemetery by a number of religious and political leaders, including the Venerable Archdeacon J.C. Davidson of the Anglican church, the Roman Catholic Archbishop Neil McNeil, Rabbi Samuel Sachs, and Controller James Simpson. Instead of paying tribute to military heroism, the participants honoured the dedication and personal sacrifice of ordinary Canadians in the pursuit of a peaceful and just society – a fireman, a policeman, a nurse, an industrial worker, and a scientist. The brief ceremony sparked the comment that an 'eventful little movement' had been started.[3]

Later that morning a young people's program featured a showing of 'High Treason,' a British film with a peace lesson, to hundreds of high-school pupils, followed by a discussion led by Earl Lautenslager, a theological student at Victoria College. Also on the program was a special poetry reading by Wilson Macdonald, the unofficial poet laureate of the peace movement. Among pacifists Macdonald was especially popular for his poems concerning war and human nature, such as the following:

WAR

His feet are rotting
  From a slow gangrene;
His tusks are yellow
  And his eyes are green.
But the church of god
  Calls him sweet and clean.
His flesh is livid
  With copper-hued sores.
He ravishes lads
  And he sleeps with whores.
But the church of god
  Lets him in her doors.
His eyes are founts
  Of greed, hate, lust.
And he killed high freedom
  With a quick, cold thrust.
But the church of god
  Had declared him just.
O Church of God,
  Where the great hymns roar,
Is that man, Jesus,
  Going from your door?
Is he going to make room
  For your red saint, War?[4]

The main speaker of the conference was J.S. Woodsworth. In the
afternoon he led a series of group discussions on the 'psychological,
political, and economic causes of war' and on proposals for pacifist action
in the light of the social and economic problems of the time.[5] That same
theme was emphasized in the major event of the day, Woodsworth's
evening address to a public meeting on disarmament sponsored by the
Toronto branch of the WIL and broadcast over radio station CFRB. The
Canadian Forum reported the general conviction of the conference: although war had its roots in almost every branch of human activity, its
'taproot feeds upon social injustice, and the economic insecurity of great
masses of people in every part of the world.'[6]
    The WIL took advantage of the Toronto conference to begin circulating
in Canada the 'International Declaration of World Disarmament,' a petition in support of disarmament that was being distributed in forty-

seven different countries.[7] Initiated by Lord Robert Cecil, joint president of the League of Nations, the declaration was publicized by the WIL in Great Britain, where it received the official support of the League of Nations, many churches, political parties, labour organizations, and peace societies. WIL groups in Winnipeg, Regina, Edmonton, and Vancouver began circulating the declaration during their respective peace conferences in 1930. Within a few months the declaration had been endorsed by the annual convention of the United Farmers of Ontario and a wide variety of women's organizations.[8]

The enthusiastic response of Canadian women to the disarmament declarations suggests that disarmament had become one of the major international issues of the day. Indeed, the worldwide petition was intended to consolidate public support for the International Disarmament Conference scheduled to commence at Geneva in February 1932. Since an earlier conference had ended in failure in 1927, the new prospect of disarmament had become the major hope of pacifists in the early 1930s and was viewed with both anxiety and urgency. In Canada the campaign for disarmament received the dedicated support of all major pacifist groups, and particularly of the WIL, which told its members that it was 'imperative that public opinion be thoroughly educated, and that the peoples be pledged to give every support to the cause of Disarmament, both before and when the Conference begins.'[9]

As part of their preparation for the upcoming disarmament conference, the WIL's Toronto branch held a special summer school or 'institute' for the American and Canadian sections at the end of May 1931. The institute was held at Wymilwood, the women's union of Victoria College, and was the first summer school in which the Canadian WIL had a direct part. The prime mover of the event was Anna Sissons, the wife of Professor C.B. Sissons of Victoria College (a cousin of J.S. Woodsworth). As the new president of the Toronto branch she played an important part in WIL activities throughout the decade. Organized around the theme 'The Economic Basis of Peace,' the institute was attended by representatives from Chicago, Cleveland, Detroit, and seven Canadian cities. Among the guest speakers were Emily G. Balch, the president of the U.S. section of the WIL, and Jane Addams, the international president. Agnes Macphail, the honorary president of the Canadian section, chaired a timely discussion on preparing for the disarmament conference in 1932.[10]

By the summer of 1931 the WIL was actively joined in the campaign for disarmament by the Canadian National Council of Women, an alliance that reflected the united demand for disarmament by the member groups of the Women's International Organizations. The Canadian local councils were particularly motivated by Lady Aberdeen, the president of the International Council of Women and the original founder of the National Council of Women in Canada.[11] Lady Aberdeen noted with pride the enthusiastic response of the Canadian National Council and its local councils to the disarmament campaign. 'It is a great satisfaction to me,' she wrote, 'how energetically the Canadian Women are promoting this great world campaign for promoting peace.'[12]

An example of this peace work was the resolution passed by the Toronto Local Council of Women urging the Canadian government to insist that any disarmament convention reached at Geneva require all signatories to assume control of industries that manufactured the 'primary equipment of war.'[13] Miss Winnifred Kydd, the president of the Canadian National Council of Women, conducted a speaking tour of eastern Canada in support of the disarmament conference and urged local councils to take an active interest in international affairs.[14] The following year Kydd was appointed an official member of the Canadian delegation to the disarmament conference. Lady Aberdeen was overjoyed with the achievement of the Canadian National Council of Women. 'I always feel it was Canada,' she confessed, 'that taught me the practicality of both NC's and of the ICW and prepared me for the further development with which I have been identified.'[15] In a broadcast from Geneva made through the facilities of the Columbia Broadcasting System, Kydd reported to the Canadian public on the progess of the conference and praised the work of Canadian women for peace: 'I am convinced that you, who have laboured so devotedly to have these petitions signed and placed before the Conference, are largely responsible for this more friendly atmosphere in which our work is proceeding. I appeal to you not to relax your efforts.'[16]

The worldwide promotion of the International Declaration of Disarmament resulted in the collection of over eight million signatures from fifty-six countries.[17] In Canada the WIL collected almost half a million signatures on the disarmament petition. The petition and the Geneva Conference in general received both encouragement and publicity from pacifist and internationalist elements. Violet McNaughton proudly reported that over two thousand signatures were collected in Saskatoon alone, and the United Church's *The New Outlook* devoted the cover of one issue to Lord Cecil and the disarmament petition.[18]

The United Church was a strong supporter of the peace campaign and of disarmament in particular. While international discussions took place in Geneva, a special committee of the general council of the United Church was appointed to consider the issue under the leadership of Richard Roberts. Asserting that 'war is contrary to the mind of Christ,' the committee called upon ministers and members of the church to 'redouble their efforts everywhere to stir up such a conviction in these matters as has never been known before.'[19] The committee advocated the abolition of the private manufacture of armaments, but confessed that it would take 'something sterner and more influential than mere resolutions' to influence one of the largest and richest of industries.

A year later, when it became apparent that the Geneva Conference was headed for failure, Roberts told Prime Minister R.B. Bennett that the Disarmament Conference was bound to miscarry 'because of the absence of a thorough-going realism in its proceedings.'[20] Roberts argued that the disarmament discussions were 'far too much occupied with questions that are hardly more than academic in view of the new and awful possibilities' of the one dominant threat in any future war – the bombing aeroplane. Since there was little defence against air attacks and *'no means of defending a city from a night attack by air,'* the new military strategy would concentrate upon the element of surprise – striking the first blow – 'in which case such a formality as a declaration of war would hardly be considered.' The ultimate significance of this revolutionized theory and practice of war, Roberts concluded, was that the brunt of the next war would fall upon non-combatant populations, 'and in particular upon the dwellers in cities.'[21] Consequently, traditional arms and the strategy and tactics appropriate to them were no longer relevant to meaningful disarmament talks. Given this 'prevision of future war,' Canada should take the lead in organizing another disarmament committee 'for the single purpose of getting the nations to look frankly' at the threat of aerial warfare and thereby 'envisage the situation which would immediately be created in the event of an outbreak of war.'

Not only did Prime Minister Bennett fail to act upon Roberts's suggestion, but the popularity of disarmament itself began to wane by mid-decade as the attention of the peace movement turned to the question of imposing sanctions against aggressor nations. Roberts was one of the few pacifists who came close to articulating the stark reality of the disarmament question; the peace movement as a whole sublimated the failure to disarm nations in an upsurge of interest in individual war resistance and the quest for social justice.

II

As is evident from the disarmament campaign, the Women's International League for Peace and Freedom was one of the groups most active in the Canadian peace movement and one that came to embrace social radicalism during the early years of the depression. At first, however, the WIL continued to emphasize practical issues such as the question of cadet training in the schools. The campaign launched during the 1920s to replace the cadet system with classes in physical education met with some success in the 1930s, particularly in Winnipeg and Toronto.[22] In both instances the final outcome resulted from a concerted effort by WIL members to separate militarism from education. One of the tactics of the Toronto branch was to nominate members as candidates for the board of education.[23] Once on the board, however, it was not easy for members to persuade Toronto's civic leaders, many with imperialist sympathies and military memories, to abolish the cadet system. The issue finally came to a head when Mrs Ida Siegel, the member of the Toronto board of education for Ward Four and a WIL activist, publicized the practice of financially rewarding teachers according to the number of cadets in their classes, which resulted in favouritism being shown to cadets over other students. When the Toronto board of education discontinued cadet training in 1931, the cadet uniforms were distributed to boys in the poor areas of the city.

The moving spirits of the Toronto WIL during the 1930s were Anna Sissons and Alice Loeb.[24] Under their guidance the Toronto branch organized annual Armistice Day peace demonstrations in which numerous organizations participated. Such demonstrations, which often featured a parade of banners and posters renouncing war, were characteristic of pacifist efforts to keep alive the public demand for peace. In 1936 the Toronto WIL and the Society of Friends sponsored a one-day national meeting concerning the special Geneva Conference on peace called by Lord Cecil. Their special guest was a well-known British pacifist, Maud Royden.[25] Rose Henderson, a member of the Toronto board of education and the Toronto WIL, was selected to represent Canada at the international WIL congress also slated to meet in Geneva. Dr Henderson, who had served as the Canadian delegate to the WIL congress at the Hague in 1922, had helped to organize a competition for peace posters in Toronto's technical schools. Over 150 posters were submitted and exhibited in a new art gallery opened by Arthur Lismer, a member of the famous Group of Seven, which included several painters, such as Lawren Harris, with pacifist sympathies.[26] Other peace-oriented school competitions included the writing of essays and plays.

Violet McNaughton remained a leading figure in the western WIL, and it may have been through her inspiration that a schoolgirl from Saskatoon won second prize in an international peace essay competition. Throughout the 1930s McNaughton maintained regular correspondence with WIL women across Canada and was in 'fairly constant' contact with Katherine D. Blake, the chairwoman of the Committee on International Relations for the New York City Federation of Women's Clubs.[27] Through Blake, McNaughton was kept abreast of the current drift of international peace activities, which she relayed in turn to other prairie women.[28]

Some headway was made by the WIL in western Canada during the 1930s. For instance, in 1930 the Edmonton Peace Study Group, under the leadership of Nellie McClung, became a full-fledged branch of the WIL, bringing the number of Canadian branches to four (in addition to peace groups in Brandon, Regina, Saskatoon, and Calgary). As a direct result of McNaughton's influence a peace group in Moose Jaw became affiliated with the WIL in 1934, and by 1938 two new WIL groups were formed in Jasper and Edson, Alberta.[29]

The women of the WIL, however, had other rows to hoe during the depression. McNaughton continued to draw much of her inspiration and many of her ideas about current affairs from the dynamic Vancouver WIL branch and its president, Laura Jamieson.[30] By 1932, however, Jamieson was devoting less time to the WIL than to radical political pursuits that combined her interests in peace and social justice. She was particularly active in the Vancouver section of the League for Social Reconstruction (LSR), a newly formed national organization dedicated to the establishment of socialism in Canada, and eventually she became a CCF member of the British Columbia legislature.[31]

Jamieson joined a co-operative composed mainly of the unemployed in Burnaby, British Columbia, because she felt strongly that 'co-operative associations are the intermediate steps between the present order and the socialist state.' The Social Reconstruction clubs, however, were not radical enough for McNaughton, who described them as 'fifty years behind the time.' 'The crisis is so acute here,' she wrote to Jamieson, 'that one hardly feels like studying academic measures when what we need is something dynamic and immediate.'[32] Similar sentiments were echoed in Toronto, where numerous WIL members were active in radical politics. Alice Loeb, for instance, headed a CCF membership drive under the slogan 'Socialism for Canada in Our Time.'[33] Rose Henderson went even further, and by 1936 had become a leading figure in the Toronto CCF Women's Joint Committee, a brief flowering of feminist support for the radical left, as she and other women wedded their interests in women's rights and peace to socialism.[34] The increasing sympathy of Henderson, McNaughton, Jamieson, and other WIL women for radical social change was typical of the transition of the entire Canadian peace movement during the depression.

III

The worsening economic situation in Canada, with its accompanying personal hardships and widespread discontent, increased the popularity of radical social, economic, and political alternatives throughout most levels of Canadian society. Those Canadians deeply involved in the peace movement found socialism to be a natural extension of their desire for a new social order, and in effect combined the basic ingredients of pacifism and socialism in their dream of a peaceful, co-operative, and just society. But the association of pacifism and socialism carried with it the responsibility for a new level of social criticism, and when the authorities began to persecute those – such as communists and 'communist sympathizers' – who advocated radical social alternatives, pacifists were quick to speak out in defence of free speech and endangered civil liberties.

In January 1931, for instance, the Toronto branch of the Fellowship of Reconciliation planned to hold an open forum on the topic of free speech.[35] Speakers for the occasion were to be Dr Salem Bland and the Reverend John Lowe of Trinity College, Toronto. Invitations were also sent to Gen. Dennis Draper, the Toronto chief of police, and Judge Emerson Coatsworth, a member of the Police Commission, to present their case to the audience. Instead, the Police Commission blocked the meeting on the pretence that FOR members were 'thinly-veiled Communists.'[36] When the FOR learned it would be denied the use of a hall, its executive secretary, Richard Roberts, complained to Judge Coatsworth and warned General Draper that the police department would be in a 'wholly indefensible position' if it forbade the proposed meeting of the FOR. 'There will be no more communism there,' he assured Draper, 'than in your own office.'[37] Roberts'splea was ignored by the authorities, and the FOR sent a delegation to the Toronto City Council demanding the restoration of their rights of free speech and assembly which had been denied by the Police Commission. They also presented a petition asking for a judicial inquiry into the activities of the commission.

To the editors of the *Canadian Forum*, the inference that the Fellowship of Reconciliation was communist-inspired was so 'manifestly absurd' that 'even those who would give their moral support to the campaign for "stamping out the reds", will be inclined to doubt whether the Commission has sufficient intellectual ability to distinguish between the "disruptive" and "respectable" elements in the community.'[38] The Police Commission, charged the *Forum*, represented an alliance of militaristic and religious fundamentalist bodies, while the FOR was backed by liberal elements, and the clash between the two groups reflected the economic developments of the depression. 'At no time in the past history of Canada has there been such an accumulation of wealth at the top of the social scale, and such an accumulation of distress on the lower levels. This sudden increase of inequality must inevitably produce unrest on the one hand and uneasiness on the other.'

The *Forum*'s analysis was shared by an increasing number of pacifists. Canada would not be freed from the threat of political revolt by jailing communists or silencing pacifists, said FOR president Maurice Eisendrath, but by establishing equitable conditions of labour, a decent standard of living for all, and fellowship among all classes of people.[39] Inevitably, the defence of the liberal tradition of free speech had a radicalizing effect upon Canadian pacifists.

One of the earliest manifestations of radical social criticism in Canada to attract pacifist support was the League for Social Reconstruction (LSR), which was founded by two small groups of intellectuals, mainly university professors, in Montreal and Toronto. The new organization was formally launched in January 1932 following the adoption of a manifesto or plan of action that endorsed the 'establishment in Canada of a social order in which the basic principle regulating production, distribution and service will be the common good rather than private profit.'[40]

Largely modelled on the Fabian Society in Britain, the LSR was designed primarily as a research and education organization. By 1933, for instance, seventeen LSR branches with a total membership of five hundred met monthly across Canada. Besides its branch activities, the LSR also sponsored public meetings with guest speakers such as Fenner Brockway, the British pacifist and socialist, and Reinhold Niebuhr and Harry F. Ward, the radical American theologians. In this manner, perhaps inadvertently, the LSR spread the gospel of pacifism as well as that of socialism.

The LSR also undertook important research work. By 1934 four pamphlets had been produced by the research committee, and the following year marked the appearance of *Social Planning for Canada*, the first comprehensive blueprint for democratic socialism in Canada. The book presented a survey and analysis of the Canadian economic system and discussed the application of socialist reconstruction to the Canadian scene; it advocated both public ownership of major capitalist industries and the reform of the remaining private sector. Concerning international affairs, the authors took the socialist view that war was the 'inevitable outcome of capitalist imperialism.' Not surprisingly, the book was generally condemned as a 'major heresy' by those in government and in the business community.[41]

Besides J.S. Woodsworth, who was the honorary president, the LSR national executive was composed of Frank Underhill, J.F. Parkinson, and Eric Havelock, all professors at the University of Toronto, Frank R. Scott, a professor of law at McGill University, and J. King Gordon, a professor of Christian ethics at the United Theological College in Montreal. Probably the strongest pacifist statements came from G.M.A. Grube, a professor of classics at Trinity College.[42] Grube maintained that pacifism was 'the only solution' to the economic and psychological difficulties that were driving the world towards another war.[43] He defined pacifism as 'the refusal to resort to arms accompanied by a sincere willingness to solve international problems by genuine and friendly cooperation between nations,' a positive approach not to be confused with passive non-resistance or isolationism. 'It should be clear that the advice to turn the other cheek means something far nobler and far more active than merely not to strike back ... It clearly refers to an attitude of mind, and the exercising of a positive, restraining influence.'

Grube also maintained that to be a pacifist required a great deal of will-power and 'not being afraid of being thought afraid.' 'It is far less of an effort to follow the crowd into uniform,' he wrote, 'than to stand out against it.' The modern pacifist's strength of conviction came from religion as well as social utilitarianism. Pacifism, above all else, was a religion of the individual conscience. Rejecting the charge that pacifism was contrary to human nature, Grube asserted that it was war that was incompatible with both humanity and the Christian civilized world.[44]

Grube also had a word of warning for his fellow socialists with respect to the growing approval of the use of violence in the movement for social change. He defended pacifism as the best course of action in class wars of social liberation as well as in imperialist wars; in fact, he thought the power of the proletariat would be irresistible if organized into a pacifist program of mass resistance and non-co-operation similar to that carried on by Gandhi in India, including 'the general strike and refusal to bear arms or pay taxes.'[45] Grube and other pacifists considered the revolutionary potential of pacifism an important new dimension of the social struggle. Despite his fairly realistic analysis of international conflicts, however, Grube still shared the liberal pacifist faith that it was 'quite possible' that wars would disappear from the face of the world in a few generations.[46]

Meanwhile, the demand for social reconstruction had been given political expression in 1932. Under the leadership of J.S. Woodsworth, representatives of the farm and labour parties of the four western provinces and the Canadian Brotherhood of Railway Employees formed the Co-operative Commonwealth Federation (CCF). The new political movement, taking its cue from the LSR, aimed to establish a co-operative economic system in Canada whereby 'the basic principle regulating production, distribution and exchange, will be the supplying of human needs instead of the making of profits.'[47] From the very beginning the basic philosophy of the CCF incorporated Woodsworth's particular blend of socialism and pacifism. The Regina Manifesto, for instance, called for a foreign policy dedicated to international economic co-operation, disarmament and world peace. The CCF declared that 'Canada must refuse to be entangled in any more wars fought to make the world safe for capitalism.'[48] Moreover, the social and economic transformation prescribed to create the co-operative commonwealth was to be brought about by non-violent political action, and the CCF registered its outright opposition to 'change by violence.' Canada's legal system, which social critics claimed was based upon vengeance and fear, was to be remodelled in accordance with a modern understanding of human behaviour and relationships. By replacing fear with trust and understanding, vengeance with justice, competition and exploitation with co-operation, most CCF goals, from the socialization of finance and ownership to the development of a fair labour code, were intended to eliminate the causes of violent conflict in the new social order. It was in this light that some members looked upon the CCF as the political embodiment of pacifism.[49]

Indeed, pacifism and socialism were inseparable in the general movement for social democracy in Canada during most of the 1930s. As Michiel Horn has explained, 'The introduction of socialism in Canada required peace; peace required non-involvement in international capitalist rivalries which the League of Nations was doing nothing to resolve. And the best service which Canada could render to the cause of peace abroad was to introduce socialism at home.'[50]

Similar reasoning characterized the more radical elements of the Canadian left, including the Communist party in Canada, which insisted war could be prevented by the 'might of the people.'[51] According to the Marxist view, to work for peace was to oppose capitalist imperialism; therefore, the radical left supported the peace movement and some adherents actually joined pacifist societies. In the eyes of the authorities, however, the association of the radical left with anti-war activities tended to discredit the entire peace movement. In this same regard, both the moderate and the radical left were considered a common threat even though there were fundamental differences between them. For instance, neither the LSR nor the CCF adopted a Marxian approach; instead, they made a broad appeal to 'industrial workers, farmers and the middle classes' by using a mixture of liberal humanitarian, democratic socialist, and Judaeo-Christian arguments that capitalism was immoral because it exploited, for personal gain, other peoples and nations.[52] Although it was not directly affiliated with the CCF, the LSR became an unofficial 'think tank' responsible for the 'core ideology' of the CCF.[53] In addition to this unofficial advisory role, individual LSR members took an active part in CCF activities.

In keeping with their social gospel roots, many LSR members, including some key figures, held dual memberships in the Fellowship for a Christian Social Order (FCSO), a newly formed Canadian organization that viewed socialism as the practical application of radical Christianity.[54] Christian socialists believed that the social crisis confronting Canadians during the depression was ultimately a spiritual problem that required a religious interpretation and response. The social gospel movement, which might have attacked this problem, was, they believed, too infected with liberal optimism to provide a base for the radical changes required by the crisis at hand.[55]

The roots of the movement can be traced back to 1930, when J. King Gordon, R.B.Y. Scott, and a Vancouver study group that called itself 'The Fellowship' began to work for the replacement of capitalism with Christian socialism.[56] Subsequent communication between the Vancouver activists and a Toronto group headed by John Line, a professor of history and religion at Victoria College, resulted in the formation of the Movement for a Christian Social Order in 1931; the two groups were consolidated in January 1932 as the 'Christian Socialist Movement.'[57] The British Columbians were now organizing themselves as the League for Christian Social Action under the presidency of Harold T. Allen, and the Christian Commonwealth Youth Movement (CCYM) was being promoted by Warwick Kelloway of Dominion United Church, Ottawa, and later of Calgary. As J. Russel Harris, secretary of the Movement for a Christian Social Order, told Allen, the objective was to establish 'a left wing group within the Church to arouse a new conscience.'[58] Finally, in April 1934 a number of United Church members, both lay and clerical, met at Queen's University in Kingston to found a national Fellowship for a Christian Social Order.[59] The founders, familiar names in the LSR and the peace movement, described the FCSO as 'an Association of Christians whose religious convictions have led them to the belief that the creation of a new social order is essential to the realization of the Kingdom of God.'

In order to convert fellow Christians to their cause, FCSO members organized study groups and social action groups across Canada, released statements on various social and economic problems, gave lectures to public gatherings and summer schools, contributed articles to the religious and secular press, and published a bulletin, *Christian Social Action*, which reached a circulation of thirty-five hundred.[60]

The Fellowship for a Christian Social Order hoped to attract young people through the Christian Commonwealth Youth Movement founded by Warwick Kelloway. As president of the national council, Kelloway urged Canadian youth to help Christianize the social order and thereby avoid the dangers of 'violent revolution or Fascist dictatorship.'[61] The FCSO helped initiate young people's units across the country and cooperated with them in joint projects. By 1933 the bulk of the new movement's membership was centred in Montreal and Ontario under an eastern council in Ottawa and in Alberta under a western council in Calgary. The Calgary group also served as the national council and sponsored a weekly radio program entitled 'The Voice of Youth.'

Central to the youth movement was its 'unqualified opposition to war.' To further that cause, it advocated two types of action. First, the movement called for support for the League of Nations, qualified by refusal to approve the use of military sanctions. The CCYM believed that sanctions were identical with the methods of war and would result in 'mass murder and destruction.' According to the young socialists, peace could be built only on a foundation of social health, and sanctions were merely 'an attempt to repress from without the irruption of disease from within.' That disease was imperialism, economic nationalism, militarism, and anarchy.[62]

Second, the CCYM urged affiliation with the War Resisters International and endorsed its declaration: 'War is a crime against humanity. We therefore are determined not to support any kind of war and to strive for the removal of all causes of war.'[63]

Those young Canadians who wished to join the movement were asked to complete a questionnaire in which they were asked if they would bear arms or otherwise support war, if they favoured the use of military or economic sanctions by the League of Nations, if they would use violence in a class war or strike, and if they favoured the socialized state.

The CCYM's emphasis on pacifism and socialism reflected the particular radical approach of the FCSO, the LSR, and the CCF. In his study of the FCSO Roger Hutchinson states that the 'radical ethic of absolute ends – the Kingdom of God as an imminent possibility; and the pacifist ethic of absolute means – non-violence and the abolition of war, co-existed in the same movement.'[64] The FCSO constitution, for instance, condemned the capitalist economic system not only as being responsible for war but also as being entirely contrary to the Christian ethic, and suggested that salvation rested in the creation of a new society that would offer the 'opportunity to practice the ethics of the Sermon on the Mount.'[65] Rather than the historic 'non-resistance to evil' of Jesus, however, the pacifism extolled by the FCSO was the modern version of non-violent resistance or, as they called it, 'non-co-operative action.' The FCSO maintained that only the 'pressure of publicly-expressed non-co-operation' would force capitalist governments to settle international disputes peacefully. Therefore, FCSO members pledged themselves to 'the most effective non-co-operative action in which we can engage in the event of war and in times of peace.'[66] Their declaration was nothing less than a commitment of united Christian socialists to the contemporary pacifist ethic, and it represented one of the first direct calls for non-violent resistance as a realistic means of social action in Canada.

In another vein, pacifism was also viewed as the best method by which the church could ease the impact of radical change upon society. According to the FCSO's first chairman, J. King Gordon, the function of religion was 'to mitigate acts of violence in social change by introducing ethical aspects to offset hatreds, cruelty, etc which are inevitably associated with social conflicts.'[67] Thus, the radical Christianity proposed by the FCSO included inseparably intertwined aspects of socio-political radicalism and pacifism.

This overall radicalism was underlined when Gordon was dismissed in controversial circumstances from his position at United Theological

College. A bright young Christian socialist, Gordon had studied under Reinhold Niebuhr and Harry Ward at Union Theological Seminary in New York.[68] After joining the faculty of United Theological College in Montreal, Gordon became active in both the LSR and the FCSO, and was at times extremely vocal in his criticisms of the capitalist order.[69] In 1932 he joined Eugene Forsey and J.A. Coote on a social and economic research committee for the Montreal Presbytery of the United Church. The committee publicized its findings on civil liberties, unemployment, penitentiaries, and wages and dividends in the Quebec textile industry. The last area was highly sensitive, since the chairman of Canadian Cottons, A.O. Dawson, and other prominent businessmen were members of the board of governors of United Theological College.

In 1933 the board members dismissed King Gordon, saying that they were implementing a decision of the general council to economize. Many ministers, particularly those in the FCSO, rushed to Gordon's defence on the grounds of academic freedom. The college finally agreed to keep him on for one more year when his supporters raised fifteen hundred dollars to pay his salary.[70]

Among those who defended Gordon was Richard Roberts, who now lived in Toronto. Putting his pacifism into practice, Roberts renewed contacts with his old Montreal acquaintances in order to help lessen the hostility that existed between the business community and the young social activists within the church. In a letter to A.O. Dawson, Roberts warned that 'profound changes in the social structure' could not be averted. 'But it is still open to us to say what changes are to come and how they will come.'[71] Roberts appealed to Dawson to bring together 'those leaders in commerce and industry who are Christian men of good will' to reason together and discuss the subject of social change and the church's role in 'the ethical aspect of social processes whether economic or political.' Roberts suggested Dawson approach R.B.Y. Scott, a professor of Old Testament literature at United Theological College and chairman of the FCSO, to begin the dialogue.

In addition to Scott, the central figures in the FCSO were John Line and Gregory Vlastos, a professor of philosophy at Queen's University. Philip Matthams, a pacifist minister from Montreal, served as FCSO national secretary until 1937. Another prominent member of the national executive was the radical pacifist Edis Fairbairn.

Following his last year at United Theological College, King Gordon became the travelling secretary for the FCSO. Later, similar duties were assumed by J. Stanley Allen, a professor of natural sciences at Sir George

Williams University. Known to his friends and associates as the 'pamphleteer of Canada,' Allen operated the Associated Literary Service from the basement of his home in Montreal and distributed FCSO and pacifist literature throughout Canada. Allen, like so many others in the FCSO, leaned towards the pacifist position in the early 1930s.[72]

In 1936 the intellectual leader of the FCSO pooled their resources to produce a book entitled *Towards the Christian Revolution*.[73] Something of a religious counterpart to *Social Planning for Canada*, the book was a symposium of radical Christian thought that spanned the philosophical spectrum from liberal utopianism to a new radical realism. The authors promoted socialism as a natural derivative of Christian social ethics. In his analysis of contemporary economics, for instance, Eugene Forsey emphasized that there was no 'painless substitute for socialism ... Until Christians learn to understand and apply the lessons of Marxism, they cannot enter the Kingdom of Heaven – nor, probably, can anyone else.'[74]

The FCSO's alignment of socialism with pacifism was underlined when King Gordon suggested that the political task of his generation was to organize the socialist state in order to save civilization 'from the devastation of war brought on by the desperate imperialist excursions of the fascist states.' 'It is a matter of ironic interest,' he added, 'that the reactionary opponents to the Church's participation in the field of social reform ... are the same individuals who applauded so lustily the Church's activity in furthering the war aims of modern nations.'[75] Edis Fairbairn emphasized the revolutionary evangelism of the Christian gospel, arguing that the distinct function of the Judaeo-Christian religion was to generate 'the negative dynamic of indignation, resentment, and revolt against the immoral and insane elements in our social structure.'[76] To Fairbairn the most 'immoral and insane' element was war.

The authors agreed that Christianity was essentially revolutionary and that the duty of Christians was to follow the revolutionary spirit that originated in God and demonstrate their faith through the transformation of society. In the closing chapter Eric Havelock concluded on a note of liberal optimism, saying that the ideal socialized state was finally within man's reach.

But Havelock did not speak for all the contributors.[77] John Line, for instance, recognized the need for a new radical realism in Christian theology and philosophy that would move beyond religious liberalism and conservative orthodoxy, and especially the need to speak more deeply to the roots of sin in both the individual and society. Very well aware of the depths of human sin, Line, Forsey, and Gordon no longer viewed the Kingdom of God as a realizable historic social order, although they still believed a prophetic minority could help transform society in such a way as to bring about human fulfilment in the real world. Thus, not all the authors could be classified as liberal; in fact, they themselves rejected the label. But neither did they represent a neo-orthodoxy or the alienation of man from the ideal. What emerged from *Towards the Christian Revolution* was a radical concept of Christian social ethics based upon the realization of man's struggling existence in a sinful world. Line himself explained that their approach was outwardly similar to but inwardly different from the liberal social gospel.

In the forward, Richard Roberts endorsed the book as an important contribution to Christian thinking in a time 'of strange and rapid transition.' Most reviewers were also favourable. Gordon A. Sisco, executive secretary of the United Church, for instance, praised the book as 'a notable contribution to radical Christian teaching' and said that it contained a 'more profound theology' than the old social gospel liberalism.[78] In 1937 the Left Book Club adopted *Towards the Christian Revolution* as an optional monthly selection. In his review in the *Left News* the British socialist John Strachey claimed that the book was one 'for which many Socialists and Communists outside Church circles have been eagerly waiting.' 'If I may say so without offence,' he wrote, 'this is the first intellectually adult work, in the full sense, on the social crisis from the pens of churchmen. Its publication will leave no one of the churches untouched.'[79] According to Strachey, *Towards the Christian Revolution* marked the FCSO radicals as the leading spokesmen for Christians in the modern world, and he predicted it would have 'profound repercussions' throughout Christendom, including strong opposition from the right wing of the Church.

One of the most important critics to appear, however, was not a conservative churchman but the American theologian Reinhold Niebuhr, whose earlier Marxism was increasingly qualified by his thesis in *Moral Man and Immoral Society*. Although he described *Towards the Christian Revolution* as 'an able presentation of the faith by which these young radicals live,' Niebuhr thought that the book revealed 'little understanding for the more difficult issues of the relation of Christianity to radicalism.'[80] In contrast to Sisco's observations, Niebuhr maintained that the authors shared the illusion of the older social gospel that the socialist commonwealth was identical with the Christian vision of the Kingdom of God. Niebuhr agreed that Christians must recognize the necessity of an economic and political revolution for the sake of justice, but he also argued that these same Christians must 'not imagine that any perennial problem of the human spirit is solved by such a revolution.' The authors of the book were deeply disappointed by Niebuhr's reaction, especially those who, like Gordon, thought they had absorbed Niebuhr's particular brand of Christian radicalism, including his cautions about reducing the Kingdom of God simply to a social order. Perhaps the main difficulty was that the book did not represent one distinct view; thus, the liberal illusion criticized by Niebuhr was not precisely the same radical vision espoused by Line and others.

Regardless of its international reception, however, *Towards the Christian Revolution* had important implications for pacifists in Canada. The authors had clearly linked pacifism and socialism in their interpretation of Christian social ethics, and the pacifist witness was viewed as an important contribution to world peace. Pacifists also began to reflect the philosophical differences separating the FCSO leadership. Some pacifists shared Fairbairn's faith that a prophetic pacifist minority would help society attain the socialist and pacifist ideal. Further along the spectrum were those who, like Forsey, had a lingering sense that the pacifist way was an important social witness but, like the perfect society, probably was not historically realizable. It was a split which would become more apparent once pacifists confronted the realities of the later 1930s. In the meantime, *Towards the Christian Revolution* boosted the stature of both the FCSO and a socially radical pacifism in Canada.[81]

It was not the FCSO, however, but an agency known as the Alberta School of Religion that was the centre of radical Christian activity on the prairies. Founded in 1924 by Henry M. Horricks, a Calgary United Church minister, the Alberta School of Religion was designed as a short summer refresher course lasting a week or ten days for United Church ministers and their families.[82] During the early years the annual sessions of the Alberta School of Religion were held at Mount Royal College in Calgary, but the lack of an appropriate lecture hall necessitated the move in 1928 to St Stephen's College in Edmonton. After a few years, however, the board of governors of the college became alarmed at the radical nature of the summer sessions and assumed the right to censor the program. In response, the school moved its 1932 sessions to St Joseph's College in Edmonton and later settled at the Morley Indian Industrial School in Morley, Alberta. When opposition to the radical tone of the sessions again arose, the Alberta School of Religion finally found a permanent home at the Fairweather Christian Fellowship Camp on the Bow River, approximately twelve miles from Calgary.[83] Although somewhat primitive, the camp meetings provided a congenial and informal atmosphere for the discussion of radical Christian ideas.

The annual sessions were financed on a shoe-string budget that barely covered the travelling expenses of the guest lecturers, but over the years the Alberta School of Religion attracted some of the best speakers available and some of the most radical Christians in the country. For instance, among the Canadian speakers featured were Woodsworth, William Irvine, Richard Roberts, T.C. Douglas of the CCF, John Line of the FCSO, Watson Thomson, a 'self-styled guru of co-operative living,' Carlyle King, the radical socialist and pacifist professor from the University of Saskatchewan, James G. Endicott, a radical United Church missionary to China, and Charles H. Huestis, a United Church minister and pacifist journalist.[84] International guests included H. Richard Niebuhr, Harry F. Ward, Sherwood Eddy, Scott Nearing, Leyton Richards, Canon Stricter, and A.J. Muste. Reinhold Niebuhr and the Japanese Christian pacifist leader Toyohiko Kagawa were both interested but unable to attend because of conflicting commitments.[85]

Other than Horricks, the leading forces behind the Alberta School of Religion were Charles H. Huestis, Arthur H. Rowe, and Stanley Hunt, all of whom were United Church ministers from Alberta. The chief concern of the Alberta radicals was to 'find some Christian economic solutions for a sick world' and to 'try to do something toward a peaceful way of living together.'[86] Although the Alberta School of Religion became affiliated with the FCSO in 1935 and was the representative of the FCSO in Alberta, the Horricks movement tended to place more direct emphasis on pacifism than did the FCSO. Those who joined the 'Horricks Fellowship,' for instance, agreed not only to refrain from the use of all 'intoxicating liquors, tobacco and drugs' but made a pacifist pledge: 'I will endeavour as far as my influence goes to discourage the use of violence as a method of settling disputes among nations but will rely on love and good will as the most powerful force in all life.'[87] Despite its slightly stronger emphasis on a personal pacifist stand, the Alberta School of Religion remained affiliated with the FCSO until the pacifist issue assumed priority during the Second World War; thereafter it affiliated with the pacifist Fellowship of Reconciliation in Canada.

Having involved themselves so fully in the creation of new religious and secular radical movements like the LSR, the CCF, and the FCSO, it is not surprising that pacifists were stimulated to explore the idea of experimental co-operative communities modelled on the communities built by the historic peace sects. This contemporary interest in communal living was promoted in Canada during the interwar years by Henri Lasserre, a descendant of a wealthy Swiss family who used his personal fortune to finance various experimental communities, first in Europe and then in Canada. As early as 1911, for instance, Lasserre and Paul Passy, the leader of the French Christian Socialists, had founded *Terre Libre*, an association designed to give moral and financial support to Passy's Liéfra colony.[88] Later, in association with men like René Thury, Adolphe Ferrière, and Paul Birufoff, the Tolstoyan protégé who later assisted the Doukhobors in Canada, Lasserre organized the *Société de Coopération Intégrale* and founded the short-lived Peney co-operative colony in Switzerland.

Despite his disappointment in the failure of these early experiments, Lasserre remained dedicated to the idea of a wholly co-operative community, *coopératisme intégral*, by which he meant the total integration of consumer with producer co-operatives and agricultural with industrial co-operatives in order to form a truly co-operative community. He believed this radical application of the co-operative principle was both 'a creative and non-violent means towards the transformation of economic society and also [a] moral and psychological preparation for, and partial anticipation of the new social relations of brotherhood and justice which must replace the older order.'[89]

In effect, Lasserre believed integral co-operative communities would lay the moral foundations necessary for the realization of a new social ethic. But where would such communities best survive? Following the collapse of the Peney colony, Lasserre looked to North America, which was free from the constraining traditions and prejudices of Europe, as a fertile field for the cultivation of integral co-operatives; accordingly, he emigrated to Canada in May 1921 and within a few years he settled in Toronto as an assistant professor of French at Victoria College.

Lasserre's arrival in Canada coincided with labour and agrarian unrest and an increased interest in the co-operative solution. Initially, Lasserre was interested in co-operative experiments underway in the United States, but, once he discovered that Americans were preoccupied with the more conventional consumers co-operatives and trade unions, he confined his attention to Canada. In association with a few kindred spirits in Toronto, such as E.J. Urwick, Murray Brooks, J.O. Leitch, and Spencer Clark, Lasserre established the Robert Owen Foundation.[90] The purpose of the foundation was to assist in the establishment and operation of co-operative enterprises, whether producers' co-operative associations, industrial co-operatives, or integral co-operative communities, and to promote interest in the co-operative movement. In effect, the Robert Owen Foundation was to act as a holding company in order to allow the co-operative group to enjoy complete ownership without jeopardizing the co-operative principle.

Lasserre found that those most receptive to his philosophy of integral co-operative communities and to the Robert Owen Foundation were the radical Christians and pacifists he met through the Fellowship for a Christian Social Order and the Toronto Fellowship of Reconciliation. With their support, the Robert Owen Foundation searched for worthy projects in Canada, especially industrial experiments, in the hope of applying the co-operative solution to the industrial disruption caused by the depression. Although Canadian farmers had become imbued with the co-operative spirit, labour was not so inspired, and the foundation's sole attempt at sponsoring an industrial co-operative was the ill-fated Work Togs Limited of Toronto. The overalls-manufacturing company operated for less than a year, and with its closing the Robert Owen Foundation rapidly lost its initial enthusiasm for industrial co-operatives and turned to other co-operative pursuits.[91]

Canadian pacifists were attracted to the utopian communalism promoted by the Robert Owen Foundation because it seemed to promise the ideal socialist and pacifist lifestyle at a time where they were searching for experimental alternatives.[92] For the same reason they responded enthusiastically to the CCF and its political route to a new co-operative social order. By mid-decade, through the efforts of such avant-garde groups as the League for Social Reconstruction, the Fellowship for a Christian Social Order, and the Fellowship of Reconciliation, the Canadian peace movement had come to represent the quest for both radical social change and peace.

IV

The active promotion of pacifism as well as socialism by a number of influential churchmen, especially those within the Fellowship for a Christian Social Order, had an important impact upon Canada's churches even though pacifists remained a distinct minority in Protestant churches and an almost insignificant force in the Roman Catholic church. Neither the Catholics nor the continuing Presbyterians, for instance, showed much interest in pacifism, and it was only after T.T. Shields of Toronto's Jarvis Street Baptist Church and his arch-fundamentalists were purged from the Baptist convention in 1927 that Ontario and Quebec Baptists began to show 'a more unreserved interest in social relations,' although they still remained wary of such a controversial issue as pacifism.[93] Other denominations, most notably the Anglican and United churches, found it increasingly difficult to escape the question of war and the Christian conscience.

For the most part, Anglicans accepted the general declaration of the 1930 Lambeth Conference in England that war was incompatible with the teachings of Jesus, but they stopped short of adopting a strictly pacifist approach. For instance, although they criticized and opposed all defence programs, Anglicans specifically recognized the right of Christian citizens to bear arms while serving their country.[94] Despite the Anglicans' uneasiness with pacifism, there were a few leading Anglican pacifists in Canada, such as John Frank, the rector of Trinity Anglican Church in Toronto and the father-in-law of the British pacifist organizer Dick Sheppard. Another was Frank's assistant at Trinity, John F. Davidson, who had been influenced by the SCM and who was associated with Upper Canada College during the 1930s and 1940s.[95]

Of all the Protestant churches in Canada, the United Church was the one most profoundly affected by pacifism and the one that ultimately became seriously divided over the issue. Because of its close association with the social gospel and its concern with contemporary social ills, the United Church was naturally attracted to the peace movement as another field for responsible Christian action, and it was the increasingly vocal left wing of the church that supplied the movement with some of its most radical spokesmen. Another factor central to this development was the commanding presence in the church of Richard Roberts, one of the most distinguished pacifists of the day.

Roberts had advocated 'radical religion' since he was first attracted to socialism as a youth in the 1890s.[96] He had written more than twenty books and pamphlets and numerous articles in religious journals, and he enjoyed a wide American and British readership. Roberts was known as one of the leading socially concerned intellectuals in the church. Perhaps for this reason he was named moderator of the United Church of Canada in 1934. As moderator, Roberts turned his attention to the devastating effects of the depression upon Canadian life and the need for radical social and economic change. Speaking to a meeting of unemployed men at Toronto's Church of All Nations in April 1936, he proclaimed that the church was committed to the establishment of a new social order based upon economic and moral prerequisites.[97] It was not only the church's business but also its right to guarantee that society allow man to rise to 'his full spiritual height,' a condition prevented by the capitalist order. Roberts admitted that he was sceptical of Canadian political processes to achieve social and economic justice, but he warned against violent revolution. Roberts was hardly a Marxist, and had actually opposed the FCSO position in 1933. Although he endorsed the Antigonish Co-operative Movement in Nova Scotia as a step in the right direction, he left his vision of future social and economic reconstruction open-ended.

Nevertheless, the socialist and pacifist views of the moderator were unmistakable, and Toronto newspapers publicized Roberts's 'cry for a new social order' and for a united Protestant declaration against the furtherance of any future war effort. In his farewell address as moderator, Roberts warned the general council that resolutions condemning war were not adequate and called upon the United Church to join with other Protestants in a specific stand against war.[98] The opportunity for such common action, he hoped, would be provided by the Oxford Conference of the Universal Christian Council for Life and Work scheduled for 1937.

Although the general council refrained from adopting a strictly pacifist position as Roberts suggested, it did encourage the growth of pacifism. In each of its sessions during the 1930s the council openly debated the issue of peace and passed successive resolutions condemning war as contrary 'to the mind of Christ.'[99] In 1934, for instance, the sixth general council declared: 'We believe armed warfare between nations to be contrary to the spirit and teachings of Christ, and that it is the duty of the Church to promote a Christian public opinion in opposition to war, to seek a complete abolition of national armaments and the placing under international control of whatever armed forces may be necessary to protect the world's peace in an emergency, with the cultivation of true international conscience.'[100] Furthermore, all ministers were 'earnestly requested' to promote the concern for international peace within their congregations, especially among young people.

Ernest Thomas later reported that the most difficult task faced by the council was not the consideration of its opposition to war, but the question of conscientious objection to military service. Two proposals were presented for debate: one favoured 'an official register of those who will pledge themselves in advance to render no military obedience'; the other suggested that 'membership in the United Church should be a guarantee of conscientious objection to armed service.'[101] While the latter was quickly rejected, the first idea raised the question of sanctioned civil disobedience and resulted in a lengthy debate. In the end, the council overruled a vocal minority and decided that the church could not 'take a step which savored of organized "concerted disobedience." ' The general council did uphold the principle of conscientious objection as long as the conscientious objector was a person who 'is so clearly governed by conscience as supreme that he will accept the civil consequence of disobedience.'[102]

Regardless of whether they shared these views or were 'unable, as yet, to take a thoroughgoing pacifist position,' the council members expressed thankfulness for the 'amazing outburst of hostility to war, particularly in colleges, which has of late startled the English-speaking nations.'[103] In conclusion, the council suggested that the peace movement 'may be the agency through which war may be made impossible, at least among Christian peoples.'

Despite repeated resolutions, the United Church hesitated to provide its members with a more specific sense of direction concerning Christian responsibility in time of war. In 1936 W.A. Gifford, the chief author of *The Christian and War*, the Canadian pacifist statement of the 1920s, accused the United Church of not having the 'moral authority to implement her declarations of principle' and suggested that the public was 'paying less and less attention to them.'[104] In reference to the deteriorating international situation, Gifford challenged the seventh general council, which was about to convene, to 'guide the public mind' on the question of war, and asked more specifically, 'What shall we say to our boys?' Concerning the chaplaincy, Gifford urged the council to take immediate action to obtain government assurance that ministers would be free to serve men at war 'in the habiliments of the priesthood, not of the military' and therefore would not have to compromise their personal witness against war.

Instead of producing any specific prescriptions for Christian action in time of war, however, the seventh general council merely reaffirmed its loyalty to the pledged word of Canada in the Pact of Paris, 'renouncing war as an instrument of national policy,' and recognized the need to define and demonstrate 'the things that make for peace, and our determined opposition to war.'[105]

In a proposal of outright pacifist tone, however, the council suggested that Christians 'must be prepared to follow Christ in turning from war.' Furthermore, the council echoed the pacifist argument that the roots of war could be destroyed 'only as we humanize commerce, moralize society, spiritualize education, and build an international order of equity and love.' But while encouraging the pacifist ethic and the Canadian search for peace, the United Church never really endorsed an outright pacifist position. Neither did it provide clear guidelines for Christians confronting the issue of war. In reference to the general council's numerous declarations condemning war, J.S. Woodsworth asked, 'Precisely what is meant by these statements? ... In the event of war – which may not be so removed as many imagine – what is to be the attitude of the Church?'[106] As one who shared a certain responsibility in the formation of Canadian policy, Woodsworth wondered where the church would stand in the event of an international crisis. 'General statements are not enough,' he said. 'What concretely should be the policy of Canada?' He particularly wished to know if the church would advocate civil disobedience, and if so whether such a policy would extend to active participation in war, the making of munitions, and assistance to those engaged in war. Echoing the earlier plea of Roberts and Gifford, Woodsworth called upon the church to 'give some guidance in these definite matters of national policy.'[107]

In some respects the United Church had attempted to offer this guidance, particularly in its open discussions of the peace issue in councils and in the church press, and in its general support for the peace movement. One of the leading spokesmen for the church in this regard was Ernest Thomas. Since the resurgence of pacifism in the mid-1920s, Thomas had demonstrated 'a notable sense of realism' in his appraisal of international questions.[108] In contrast to Fairbairn's radical condemnation of the 'war system' as the root cause of war, for instance, Thomas blamed 'exclusive nationalism directed by fallible men' and suggested that this danger could be overcome by the slow and painful process of building what he called 'institutions of social determination,' included among which were those of international co-operation and good will. Thomas welcomed the prophetic role of pacifists within the church, but he also warned that 'no one should lightly assume that his passionate revolt against some existing evil guarantees prophetic insight.'[109] Nevertheless, Thomas believed that there was 'little doubt as to the obligation of the Church to release such spiritual energies as make for the elimination of war.' The proper responsibility of the church, he argued, was to provide the 'spiritual forces' that would help man 'withstand the tendencies which made for war.'

In the 1930s Thomas continued this line of thinking in *The Quest for Peace*, a pamphlet issued by the Board of Evangelism and Social Service of the United Church to help study groups focus attention on the Christian basis for the abolition of war.[110] Thomas defined peace as the 'co-operative effort to bring about changes.' 'Peace is much more than absence of fighting,' he wrote. 'There is not so very much difference in moral quality between the spirit which fights to prevent another people achieving some required change, and that which tells the other people that their anxieties are no concern of ours. The latter is no more peaceful that the former – indifference or contempt is no better than hate.'

In regard to the responsibility of Christian citizens in time of war, Thomas claimed that he 'dare not assume responsibility for formulating the decision of his readers,' since conscientious objection to military service, something that affected the very foundations of society, was a matter of individual conscience. Thomas did suggest, however, that prospective conscientious objectors base their convictions upon Christian belief rather than on the utilitarian view that private or concerted refusal of military service would be an effective political tool to prevent war. In conclusion, he cautioned his readers not to mistake the 'glorious impatience with war' characteristic of the peace movement 'for a deep-seated change of attitude and an abiding determination that, no matter what the issue may appear to be, war shall not be recognized.' While in sympathy with the latter aim, Thomas argued that, in the reality of another world crisis, 'it will take more than an emotional dislike to overcome the new urge.'[111]

In contrast to the prevailing pacifist mood of the social gospel, Thomas represented a new philosophy of 'international realism' similar to that which was later called Niebuhrian.[112] At times he was sharply critical of outright pacifism and those who espoused it. In 1934 Thomas criticized 'quite adversely' Kirby Page's plea to the Federal Council of Churches for 'an out-and-out pacifist pledge', and accused pacifists of 'philosophical anarchism.'[113] The opposite view was taken by William B. Creighton, the editor of the New Outlook. Creighton accused Thomas of being caught up in the 'argumentative soundness' of the pacifist campaign for an anti-war enlistment when what was really important was whether or not it 'would help to make war less possible.'[114] Creighton questioned Thomas's criticism of Christians for 'striving to reach what they believe to be their high principle touching this issue' and suggested that if a large percentage of Christians shared the pacifist stand of Quakers 'a world war would become very shortly an impossibility.'

Creighton's continued enthusiasm for the peace movement was characteristic of the New Outlook during most of the interwar period. The editorial page, for instance, often endorsed pacifist works by such writers as A.A. Milne, Max Plowman, and Aldous Huxley.[115] Huxley's 'The Case for Constructive Peace' was hailed as a 'sane pacifist philosophy' built on a 'firm and convincing base.' The popular British pacifist Vera Brittain adorned the cover of the *New Outlook* when it featured her article on 'Youth and War.'[116]

Overall, Creighton believed that the Christian church was the best force to undertake a 'powerful and desperate' campaign against war, but he wondered if the church still had what it took 'to do that sort of thing any more – to fight against vested interests and strongly entrenched prejudices.'[117] He suggested that individuals and organizations outside the church were now campaigning 'more aggressively and effectively' than Christians, and he called upon his readers to join that movement and wage peace 'as men have waged war.' Pacifism had been 'too long confined to the halls of academic discussion, and to the pulpits and platforms of the churches.' Despite the increasing pacifist sympathies of the church, as reflected in its official resolutions as well as in the public pronouncements of prominent churchmen, the time had come to take the discussion into the crowd, since the cause of peace, like that of social justice, demanded the determined commitment of individual Canadians. 'We need to get down to individual study of the causes and effects of war and individual enlistment in the cause of peace.'[118]

v

The peace movement in Canada took a new turn in the autumn of 1934 when it launched a campaign to encourage individual war resistance. W.B. Creighton had already recognized the need for such a tactic; it was no surprise, therefore, when the *New Outlook* endorsed Dick Sheppard's peace pledge petition in Britain and urged Canadians to sign a similar pledge initiated in Canada by J. Lavell Smith, the minister of Westmount Park United Church in Montreal.[119]

As a member of both the Fellowship for a Christian Social Order and the Fellowship of Reconciliation in Montreal, Lavell Smith was one of those young radical ministers intent on taking some direct action in order to help achieve peace and social justice.[120] For some years he was convinced that his greatest service to the cause of peace would be simply to declare himself 'utterly and unalterably opposed to war.' 'The evils flowing from war are so terrific', he wrote, 'that I am determined that war shall never again have my support.'[121] But Smith also agreed with Creighton that what was needed was 'some convincing demonstration' of public opinion in favour of pacifism. Once convinced that the time was 'more than ripe for such an appeal here in Canada,' Smith challenged his fellow members of the United Church, both lay and clerical, and all Canadians to join him in a peace pledge modelled after Dick Sheppard's famous pledge of war renunciation: 'I renounce war and never again, directly or indirectly, will I support or sanction another war.' Smith urged all who were willing to take the pacifist stand to sign the pledge and send it to him without delay in order that Canadians 'may have the encouragement of knowing that many others stand with them, and in order that our Government may be aware of this body of opinion.' In the end, Smith collected between three and four thousand signatures.

Smith had shown his pacifist pledge to his FCSO associate John Line of Toronto. Line agreed 'heartily with every word' and insisted that the refusal of individuals to participate in war was the 'only means finally to prevent its recurrence.' Moreover, Line suggested that 'the people who will never again assist in war are now a large body, and I think it only right that our rulers should know of this.'[122] If war came again, Line declared, he would have no part in it himself and would urge that course upon others, 'including potential combatants.' Line believed that the pledge would serve as a warning to the Canadian government not to get involved in war.

Another who publicly endorsed the pledge was the social gospeller Stanley Knowles. 'It is my feeling,' he wrote, 'that our governments ought to know something of the extent of pacifism amongst individual citizens.'[123] While he agreed with Line that the awareness of widespread pacifist sentiment would 'have some effect as a deterrent' to Canada entering war, Knowles felt there was 'something further that our governments ought to know.' There were hundreds of pacifists, he claimed, who would not only withhold their support in the event of war but would actually do all within their power, without violence, to hinder the war effort. What specific action would pacifists take? Knowles suggested that they 'would seek to persuade others, including potential combatants, to desist. We would be strike-organizers at munitions plants,and would encourage the crippling of domestic economic processes. We would use our pulpits, or whatever means might be available, to put barriers in the way of carrying on the war.'[124] A declaration of war would be 'a signal for drastic, positive action on the part of pacifists prepared to pay any personal price for peace.'

The 1934 peace pledge campaign was paralleled by a similar drive among Canadian youth. That autumn the World Student Christian Federation, the international scm, sponsored a questionnaire among Canadian university students to determine what students thought about war and 'under what circumstances, if any, they would support their country in a war.'[125] The survey, initiated by the *McGill Daily*, was conducted through student newspapers across Canada. Students were asked if they believed there would always be wars and whether they would support the Canadian government in any war, in certain wars, or in no war at all. The questionnaire also attempted to discover what specific actions students would take in the event of war, such as enlisting voluntarily, refusing all service, or actively opposing the war in other ways.[126]

The results of the poll indicated that the majority of respondents did not believe that wars were inevitable.[127] Out of 497 respondents at McGill, 233 would support the Canadian government in a just war, 134 would support no war, and 83 would support Canada in any war.[128] At McMaster University the anti-war position was even more pronounced. Out of a total of 275 students, only 8 declared unreserved support for Canadian participation in war. One hundred forty-eight agreed to support a just war, while 89, or 35 per cent of those polled, refused to support Canada in any future war.[129] At both McGill and McMaster the majority of respondents revealed that in the event of war they would either 'refuse military but render humanitarian service' or refuse all service. A large number of the students also agreed actively to oppose a war effort by refusing to pay taxes, engaging in a general strike, or – the most popular action – organizing peaceful mass protests and petitions. Results were similar at the University of Alberta, the University of Saskatchewan, and the University of Western Ontario.

A few months later, Queen's University students took part in a slightly different peace poll conducted across North American campuses by the Association of College Editors. Perhaps because it was emphasized that they were the only Canadians to participate, the Queen's students scored a remarkably high response, with over 50 per cent of the student body casting ballots. The final results were much the same as those of the scm questionnaire at other universities. The headline of the *Queen's Journal* read: 'War Only in Self Defence, Student Verdict.' While over 80 per cent of those polled agreed to fight to defend Canada, the vote was seven to one against bearing arms in defence of another country.[130] As well, the majority of respondents opposed military preparedness as a deterrent to war, favoured the conscription of wealth in the event of another war, and favoured government ownership of armament and munitions industries. But the most striking revelation was that two-thirds of the Queen's respondents were confident that Canada could stay out of another war.

Overall, the war questionnaire and the peace poll of 1934 revealed that Canadian university students were, indeed, in sympathy with the general peace movement. In fact, the campaign for disarmament and war renunciation captured the attention of students as much as if not more than the effects of the depression. There were frequent peace lectures and meetings on campuses, and on at least one occasion Queen's University students jammed into Convocation Hall to discuss questions of peace and the future of the League of Nations.[131] While not necessarily radical, student opinion was strongly opposed to war.

During the 1930s, as during the 1920s, university students were most often drawn into the peace movement through the Student Christian Movement. In order to create public support for disarmament in 1931, for example, student committees across the country organized public meetings and presented an SCM-initiated petition to Prime Minister R.B. Bennett. Signed by ten thousand Canadian university students, the petition urged Bennett to 'ensure that Canadian influence will be exerted vigorously on behalf of significant reduction of armaments' at the 1932 Geneva Conference.[132]

Reflecting the general public mood of the early 1930s, the SCM involvement in the peace movement continued. By 1935 its national council had appointed a special committee to formulate the SCM position on peace and war. The committee report affirmed the SCM's opposition to war 'as contrary to the mind of God and his purpose for man as revealed in Jesus Christ' and endorsed the 'power of Love as expressed in and operative through human relationships' to bring about the new social order.[133] The logical implication of this position, the report stated, was the personal renunciation of war. In recognition of the SCM's responsibility for peace education, the report recommended several courses of action for local SCM units: co-operation with the League of Nations Society; protests against militarism, narrow patriotism, and fanatical nationalism; the use of questionnaires and peace ballots; and the utilization of Armistice Day for meetings and parades to arouse peace consciousness. Quick to respond, the SCM unit at the University of Toronto initiated what was to become an annual Armistice Day peace service as an alternative for those students who did not wish to participate in the traditional military ceremonies. The first such SCM service in 1935 drew a capacity crowd of seven hundred.

The SCM also supported another peace activity of North American youth known as the 'peace caravan.' Begun by the American Friends Service Committee in the 1920s, peace caravanning was an annual summer custom of university students who toured the United States, stopping in small towns to hold public meetings on peace and international issues.[134] In 1934 Canada was added to the tour, and John Copithorne, a young Canadian Friend and a member of the Toronto Youth Council, joined the caravan.[135] Following two weeks of training at the Institute of International Relations in Durham, North Carolina, Copithorne teamed up with a young American and toured Ohio, New York, and Ontario. They spent the summer spreading the gospel of pacifism to political, social, and religous groups meeting in churches and clubs and on street corners.[136] The New Outlook praised the peace caravan for its enthusiasm and idealistic spirit and suggested it would give the peace movement 'a little of the glamour or romance that great and good movements sometimes lack … It is quite true that idealism and romance may not be able to establish world peace and far-reaching international goodwill on a secure and safe basis, but they may be used, and used very effectively, toward that end.'[137] Although it was not always an annual event in Canada, the peace caravan remained a popular activity throughout the 1930s and received the financial support of Canadian Friends and the SCM.[138]

In their attempt to raise the peace consciousness of Canadians, SCM members adopted the radical critique linking war with capitalism and argued that as long as that connection existed there would be a continuous de facto war. 'In the end of the day, having done all we can to mitigate or avoid an open holocaust, we peace-makers are exactly what the militarists say we are – naïve visionaries – unless we are willing to kill war where it is born.That is the private ownership of machines.'[139]

The same analysis appeared in the McGill Echo. The author, C.T. Howell, blamed war on nationalism, war debts, capitalism, and the breach between capital and labour. 'For the safety of civilization and the survival of humanity,' he wrote, 'present world economic relations must change … the war-system has got to be smashed.'[140] Like Fairbairn and Grube, Howell argued that true pacifism did not 'merely involve non-resistance in war time,' but also included constructive peacetime programs designed to 'remove the basic causes of war, and to strengthen the permanent peace-system now growing.' It was a 'challenge anything but simple, cowardly, or negative;' in fact, he concluded, it was the 'expression of true patriotism stripped of its flags and bayonets.'

By mid-decade the pacifist spirit described by Howell was being registered in a variety of peace pledges and peace ballots across the country. Whether in the peace caravan or the scm, Canadian youth had assumed a leading role in this campaign for 'individual enlistment in the cause of peace.' Moreover, the personal pledges of university students to resist war and their growing demands for social change appeared to be further evidence of the revolutionary potential of the socially radical pacifism taking shape.

VI

No Canadian group was more committed to the development of a socially radical pacifism than the Society of Friends, which had moved even further towards the left under the impetus of the depression. The Quakers were in accord with the student peace movement. They could hardly object to the deepening interest in peace issues manifested in the lively debate in the United Church. The communal aim of the Robert Owen Foundation was too much like a page from their own past to be ignored, and increasingly their own statements sounded like those of the Fellowship for a Christian Social Order.

The involvement of Quakers in the movement for peace and social reconstruction was now the responsibility of the Canadian Friends Service Committee, founded in 1931. At first the committee represented only the Canada and Genesee Yearly Meetings, but subsequent support from the Conservative Friends meant that for the first time all three branches of Canadian Quakers were united behind one committee and spoke with a unified voice.[141] One of the first actions of the new committee was an appeal to Prime Minister Bennett for the appointment of suitable Canadian delegates to the Geneva Disarmament Conference in 1932.[142] Its second annual meeting reaffirmed the Quaker peace testimony and emphasized that pacifism was a 'positive, practical recognition of the universal fatherhood of God, brotherhood of man and sacredness of human personality.' Pacifism, the committee declared, was the full and practical application of the Sermon on the Mount.[143]

One example of a practical activity was the creation of a peace library and reading-room in the Toronto Friends Meeting House. With the assistance of Raymond Booth, the secretary of the Toronto Monthly Meeting, an interdenominational committee representing Toronto's religious and social organizations was formed in 1931 to establish a special free library of books dealing with peace and war.[144] The Toronto Peace Library Committee was made up of, among others, Norman Mackenzie, a professor of international law at the University of Toronto who had been active in scm peace activities during the 1920s, Raymond Booth, and Fred Haslam.[145] The peace library mimeographed articles and sent copies to interested study groups, particularly in the rural districts of Ontario.[146] By 1938 approximately 1,055 copies of articles and 116 books had been distributed across Canada.[147] That literature, together with an annual subscription to *Goodwill*, the publication of the World Alliance for Friendship through the Churches, accounted for the major expenditure in the section of the Friends Service Committee budget allocated to peace work.

In conjunction with the peace library, the service committee issued several pamphlets of concern to pacifists.[148] One such leaflet, entitled 'An Alternative to Sanctions,' proposed the 'reconsideration of the common rights of nations and peoples to share equitably in the resources of the world.' It was sent to members of Parliament and to the press, and received a limited but negative response. Another pamphlet, 'The Economic Crisis' by Fred Haslam, the general secretary of the service committee, called for fundamental social and economic changes in Canadian society, and was described as 'the most intelligent and also ... the most radical statement thus far produced by Canadian Friends.'[149]

A major part of Quaker activities during the 1930s was their co-operation with a broad range of Canadians in the consideration of radical solutions to economic and international problems. Through the initiative of Arthur Dorland and Raymond Booth, for instance, the Friends joined with several other organizations to found the annual Institute of Economic and International Relations. The first Institute was held in August 1932 at the ymca camp at Geneva Park, Lake Couchiching, Ontario. The annual event received especially strong support from the United Church, the Fellowship for a Christian Social Order, and the League for Social Reconstruction, and in the summer of 1933 Eugene Forsey joined the staff of the institute.[150]

Since the idea of inherent violence in capitalism pervaded pacifist thought during the interwar years, Canadian Friends instinctively related their pacifism to the need for radical economic change. Such radical sympathies were evident in Quaker praise of the ccf as being 'in the vanguard of the great forward advance' of mankind.[151] Another commendation went to the Antigonish Co-operative Movement under the direction of Father M.M. Cody, an experimental but promising socio-economic reorientation of Nova Scotian farmers, fishermen, miners, and industrial workers.[152] Pacifists were particularly interested in the adult education phase of the movement. From their support of radical alternatives to specific activities such as the Toronto Peace Library and the Institute for International Relations, Canadian Quakers were instrumental in the quest for both peace and social justice during the 1930s.

VII

During the first half of the 1930s pacifist feeling thrived in Canada as pacifists cemented their bonds with social radicalism. Although specific peace organizations were largely limited to the Society of Friends, the Women's International League, and the Toronto Fellowship of Reconciliation, the peace movement in general was composed of a broad range of groups and individuals, and peace activities received wide popular support, from League of Nations internationalists to committed socialists. While the large majority of these peace advocates, therefore, were not strictly pacifists, they eagerly accepted the label that had become synonymous with the abhorrence of war and the peaceful settlement of international disputes. Disarmament continued to receive enthusiastic support as one of the best ways of relieving international tensions. Otherwise, the peace movement was largely preoccupied with the domestic crisis caused by the depression, and pacifists joined in the growing demand for radical solutions to the social and economic ills facing the nation.

The alignment of pacifism and socialism had been building since the Great War, but it was not until the urgency of the depression years that pacifists concentrated on the necessity to eliminate or reform capitalism in order to secure both peace and social justice. Accordingly, pacifist influence was present within the various groups promoting radical alternatives: the League for Social Reconstruction, the Co-operative Commonwealth Federation, and the Fellowship for a Christian Social Order and its western affiliate, the Alberta School of Religion. All these groups attempted to grapple with ways to effect radical social and economic change as well as the pacifist alternative.

Churches also endorsed the movement for peace and social justice, as did student groups such as the Student Christian Movement, the YMCA, and the YWCA. During the 1930s hundreds of young people were attracted to the peace movement and toyed with the idea of refusing to fight in any future war. In fact, the personal pledge of individual war resistance was an important pacifist tactic in Canada, although it was never as popular as it was in Britain.

The exuberance of the peace movement in the 1930s, however, was short-lived. By mid-decade, as national attention again turned to the international scene, the ideals of peace and social justice were threatened by increased fascist aggression. As a result, the liberal democracy that had seemed the route to world peace was increasingly in need of defence – ultimately, it would be argued, by armed resistance. Socially radical pacifists would find it difficult to evade the approaching crisis.

6

Crisis and consolidation

During the latter half of the 1930s increasing international violence challenged the viability of the peace movement. The civil war in Spain, the
Sino-Japanese war, and German aggression all forced pacifists to make
an agonizing choice between the preservation of democracy and social
progress in the world and the ideal of non-violence. To many pacifists
the two goals seemed so closely interrelated that choice was impossible;
yet the ineluctable march of events appeared to force the impossible
choice. Concurrent with the challenge of world events, and aggravating
the pacifists' dilemma, was a transition in the world of theology that
was now beginning to have its effect upon the theological underpinning
of twentieth-century pacifism. As a result of these combined influences,
many leading liberal and modernist Protestants began to doubt, and
some to abandon, their theological position in favour of neo-orthodoxy
and to adopt what they considered a more realistic approach to international violence. Following such heart-searching over a period of years,
a large number of these persons left the peace movement. A more general
slippage in public support became evident as the latter half of the decade
progressed and as, in reaction, those Canadians who remained pacifists
attempted to consolidate their forces and prepare for approaching world
disaster.

A rift within the peace movement separating pacifists from their temporary alliance with League of Nations internationalists and left-wing
anti-imperialists began to develop in response to the increase in fascist
aggression at mid-decade and, in particular, to the Spanish Civil War.
The debate in the former case centred on the use of economic and military
sanctions to enforce the principle of collective security. Some pacifists,
such as J.S. Woodsworth, approved the use of economic sanctions against

aggressors, and for a brief time, in response to the Italian invasion of Abyssinia in 1935, it appeared that the Canadian government agreed.[1] But as the 'Riddell incident' eventually proved, government officials, perhaps reflecting an isolationist tinge in popular peace sentiment, were not ready to take such decisive action.[2] Accordingly, Canada joined with member nations in removing the League's economic sanctions against Italy. The League of Nations' failure to employ economic sanctions successfully meant that internationalists who still valued collective security as the route to world peace now looked to military sanctions. On this point, however, they lost the support of committed pacifists, and the fissure in the peace movement widened.

A more serious question arose in response to the Spanish Civil War in 1936. Besides being another instance of fascist aggression, the war also posed a threat of extinction for all left-wing groups struggling in a newly established democracy.[3] Predictably, the radical left rallied to the support of Spanish democracy and began to call for a military response. The peace movement, especially that element in the vanguard of the quest for social and economic justice, found itself in an inescapable dilemma: its commitment to non-violence was in danger of being compromised by its commitment to social justice, which some interwar pacifists had already begun to equate with the necessity to resist fascism, if need be, by armed resistance. Failure to resolve that dilemma left the pacifist movement severely weakened by the end of the decade.

I

The first branch of the peace movement to adopt a more militant stance in the campaign against fascism was the radical left. The tenuous alliance between pacifists and radical leftists was exemplified by the League against War and Fascism under the direction of A.A. MacLeod, a Canadian radical and a former executive editor of the *World Tomorrow*. McLeod, who had a strong Christian background, had served as the YMCA secretary in Halifax and Chicago before joining the staff of the *World Tomorrow* as business manager in 1929.[4] Based in New York City since before the First World War, the *World Tomorrow* had become the leading exponent of the pacifist-socialist alignment among radical Christians. Its editors included such leading radicals as Devere Allen, Kirby Page, and Reinhold Niebuhr. Their call for a militant pacifism reflected the popular view of pacifism as the best means to achieve a socialized state. Although it was published in the United States, the journal regularly carried reports by foreign correspondents, including Canadian contributors such as Agnes Macphail and Jack Duckworth, a young pacifist from Montreal.[5] the *World Tomorrow* also followed closely the progress of the CCF and the Antigonish Movement in Canada.[6]

Because MacLeod had been born and raised in Nova Scotia he was in direct sympathy with the plight of the idle coal miners there, and in 1933 he returned to Cape Breton to establish a worker's school.[7] Two years later, following his resignation as executive editor of the *World Tomorrow*, MacLeod arrived in Toronto to assume the chairmanship of the Canadian League against War and Fascism.[8] Launched by Canadian communists in 1934, the League against War and Fascism was the Canadian branch of a worldwide movement 'to mobilize intellectuals prepared to combine opposition to war and fascism with support of Soviet foreign policy.'[9] It was, in MacLeod's view, an organized effort to steer the peace movement away from pure pacifism and towards a 'more realistic understanding of the struggle for peace' characteristic of the Soviets.[10] Support for the league formed around a nucleus of intellectuals: professors at the University of Toronto, Protestant clergymen, and pacifists in the Fellowship of Reconciliation and the Women's International League for Peace and Freedom. Members of the league's national council, for instance, included Dr Salem Bland, the social gospel spokesman; T.C. Douglas and William Irvine, CCF members of Parliament; John Line and J.W.A. Nicholson of the FCSO; Rabbi Maurice N. Eisendrath, president of the Toronto FOR; and Peter G. Makaroff, the pacifist Doukhobor lawyer from Saskatoon.[11] The Communists stayed out of the limelight as much as possible in order to reassure sceptical liberals and socialists. For a time, T.C. Douglas and Frank Underhill, a history professor and socialist intellectual in the LSR, were vice-presidents of the league. Overall, however, MacLeod was the moving spirit behind the league and its nationwide campaign against fascism as the major threat to peace and democracy.[12]

It is doubtful that MacLeod ever embraced pacifism, but, as a socialist and one of Canada's leading Communists, he was active in the general peace movement of the time. In the summer of 1935, for instance, MacLeod embarked on a national tour that included peace rallies, protest meetings against the persecution of Jews in Europe, and conferences on the use of sanctions against Italy. Most meetings were held in co-operation with other organizations such as the WIL or the FOR. In August the league co-operated with the Canadian Youth Congress in organizing a torchlight parade for peace through downtown Toronto that ended with a speech at Queen's Park by John Copithorne of the student peace caravan.[13] Over the years the league sponsored visits to Canada by such international figures as André Malraux, Thomas Mann, Harry Ward, and Lord Cecil. In 1936 MacLeod headed a fourteen-man Canadian delegation to the First World Peace Congress in Brussels. There he was elected to the general council of the International Peace Campaign inspired by Lord Cecil.[14]

In that same year, however, the league's sympathy with Canadian pacifists began to change as MacLeod and others in the league adopted a more militant response to fascist aggression. Their support for military sanctions and their disregard for proper democratic procedures in meetings ultimately resulted in a breach between the league and other peace organizations such as the WIL. The Toronto branch of the WIL in particular discontinued all association with the League against War and Fascism, while other branches continued to work with the league for a time but without affiliation.[15]

In order to project a more positive image, the league changed its name in 1937 to the League for Peace and Democracy and claimed that its aim was to 'protect democratic rights for all sections of the Canadian people. Save Canada from war by helping to restore world peace.'[16] Regardless of its name, however, the league's position remained clear-cut: support for a military victory of the International Brigades over General Franco's fascists. While it obviously was never a pacifist organization, the League for Peace and Democracy capitalized on popular peace sentiment by equating the fight against fascism with the preservation of peace and democracy. As a result, pacifists were tempted to support the fight for international justice at the expense of their pacifist beliefs.

Although it represented an indirect endorsement of international violence, the call to aid Spanish democracy succeeded in attracting considerable support within the peace movement. Leading liberal and socialist peace advocates joined with the League for Peace and Democracy to establish the Canadian Committee to Aid Spanish Democracy under the honorary chairmanship of Salem Bland. Later, the same coalition lent support to the group of young Canadian men who joined the International Brigades in Spain as the Mackenzie-Papineau Battalion.[17]

The Canadian Committee to Aid Spanish Democracy also received enthusiastic support from various youth organizations, including the Christian Co-operative Youth Movement, the Student Christian Movement, and the YMCA and YWCA, which had recently joined forces to form the Canadian Youth Congress.[18] The Canadian Youth Congress was organized in Toronto in May 1935, with approximately six hundred observers and delegates from over two hundred organizations, largely from Toronto, in attendance. Discussions centred on the topics of peace, unemployment, and education, and the congress elected a continuing committee known as the Canadian Youth Council to pursue peace activities and organize educational forums in Toronto and other cities.[19] The idea of the congress began to spread, and local youth councils sprang up in most of the larger centres across the country. The local councils supported peace activities and staged youth peace parades in various cities during the summer of 1935.[20]

The Canadian Youth Council also invited all candidates in the 1935 general election to complete a questionnaire designed to provide a profile of the candidates vis-à-vis pacifism, the question of sanctions, and social welfare programs. Although he complied with the request, J.S. Woodsworth appeared somewhat annoyed by the tactic, and commented critically 'Why does the Canadian Youth Congress stand on the sidelines and content itself with cheering and booing those in the game? Resolutions not fierce enough – Get into action!'[21] Perhaps with Woodsworth's challenge in mind, the youth councils began to take steps to form a national body that would co-ordinate their various activities into an effective program of action. This plan was accelerated when the Canadian League of Nations Society asked the Canadian Youth Council to call a national convention of all youth organizations. The purpose of the convention was to select delegates to represent Canada at a World Youth Congress scheduled to meet at Geneva in the fall of 1936 under the auspices of the International Federation of League of Nations Societies.[22]

In May 1936 the first national meeting of the Canadian Youth Congress convened in Ottawa, with 455 delegates from across Canada representing over twenty different youth organizations.[23] The major goal of the young delegates was to draft a program to improve the living conditions of all young people through education and affirmative action on such issues as unemployment, social justice, and peace. Accordingly, the main topics of discussion were 'Canadian Youth and World Peace' and 'Youth in the Canadian Economy.' One delegate, Wilfred Cantwell Smith, reported that the impressive fact of the conference was the overriding spirit of co-operation and compromise in spite of some incompatible attitudes. Even the communists, he wrote, 'were conspicious by their mildness.'[24] Smith also reported that the tenor of discussion was radical 'in the sense that the delegates were trying to get at the root of things,' but he refuted the rumour that the congress was merely an attempt by extremists to attain respectability: 'Revolutionary suggestions were not disputed but laughed at merrily; the absolute pacifist, though applauded, was voted down.'[25]

The congress endorsed a proposed Canadian Youth Act, which recommended government-sponsored youth projects, and adopted several resolutions, including one that condemned war as primarily an economic issue and urged Canadian participation in international discussions and action to eliminate war's causes. While most motions received virtually unanimous approval, a resolution that supported military sanctions by the League of Nations was opposed by 20 per cent of the delegates. In the end, the congress issued a 'Declaration of Rights of Canadian Youth' that set out its demands for work, security, recreation, knowledge, training, freedom, and justice. Concerning peace, the Canadian Youth Congress declared:

We want our country continually, and with all its resources, to struggle to promote collective security and peace among all the nations and peoples. This will be the best guarantee of our peace. We want our government to establish responsibility to the people in matters of foreign policy, and demand that on these matters the people shall be asked to decide by vote. We also declare intolerable any and all acts, bills and laws which would or do provide the breach of the state of peace either within or without our borders.[26]

The issue of peace was considered to be of primary importance to Canadian youth, and to a certain extent the Canadian Youth Congress pronouncements on peace served as an indication of youth opinion for the delegates selected to attend the World Youth Congress, also billed as the International Congress against War.

In September, over 700 delegates from 36 nations gathered in Geneva; Canada sent 32 delegates and observers, one of the largest delegations. The Canadians, who represented every region of the country, were members of the YMCA, the YWCA, the SCM, the United Church, the Baptist church, the Christian Co-operative Youth Movement, the Communist Youth League, and several regional groups. Among them were William Kashtan, secretary of the Communist Youth League, Paul Martin, a future member of the Liberal government, and T.C. Douglas, a future CCF premier of Saskatchewan.[27] Kenneth Woodsworth (the nephew of J.S. Woodsworth), the chairman and chief spokesman of the Canadian Youth Congress and one of the Canadian delegates, felt that the Canadian delegation gave 'constructive leadership' to the World Congress.[28] He was especially proud that the proposed Canadian Youth Act was used as a model by the world youth movement.[29]

The major accomplishment at Geneva was the establishment of the World Youth Congress as a 'permanent continuing body' dedicated to achieving 'unity of action on an international scale.' The congress issued a call for a collective peace system that would provide real security against aggressors, 'a system having its roots deep in the mass movement of the people for peace; not in support of an abstract ideal of collectivism, but to create a potent instrument to maintain the peace of the world.'[30]

The young delegates hoped to direct the enthusiasm of youth away from fascism towards a constructive peace movement. Peace could be established, they believed, 'through the unified will of the whole people, organized in their own popular movement, consistently directed against any and every force which might lead to war.'[31] The World Congress concluded that economic reform was essential to lasting peace, and outlined specific proposals delegates might adopt in their respective countries, particularly in regard to the economic distress of young people.

Upon his return home, Kenneth Woodsworth boasted that the Canadian delegates were infused with a 'spirit which will blossom forth in still greater accomplishments.' During the next few years the Canadian Youth Congress accelerated its campaign on behalf of a Canadian Youth Act and took the lead in organizing Youth Peace Day demonstrations across the country every Armistice Day.[32]

The Canadian Youth Congress had also begun to re-evaluate the proper response for Canadian youth to increasing fascist aggression, and by 1937 it was involved in organizing a special Canadian Youth Committee to Aid Spain. The national chairman, Ken Woodsworth, welcomed the new activities, such as assisting war refugees in Spain, as the type of practical peace work that ought to be undertaken by the youth councils.[33] Later, during the Sino-Japanese conflict, the Canadian Youth Congress broadened its appeal for aid to include refugees in China, and called for a boycott of Japanese goods. The congress maintained that it was inconsistent on the part of the Canadian goverment to build up defence on the Pacific coast while at the same time permitting the shipment of war materials to Japan, Canada's only potential enemy in the Pacific.[34] A similar position was taken by other groups such as the Women's International League for Peace and Freedom.

In the face of continued international aggression, the Canadian Youth

Congress began to argue that a meaningful movement for peace demanded sterner measures than mere demonstrations and humanitarian services. In a letter to local youth councils in November 1938, Ken Woodsworth lamented the impotence of the peace movement. Despite another year of peace rallies by youth, Czechoslovakia had fallen and Canton and Hankow were destroyed. 'The crisis through which we are now passing,' he wrote, 'has tried the peace movement severely and has found it wanting in many respects.'[35] Woodsworth challenged the local councils to seek a new approach of practical activity for the peace movement. Furthermore, while reaffirming its faith in the principle of collective security, the Canadian Youth Congress called upon Canadian authorities to formulate a peace policy for Canada that would include the type of action necessary to halt fascist aggression.[36] Clearly, in the eyes of the Canadian Youth Congress, the popular peace movement had come to be associated with something quite different from pacifism.

The crisis in the peace movement marked by the abandonment of non-violence by the Canadian League for Peace and Democracy and the Canadian Youth Congress was also reflected in the CCF and its gradual move away from a strictly neutral foreign policy position.[37] From its inception the CCF closely followed J.S. Woodsworth's pacifist-socialist philosophy and endorsed a strict neutralist foreign policy for Canada. In effect, the CCF echoed the socialist argument that the best way to rid the world of war was through the elimination of capitalism with its social injustice and imperialist aggression. For a time there appeared to be no conflict between pacifism and socialism, since it was generally assumed that future wars would be primarily capitalist wars. The outbreak of civil war in Spain, however, severely challenged the socially radical pacifist analysis and triggered a shift among socialists away from a neutral or pacifist position. When CCF members became active in the Canadian Committee to Aid Spanish Democracy, the party was in a dilemma. On the one hand, it opposed Canadian participation in any foreign war; on the other hand, it championed the individual right of Canadians to go to Spain to fight fascism. The ambiguity of this stand was underlined in 1937 when the CCF national council rephrased its 1936 foreign policy resolution, which urged neutrality in the event of 'any war,' to read 'any imperialist war.'[38] Did this mean that the CCF would support a war to resist fascist aggression, as in Spain? Woodsworth, of course, continued to call for a policy of strict neutrality, and the CCF endorsed that position in regard to the Sino-Japanese conflict. Nevertheless, unrest continued to mount, and in 1938 the CCF reversed an earlier stand and recognized the need for home defence as the struggle intensified between the pacifists and non-pacifists within the party. The neutralist platform was doomed.

The Spanish Civil War was causing a crisis of major proportions in the peace movement. Relations with the League for Peace and Democracy were strained; the Canadian Youth Congress response to the Spanish Civil War pressed hard upon pacifists; and the ccf foreign policy alliance of anti-imperialists, anti-militarists, neutralists, and pacifists was threatened. A widespread re-evaluation of the use of armed force to defend liberal democracies from the encroachments of totalitarian regimes was underway. The threat of fascism had shaken to their very foundations the pacifist convictions of many social radicals, including M.J. Coldwell, Stanley Allen, and Eugene Forsey, and resulted in their defection from the peace movement as the crisis ultimately came to a head.

II

Central in the pacifist crisis of conscience was the increasing re-examination of the proper Christian response to war, especially in the light of a new stream of theological thought that actually appeared to endorse the use of armed force. To some extent, the change of heart exemplified by many Canadian pacifists during the later 1930s followed the lead of the American theologian, Reinhold Niebuhr, who raised one of the most serious philosophical challenges to pacifism.

Niebuhr, the former chairman of the Fellowship of Reconciliation in the United States, left the FOR in 1934 when its pacifist membership refused to declare total allegiance to the class struggle.[39] Soon afterward he rejected pacifism altogether as an ineffective and unrealistic philosophy of social change. As Niebuhr considered a Marxist interpretation of political and social questions, he launched a far-reaching critique of theological liberalism and moved towards a reformulation of theological orthodoxy. Niebuhr concluded that only a neo-orthodoxy that emphasized the depth and continuity of the sinfulness of man in human history could come to terms with the realities of the twentieth century and provide the philosophic base for radical social thought.[40] He looked on liberal Protestantism and pacifism as heretical developments that had substituted faith in man for faith in God. Although individual man was moral, he argued, society on the whole was immoral and therefore incapable of perfection.[41] Neither the perfect means nor the perfect end were real options in social action, and to act as if they were was not only unrealistic, it was to invite disaster. In contrast to the absolutism of pacifists and many social radicals, the moral relativism of Niebuhr required Christians to choose the least possible evil relative to their particular situation.

Although the real impact of Niebuhr's thought was not felt in Canada until after the Second World War, his changing philosophy was already being publicized in Canadian religious journals. Niebuhr's rejection of pacifism and his call for a more realistic Christian approach to international conflicts was an important influence on those Canadian pacifists who were rethinking their pacifism in response to the anti-fascist mood of the late 1930s. But the loss of his support was a major setback to the peace movement, and, coupled with the emotional issue of Spain, revealed the vulnerability of the socially radical pacifism of the twentieth century.

There was no serious attempt by a Canadian pacifist to answer Niebuhr directly until the Second World War,[42] but the dilemma of the Christian pacifist was clearly recognized in 1937 by Arthur G. Dorland. In an article in the *Canadian Friend* Dorland urged his fellow pacifists to maintain their trust in the redemptive power of love in bringing about the Kingdom of God. Many Christians, he warned, were abandoning this faith with the excuse that 'man is fundamentally wicked and untrustworthy.' That attitude may have been in line with the teachings of Calvin but was not according to the teaching of Jesus.[43] Dorland recognized, however, that Christian pacifists who did rely on spiritual forces and who sought to apply the principles of the Kingdom of God to 'every relationship of life' found themselves in a dilemma. 'This dilemma is of far greater complexity than just the question as to whether shooting out the brains of an opponent – either individualy or in mass – is a Christian or reasonable way of settling a dispute.' The dilemma of war was inextricably linked with the pressing social and economic problems of the day. On this point Dorland made himself perfectly clear: 'Those Christians who seek to dodge the dilemma of economic and social justice in a Christian society and who refuse to do anything to remove these injustices or to construct a more equitable and truly Christian order, actually become by their timidity and inertia the upholders and defenders of the existing injustices and social evils.'[44] Christians could face the dilemma and seek to remove the causes of injustices and evils in contemporary society. What was needed, Dorland suggested, was the establishment of a society 'in which man will live by something better than the rule of profit and self-aggrandisement.'

The heart of the dilemma, however, concerned the extent to which the Christian pacifist should pursue the new social order, especially since there was a real danger that pacifism would be sacrificed if the end goal of social and economic justice was carried to the extreme. Dorland noted that, in their dedicated campaign for social and economic reform, some social gospel radicals had already lent support to persons and causes that were 'activated by hate and revenge against those who control our present social and economic system' and who favoured class warfare.[45] There were a 'rapidly growing number' of Canadians, he reported, 'who have been so won by the avowedly idealistic appeals of the ... Fascist or Communist as the case may be ... that they are ready to go out to kill their fellow men to secure these desirable social ends in a class war, if not in an international war.'[46] Dorland hoped that his fellow pacifists would recognize the hidden danger in supporting radical alternatives. In reality, Christian pacifists were being asked to support causes 'that would justify the use of the war method in a bloody class war to attain ... particular economic and social ends.'[47] In conclusion, Dorland reminded his readers that if they wished to bring in the Kingdom of God they would have to use the methods of the Kingdom and not violence and hate, 'however praiseworthy or desirable the end to be attained may appear to be.' 'We cannot further Heaven's end,' he wrote, 'by breaking Heaven's laws.'

Dorland was realistic up to a point. He recognized the need to pursue peace through social and economic justice, and saw that if followed to extremes that approach could compromise pacifism. What he did not seem to recognize was that it was not extremists who were drifting away from pacifism, but committed liberal, labour, and social democrats who had had pacifist inclinations but now feared that the defence of their primary values might entail a war they could not reject. Dorland did not comment on that aspect of the crisis. He remained a committed absolute pacifist and, still basically liberal in his thinking, he was unable to turn the last screw in analysing the dilemma. Niebuhr remained to be reckoned with.

The questions raised by Niebuhr and Dorland concerning the proper Christian response to war became one of the major issues considered by the world's leading Protestants at the Oxford conference of the Universal Council for Life and Work. Over four hundred delegates and four hundred associate members and visitors representing almost every branch of the Protestant church throughout the world gathered at Oxford in 1937 to consider the relationship between the church and the social and economic order. On the whole, the conference reflected a growing realism in Christian social thought, 'and a more resolute determination that the Church should bear its witness in the world as it was, rather than remain in the realm of utopian idealism.'[48] This was especially true concerning the issue of pacifism, perhaps in response to the worsening international situation.

As one of the Canadian delegates to the Oxford conference, Richard Roberts was primarily concerned with the question of war. In fact, prior to his departure for England, Roberts confided to John Nevin Sayre, the international chairman of the Fellowship of Reconciliation, that he felt the most urgent question at Oxford would be that of peace: 'I am not at all sure whether it isn't the most immediately critical issue for the Church at this moment. Anything short of a stark condemnation of war, root and branch, will stultify the church in the face of the world.'[49] As a member of the Group on International Order and War, Roberts worked in close association with the British pacifist Canon Charles Raven in drafting the statement on war. It was not a pacifist document, but he thought it was 'the strongest thing that has yet come from a church body on war.'[50] In effect, the Oxford pronouncement recognized three possible positions for a Christian in time of war: Christian submission to the state's declaration of war; support only for a just war waged according to Christian principles; and a strict pacifist rejection of all war.

Roberts was particularly pleased with the official recognition of absolute pacifism as a legitimate Christian stand because he realized the report of the Oxford conference would influence subsequent declarations of Canada's churches. Indeed, when the general council of the United Church reiterated its opposition to war in 1938 it mentioned only two of the three possible Christian alternatives upheld by the Oxford conference: absolute pacifism and selective abstention from war. Omitted altogether was any reference to legitimate grounds on which the state or Christians might wage war.[51] In effect, the general council reached a compromise between absolute pacifism and the growing Christian realism regarding international affairs.

When Roberts returned to Canada he became the centre of a controversy arising from the Oxford pronouncement on war. While speaking at the twentieth annual pastors' conference at the Hartford Seminary in Connecticut, he stated that if the Oxford report on war was to sink into the mind of the church, there would be 'no more recruiting and drum-beating in the pulpits and no more prayers for victory.'[52] His comments were reported in Toronto newspapers, and provoked a flurry of letters to the editors. Roberts's most venomous critic was H.A. Kent, principal of Queen's University. In a letter to the *Globe and Mail*, Kent branded Roberts's statement a 'foolish utterance ... only possible in the mouth of someone who sits by while other people may be in agony.' 'The tongue is a little member,' Kent concluded. 'In the mouth of Moderators and ex-Moderators it should be bridled against foolish utterance.'[53]

The controversy that resulted from Roberts's speech and Kent's rejoinder lasted for several months. Most contributors either vilified Roberts or spoke out whole-heartedly on his behalf. One of the most penetrating comments came from the radical pacifist Edis Fairbairn. In his usual caustic manner, Fairbairn agreed with Kent that Roberts's statement was a 'foolish utterance' since, regardless of any anti-war position taken by the church, individual ministers would 'certainly recruit from the pulpit and pray for victory ... in the next war, as in the last.' 'Dr Roberts' misguided optimism,' he wrote, 'seems to me as dangerous as Dr Kent's naïve unrealism.'[54] Fairbairn predicted that Mammon and Mars, the twin gods of civilization, would have no difficulty swinging the churches into line in time of future crisis. Another well-known pacifist minister, G. Stanley Russell of Deer Park United Church, stated that it was not Roberts but Kent who needed to defend his position.[55]

In a personal letter to Roberts, Gordon Sisco, general secretary of the United Church, said that he felt Kent had missed the point. He then continued:

What I do want to say is that in this difficult time, when many of us are trying to think our way through a Christian conclusion, and the relation of Church to state, especially in times of war, we are heartened by what you said at Hartford, Connecticut. There are many of us who know exactly what you mean when you speak of the Church as a body of believers who must be true to the Christian ethic as far as possible in time of international strife. I do hope you will be encouraged to feel that many are with you. Don't budge a damn bit![56]

Roberts did not move from his pacifist position in the years to come. He left Toronto in 1938 after having worked there slightly over a decade. During that time he had become well known and respected for his constant but reserved call for pacifism and social action both within the United Church and throughout Canada as a whole. It was he who later

made the strongest Canadian pacifist response to Niebuhr. Nevertheless, the response to Niebuhr's challenge, the Oxford pronouncement
on war, and the Kent-Roberts controversy underlined a growing dilemma within the Church, the peace movement, and Canadian society
in general concerning the proper role of Canadians in a war against
fascism.

III

The latter half of the 1930s was a time of crisis for the peace movement
as numerous Canadians drifted away from pacifism in order to support
the fight against fascist injustice. Alarmed, committed pacifists, especially those in the Society of Friends, the Women's International League
for Peace and Freedom, and the Fellowship of Reconciliation began to
regroup and consolidate their organizations. In 1938, for instance, all
three branches of the Society of Friends in Canada issued a joint statement reaffirming their ancient peace testimony and sent copies to the
prime minister, the minister of national defence, and the leaders of both
opposition parties.[57] Since Canadians were again preoccupied with the
thought of war, Quakers felt impelled to remind the government of
Christ's message: 'But I say unto you that ye resist not evil, but overcome
evil with good.' To oppose force with more force, they argued, would
accomplish nothing; 'it is like using frost to destroy frost, hate to destroy
hate, or evil to destroy evil.' Although they offered their loyal assistance
in arriving at crucial decisions, Friends warned that 'under no circumstances' would they take part in war or preparation for war. They placed
their faith in 'the spirit and principle of love' to bring about real peace
on earth.[58]
    Such pleas might suggest that Canadian Quakers were entirely out
of touch with the enormities of political and racial persecution that were
becoming a hallmark of the 1930s, but they were in fact among the first
to respond with humanitarian services in response to the suffering in
war-torn countries and those under fascist regimes. After the outbreak
of civil war in Spain, for instance, the Canadian Friends Service Committee and the Canadian Committee of the Save the Children Fund
issued a joint appeal for assistance for Spanish children. When war broke
out in China in the following year, the two organizations acted together
again.[59]
    As early as 1933 Friends had voiced their concern for the growing
number of those fleeing Nazi Germany and pledged their assistance. It

was believed that most of the exiles were German pacifists, Jews, or Christians of Jewish descent.[60] By 1936 the Quakers had joined a group of Toronto churchmen in a demand that the Canadian government offer asylum to the refugees. Canada, they proposed, could become a sanctuary for those escaping Nazi terror;[61] they warned that Hitler and his Nazi supporters would never restrain their persecution of German Jews.[62] In order to create an effective network of refugee work, Quakers cooperated with other religious and pacifist organizations such as the Canadian Conference of Christians and Jews and the Women's International League for Peace and Freedom.

The WIL took a keen interest in the problem, and was particularly instrumental in the movement to assist German refugees in Canada during the war. In fact, the Toronto branch of the WIL received credentials from a few refugees seeking permanent residence in Canada as early as 1936.[63] Most refugee work required that careful personal attention be paid to each individual being considered. It proceeded slowly, without publicity, and generally did not meet with much success until Canada became directly involved during the Second World War.

In addition to its refugee work, the WIL launched an active opposition to increased military spending and the shipment of war materials to Japan.[64] In February 1937 the Toronto branch sponsored an emergency peace meeting in an attempt to organize sentiment against increased military expenditures. The meeting sent five thousand cards to members of Parliament asking them to vote against any such increases. Anna Sissons, president of the Toronto WIL, urged other branches to take similar action.[65]

Most of the WIL activity in the late 1930s, however, was devoted to national reorganization and consolidation in the light of the growing challenge to world peace and to pacifism. During the course of the decade national co-ordination of the WIL had fallen into disarray, especially since Laura Jamieson, the leading national figure, devoted more and more of her time to CCF political activities in British Columbia. Anna Sissons made an effort to keep the organization together by assuming the post of national secretary and distributing a national WIL newsletter.[66]

Following the international events of the mid-1930s, however, it was evident that closer national organization was necessary if the WIL was to lead an effective peace program. Violet McNaughton of Saskatoon and Lila Phelps of Winnipeg agreed on the urgent need for national leadership, and in June 1937 the Winnipeg branch of the WIL sponsored a national organization conference.[67] The conference delegates included Anna Sissons from Toronto, Laura Jamieson from Vancouver, Mrs V.A. McConkey from Edmonton, Laura Goodman Salverson and Rachel Coutes from Calgary, Mrs G. Hartwell and Mrs G.W. Hutchinson from Regina, and Beatrice Brigden, Mrs F.L. Lloyd, and the chairwoman of the conference, Lucy Woodsworth, all from Manitoba.[68] From this list of prominent members, the WIL appears to have been the women's peace arm of the CCF.

Reports on the various activities of local branches revealed that WIL-women across Canada were involved in the sponsorship of local peace conferences, radio programs, essay and poster contests in schools, theatrical productions, and Goodwill Day celebrations. The Regina women were particularly proud of their recent success in ending cadet training in schools.

Following an enthusiastic agreement to organize on a strong national basis, the new Canadian section passed resolutions in favour of numerous issues ranging from birth control to peace. One example was the proposal for a national referendum to decide on Canadian participation in an imperial war: 'Resolved: That the Women's International League for Peace and Freedom, Canadian Section, urges the Government to take necessary steps to ensure to Canada her right to decide as to participation or non-participation in any war in which the United Kingdom may become involved.'[69] The WIL also declared its support for the creation of a select standing committee in the House of Commons to investigate the entire question of the manufacture, purchase, and sale of armaments in Canada and the effect upon the Canadian economy.

Although unable to attend the national WIL conference in Winnipeg, Violet McNaughton actively promoted WIL objectives in Saskatchewan and was involved in the creation of the Saskatoon Peace Group, a forerunner of the Fellowship of Reconciliation in Saskatoon. WIL efforts in Saskatoon, however, appear to have met only limited success. McNaughton, depressed by their rather poor showing, complained in April 1937 that 90 per cent of the inhabitants of Saskatoon did not have the least interest in the peace question, 'and yet we've tried all kinds of methods of reaching them.'[70]

Pacifists in Toronto appeared to have fared a little better. In May 1937, for instance, the WIL joined with the FOR, the LSR, and the FCSO to sponsor a special Peace Day celebration, featuring the American pacifist Harry Emerson Fosdick, commemorating 120 years of peace between Canada and the United States. Such pacifist efforts notwithstanding, it became increasingly evident that, whether in Toronto or Saskatoon, that the public appeal of pacifism was in decline.

IV

As popular support for the peace movement began to wane, pacifist groups accelerated their effort to unite their members and maintain some semblance of pacifist activity. The organization of the WIL on a national basis was an important step in that direction. Similarly, the Fellowship of Reconciliation began to organize nationally, and before the end of the decade the FOR became the leading inter-pacifist organization in Canada. Prior to 1938, however, small FOR groups in various Canadian cities functioned without national co-ordination or even affiliation with the international organization. What little contact they did have with the official FOR was largely through the American branch and its publication, *Fellowship*, and other journals such as the *Christian Century* and the *World Tomorrow*.

During the 1930s the largest FOR group was in Toronto. It was a popular but loosely organized society through which a variety of pacifists co-operated in the promotion of peace demonstrations and other events. Its wide range of supporters included members of the Society of Friends, the United Church, the WIL, the Jewish community, and other interested parties. For years major leadership was exercised by Maurice N. Eisendrath, rabbi of Toronto's Holy Blossom Temple, and Raymond Booth, chairman of the Toronto Monthly Meeting of Friends. But even Eisendrath, after firsthand exposure to Nazism during several trips to Europe, painfully reappraised his pacifism and left the FOR.

In Montreal a small FOR group functioned under the leadership and guidance of J. Lavell Smith of Westmount Park United Church, Clarence Halliday of West United Church, Philip Matthams, national secretary of the Fellowship for a Christian Social Order, Jack Duckworth, general secretary of the Notre Dame de Grâce YMCA, and various McGill University students. Eugene Forsey, a professor of economics at McGill, J. Stanley Allen, a FCSO travelling secretary, and other members of the FCSO were also active in the Montreal pacifist circle, although they too began to re-evaluate their pacifist stand in reaction to the Spanish Civil War.[71]

On the west coast the FOR developed primarily around a nucleus University of British Columbia students and counted among its members the western secretary of the United Church Department of Evangelism and Social Service, Hugh Dobson.[72] In Alberta and most of the prairies the major interwar Christian pacifist organization was still the Alberta School of Religion, the FCSO affiliate. By the late 1930s, however, the FCSO had become clearly divided over the pacifist issue, and its pacifist members, while not bitter, became uncomfortable and gradually gravitated to the FOR. In fact, FCSO members desiring a more specifically pacifist affiliation were largely responsible for the active FOR groups across Canada. Aware of the developing rift, and sensing the need for a closer bond among pacifists, the Alberta School of Religion finally cut its offical ties to the FCSO in favor of affiliation with the FOR.

The FOR in Saskatchewan developed out of the Saskatoon Peace Group, a small society devoted to the study and discussion of questions of concern to pacifists, such as the reorganization of the League of Nations, Canada's defence policy, and conscription. The Saskatoon Peace Group also sponsored public forums for the discussion of topics relevant to world peace and endorsed numerous resolutions favouring such measures as the nationalization of the munitions industry, conscription of all wealth in the event of war, and a national referendum on the question of Canadian participation in war.[73]

The leading figures in the Saskatoon pacifist circle were John and Violet McNaughton, Peter Makaroff, the Doukhobor lawyer, Nelson Chappel of Westminster United Church, Carlyle King, professor of English at the University of Saskatchewan, and Cleo Mowers, a theological student.[74] The group met regularly in Makaroff's law office, where they studied pacifist works, such as Richard Gregg's *The Power of Non-violence*, chapter by chapter, learned about the peace movement abroad, and organized activities for Saskatoon.[75]

According to Carlyle King, the group began to call itself the Fellowship of Reconciliation chiefly because the participants 'liked the sound of it' and because it seemed more positive than War Resisters International or Peace Pledge Union. 'We had no written statement of purpose,' said King, 'but we had unity of purpose although we had come to pacifism by a variety of roads. There were Doukhobors who had left the faith, Friends who had no meeting, Bahaists, Jews, Mennonites, United Church people, and others without formal church or religious connection.'[76] With a membership roll of thirty in 1937, the Saskatoon branch was one of the largest FOR groups in the country.

Although a number of Canadians were members of the American FOR, increased correspondence between the various pacifist groups revealed a growing desire to organize the FOR on a national basis within

Canada. The move towards this end was initiated by the Montreal group and accelerated when Percy Bartlett and John Nevin Sayre, secretary and chairman, respectively, of the international FOR, toured Canada in the summer of 1937 under the sponsorship of the Canadian Friends.[77] By autumn of that year, Sayre, chairman of the American branch and of the international organization, assured the Montreal spokesmen, Lavell Smith and Jack Duckworth, that he would personally endorse their application for affiliation with the international FOR if there was a 'satisfactorily functioning Canadian section.' 'I must certainly favor it,' Sayre told Smith, 'provided you find that there are convinced and capable converts of Christian Pacifism in several Canadian cities who favor the move.'[78] It appears that Sayre had co-operated on several occasions with the Canadian League of Nations Society and appreciated their support, but he warned Smith that it was 'not a good thing to have most of the organized peace movement in Canada under the League of Nations Society.' Experience in both the United States and England demonstrated that Christian pacifism could not be propagated adequately under the society's auspices. Consequently, it was Sayre's wish that 'there might one day be in Canada a variety of peace organizations, each fulfilling the function and spreading the message for which it is fitted, but all of them sending their executive to such meetings for continuing conference and consultation ... Perhaps such a development would be hastened if there was a Canadian FOR strong enough to put its case against sanctions and for completely peaceful measures, before your Country.'[79]

Sayre was not in favour of 'purely a paper organization,' however, and he recommended that the Montreal group establish a national office and select officers who were known and trusted. If this minimum level of organization could not be effected, he concluded, 'it would probably be best for the FOR headquarters in the United States to continue serving members in Canada as at present.'[80] In any case the American FOR was ready to send its literature to Canada and route some of its speakers to various Canadian cities.

Sayre's presumption in suggesting that a Canadian FOR should affiliate with and thus become an arm of the American branch annoyed the Montreal group. Lavell Smith, in particular, rejected the idea in favour of a Canadian organization independent of both American and British connections. Consequently, the Montreal group shelved Sayre's proposal and turned their attention to more immediate issues. In July 1938, for instance, they distributed a leaflet drafted by Smith, Halliday, and Duckworth protesting the proposed increase in training centres for military aviators and construction plants for fighter and bomber planes as contrary to the Canadian government's claim to be rearming for defence only.[81] As far as the consolidation of Canadian pacifists was concerned, Halliday and Duckworth admitted that the job was too much for their small group and they suggested it be assumed by a larger FOR unit, preferably the one in Saskatoon.[82]

The first step in that direction occurred when a national FOR organization conference convened in Toronto during the sessions of the general council of the United Church in September 1938. Approximately thirty people, representing Toronto's peace groups and pacifists within the United Church and the FCSO in particular, gathered at Toronto's Diet Kitchen on 27 September and resolved to establish an official Canadian section of the FOR.[83] The participants named a national committee consisting of three members from Toronto (Booth, Joseph Round, and Ted Mann), three from Montreal (Smith, Halliday, and Thelma Allen), three from Saskatoon (King, Mowers, and F. Blatchford Ball), two from Alberta (W.F. Kelloway and W.H. Irwin), and two from Northern Ontario (C. Clare Oke and J.W.E. Newbery). It was announced that the Saskatoon unit was 'willing to co-operate in organizing a National FOR Movement' and the new committee was instructed to communicate with Carlyle King in that regard.[84]

Although King and Mowers did not attend the meeting and therefore were named to the committee without their knowledge or consent, it appears that Mowers had implied their willingness to undertake the task when he was in Montreal earlier that year,[85] and King and Mowers accepted the challenge.

Since they received no further word from the national committee, King and Mowers appointed themselves chairman and secretary respectively and then sought committee approval of their unilateral action. It turned out that the other committee members 'were only too happy' with the new national executive, and a November meeting of those members from Ontario and Montreal adopted the following resolution:

That this group, representative of Montreal, Toronto and North Bay, concur in the suggestion that there be set up a National Council of the Canadian Fellowship of Reconciliation with the following Executive Officers: President: Professor Carlyle A. King, University of Saskatchewan. Secretary: Mr C.W. Mowers, University of Saskatchewan, and that these Executive Officers proceed to complete the formation of the Council. It was further moved that steps be taken to secure the ratification of local units of the FOR in Canada, of these appointments.[86]

One of the first tasks of the executive was to be the formulation of a statement of purpose acceptable to groups across Canada. King had already begun to draft a 'Statement of Basis and Aims,' and in late November he sent copies to the various units for approval.[87] The response of council members was completely favourable, and King proceeded to incorporate the 'Basis and Aims' in a leaflet for use in a membership drive.[88]

From the very beginning King's most ardent support came from Smith, Halliday, and Duckworth in Montreal. They were always prompt with suggestions and offers of assistance. In January 1939, for instance, Smith sent King a list of approximately four thousand names of Canadians who had signed the War Renunciation Pledge of 1934. Smith confessed that the list was not entirely reliable, since many signatures had probably moved and undoubtedly some had renounced pacifism, but he hoped it would be of some use.[89]

Elated over the prospect of an organization incorporating a thousand or more prospective pacifists in Canada, King and Mowers launched a membership drive. In the spring of 1939 Mowers recalled their experience: 'First we compiled a list of about one hundred names of people in all parts of the nation, people whom we thought were *sure* bets. We sent each of them copies of our printed leaflet. Only a very few replied. We wrote many personal letters and still very few replied. We sent circular letters, with the leaflets, to 120 United Church ministers who signed the Peace Pledge about four years ago, and still only a very few replied.'[90] Disheartened with their enrolment of only sixty new members in four months, King and Mowers concluded that they had made a 'gross error in judgement' concerning the popular demand for a Canadian FOR. Clearly, the heightened international tensions of the later 1930s were taking their toll of pacifist sentiment.

Still, King and Mowers were encouraged by the formation of some new units, especially among FCSO members. J.W.E. Newbery of All Peoples' Mission in Sudbury organized an FOR unit, and in the North Bay area the Fellowship for Constructive Peace headed by Clare Oke of Sundridge, Ontario, announced its support for the FOR.[91] On the east coast Fred Young, a United Church minister in Tryon, Prince Edward Island, promoted both the FCSO and the FOR as the means to convince people of the underlying economic causes of war.[92] Young was one of the few FOR supporters in the Maritimes.

In their leaflet entitled 'Our Battle for Peace,' the Toronto branch of the FCSO endorsed the FOR as well as other peace organizations in an urgent appeal for all Christians to work for peace in spite of the 'apparently unbridgeable gulf of opinion as to the methods of peace-making' within the FCSO.[93] Some members, such as Eugene Forsey and Stanley Allen, had begun to move away even from the FCSO because of their CCF commitments and the FCSO's willingness to continue a broader front of operations, including support for MacLeod's League for Peace and Democracy, which Forsey and Allen, among others, saw as a Communist party front. Obviously, the pressure of international events of the second half of the decade was fragmenting the peace movement once more, and there were now a number of options for achieving an ultimately peaceful world; the FCSO could barely hold together, and pacifists were forced to look for another home. Indeed, their non-pacifist colleagues such as R.B.Y. Scott and Gregory Vlastos supported the validity of the absolute pacifist position for some people and encouraged pacifists to join the FOR.[94] But the divisions were deepening. In the spring of 1939 Clare Oke reported that the Peace Committee of the FCSO had decided that the best contribution a divided FCSO could make to world peace was to attempt to bring about a more equitable social order. 'I have a growing conviction,' Oke concluded, 'that the FOR with its pacifistic method is perhaps the wiser in its policy even in relation to the evolving of a better society.'[95]

A similar criticism of the FCSO's retreat from pacifism was levelled by Stanley Knowles. In regard to the FOR, Knowles welcomed 'the possibility of uniting and consolidating pacifist opinion' and pledged his support. He also predicted that the majority of the FCSO members in Winnipeg would join the FOR, since they were in 'full sympathy' with its basis and aims.[96]

The prospect of a new FOR unit in Winnipeg and a report of similar action in Edmonton was welcome news to Canadian pacifists in 1939. In addition, a stronger FOR unit was being organized in Vancouver, largely through the efforts of Robert Tillman, the SCM chairman in British Columbia, and Ernest Bishop, a theological student. What seemed to be the most encouraging news, however, came from Toronto, where the FOR unit of approximately thirty-five pacifists elected R.J. Irwin, an FCSO minister, and Raymond Booth chairman and vice-chairman respectively. According to the secretary, Joe Round, the Toronto group planned to launch a 'militant! pacifist effort.' 'I would like to express the private hope,' Round told King, 'that you will bombard us with all sorts of proposals for pacifist action.'[97] Despite Round's pledge to 'drop all other activities in favour of the peace work,' his optimistic appraisal of the

Toronto organization and rumours of a thousand pacifists active there, Mowers feared that the Toronto unit was 'practically dead.'[98] And in truth, the FOR in Toronto was disorganized and beset with dissension until well into the war years.

Although finally organized on a national basis, the Canadian FOR was still a relatively small, weak entity. Moreover, the gradual defection of FCSO allies further heightened the sense of isolation among pacifists. It was not surprising, therefore, that the national organization in Canada sought a closer association with fellow pacifists in other countries, particularly the neighbouring United States. The move in that direction was apparent by autumn 1938, when the American FOR publication *Fellowship* began to feature a regular report on the Canadian movement from an official Canadian correspondent, Jack Duckworth.[99] It was also at that time that efforts were renewed to affiliate the Canadians with the American branch, an arrangement favoured by John Nevin Sayre for several years. In November the executive secretary of the FOR in the United States, Harold E. Fey, reminded Duckworth that the American council planned to consider the affiliation of the Canadian group the following month and therefore needed a copy of the Canadian statement of purpose. If it was 'sufficiently near' to the American statement he foresaw no objections to the idea.[100] Fey also outlined what he thought would be the basis of such an affiliation. The Canadian fellowship would receive a special group membership in the American FOR and would have official representation at American meetings; in return, the American branch would continue to supply various services and guest speakers as well as its magazine *Fellowship*. A few days later Sayre reassured Carlyle King that despite the failure of the Montreal group to act upon his proposal in the previous year, 'the way is open today, as it always has been, at this end for some form of affiliation, if that is what our Canadian brothers want.'[101]

It appears that most of the Canadian members did favour affiliation with the American branch, perhaps because they were already familiar with the American organization or because they felt the need to consolidate pacifists in North America. In any case, King informed Sayre that the Canadian council had agreed to affiliate with the American FOR on the basis of Fey's letter to Duckworth, and he enclosed a copy of the Canadian Statement of Basis and Aims for American approval.[102]

The statement, however, revealed a conflicting difference between the Canadian and American sections. It identified the Canadian FOR as 'an association of men and women who believe in the non-violent settlement of all conflicts' and listed several ways in which they could express their faith, from personal relationships to the refusal to sanction war. The most controversial part concerned the omission of a predominantly Christian basis of belief: 'Many of the members have joined because of their desire to follow unswervingly the way of life exemplified by Jesus; some have received their inspiration from other religious leaders, and some have reached their faith in love and non-violence in still other ways.'[103]

In his letter to Sayre, King had pointed out that Canadians desired a broad statement in order to attract all pacifist groups. 'We have felt that there is room in Canada for only one pacifist organization and accordingly have drafted our statement of Basis and Aims in such a way as to make it acceptable not only to Christian pacifists but to people who are pacifists on other grounds.'[104] Since the statement closely followed the American version in all other respects, King felt there was likely to be no problem.

Nevertheless, Sayre was dubious about the Canadian movement and criticized the Canadian statement for its lack of emphasis on Christian belief. He advised the Canadians to revise their statement, especially since Canadian-American affiliation was contingent upon the international FOR's granting official recognition to their group. As it stood, Sayre warned, the international FOR executive committee, of which he was chairman, might wonder if the Canadian statement 'does not relegate Jesus to the periphery of the Canadian Fellowship instead of having him at the center.'[105] What Sayre wished to see inserted in the Canadian statement was some reference to Jesus, perhaps something similar to the American assertion that FOR members 'believe that love, such as that seen preeminently in Jesus, must serve as the true guide for personal conduct under all circumstances; and they seek to demonstrate this love as the effective force for overcoming evil and transforming society into a creative fellowship.'[106] Sayre closed by reminding Canadians that the international FOR was convinced that its affiliated branches 'must be definitely and predominantly Christian.'

Annoyed and offended at the tone if not the content of Sayre's letter, King shared his thoughts on the matter with the other members of the national council:

Mr Sayre insists that the FOR should be primarily a Christian pacifist movement. Our Council agreed that in Canada we should try to unite Christian and non-Christian in a pacifist program, and agreed to a statement of basis and aims which should be acceptable to both. We have been able, as you know, to work out such a statement – a statement which embodies a whole philosophy of life embracing personal, social, national and international conduct. That is, we have been about our business of reconciling diverse points of view and uniting people of differing religious attitudes around a program of good will to all men. We have succeeded in that, only to be told by Mr Sayre that we ought to be sectarian. He asks us to revise our statement to make it specifically Christian.[107]

King also maintained that Sayre's letter 'politely but clearly' implied a lack of confidence in the Canadian chairman, underlined by the fact that copies of the letter were sent directly to the other members of the national council. Consequently, King felt compelled to resign as chairman unless he was reassured of the continued support of the council.

Reports from the national council unanimously supported King as chairman and expressed surprise at the whole affair. The Montreal group was particularly puzzled and wrote Sayre asking him if there was not some mistake and if he had received the final version of the Canadian Statement of Basis and Aims. With respect to their relegation of Jesus to the periphery, Duckworth emphasized that they did 'not so interpret it.'[108] In reply, Sayre reiterated his view that the Canadians should demonstrate that they regarded Jesus as 'more authoritative for the Fellowship than other teachers of non-violence – for instance, Gandhi.'[109] Sayre also reported that he had been assured by Raymond Booth that the Canadian fellowship was 'definitely and certainly Christian.' If that was indeed the case, he argued, 'in the interests of frankness and clarity, it should be so indicated in your statement of basis.'

After meeting with Sayre in New York, Booth notified King that he was in sympathy with Sayre's demand for a strictly Christian statement, since it stemmed from the past experience of the American FOR with an infiltration by 'Communists and other borers-from-within.'[110] Booth confided that the Toronto group had suffered a similar experience when it was first organized. 'Our Toronto FOR was organized upon such a broad basis,' he wrote, 'and for this I am quite largely responsible, that we attracted to ourselves all the people who were itching for a fight.'[111] Booth concluded that he agreed with Sayre that only those with 'an abiding conviction of the fundamentally spiritual nature of the universe' would be loyal to the pacifist cause.[112]

Despite assurances from Canadian members of their strong Christian bias, Sayre remained sceptical of the Canadian movement and King's leadership in particular. Since it appeared that King did not wish to revise the Canadian statement, Sayre suggested that Canadians try to organize along the lines of the Peace Pledge Union or the War Resisters International. 'But, obviously ... if you want your organization to be the all-inclusive pacifist type,' wrote Sayre, 'you should not use the name "Fellowship of Reconciliation," which stands for something different.'[113] Sayre reminded King that a Christian pacifist organization such as the FOR could include a minority of non-Christian members as long as its statement of purpose was appropriately Christian.

Although Booth favoured amending the Canadian statement according to Sayre's suggestions, most of the other members on the national council did not. Neither did they consider the Peace Pledge Union or War Resisters' International as real alternatives to the FOR. Sayre obviously did not understand conditions in Canada, where the peace movement was predominantly Christian and yet so small that it required no more than one national organization to consolidate pacifists. Canada's Christian pacifists wanted that organization to be the FOR, but they agreed with King on the importance of sheltering all those who embraced pacifism, regardless of their religious beliefs. Ironically, Sayre's pressure for a Christian statement came at a time when Christians in Canada were dividing precisely over the Christian response to the looming prospect of war.

In May 1939, Clare Oke wrote King that the members of his local group in the North Bay-Sundridge area recommended that 'the Canadian FOR apply for affiliation with the International FOR at once on the basis of our present statement of principles and aims.'[114] They felt that any revisions should be considered only if the international council indicated its dissatisfaction. King was also encouraged in this regard when Halliday reported that the British pacifist leader, Canon Charles Raven, had intimated that he saw nothing wrong with the Canadian statement.[115]

Consequently, on 19 May 1939 King formally applied for affiliation of the Canadian organization with the international FOR. In his letter to Percy Bartlett, secretary of the international body, King expressed the hope for a favourable reception despite Sayre's doubts concerning the Canadian statement.[116]

The Canadian request was laid before the international FOR executive council meeting at Fanø, Denmark, on 9 June. A few weeks later Bartlett reported that the council had rejected the Canadian bid for affiliation because the Canadian statement of basis 'did not approach quite closely enough to the definitely Christian phrasing required of an officially recognized branch of the International Fellowship.'[117] Although he had not been present at the Fanø meeting, Sayre reported that the international council did desire fellowship with the Canadians; he patronizingly expressed the hope that the Canadian group would overcome their difficulty with their statement in the near future.[118]

The Canadian council, while disappointed, generally favoured revision of the Statement of Basis and Aims. Lavell Smith wrote King that he believed the majority of Canadian FOR members now supported the idea of a specifically Christian movement.[119] Smith also warned that pacifists who lacked a religious foundation for their convictions were already falling out. As an example he cited G.M.A. Grube, the editor of the *Canadian Forum* and a founding member of the LSR, who had written numerous articles in support of pacifism during the 1930s. By the end of the decade, however, Grube confessed that he lacked the type of religious conviction necessary to sustain a pacifist stand in the light of contemporary problems.[120]

Despite Smith's interest in a revised statement, council members failed to take any action in that regard or to make further suggestions to King.[121] Instead, pacifists began to turn their attention to more immediate issues such as plans to unite conscientious objectors in Canada – a hint of what was on the horizon.[122] As far as the Canadian FOR was concerned, its statement remained unchanged as it hobbled along, with King's assistance, in an attempt to serve Canadian pacifists in the face of approaching international disaster.

v

Besides causing a loss in prestige, the FOR's failure to become an official part of an international pacifist network left Canadian pacifists isolated and loosely organized at the close of the decade. The last pre-war display of pacifist solidarity occurred during the summer of 1939 as representatives of various pacifist and youth organizations gathered on the shore of Lake Simcoe for a weekend peace conference. The purpose of the meeting was to discuss ways and means of spreading the pacifist answer to modern violence and war. Conference participants, largely young people, expressed the conviction that it was 'high time pacifists made overtures to producer groups, co-operatives, and labour unions, as well as campaigning in the churches.'[123] Dr Willard Brewing of St George's United Church in Toronto reminded the pacifists that they were 'pledged to refuse participation in all wars, whether civil, class, or imperialist.' Other participants argued that the major task of pacifists was to work for a new social order without the competitive profit-motivated tensions that lead to war. The suggestion was also made that 'sincere pacifists should express their sympathy with the underpriviledged, by living on a minimum allowance and giving away the rest of their salary.'

Speaking in a personal vein and revealing his recent change of heart, George Grube emphasized how difficult it was to be active in politics and still hold pacifist ideals. He told the crowd that pacifists 'could have little influence in politics and should be content to play the role of the social prophet in society.' Grube evidently had reached that conclusion earlier in the year when he was at the centre of a controversy concerning free speech. It erupted after he sponsored a motion at an Ontario CCF convention condemning Canadian defence expenditures as a waste of money in the interests of British imperialism. When the issue was raised in the Ontario legislature, Premier Mitchell Hepburn branded Grube a foreigner and a communist and threatened to cut off financial support to Trinity College if Grube was not removed from its faculty. Although Grube rode out the storm, his defence of free speech strengthened his commitment to democracy at a crucial time. He concluded that, although he believed non-intervention in any European war was the best policy for Canada, as a democrat he would support the majority decision of his countrymen even if it meant supporting a war.[124] His critical analysis of the weakness of the pacifist answer to political and international tensions sparked considerable discussion among the delegates.

By the time it closed, the conference was credited with arousing 'enthusiasm and renewed vigour' in the peace movement. Plans were formulated to begin training people in the ideas and methods of non-violence and a motion was passed to encourage the Fellowship of Reconciliation to organize an even larger pacifist convention in Toronto the following year in order to launch an extensive peace campaign. Although these ambitious plans were later curtailed by the outbreak of the war, the *United Church Observer*, caught up in the spirit of the moment, concluded that 'Toronto pacifists have a close knit body who mean to translate their theories into action and have decided to move from the realm of talking, into the realm of action!'[125]

At about the same time, a controversy was raging in the *Observer's* reader's forum which pointed out the sharp divisions within the United Church over the pacifist issue and the proper Christian attitude to war. The barrage of letters was incited by a statement by William Iverach of Isabella, Manitoba, that war was not unchristian. One contributor argued that war 'in defence of international law and order or in resistance to lawless aggression' was the proper Christian response. Another writer suggested that Christians could wage war, but not in the name of Christ. Still another accused Iverach of committing a 'great sin' in attempting to link the New Testament with war.[126] Cleo Mowers, the national FOR secretary from Saskatoon, maintained that pacifists did not need biblical authority since it was enough that the hate and killing of war were contrary to the spirit of Jesus.[127] Edis Fairbairn suggested that Iverach had inadvertently 'rendered a service to the whole Church in expressing bluntly and forcibly the average man's reaction to the Church's repudiation of war.' Iverach was not to be blamed because the pulpit had failed to explain the latest developments in Christian thinking on the problem of war. In particular, Fairbairn referred to the Oxford pronouncement's allowance of the absolute pacifist position.

In his response to the controversy Iverach thanked the *Observer* for opening the 'all-important question' for discussion, thereby showing 'the every-day members of the United Church where a section of its ministers stand on some great national questions ... It exposes, too, the attempt of the pacifist section of our ministry to set themselves up as a sort of super-Christian.'[128] Despite the eleventh-hour surge of enthusiasm among Toronto pacifists, Iverach's defence of Christian participation in war probably reflected accurately the public mood at the end of the decade.

VI

During the second half of the 1930s, the Canadian peace movement was reduced to a shadow of its former self. A wholesale abandonment of pacifism occurred as the suppressed inner divisions inherent in any broad movement surfaced in response to increased international tensions and the theological search for political realism. The fascist threat to world peace began to sort out the supporters of collective security and possible military action from the absolute pacifists, while the Spanish Civil War further disrupted the alliance between pacifists and the radical left. Consequently, internationalists and social radicals began to abandon their pacifist ideals, particularly as they re-evaluated the proper Christian response to war. The churches themselves had refused to endorse a strictly pacifist position and some churchmen again began to advocate the armed defence of Christian civilization.

In response to this crisis, committed pacifists in the Society of Friends, the WIL, and the FOR reorganized and consolidated their forces. Furthermore, since the political relevance of pacifism appeared to dwindle with each instance of international violence, socially radical pacifists gradually retreated to the position that war was absolutely and always wrong – not entirely unlike the sectarian creed of the historic peace churches. Indeed, by the end of the decade the once broadly based peace movement had contracted to the point where it often resembled a quasi-religious sect. This was especially true of the FOR as its membership moved towards a strictly Christian basis of organization. Nevertheless, the Canadian FOR was destined to become the core around which Canada's non-sectarian pacifists would coalesce during the war years.

7

The courage of conviction

The Second World War began on 1 September, 1939, when Germany invaded Poland. Two days later Britain declared war. Legally, Canada was also at war, but, in contrast to the 'Ready, aye, ready' attitude of 1914, the Canadian government symbolically maintained a policy of neutrality for a week before it committed Canada to participating in the world conflict.[1] From the pacifists' perspective the worst had happened: they were isolated in a world that had gone to war despite their own best efforts. The consequences in human suffering were nightmarish to contemplate. As suspect members of the national community, what could they now do? The depression had sharply honed their social consciences, but what could now be accomplished on that front? The first two years of war were especially agonizing for Canadian pacifists: they would protest and debate in the columns of the church press, outspoken pacifist clergy would find their pastorates challenged, even the Fellowship for a Christian Social Order would experience a hardening of lines, and Niebuhrian neo-orthodoxy would have to be confronted anew. Much of their time, one suspects, was spent in silent agony, to which they occasionally gave expression. Of necessity they leaned on each other for mutual support and summoned what courage they could to meet the future. Survival was a critical concern, but their consciences told them that mere survival was not a sufficient role in such a time. What was really needed was the translation of their religious, social, and political convictions into some meaningful form of war resistance.

Canadian pacifists also discovered that the experience of the Second World War was to be quite different from that of the First World War. For one thing, there was a noticeable coolness in the Canadian response to the thought of war in 1939. As Donald Creighton has recorded, 'Canadians had lost, or were losing, some of their moral extremism as well as their evangelical zeal.'² In the end Canada did go to war, in part because Britain went to war, but also because most Canadians were convinced by four years of international turmoil and fascist aggression that war was unavoidable. In both respects, a sober reluctance hung over the land:

There were no crowds around newspaper offices, no bands in the streets, no impassioned singing of *God Save the King* or *La Marseillaise*. The memories of 1914–18, the terrible casualties of that war, and the divisions it left in the fabric of the nation were still too deep for that. The disillusionment over the failure of the 1930's, over the collapse of the League of Nations, and over the weaknesses of British policy – all were too clear ... Above all, the great depression had sapped the will of the people. For the first time many Canadians might even have wondered if the system was worth fighting for.³

O.D. Skelton, under-secretary for external affairs and an ardent isolationist, noted at the time that there was little enthusiasm even among the war supporters. He doubted if the majority of Canadians would have voted for war in a free plebiscite, and observed that the main reason the anti-war forces failed to muster a more significant opposition to Canada's entry into the war was because they lacked effective leadership. To be sure, support for the once-popular peace movement had dwindled in response to the growing Nazi menace. Nevertheless, the lack of Canadian enthusiasm for war reflected to a certain extent the successful growth during the 1930s of pacifist, isolationist, and socialist sentiment which pacifists still hoped to exploit in their struggle to maintain a pacifist front.

By the eve of the Second World War, therefore, pacifists had aligned themselves with isolationists and some socialists in the demand for Canadian neutrality. Despite their strong belief in the necessity of building a new social order on an international scale, neutrality was urged by pacifists as a last-ditch effort to keep Canada out of war. Amid the escalating fascist aggression of the late 1930s, however, pacifists were bound to identify with more isolationist-minded Canadians who recoiled from all international entanglements in an effort to preserve peace and protect Canada from European and imperialist violence. Thus, pacifism became irrevocably linked with isolationism.

Under the commanding influence of Frank Underhill, the League for Social Reconstruction became a leading exponent of neutral isolationism.[4] Underhill urged that Canadians refrain from lending military support to Britain in a European struggle, since such action would only assure 'the burying of 60,000 more Canadians somewhere across the ocean.' 'It may be that another such mass burial service will assure world peace, or democracy, or freedom – *after* the next war,' he wrote. 'But our experiece during and since the last war should have made us skeptical to such claims.'[5] In an attempt to help maintain neutrality, the LSR demanded a national plebiscite on the question of Canada's participation in war, similar to the referendum proposed earlier by the Women's International League for Peace and Freedom and the Saskatoon Peace Group.[6]

A slightly different type of anti-war sentiment existed in Quebec. Formed along neutralist and Quebec nationalist lines, French-Canadian opposition to the Second World War made no pretence to pacifism. As in the First World War, Quebec was worried about conscription rather than the principle of non-violence. A similar stand in favour of neutrality was taken by Canada's communists, especially after the signing of the Hitler-Stalin pact of August 1939. Nevertheless, despite such diverse support, an official policy of neutrality was totally unacceptable to most Canadians. Pacifists clearly recognized this fact, and yet they still believed there was room for dissent in a liberal society at war.

I

The political reaction to the Canadian entry into war was varied. The Liberal party was divided, primarily because of French-Canadian opposition to war, but the cabinet, including the ministers from Quebec, was solidly behind the prime minister. Likewise, consistent with their Tory heritage, the Conservatives vigorously supported the decision to go to war, and their leader, Dr R.J. Manion, pledged his co-operation with the government. The party most seriously torn by the war issue was the CCF. As early as 1937 the CCF had begun to modify its pacifist policy; a committee of the national council rephrased the party's foreign policy statement so as to urge neutrality only in the event of an 'imperialist' war.[7] Although Woodsworth continued to press for strict neutrality, the party's interventionist forces, led by George Williams, president of the party in Saskatchewan, mounted an undercurrent of opposition to a party policy of pacifism and neutrality which finally surfaced in the 1939 debate on the war.[8]

The CCF national council met in emergency session from the sixth to the eighth of September. The council was sharply divided over the issue. In the end, a committee worked out a compromise between the all-out war effort advocated by Williams's faction and the absolute neutrality of Woodsworth and his fellow pacifists; the result was qualified support of the war but opposition to sending men overseas. The decision of the party was a complete reversal of its previous official policy of neutrality and a repudiation of Woodsworth's pacifism. It was decided that the party's new position would be stated in the House of Commons by the national chairman, M.J. Coldwell, thus freeing Woodsworth to voice his unyielding personal opposition to war.

The CCF council was in the midst of reaching its compromise position when the special war session of Parliament was convened on 7 September. In the Speech from the Throne the government sought approval for Canadian entry into the war.[9] It was no surprise to the House, and, assured of the support of both the Conservatives and the CCF, the prime minister knew there would be little opposition to the request. In the brief debate that followed there was a steady stream of support for war; even one-time peace activists such as Agnes Macphail sided with the government. Despite almost two decades of pacifist rhetoric and pledges of 'never again,' Canada was at war three days after the special session opened.

Only one voice was raised in the House in opposition to Canada's entry into the war. J.S. Woodsworth, freed from the constraints of his party's position, spoke out on behalf of his own conscience and the pacifist minority in Canada. His address was an eloquent appeal for neutrality and pacifism. Woodsworth began by questioning the meaning of the government's statement. He argued that the House had a right to know every aspect of government policy. Would an expeditionary force be sent to Europe? Would wealth be conscripted? Woodsworth also maintained that if Canada was not already at war there was no reason to have reinstated the War Measures Act.[10]

Most of Woodsworth's remarks, however, were devoted to his unswerving pacifist conviction. In his biography of Woodsworth, Kenneth McNaught argues that in 'the final analysis' it was Woodsworth's 'estimate of capitalism that produced his pacifism.'[11] While McNaught admits that this pacifism 'came to have a high emotional content not dissimilar to that of a religious pacifist', he seems to overstate the material aspect of Woodsworth's beliefs. To be sure, Woodsworth's socialism and pacifism were probably inseparable; nevertheless, it appears that in 'the final analysis,' at least judging from his famous address to the

House, the basis of Woodsworth's pacifism was religious. While it is true he argued that war was 'the inevitable outcome of the present economic and international system with its injustices, exploitations and class interests,' he also emphasized that pacifism, although not necessarily Christian, was a religious and moral force.[12]

Discussing the nature of his own pacifist belief, Woodsworth recalled that he had left the ministry of the church during the First World War because of his opposition to war. Although he no longer had any particular church affiliation and his creed was 'pretty vague,' he claimed that he still believed in the principles 'underlying the teachings of Jesus and the other great world teachers throughout centuries.' For him and for a 'growing number of men and women in the churches' war was an 'absolute negation of anything Christian.' Of course, it required a great deal of courage to trust in moral force, but he reminded the House that there was a time when people thought 'there were other and higher types of force than brute force.' 'That,' he explained, 'is what the church fathers used to call faith. It requires a great deal of courage to carry out our convictions; to have peace requires both courage and sacrifice.'[13]

Woodsworth also spoke in defence of individual pacifist dissent and extended encouragement to young Canadians contemplating the alternative of conscientious objection to military service. 'I do not care whether you think me an impossible idealist or a dangerous crank,' he stated. 'I am going to take my place beside the children and those young people, because it is only as we adopt new policies that this world will be at all a livable place for our children who follow us.' He continued, 'I have boys of my own, and I hope they are not cowards, but if any one of those boys, not from cowardice but really through belief, is willing to take his stand on this matter and, if necessary, to face a concentration camp or a firing squad, I shall be more proud of that boy than if he enlisted for the war.'[14]

Interrupted at this point by cries of 'Shame', Woodsworth emphasized that pacifism was not only his belief but the conviction of a growing number of Canadians as well. He then thanked the House for the courtesy shown him, recognizing that it was possible to make statements in a Canadian parliament that would not be possible in Germany. In fact, he said, he believed the only way 'to maintain the very essence of our British institutions of real liberty' was by 'an appeal to the moral forces which are still resident among our people, and not by another resort to brute force.'

So ended Woodsworth's last major speech in the House. In a sense it was his farewell to his party and his country, neither of which followed him on the pacifist trail he had blazed in Parliament. Within two years the pacifist-socialist pioneer was dead. While he had not assumed the role of Canadian pacifist leader during his last years, Woodsworth had reiterated his warnings against conscription and his demand for the nationalization of war industries.[15] Above all, his address to the special war session became an inspiration to Canadian pacifists in a time of crisis. Fred Haslam, as an adviser to prospective conscientious objectors in the Society of Friends, kept a copy of Woodsworth's speech on hand throughout the war.

In his address Woodsworth had expressed confidence, from the scores of telegrams and letters he had received, that there were 'thousands upon thousands' of Canadians who shared his pacifist conviction;[16] he felt he had voiced their feelings as well as his own. A further avalanche of mail followed the speech, the bulk of which, if not in complete agreement with his pacifism, at least commended his stand.[17] For example, C.C. Annett of Winnipeg wrote Woodsworth that he approved heartily of his position and added that many others also agreed with him 'even though they may lack the moral courage to stand up and say so.'[18] From the Canadian legation in Washington, Escot Reid wrote, 'I have read with the greatest admiration your most moving speech in the House of Commons. That is a speech of which you and your friends will always be proud. Their pride will increase as time goes on and we can see the events of these days in better perspective.'[19] A young man from Calgary expressed admiration and appreciation of Woodsworth's pacifist stand and offered his assistance in furthering the cause of peace. The writer, Howard Patton, claimed he shared similar pacifist convictions, as did the majority of young people with whom he had associated over the last two years.[20] A somewhat different letter of praise came from H.G.L. Strange, director of agricultural research for the Searle Grain Company of Winnipeg. Although Strange was not a pacifist, he found himself in 'complete agreement with almost everything' Woodsworth said. 'Just as I feel it my duty to do all I can to win this war,' wrote Strange, 'so likewise do I feel it my duty to do everything I possibly can to respect and esteem the stand that true Christians like you take.'[21] Obviously, Woodsworth's stand in no way threatened the solidarity of political support for the war effort, but the outpouring of 'deep admiration' for his moral courage and faith revealed that he had succeeded in setting an important, albeit isolated, example of pacifist dissent within the political arena.

II

Admiration for Woodsworth's pacifism was not reflected in the churches' official reaction to the war. Prior to the war, pacifism had been a popular topic of debate among Canadian Protestants; but it was a muddled debate, because few churchmen were prepared to argue forcefully that war was unchristian without implying absolute pacifism. In effect, they tended to condemn war per se while at the same time sidestepping the whole issue of what to do 'when the bombs begin to fall.'[22] Despite their concern with peace, therefore, they remained unprepared to support a pacifist or even semi-pacifist course of action for Christians confronted with the reality of war. In the autumn of 1939 Protestants began to repudiate their 'unrealistic' flirtations with the pacifism of the 1930s. In his study of the churches and Canada's war effort, Thomas Sinclair-Faulkner has shown that the major churches in Canada, Protestant and Roman Catholic alike, accepted the war as a fight 'for Christian civilization.' Shortly after the beginning of the war, Canada's major Protestant denominations – Anglican, Baptist, Presbyterian, and United Church – issued a joint statement on the war: 'We believe that our cause is the cause of Christian civilization, and that Divine power and guidance will be given to us to win victory for it, however hard the road we must first travel.'[23] In general, the Roman Catholic church abided by the doctrine expounded by Bishop Briand in 1775 of obedience to oath and king. Nevertheless, although it did not believe the war raised the issue of pacifism or even of 'just war,' the Catholic church in Quebec displayed little enthusiasm for the war. For instance, Cardinal Villeneuve, the archbishop of Quebec and the head of the Canadian hierarchy, remained relatively silent on the question of war.[24] English-Canadian Catholics, were more vocal in their support, and many criticized the isolationist sentiment.

The mainstream Protestant churches all supported the declaration of war, but they differed in their reasons for doing so and in the degree of their enthusiasm. Contrary to their extreme zeal during the later years of the First World War, most Protestant newspapers urged respect for pacifists even while they lent encouragement and support to those who chose to fight in a just war. Baptists, especially fundamentalists like T.T. Shields of Toronto's Jarvis Street Baptist Church, were the most vocal in their demand for a maximum Canadian war effort, and even advocated conscription.[25] Anglicans and Presbyterians supported the war with a little less enthusiasm, but, like the Baptists, their decision was never really complicated by pacifist considerations.

It was the United Church that was the most deeply torn between pacifism and support for the war. The mid-depression posture of the United Church was difficult to reconcile with an all-out war effort. Throughout the interwar years the general council had adopted successive resolutions condemning war, but its open debate over pacifism 'offered little practical help in giving leadership during actual war conditions.' Apparently aware of the confusion, J.R. Mutchmor, secretary of the United Church's Board of Evangelical Social Service, called a series of meetings the week before Hitler invaded Poland in order to consider a proper course of action for the United Church in the impending crisis. The participants agreed with Mutchmor that war was 'contrary to the mind of Christ,' but questioned the 'practical value of such an ultimate ethic' as pacifism in the present circumstances. Furthermore, while they agreed that citizens had a duty to disobey 'unjust and tyrannical' governments, they were strongly against basing such civil disobedience solely on an individual's private judgment.[26] These deliberations appeared to weaken the 1938 general council's sanction of conscientious objection to military service. A week later, however, the moderator of the United Church, John W. Woodside, sent a pastoral letter to the clergy concerning the church's response to the war in which he reiterated official church support for the right of conscientious objection: 'We must affirm for ourselves and our brethren the paramount authority of conscience under the leadership of Christ. We are at war with a power which seems to disregard conscience; and we must not fall into what we hold to be its error.'[27]

At first the moderator's letter appeared to calm those who feared that the United Church would take too militaristic a stand, including the well-known pacifist, Richard Roberts. Roberts wrote his daughter that he had been made particularly hopeful by the moderator's stand. 'It is very cheering to me ... I had to resign from my congregation in 1914 for saying the things that apparently all the United Church ministers are saying these days. It is not that they have become pacifists, but that they have come to see that the Gospel and war are at extreme antipodes from one another.'[28] Jack Duckworth, general secretary of the Notre Dame de Grâce YMCA, told Roberts that a group of laymen and YMCA directors in Montreal had agreed that the business of the church in wartime was to preach peace and good will, not to foment a warlike spirit. Perhaps because of its earlier pacifist inclinations, the United Church appears to have been somewhat uncomfortable in its internal support of the war. But the optimism of Roberts and Duckworth was not completely warranted, especially in the light of the church's ambiguity in defining its exact position with regard to pacifist dissent. Nevertheless, shortly after the Canadian declaration of war on 10 September 1939, the presbyteries of the United Church unanimously endorsed the general council's expression of loyalty to the government of Canada.[29] Unlike similar statements by the other major churches, however, the United Church's announcement was not without serious repercussions.

III

Although clearly in a minority, pacifists within the United Church were in a defiant mood, especially since it appeared that their church was about to surrender to the war spirit and perhaps repudiate its declared support for the pacifist alternatives, if not actually repeat its over-zealous crusade of the Great War. Pacifists were also repelled by the behaviour of the church during the first few weeks of war, particularly when a newly formed War Services Committee actually met four days before Canada officially declared war. Consequently, the likely prospect of the United Church's war effort ultimately leading to a complete apostasy compelled the pacifist minority to speak out against the war in radical defiance of the authority of their church. Their protest took the form of a letter to the editor of the *United Church Observer*.[30] It was the first instance of an organized public declaration of pacifist dissent within a Canadian denomination.

Entitled 'A Witness against the War,' the pacifist manifesto was signed by 68 United Church ministers, mostly from Toronto and Montreal but representative of the whole country. It included an invitation to others to forward their names for later publication. A month later the *Observer* published an additional 64 names, lay and clerical, which brought the total of published signatories to 132.[31]

The manifesto began with reference to the declaration of the general council of 1938, which officially recognized pacifism as a legitimate Christian alternative in time of war. Accordingly, the ad hoc committee of ministers felt they were merely exercising their right as pacifists to disapprove of the war. They recognized that other ministers and church members, 'equally sincere,' felt duty-bound to support the war and they respected their right to do so. Nevertheless, they believed their own pacifist convictions, 'characteristic of the earliest Christian Church, and of many reform movements throughout the centuries,' represented a truer Christian position. 'It is generally agreed and confessed that Christendom has through the centuries sadly and seriously fallen short in faithfulness to Christ. We are convinced that at no point has Christendom departed so radically from the mind of Christ and its own original faith as in its acceptance of war.'[32] As to the question of war itself, they stated forcefully that 'the will and Kingdom of God must take precedence over the national convenience or policy' and emphasized that the nature of modern warfare was especially incompatible with Christianity. The manifesto quoted the British prime ministers Baldwin and Chamberlain on the futility of war.

The most important point of the 'Witness against War' concerned the signatories' desire to preserve the soul of the church. They pointed out that 'the Churches lost heavily in spiritual authority because of their general surrender to the war spirit' during the First World War. 'We think it ought to be placed on record now, in view of the further loss of spiritual authority, probable if the Church sanctions this present war, that at least some representatives of the Christian Churches disapproved and uttered their protest.'[33] The manifesto concluded by emphasizing the desire on the part of the signatories to perform some constructive pacifist action in the days ahead: 'We affirm that we are not seeking escape from the burden or sacrifice, and we profess our readiness to implement our citizen loyalty in some form of service equally as taxing, difficult, and dangerous as military service, providing it does not contribute directly to the war effort.'[34]

Although it was publicized as a joint effort, the drafting and circulation of the 'Witness against War' manifesto was almost entirely the work of Edis Fairbairn of Bracebridge, Ontario, assisted by his Montreal and Toronto associates in the Fellowship for a Christian Social Order and the Fellowship of Reconciliation. Well known for his radical pacifism, Fairbairn was also acquainted with the nature of church politics. He had long realized that the United Church was not pacifist, but he was dismayed by the speed with which church officials were diverting their energy into moral support of the war. The manifesto was intended to 'force the Church to recognize the moral dilemma posed by the war' and to advertise the conscientious commitment he and some others shared.[35] Despite Fairbairn's radical nature, the 'Witness against War' was a temperate pacifist statement. It made no attempt to undermine the authority of the general council of 1938, nor did it advocate any type of civil disobedience.

Following initial approval of the statement, Fairbairn and his FCSO and FOR associates, including James M. Finlay and R.J. Irwin of Toronto and Lavell Smith and Clarence Halliday of Montreal, set out to collect as many signatures as possible. Twenty-two pacifists from the Toronto-Ottawa-Montreal area were the first to sign the manifesto before it was circulated under a cover letter signed by Finlay to other clergymen across Canada. Since the manifesto was given the widest possible circulation, it seems evident that the 'Witness against War' was also part of a continuing effort to consolidate or 'bring into fellowship' all Christian pacifists in the United Church as well as to organize some type of appropriate emergency pacifist action.[36] A meeting of the signatories from the Toronto area was held on 20 October 1939 at Carlton Street United Church in Toronto. Under its pacifist minister, James Finlay, the Carlton Street church, known as the 'House of Friendship,' often served as an unofficial meeting place for Toronto pacifists during the war. The meeting was held behind closed doors 'for freer discussion' with Finlay presiding, assisted by R.J. Irwin, minister of Donlands United Church and president of the Toronto Fellowship of Reconciliation, and Gordon Lapp, assistant minister of Westminster-Central United Church in Toronto.[37] The meeting succeeded in obtaining several more signatories to the list, boosting the total number of signatories to over seventy-five. Thereafter, the manifesto became known as the 'Protest of the Seventy-five.' Among the names added was that of Richard Roberts, who had mailed in his signature from Pine Hill Divinity School in Halifax.

The meeting decided to send a deputation composed of Fairbairn, Finlay, Irwin, and S.T. Martin of Hamilton to the War Services Committee of the United Church. The delegation was to urge the committee to redirect the church's war effort so as to focus attention on the future peace, to be completely honest about the causes and evils of war, to help conserve civil liberties, to assist 'refugee aliens both in the war and at home,' and to co-operate with the Society of Friends and similar pacifist groups.[38] In effect, the pacifists offered an alternative stance for the church in time of war. Before the pacifist challenge could be completely articulated, however, a nationwide controversy erupted over the 'Witness against War' manifesto.

In addition to condemnation from their peers within the church, the signatories also risked criminal prosecution under the section of the Defence of Canada Regulations pertaining to 'subversive teachings.' The office of the attorney-general of Ontario somehow received a copy of the pacifist manifesto on 10 October 1939, five days before its publication, but the attorney-general, Gordon D. Conant, did not order an official investigation until the matter made the front pages of Toronto's daily newspapers. Press reaction in Toronto and throughout the rest of the country was generally unsympathetic; editors at times argued that the war was actually caused by such pacifism.[39] The fact that the Toronto signatories met behind closed doors fuelled suspicion.

The Ontario attorney-general's staff finally concluded that the 'Witness against War' signatories did indeed violate the Defence of Canada Regulations on two counts: the publication of the manifesto was 'likely to prejudice the recruiting of His Majesty's forces,' and it would be 'prejudicial to the efficient prosecution of the war.'[40] Rather than launch a full-scale prosecution of the pacifist ministers, however, Conant referred the matter to the federal minister of justice. The reply from Ottawa expressed doubt that the pacifist statement would prejudice military recruiting, and recommended against prosecution. Accordingly, the attorney-general decided not to act. Instead, he called a press conference on 1 November, and in the presence of representatives of the United Church sub-executive and their legal counsel, he condemned the pacifist 'Witness' but announced that the government would leave it to the governing body of the church to 'render a sufficient verdict and provide the effective remedy.'[41]

The sub-executive of the general council had already met on 25 October to consider the 'Witness against War.' Their statement, published the very day of the attorney-general's press conference, steered a middle course that appeased neither the attorney-general's office nor the pacifist dissidents.[42] In effect, the sub-executive sidestepped the basic question concerning the right of Christian pacifists to concientiously object to the war. Instead, they concluded that too much attention had been given to a document that did not emanate from an official body of the church and then seized the opportunity to reaffirm that the church as a whole was completely loyal to the king and was ready 'to support him in the present dire struggle in every way which is open and proper to the Church.'[43] As far as the 'Witness against War' was concerned, the sub-executive expressed regret that the signatories had made their manifesto public, and then stated: 'The Church is determined to adhere to its previous declarations that it will protect the individual conscience, but in our judgement, by acting collectively and inviting signatures "for later publication", the signatories of this manifesto, however sincere, have gone far beyond the limits of what is wise and proper in time of war.'

Overall, the statement of the sub-executive appeared to be a prudent attempt to disassociate the Church from pacifist dissent, and it seemed inconsistent with the moderator's pastoral letter, which had urged tolerance and respect for the 'paramount authority of conscience under the leadership of Christ.'[44] R.B.Y. Scott, one of those who helped draft the moderator's letter, publicly registered his disappointment: 'The text of the Sub-Executive's statement is ... not quite the complete repudiation suggested by the press, but in effect it is a desertion of our comrades who are under fire because they have made an unpopular witness for conscience sake. The whole tenor of the official statement suggests that the Church's reputation for loyalty to the military enterprise of the State is a more important consideration than that of loyalty to religious conviction.'[45]

In reality, the sub-executive was badly split over the pacifist issue, and, after a heated debate, approved the final statement by only one vote.[46] According to a report Fairbairn received from a member of the sub-executive, there were 'threatenings of a split in the church' unless the sub-executive disowned the pacifists and supported the war.[47] In such a charged atmosphere the sub-executive could hardly settle the question of pacifist dissent, but it did attempt to protect individual con-science as long as it remained prudent to do so. This action, together with the decision of the attorney-gerneral's office not to intervene, calmed the fears that some type of disciplinary or legal action would be taken against the signatories.

Perhaps the presence of so well-respected a churchman as the former moderator, Richard Roberts, on the list facilitated that result. While it is true that his name had lent a certain credibility to the manifesto, Roberts himself had not been in favour of its publication. In fact, he had advised Fairbairn not to make a public declaration at that time, primarily because he considered the moderator's letter 'far in advance in its Chris-tian temper of any comparable document in 1914.'[48] But if a pacifist statement was publicized, he believed that he could not afford to let anyone suppose that he had 'ratted' from a conviction that he had held and publicly avowed since 1914 and that he had reaffirmed upon Canon Raven's visit to Toronto in March 1939. In any case, Roberts expected to see the final draft and receive further word before definite action was taken; however, Fairbairn and his associates had already 'taken the plunge.'[49] In a letter to Lavell Smith, Roberts remarked that the sound-ness of his 'caveat' was borne out by the fact that the 'Witness against War' had 'the effect of provoking the action of the sub-executive which virtually throws the Church on the side of war.'[50] Nevertheless, once the sub-executive released its statement, which he described as 'feeble' and 'cowardly,' Roberts expressed gratitude that his name was on the 'black list.' 'The sub-executive,' he wrote, 'should, in addition to "regretting," have affirmed the right of its ministers to hold and express dissenting convictions.'[51] Furthermore, from the deluge of letters he received following the publication of the 'Witness against War,' Roberts concluded that many others were in agreement with him: 'there is much more support in the church for the forthright Christian position on the matter than the sub-executive and the "patriotic" suppose. I wonder how long Christian churchmen are going to allow their nationalism to prevent their churchmanship – especially when the Ecumenical Church is beginning to enter into our calculations.'[52]

Roberts's reaction was shared by others. Lavell Smith, for instance, expressed disappointment that the sub-executive repudiated the pacifist witness 'without so much as a hint that the Church has ever denounced war.' At the same time, however, he was encouraged to find several men in Montreal who were 'standing staunchly' for the right of pacifists to make such a statement.[53]

The reluctance on the part of the sub-executive to come out in defence of pacifist dissent was also reflected in the general attitude of other committees as well as a sizeable portion of the church membership at large. The War Services Committee, for instance, sought no alternative ways to allow pacifists to perform non-military service related to the war crisis. Lavell Smith criticized the committee's stand as 'a trumpet call with but a single note' and pressed for some type of pacifist participation.[54] The delegation from the 'Witness against War' group made a similar plea when they attended the third meeting of the War Services Committee in October. Among their specific proposals was the recommendation that local congregations minister to the peculiar social, moral, and spiritual problems caused by the war among military personnel and their families. The pacifists also emphasized the need to maintain normal church services, and recommended that the church provide pastoral care for interned aliens and hospitality for refugee children from enemy nations.[55]

The response of the committee was generally unsympathetic. Most of the pacifists' requests were either ignored completely or merely acknowledged as unimportant and occasionally passed to other administrative divisions for consideration. The suggestion that the United Church ask the government to send Canadian pacifists overseas in order to help with reconstruction in Poland was dismissed as 'impractical.'[56] When the pacifists complained that the name 'War Services Committee' implied the church's 'wholesale support for the war,' they came close to the truth. It was soon evident that the aim of the committee was to maximize support for the war effort and to minister to soldiers, not pacifists. Having failed to convince the War Services Committee to create some type of pacifist service, the 'Witness against War' group ceased to function as an organized body.[57]

In addition to threats of legal sanctions, angry denunciations in the press, and virtual dismissal by the church hierarchy, the major fallout from the 'Witness against War' manifesto occurred in the individual congregations of the signatories. The reaction was generally unsympathetic. In most cases, a corps of wealthy congregational leaders forcefully denounced the pacifist ministers and demanded their resignations. In the end, several of the signatories were forced out of their churches; some accepted new stations, usually small northern posts, while others left the church entirely. Montreal's pacifists were seriously affected, since both Clarence Halliday and Lavell Smith were forced to resign from their respective churches, West United and Westmount Park United. During the first few years of the war, Halliday served as a voluntary chaplain to German refugees interned in camps outside of Montreal. Then, following a brief posting in the North, he left the ministry for social work, and ultimately became the head of the Children's Aid Society in Ottawa.[58]

The case of Lavell Smith was slightly different. By the time of the war, Smith had become known as one of the most promising young radical ministers in the United Church, and, although he also lost his posting because of the 'Witness against War' controversy, he remained one of the leading pacifist spokesmen in the church throughout the war years and after. Almost immediately following the outbreak of war but prior to the publication of the pacifist manifesto, Lavell Smith had reiterated his pacifism and outlined what he thought constituted a pacifist ministry in time of war.[59] Smith's outspoken pacifism had never been representative of the membership of Westmount Park United, one of the most imperialist-minded, pro-establishment congregations in the country. Following the publication of the 'Witness against War,' a powerful minority of the congregation, mainly composed of former Presbyterians, began to organize secretly against Smith and appointed a local War Services Committee in order to prove their loyalty to king and country.[60] At one point a poll taken of the congregation revealed that 80 per cent of the church members wanted Lavell Smith to remain as their pastor despite his pacifist views. An engaging, earnest man and a forceful preacher, Smith stayed on a few more years. Unlike some of his co-signers, he showed remarkable resistance to a mounting undercurrent of opposition. Finally, after nearly sixty of the wealthiest members had left the congregation and many others had refused to attend church services or to participate in their accustomed activities, Smith decided to resign.[61] On 27 April 1942 hundreds of Montrealers crowded into 'every corner of Webster Hall,' which adjoined Westmount Park United Church, to bid farewell to Lavell Smith and his wife Emily. Even at that late hour Smith received an enthusiastic show of support.[62] None the less, four days later he assumed his new duties as superintendent of Toronto's Church of All Nations, where he would remain for the next seventeen years.

Although they still enjoyed the respect of many, the Smiths endured their last few years in Montreal in an atmosphere of strain and discomfort. They were snubbed by numerous members of the congregation, closely watched by the police and visited by the RCMP. Lavell Smith suspected that his phone was tapped.[63] Through it all, he continued to speak out according to his conscience and, like Halliday, became interested in the problems of German refugees interned in Quebec. But his was not a one-sided approach, and throughout the war he kept in regular touch with the enlisted men of his congregation.[64]

This practice of writing men overseas was shared by Jack Duckworth of the Notre Dame de Grâce YMCA (NDGY) and another of Montreal's active pacifists. Duckworth sent circular letters to all the NDGY boys he knew in the military. His intention was to keep up their morale; he avoided any mention of his personal pacifism.[65] Those who knew Duckworth, however, were well aware of his pacifist and socialist inclinations. He had studied under Reinhold Niebuhr and Harry Ward at Union Theological Seminary in New York, and he and his wife Muriel were noticeably active in the SCM, the FOR, the FCSO, and other radical groups. When he joined the staff of the NDGY in the early 1930s, Duckworth became a leading moral influence in the lives of teenage boys in Montreal. He never attempted to indoctrinate the boys, but his activism and his outspokenness about his radical beliefs, including his pacifism, made him somewhat unpopular with the Montreal businessmen who controlled the YMCA board.[66] The board was particularly displeased, for instance, with his opposition to the Boy Scouts, which he viewed as a paramilitary organization, uniforms and all. Evidently, Duckworth aroused enough antagonism to cause someone to fire a shot through his office window. Despite his tense relationship with the YMCA board, however, Duckworth endured the war years in Montreal, and not until 1947 was he transferred to Halifax.

Some of the signatories to the 'Witness' met a sterner fate. In Ontario, Edis Fairbairn and E. Harold Toye lost their churches at the insistence of their congregations. Fairbairn, the instigator of the 'Witness against War' protest, was officially rebuked and ejected from his church in Bracebridge. But Fairbairn refused to leave the ministry altogether and accepted what was known ecclesiastically as an 'undesirable charge' at Windermere, a small rural community in the Muskoka region of Ontario.[67] Fairbairn had realized for some time that he would always be relegated to 'undesirable charges' because of his outspoken radicalism and impetuous nature. In fact, it appears that he even looked upon his undistinguished career in the ministry as a form of martyrdom – the penalty he had to pay for remaining true to Christianity while the church floundered.[68] At any rate, although his new congregation at Windermere did not necessarily approve of his pacifism, they were grateful for his presence and encouraged him to stay there until his retirement in 1948. In Windermere Fairbairn enjoyed a certain amount of freedom for his various pacifist pursuits. He even found 'farmers on the back concessions whose total indifference to religion dated from the shock they received when the Churches recruited for the First World War,'[69] a discovery, he felt, that proved what he had been saying for years and supported his more recent criticisms of the church.

The case of Harold Toye was similar, but Toye, unlike Fairbairn, did leave the parish ministry. Toye's trouble at Toronto's Kingston Road United Church began before the 'Witness against War' document was drafted, and was directly related to his overall radicalism.[70] For example, Toye had always supported the social gospel in his pulpit ministry but, like other members of the FCSO, his radicalism increased in response to the social conditions of the depression years. At one point, the official board of the Kingston Road United Church succeeded in bringing him before a special presbytery commission for examination. Although the presbytery ruled in Toye's favour, the officials continued in their effort to have him removed. On two occasions Toye tendered his resignation, only to have it refused by the majority of the congregation. When Toye's wartime pacifism was added to his labour sympathies and socialist politics, however, the dissatisfied minority seized the opportunity to respond to his signature on the 'Witness against War' manifesto. Eleven wealthy parishioners launched a concerted campaign to have Toye removed, employing tactics ranging from withholding their church contributions to severing completely their connections with Kingston Road United Church.[71] Confronted on the one hand with a divided congregation and on the other with what he considered the failure of the United Church to relate ethical and spiritual ideals to the social order, Toye finally resigned in 1941 and asked to be left without a station in order to engage in the work of industrial evangelism.

Although pacifism was the immediate issue surrounding Toye's resignation, it was but one expression of his radicalism. Over the next few years He joined a small group of kindred spirits – labour representatives, professional people, and social workers – in an attempt to make religion relevant to industrial society. At first Toye was urged to found a Toronto labour church,but he did not agree with that approach.[72] He strove instead to create a dialogue between organized religion and organized labour, whose co-ordination and co-operation, Toye believed, would promote social change within a moral framework. Organized religion, he argued, had failed to recognize that unions, collective bargaining, and strikes were all part of the true revolutionary character of the Hebrew-Christian religion.[73] Organized labour, in turn, had to function within the framework of a moral order prescribed by the ethical and spiritual demands of religion. The time had come 'to lift the whole struggle of the workers from the mere level of class struggle ... and view it in relation to the moral integrity of the universe.'[74]

In order to develop this spirit of co-operation between religion and labour, Toye and his associates founded the Religion-Labor Foundation. The foundation was a small organization composed of clergymen, laymen, and active unionists who thought of themselves as 'the Brotherhood of Church, Farm and Factory.' While most Canadians at the time were concerned with the war, the members of this small group turned their attention to the social economic and moral problems of industrial society, anticipating the post-war era. But that is not to say that they ignored or overlooked the war; rather, they viewed war as an important problem of industrial peoples. Toye, for instance, believed that the whole war effort of the 1940s was a humiliating and devastating experience for Canadian workers. He saw the need for a great moral crusade and hoped that the Religion-Labor Foundation would help bring about some necessary radical changes: 'The Religion-Labor Foundation is convinced that we are due for a New Reformation. The recovery of traditional revivalism, in whatever form, is not likely to help much. It will have to be truly radical ... and provide salvation from sin, not merely in the theological sense, but from specific sins,monopoly control, unfair employment practices, starvation wages, unethical and unjust profits, racial discrimination and war.'[75]

Small in size and experimental in approach, the Religion-Labor Foundation progressed slowly, at first receiving more co-operation from labour than from the church.[76] Nevertheless, it made its impact, or 'Christian witness,' in Canada's industrial society, in activities ranging from mediating in industrial disputes and strikes to lobbying for specific legislation designed to recognize and protect ethical and spiritual values in labour-management relations. The foundation held regular joint sessions of clergy and unionists in many Ontario communities. As the executive secretary of the foundation, Harold Toye was largely responsible for directing this experimental work in industrial evangelism. It became a new outlet for his radicalism when wartime pacifism forced him out of the parish ministry, and he remained devoted to the task for the rest of his life.

Other signatories to the 'Witness against War' suffered fewer repercussions because of their pacifist witness. For example, Fred Smith, a 'stop-gap' national secretary of the FCSO, was never confronted with a campaign to oust him. Nor was J.W.E. Newbery.[77] In Saint John, New Brunswick the congregation of the Reverend H. McLean unanimously repudiated his pacifism but asked him to keep his pulpit.[78] This was also the experience of Douglas Smith, who stayed on in Belleville, Ontario.[79] One of the most prominent cases involved James M. Finlay, an organizer of the 'Seventy-five,' who, with the support of his congregation, withstood a serious challenge from the official board of Toronto's Carlton Street United Church. A small but influential minority of the congegation had been unhappy about Finlay's role in drafting the 'Witness against War,' and by the spring of 1940 church officials were calling for the resignations of Finlay and his two deaconesses, Miss Bessie Irwin and Miss M. Clapham, who also showed pacifist leanings.[80] But Finlay refused, arguing that since he had accepted his pastoral duties at the invitation of the congregation it was a matter for them to decide.[81] Accordingly, on the evening of 17 June, the congregation, both 'members' and 'adherents,' and sympathetic guests crowded into the Carlton Street church to put an end to the controversy. John Coburn, president-elect of the Toronto conference of the United Church, opened the meeting by urging the congregation to 'recognize the right of other people to hold opinions diametrically opposed to ours,' and reasoned: 'We have sent our boys to fight Hitler. Hitlerism is a force that crushes individualism, freedom of thought and even the human soul. If we are fighting it in Europe, we must exemplify it [freedom] at home.'[82] Testimonials on behalf of Finlay and the deaconesses poured in, including messages from many people from across the country who listened to Finlay's nationwide weekly radio broadcasts. The meeting unanimously pledged its support to the Allied cause and Canada's war effort, but Finlay was accorded a sweeping vote of confidence. By a vote of 361 to 80 the members of the congregation adopted the following resolution: 'While we may not all agree with our minister, we assure him of our confidence in him as a minister of Christ and our whole-hearted co-operation in his efforts to win souls for Christ and to advance the Kingdom of God on earth.'[83]

A further motion to have the contentious matter brought before the presbytery was defeated by the same wide margin. After accepting a standing ovation, Finlay thanked the meeting and expressed the hope for a unified congregation in the future. But the eighty wealthy members who had opposed Finlay remained unimpressed. Many of them left the congregation in the belief that the absence of their support would force Finlay to resign.[84] Instead, young couples and sympathetic people from across Toronto came flocking to Finlay's side, and the Carlton Street United Church, in keeping with its reputation as the 'House of Friendship,' was 'reborn.'

Finlay felt a particular loyalty to the young pacifists brought up in the 'Never Again' atmosphere of the 1930s, who were completely bewildered by the church's support of the war effort and its condemnation of 'Witness against War.'[85] The previous year, for instance, a group of Victoria College students had signed their own pacifist manifesto in which they reaffirmed their belief that peace could be achieved only by 'the absolute renunciation of war by individuals, by the church, and the State.'[86] They also called upon the United Church to formulate an alternative program to military service in which conscientious Christians could take 'a positive stand without compromising their Christian faith.' By 1940 many of these young pacifists sought refuge in Finlay's church and advice on the proper role of Christians in time of war. That question, effectively raised anew by the 'Witness against War' controversy, remained unanswered by the church.

IV

The United Church had offered little guidance on the proper Christian response to war because its exact teaching on the issue was unclear. For this reason both pacifists and non-pacifists urged the church to justify its action in condemning the 'Seventy-five' and 'to show how its members could at the same time avow an allegiance to Christ while doing the necessary deeds of warfare.'[87] The 1940 general council did appoint a special committee to produce such a statement, but 'for some unstated reason it never reported.' Frustrated and angered by the 'stony silence' of church leaders, Edis Fairbairn unleashed his wrath on the pages of the *United Church Observer* and stirred up another storm. His statement, entitled 'Indictment,' condemned the United Church as 'incompetent and unworthy to serve the cause of God.'[88] In reference to the church's often repeated anti-war statements of the previous decade, Fairbairn charged that church leadership lacked the courage of its convictions. He expressed particular disappointment at the way the 1940 general council 'boldly slunk around' the war issue. 'I am therefore heartily ashamed of the United Church. Because of its cowardly failure to confess its errors and clear its standards it has brought about the farcical situation that while volubly expressing itself in support of the war, its official statement is, "we positively reject war." '

What Fairbairn objected to most was the 'unreality' or inconsistency in the situation. 'Much as I differ in conviction,' he explained, 'I could have retained my respect for the effective leadership of the Church if it could have brought itself to the point of clearly declaring its change of mind and its present approval of war.' Fairbairn accused the church of allowing its ministers to speak out on social evils only as long as their preaching was not accompanied with a demand for action. 'It is possible in this way to gain great repute for eloquent but harmless radicalism.' As one who had lost his church, Fairbairn testified that there was no freedom in the United Church for 'any utterance that annoys the good contributors to the local or general Church funds.' In other words, the United Church was 'fundamentally a financial institution' since the first and foremost duty of its ministers was to avoid upsetting their contributors.

The most damaging result of the church's position, however, may well have been a loss of credibility with the average man. Fairbairn claimed that men were already asking, 'Is there *any* issue upon which the United Church will take a stand and act on it regardless of consequences?' Besides the fact that an affirmative answer was in doubt, the real tragedy, he wrote, was that 'the average man does not believe in the Christianity of the Churches because he is unable to believe that they believe in it. And all the revivals or preaching missions in the world will not convince ordinary men, that we Christians believe in Christianity. Only a faithfulness to Jesus Christ and his Gospel of the Kingdom of God could do that ... in reality the acid test is not, Will you die for your faith? But, Will you cheerfully suffer financial loss for it?'[89]

The *Observer* received so many letters in response to Fairbairn's 'Indictment' that the editor found it impossible to publish them all. Among those writing in support of Fairbairn were two members of the Alberta School of Religion, William Irwin and Charles Huestis. Huestis agreed with every word of the article and pointed out that it was quite appropriate that the moderator's endorsement of the War Savings Certificates Plan was printed on the same page as Fairbairn's statement, since 'it so fully supports the indictment.' 'Having found that people will not adequately support the schemes of the Church from loyalty to Christ,' he wrote, 'we promise to implement their loyalty to the State in its war plans.'[90] Praise also came from Fairbairn's former FCSO colleague, Gregory Vlastos, now at Queen's University. Vlastos did not share Fairbairn's pacifism, and he eventually supported the war effort, but for the moment he opposed the war on other grounds. He agreed with Fairbairn that people lost their religion because of 'glaring contradictions between the faith we profess and the way we live.' He suggested that all those who considered themselves followers of Christ should 'read and re-read' Fairbairn's 'Indictment' and ask themselves: 'What are we to do about it?'[91]

R.B.Y. Scott, the co-editor with Vlastos of *Towards the Christian Revolution*, however, was not so kind. He argued that Fairbairn's wholesale indictment was 'as unfair and untrue as it is sweeping.'[92] Specifically, he claimed that Fairbairn misrepresented the church's attitude to war. According to Scott, there was no inconsistency in the United Church's past anti-war statements and its support of the war effort since no general council had ever equated rejection of war with complete pacifism. On the contrary, he argued, 'multitudes' in the United Church and many in its leadership still rejected war as genuinely as did Fairbairn, but that did not mean they adhered to doctrinaire pacifism. They could not escape their responsibility in the war simply by washing their hands. 'We have not chosen war and do not willingly participate in it; we reject it, but cannot now avoid it.' The way to world peace, Scott concluded, was not necessarily Fairbairn's way. And there the issue rested for the readers of the *Observer*.

Perhaps the most notable feature of the debate in the *Observer* was the disagreement between principal members of the Fellowship for a Christian Social Order which revealed the tragic fragmentation of the

Christian left in the face of the war. Such a development could only spur the growth of the Fellowship of Reconciliation, but both groups worked at keeping doors open to the other. Scott, Vlastos, and other non-pacifist FCSO members did not want their disagreement on the war issue to overshadow their overall goal of radical social change.[93] Hoping, therefore, that the FCSO could continue to encompass both pacifists and non-pacifists, the national executive encouraged freedom of conscience and expression among its members. In response to the 'Witness against War' controversy, FCSO spokesmen argued that although the church had decided to support the state at war, 'the prosecution of the war must never become its peculiar task.'[94] Furthermore, they urged the church to 'refrain from even appearing to conceal divergence of opinion among its ministers' and suggested that when a conflict arose between loyalties to God and state the church should:

1) recognize the conflict as essentially religious whatever the decision finally reached...
2) try to make clear to the public as well as to its members that the difference of opinion is merely one of method in driving towards the one supreme end.
3) widen the scope of its war time service to have it provide worthy occupations not only in non-combatant war-service but also in services which in no way contribute to war.[95]

Overall, the FCSO was sympathetic and tolerant towards its pacifist members and tried to accommodate them, even to the point of advocating some type of pacifist alternative service. Nevertheless, it was also clear that most members of the FCSO had divorced pacifist means from Christian socialist action. For instance, the annual FCSO convention in 1940 was presented with two positions on the war, the pacifists being in the minority. The majority of delegates were of the opinion that the vital task of the FCSO during the war was to preserve civil liberties at home while supporting the cause of freedom, equality, and brotherhood throughout the world. Without mentioning the challenge to Christian pacifism, they suggested the war 'verified and intensified' the need for radical social change and agreed that 'the Christian force is moving in the direction of socialism, and that only when productive resources in every nation are owned and controlled by its people will war be securely outlawed and peace established.'

Although they shared the passion for radical social change, even socialism, pacifists could hardly believe that peace could be established without commitment to pacifism, the way of peace. Pacifism and socialism were part and parcel of radical Christianity and therefore inseparable; but with the FCSO now visibly rejecting pacifism as a realistic alternative, pacifists, already uneasy in the FCSO on the eve of the war, were increasingly isolated and in need of the solidarity and strength provided by the Fellowship of Reconciliation.[96] The FOR, however, was still a weak reed and it was the good fortune of pacifists that their FCSO associates remained sympathetic. Eugene Forsey, Stanley Knowles, and Stanley Allen, for example, had changed their minds on pacifism but still showed concern for their pacifist brothers.[97] Whenever he was in Toronto during the war years, Forsey visited Carlton Street United Church to meet with Finlay. The two men obviously held each other in the highest esteem.[98] Although the United Church may not have endorsed the pacifist alternative directly, it was evident that pacifists still commanded much respect and sympathy from certain elements within the church and society at large, and especially from the social radicals in the Fellowship for a Christian Social Order.

v

There was an increasing sense of isolation among Canadian pacifists during the first two years of the war. It was visible in the United Church, having been created in part by the 'Witness against War' Manifesto, in the *Observer* debate, and in the ranks of the Fellowship for a Christian Social Order. Only the Canadian Fellowship of Reconciliation seemed to promise pacifists some solace; but, after the Canadian group lost its initial bid for affiliation with the international FOR in 1939, it remained weak and loosely organized until well into the war years. Until then the first national chairman, Carlyle King, carried on as best he could in his leadership of the various FOR groups scattered across the country. Almost single-handedly he kept the sole Canadian pacifist organization afloat during its darkest days. Once the War Measures Act was in force, the FOR could do little 'in a public way to advance the cause of peace.'[99] Nevertheless, within a few weeks of Canada's entry into the war, FOR members in Vancouver, Toronto, and Montreal began organizing opposition to the possible introduction of conscription and the curtailment of civil liberties. King had singled out conscription as the most immediate danger, and he urged all FOR units to draw together religious, political, labour, youth and other groups to pressure the government to stand by its word that conscription would not be introduced.[100] The Vancouver group took the lead when they set up a 'Committee for the Maintenance of Peace Time Liberties' composed of representatives from the FOR, the WIL, the YWCA, the CCF, and the Christian Commonwealth Youth Movement. A similar scheme was organized in Toronto.

By necessity, the activities of such committees were somewhat limited. The Toronto group, for instance, met weekly, and convened a study group every other week; otherwise, they 'kept fairly under cover' with 'no publicity of any kind.' Their main purpose was merely to send 'letters of congratulations and of protest to various government officials' and to co-operate with the CCF, the LSR, and other left-wing groups. In addition, the Toronto WIL reported that they had remained on friendly terms with the League of Nations Society and were in contact with the American WIL in the hope of convincing the United States to convene a world peace conference.

Toronto pacifists also hoped to co-operate with the Quakers in some type of humanitarian relief project similar to the work done by the American Friends Service Committee in the Great War and the Spanish Civil War. The idea was to provide Canadian pacifists with 'an alternative to military service and a chance for a positive witness to their idea of human brotherhood in wartime.'[101]

Carlyle King offered the following advice on the proper wartime role of the individual pacifist:

[His] main task is to keep sane and preserve in himself and his friends the spark of friendship and decency. He must guard against hysteria, hatred, and indignation; he must be an island of sanity in the midst of surrounding chaos, so that when the madness passes there may be some people who can give us leadership in seeking to establish human unity, understanding and good-will. Perhaps he can damp down the hatred of the 'enemy' in the people he meets, minimize atrocity stories, and check harsh treatment of alien folk in his own community. In a quiet and private way he can give sympathy and counsel to young people perplexed and harassed by 'patriotic' pressure.[102]

King also suggested that pacifists meet regularly in small groups, such as those in Vancouver, Toronto, and Saskatoon, to discuss peace literature and its relation to the war. He felt such a practice would not only strengthen and encourage their pacifism but would provide an opportunity for them 'to exchange ideas and feeling frankly.' Above all, he reminded Canadian pacifists not to speak out publicly against the war and to refrain from arguing with the 'belligerently minded.'

King was well aware of the dangers of making unpopular public statements. The previous year he himself had come under fire because of his outspokenness. At a meeting of the Saskatoon Young Communist League King had advised Canadian youth to 'refuse to fight to maintain the profits of the British plutocracy' and had expressed his opposition to Canada's entering the war merely because of its connections with the British empire.[103] His remarks were given front-page coverage in the press, and they triggered a minor furore as organizations and individuals throughout the province condemned his unpatriotic utterances. The Moose Jaw branch of the Canadian Legion and many parents of university students demanded King's dismissal from the University of Saskatchewan faculty and called for an investigation into the overall teachings of the university.[104] He was labelled anti-British, anti-Canadian, and communist.[105] The *Regina Daily Star* condemned him as dangerous and dogmatic and suggested that the Young communists who had arranged the meeting must have been pleased.[106] In his defence King released a statement in which he declared that he was not and never had been a communist and did not accept their philosophy. As a member of the FOR he rejected the use of violence in settling disputes between nations or between classes, creeds or races within nations.[107] He asserted that his criticism of British imperialism was not necessarily anti-British and definitely was not anti-Canadian. On the contrary, his brand of patriotism or nationalism, although the exact opposite of blind allegiance to the British empire, was entirely sincere.

My love of Canada takes the form of working to see that every Canadian has good food, good clothes, good housing, a permanent job and an income that will permit him to enjoy those forms of recreation and culture he likes; of urging our Government to co-operate with other nations to remove the causes of war and to establish a just peace; and of being willing to make personal sacrifice toward those ends. I leave it to candid minds to say which form of patriotism is more Canadian or more in harmony with our professed religion.[108]

Support for King's right to free speech and academic freedom came from all sides. Numerous individuals praised King's stand in letters to the press.[109] University students, while not necessarily endorsing his specific opinions, pledged their support for King and lauded his 'unbiased views.'[110] Tracing the history of opposition to free speech back to biblical times, W.G. Brown, minister of St Andrew's Presbyterian Church in Saskatoon, defended the right of a university professor such as King to offer criticisms. The *Leader-Post* of Regina helped to defuse the issue by observing that 'the core of his speech was an attack on war.' The editor emphasized the necessity to protect free speech and concluded: 'If the present social order and its views on war cannot stand up against the views, here and there of a pacifist or of a Communist, then it will collapse sooner or later of its own weakness.'[111]

The controversy died down when the university board of governors refused to take action, but flared up again six months later when King, addressing the Kinsmen Club of Saskatoon, was critical of the Chamberlain government in Britain.[112] A new barrage of attacks and demands for King's dismissal erupted almost immediately. In order to prevent further embarrassment to J.S. Thompson, the president of the university and a staunch defender of academic freedom, King voluntarily decided to refrain from speaking publicly on the subject of peace. Accordingly, on 29 September 1938 he cancelled his plans to speak that evening to a meeting sponsored by the Saskatoon branch of the Canadian League for Peace and Democracy. In his letter to the local secretary of the league, King blamed his decision on the harassment of President Thompson and accused his critics of condemning him from inaccurate newspaper reports. The major question raised by the whole affair, he argued, was why a professor in Saskatchewan could not repeat what members of the House of Lords stated freely in England. In the first draft of the letter, but omitted altogether from the public statement, was King's personal interpretation of his public utterances:

For two years my public speeches have had one object, and one only: to keep my Country out of European war: I had thought to do what I could to keep Canadian boys, particularly my students, from the moral iniquity of burning and torturing the women and children, the aged and the infirm, of 'enemy' nations. I had hoped to use my knowledge and my ability to that end. In my speeches I have never once objected to Canada's membership in the free and voluntary association of Nations. Would that there were more such associations![113]

King faithfully refrained from speaking out on international issues, even though he was implicated in bitter attacks on the FOR and its leadership. In a lengthy front-page article that appeared on 9 December 1939, and in subsequent articles, the Toronto *Financial Post* attacked the Canadian FOR alleging that its leaders were either communists or communist-inspired, charges the Vancouver *Financial Post* readily echoed.[114] As a result of such accusations, King's assistant, Cleo Mowers, was forced to resign as national secretary of the FOR and to sever all connections with the organization in order to save his job on the Saskatoon *Star-Phoenix*.

Mowers's resignation placed King in a difficult position, since he could not find a suitable replacement for him and could not carry on the executive work of the FOR alone. He therefore offered his own resignation to the national council. In doing so he recommended strongly that the executive work be taken over by either the Toronto or Montreal organization. By this time, however, the other members of the national council were caught up in their own troubles stemming from the 'Witness against War' controversy and were unable or unwilling to assume further responsibility in the FOR. With the promise of extra money for stenographic assistance, Lavell Smith once again persuaded King to continue to serve as national chairman.[115] Smith also added that, however lamentable, the policy of silence was 'the only one which can now be followed.'

Although it was not exactly the kind of silence that Smith had in mind, the national chairman heard very little from other members of the national council over the next year.[116] King was aware, however, that the Canadian FOR was not in the healthiest of conditions. Both Thelma Allen of Montreal and F. Blatchford Ball of Saskatchewan renounced their pacifism and resigned from the national council. The Toronto group, supposedly one of the most important units in Canada, was weak and disorganized. For all practical purposes, the Toronto FOR came to a standstill when its president, R.J. Irwin, resigned on the heels of the 'Witness against War' controversy.[117] To some extent, however, the slack was taken up by the work of the Toronto Pacifist Council, an alliance of twelve groups including the FOR, the WIL, the Quakers, United Church Youth, and the Christian Commonwealth Youth Movement. Under an executive that included James M. Finlay, Anna Sissons, and Ted Mann, the Toronto Pacifist Council counted approximately two hundred pacifist members.[118] Many, such as Mann, Joe Round, and Gordon and Kay Yearsley, were young social activists who had come together in youth groups organized and supported by Finlay and Irwin at their respective churches.[119] The major activities of the Pacifist Council were assisting German aliens in Toronto, supporting the No-Conscription League, and lobbying to amend the Defence of Canada Act so as to protect the rights of pacifists.

Such activity on behalf of civil liberties notwithstanding, the majority of Canadian pacifists appeared for a time to have followed Lavell Smith's advice and adopted a policy of silence. As the FOR national chairman, Carlyle King remained the official voice of Canadian pacifists and single-handedly corresponded with would-be converts and prospective conscientious objectors scattered across the country. He never received the promised financial help for stenographic assistance. Then, in June 1941, King was encouraged by an inquiry from Fairbairn about the possibility of reorganizing the FOR. 'I had begun to think that nobody was going to take any interest any more in the infant,' King replied. 'Now that some people feel a definite [need] for a fellowship of war resisters, perhaps the under-nourished babe can be revived.'[120] After providing Fairbairn with a brief history of the Canadian organization, King expressed his feeling that the time was 'ripe for a new deal and a new slate of officers' and suggested that Fairbairn and others in eastern Canada who were 'close enough to work together easily' should take over the organization. He sent Fairbairn the FOR membership lists and other lists of contacts, the balance in the treasury, (no more than fifteen dollars), and a bundle of FOR statements. Concerning the Canadian Statement of Basis and Aims, King conceded that since the other scheme had failed, the Canadian group should conform to the regular pattern of the international FOR and 'make our body a specifically Christian one.' When King finally relinquished the national chairmanship he advised Fairbairn that if he was really serious about reviving the FOR he should elect himself 'president, or dictator or what have you, *pro tempore*, and afterwards conduct a ballot by mail at your leisure.'[121]

It appears that Fairbairn's interest in the FOR coincided with a renewed concern among remaining members of the FOR national council to strengthen the fledgling pacifist organization. In the spring of 1941, for instance, Lavell Smith, James Finlay, and Clarence Halliday sent a letter to those on their old mailing list in an attempt to renew contacts and 'keep alive a sense of fellowship' among Canadian pacifists.[122] Forty of the forty-six who replied were standing firm in their pacifism. In September Clare Oke distributed a similar letter in which he suggested the desirability of revising the Canadian Statement of Basis and Aims according to the international FOR guidelines. Twenty-four individuals replied; two-thirds of those agreed that the Canadian statement should be made more specifically Christian. No further initiative was taken to reorganize the FOR, however, until the beginning of the new year, when Lavell Smith again called for a renewed commitment from 'Canadian Lovers of Peace.' In reference to the rather poor response to Oke's letters, he asked: 'Does that mean we ought to stop writing? Some of us think not, for there is all too little here in Canada to hold us together.' In contrast to the American FOR, which had over ten thousand members, the Canadian organization faced peculiar problems: 'Here in Canada our members are few; great distances separate us; some are cut off from fellowship with sympathetic spirits; the columns of our journals are largely closed to 'peace propaganda'; many of us are under too great pressure to venture to express ourselves in print. It would appear that we ought at least to circulate an occasional letter in the interests of fellowship.'[123] Furthermore, since the Canadian FOR no longer had either an executive or a complete national council, Smith emphasized the need for a total reorganization and proceeded to request nominations for a new national council, 'as representative as possible of the various Provinces.'

Despite the plea for national representation, the revived FOR was largely dominated by United Church pacifists in Ontario, especially after Lavell Smith's move to Toronto in May 1942. It appears that they wanted a specifically Christian pacifist organization, and hoped to follow Richard Roberts's suggestion to organize pacifist cells within the church for fellowship and prayer, with the prospect of leading toward the spiritual renewal of the church. James Finlay, for example, agreed that the brand of pacifism most likely to endure was that based upon the Christian faith rather than some other foundation. The focal point of pacifist thinking, words, and deeds should not be pacifism as such but a 'positive dynamic witness in all situations' as Christians.[124]

By September 1942 the reorganization of the Canadian Fellowship of Reconciliation was complete. Despite the fact that the national council was expanded in order to encompass representatives from across the country, the hub of the revived organization was Toronto. The new executive included Lavell Smith as chairman, J.W.E. Newbery as secretary, and Clare Oke as treasurer, all of whom had resettled in the Toronto area.[125] While Carlyle King's continued membership on the national council offered a certain element of continuity with the early days, the new organization clearly reflected a stronger Christian bias. The Canadian Statement of Basis and Aims, revised by Oke and renamed the 'Statement of Purpose,' adhered more closely to the Christian format of the international statement. Included was a version of the Christian 'Basis' requested by John Nevin Sayre in 1939 as a prerequisite for international recognition of the Canadian group.[126] The remainder of the statement outlined the responsibility of members to abolish war and build a new social order. With this revised statement, and with encouragement from Sayre, the Canadian FOR proceeded to reapply for affiliation with the international organization. Finally, almost four years after their initial bid, Canadian pacifists were accepted into the international FOR fold.[127]

VI

At long last Christian pacifism in Canada had begun to gel, from the public protest of United Church ministers in the 'Witness against War' manifesto to the long-awaited affiliation of Canadian pacifists with the international Fellowship of Reconciliation. In effect, this surfacing of a Christian pacifist front, weak as it still was, was a tribute to one of its most devoted proponents, Richard Roberts. A co-founder of the original Fellowship of Reconciliation in 1914, Roberts had become a perennial pacifist influence in Canada since his arrival in 1922. First in Montreal and then in Toronto, where he also served as moderator of the United Church during the depth of the depression, Roberts aroused public interest in Christian pacifism and social action. By 1940 he had retired from the active ministry and accepted a lectureship at Pine Hill Divinity School in Halifax. Halifax was the Canadian port most directly involved in the war, and it was an uncomfortable place for a pacifist, especially for one like Roberts who, in 'both sentiment and judgment,' was in complete sympathy with the Allied cause and yet remained committed to pacifism. 'The ethical disparity of the two sides is hardly measureable,' he wrote. 'But I am sure the church should stick to its own job – if everything is not to go with the flood.'[128] Perhaps because of this personal dilemma, Roberts became particularly annoyed with what he called the 'hoity-toity pacifism' professed by such people as Muriel Lester. He believed that they lacked 'any realization of the actual and tragic failure of pacifism which the war indicates; and that the proper wear of pacifists at this time is sackcloth and ashes.' Roberts was convinced that in the world as it was in 1940 anything that seemed easy was suspect, including pacifism.

Nevertheless, Roberts spoke out strongly in defence of radical pacifism in response to the challenge of Reinhold Niebuhr's 'Christian realism,' which seemed to him more like moral relativism. In fact, his major contribution to the pacifist debate during the war was his open dialogue on the topic with Niebuhr himself. It began in the winter of 1940 when Niebuhr, writing in *Radical Religion*, castigated the pacifist position as self-righteous.[129] Roberts took Niebuhr to task in an open letter published in *Christianity and Society*. The use of the term 'self-righteous,' said Roberts, was a 'boomerang,' since it betrayed that unpleasant condition in Niebuhr himself and raised the suspicion that he was not too sure of his own position.[130] Although Roberts admitted that there were 'all sorts of faults and perversities in the pacifist movement,' there were more of them in the case for Christian participation in war. He confessed, however, that he could not find an easy answer to Niebuhr's arguments and consequently was 'caught in a lacerating conflict of loyalties': 'Frankly, I would give a good deal to be able to accept your [Niebuhr's] doctrine. It would make life a good deal easier for me; there's the sense of alienation from my people, the coolness of friends, the suspicion of disloyalty, the spite of the intolerant, and the like, all of which hurt me deeply.'[131]

To Roberts, pacifism was a difficult and complex principle; it was neither the 'simple Christian moralism' that Niebuhr had described nor the 'equally simple' moral relativism that Niebuhr professed. Roberts warned that, contrary to the strict Christian basis of the pacifist doctrine, 'moral relativity' made a 'virtue or a sort of philosophy' out of the failure to follow Christ. While it appeared to solve a momentary and isolated problem, moral relativism was perhaps the 'first step down a very slippery slope.' In effect, Roberts suggested that Niebuhr's dialectic had led to what Plato called 'making the worse appear the better reason.' Although he himself detested 'Hitlerism and all its works', Roberts argued that the chief duty of Christians was not to discriminate between parties in the present war but to judge the 'whole business of war' against the 'revealed righteousness of God.' Unless that was done, he warned, the evil of war would perpetuate itself throughout society: 'Nations at war tend to grow like each other; and the restoration of civil rights and liberties suspended in wartime has generally been slow and grudging. The longer this war lasts and the more fiercely it is fought, the more dangerous will become the menace of Hitlerism, even though Hitler be destroyed.'[132]

Niebuhr praised Roberts's letter as the first communication he had received from a pacifist that was not 'ill-tempered' and said that it neatly revealed the theological gulf between pacifism and non-pacifist Christianity. Roberts's casual reference to war as an 'incident' in history conflicted with Niebuhr's view of war as 'a final revelation of the very character of human history.'[133] Although Niebuhr conceded that Roberts was correct in his observation that moral relativism could easily degenerate into opportunism and 'unprincipled conduct,' he maintained that at times it was the duty of christians to 'preserve some relative decency and justice in society' and thus participate in war despite the sinful character of the action. In effect, Niebuhr accused Roberts and his fellow pacifists of trying to attain the impossible dream of living in history without sinning. The bulk of Niebuhr's criticism, however, was directed toward isolationism and those American pacifists 'inclined to identify neutrality with the "Sermon on the Mount."' On the whole, the dialogue between Roberts and Niebuhr revealed little that was new; and yet it served as an important reminder that, despite the loss of Niebuhr, Christian pacifism was not intellectually stalemated by the war.

VII

Niebuhr had seriously challenged liberal and socially radical pacifists to face reality rather than retreat behind the confines of a religious ideal like a millennial peace sect. For the most part, Canadian pacifist leaders were sensitive to Niebuhr's criticism. No one was more aware than they of the dangers of irrelevance. They realized that pacifist protests alone were not a satisfactory answer, but they could not condone what Roberts called Niebuhr's dangerous policy of moral relativism. Instead, pacifists attempted to face reality in their own way, and what could be more real than the heightened experience they had been through by 1941 in the course of maintaining the courage of their convictions? Although the 'Witness against War' manifesto appeared to have cast United Church pacifists in the role of rebels, for instance, it was primarily an attempt to provide a realistic pacifist alternative within the existing framework of the church. Failing in that, they began to rebuild pacifist solidarity through the Fellowship of Reconciliation and turned to the implementation of the pacifist witness within the historical context in which they found themselves. Thus, during the remaining war years pacifists would respond to Niebuhr's challenge to face the reality of the times by assuming an active role in various humanitarian activities, the defence of civil liberties, and, above all, the struggle for alternative pacifist service for conscientious objectors. If it did not meet the demands of Niebuhr's neo-orthodoxy, the course they would take required its own heroic assumption of the tragic burden of the war.

8

Alternative pacifist service

From the very beginning of the Second World War Canadian pacifists faced one major threat: conscription. Above all else conscription exposed the vulnerability of the individual conscience, and forced pacifists to declare their personal opposition to the nation's war effort. From the beginning, too, some pacifists recognized the need to make a positive response to the conditions war brought in its train. Perhaps the latter was construed as a means of coping with the former. Whether it was or not, it was necessary to demand that Canada show some measure of moral progress on the question of conscientious objection. Pacifists became almost completely absorbed in an effort to ensure their exemption from military service while at the same time attempting to pursue some form of non-violent social action. For many non-pacifists, too, freedom of conscience was what the war was about – the pacifist at home stood at the crux of the matter. Many more Canadians saw it differently, however, and therein lay the danger and the struggle.

Mindful of the potentially explosive opposition of Quebec, the Liberal government of Mackenzie King tried to avert a repetition of the 1917 conscription crisis by gradually introducing compulsory military service in two stages. At first limited to home defence, conscription was broadened to include overseas service at the eleventh hour. Such a course of action reflected the mood of the House of Commons prior to the outbreak of war. In March 1939, for instance, both King and the leader of the opposition, R.J. Manion, had declared their opposition to conscription for overseas service.[1] At that time the prime minister actually promised that as long as his government was in power no such measure would be enacted, a pledge he later repeated in the House during the special war session.[2] Accordingly, the King government pursued an initial policy of 'limited liability' that emphasized home defense and thus keeping the participation of Canadian forces abroad to a minimum. Canadians were told that their major responsibility would be the provision of munitions, raw materials, and foodstuffs rather than men.

Gradually, however, government policy began to change. Alarmed by the end of the 'phoney war' and the collapse of France in the spring of 1940, the government initiated a more aggressive war effort marked by the adoption in June of the National Resources Mobilization Act (NRMA). In effect, the NRMA authorized restricted conscription for home defence. Thereafter, the debate centred on the question of conscription for overseas duty.

Again, government policy reflected the course of the war. The Japanese attack on Pearl Harbor and the defeat and capture of Canadian forces at Hong Kong in December 1941 increased calls for 'Total War Now' and for an end to the restrictions on the service of NRMA men, who were derisively known as 'Zombies.'[3] In the spring of 1942 King decided to ask the Canadian public in a plebiscite to release the government from former pledges 'restricting the methods of raising men for military service.' It was at this point that French-Canadian opposition to conscription solidified in La Ligue pour la défense du Canada under the leadership of its secretary, André Laurendeau.[4] The league appealed to all Canadians to vote 'no' in the plebiscite, but it was no surprise when Quebec stood alone in its opposition to releasing the government from its past commitments.[5] Despite the favourable outcome of the plebiscite, King remained reluctant to force conscripts into regular service. Ultimately, however, the voluntary system failed to meet the needs of the army, and the King government finally instituted overseas conscription in November 1944, only a few months before the end of the war in Europe.[6]

In the long run the government's five-year delay in adopting conscription for overseas duty was relatively successful in defusing an historically explosive issue. It was also effective in undermining any possible development of an anti-war coalition by dividing along philosophical lines those opposed to military service overseas from those opposed to military service in any form. As long as conscripts were not sent outside Canada many Canadians initially opposed to conscription were mollified, and those with conscientious objections to military service were further isolated.

The program of national registration begun in each federal election district in August 1940 was therefore implemented smoothly in an 'atmosphere of calm and resignation.'[7] The only major incident occurred when the mayor of Montreal, Camillien Houde, publicly declared his opposition to registration as 'unequivocally a measure of conscription' and was swiftly seized and shipped off to an internment camp by federal authorities. The government's draconian reaction served as a clear indication that public criticism of the nation's war effort would not be tolerated, and pacifists took heed.

During the First World War registration and conscription had been passionately denounced by such radical pacifists as J.S. Woodsworth and F.J. Dixon, but in 1940, except for some Doukhobors, particularly the Sons of Freedom, pacifist groups accepted national registration without protest. They concentrated instead on securing two major concessions from the government: the right to conscientious-objector status of all individuals who conscientiously opposed military service regardless of religious affiliation, and the establishment of some form of alternative service in the national interest. Although of minor importance during the first war, both demands had become crucial by 1940 because of the increased number of pacifists in Canada's regular Protestant denominations who were determined to assume an active role during the war and because the restrictive language of the law meant that alternative service was seen as possibly the only way to ensure the rights of all conscientious objectors, including some within the historic peace sects. In time, following concerted pacifist pressure and the initial wartime mobilization of manpower, government authorities came to share this view and made allowances for pacifist service. The volatile issue of conscription for overseas service, on the other hand, was never really relevant to the personal dilemma of pacifists. While the nation at large was debating the pros and cons of the plebiscite, for instance, pacifists were arguing for an expansion of alternative service, and while the question of overseas service for conscripts was still under discussion Canadian conscientious objectors were already serving overseas in a humanitarian capacity. The Canadian pacifist response to conscription was much less resistance than an affirmative pacifist witness.

I

The decision of pacifists to seek some acceptable form of alternative service was unquestionably linked to the government's limited provision for conscientious objection. Although the National Resources Mobilization Act authorized the government to adopt conscription for home defense, it was the National War Services Regulations (Recruits) that defined the ground rules for the actual call-up of men and for exemptions.[8] Accordingly, divisional registrars responsible to the minister of national war services were appointed to select men for military training in each of the thirteen military administrative districts across the country. In keeping with historical precedent, provision was also made for the exemption of those with special occupations such as judges, clergymen, policemen, firemen, and prison and mental asylum workers as well as for the deferment of Doukhobors, Mennonites, and conscientious objectors. Unlike the Military Service Act of 1917, however, which either exempted or excepted the historic peace sects, the 1940 regulations merely provided for the postponement of their military training.

In order to be granted a postponement, Mennonites, Doukhobors, and others with conscientious objections were required to submit a written application to their divisional registrar and to appear before the National War Service Board (often referred to as the Mobilization Board) in their military administrative district. If the board was satisfied that the applicant conscientiously objected by reason of religious training or belief to war in any form, his military training was postponed. In practice, however, the ease or difficulty of obtaining a postponement as a conscientious objector (CO) varied from one division to another since each mobilization board was autonomous and its decision depended on a variety of factors such as the attitude of the local populace or the personality of the board chairman. For example, Justice J.E. Adamson, chairman of the Manitoba board, refused to recognize numerous young Mennonites as bona fide COs, and the fact that all Mennonites were not treated in the same manner also reflected the divergence of opinion within the Mennonite community itself.

Generally speaking, the various Mennonite groups ranged in belief from a conservative adherence to the doctrines of non-resistance and non-conformity to a more progressive acceptance of and adaptation to modern society, it was along these lines that they were divided in their initial response to the prospect of alternative service in lieu of military training.[9] The internal debate was aggravated when the law appeared to limit those who could qualify for an automatic postponement from military service.

According to the War Service Regulations, Doukhobors and Mennonites were specifically guaranteed an indefinite postponement of military training, but the term 'Mennonites' was restricted to the *Kanadier* group largely centred in Western Canada, the descendants of the seven thousand Mennonites of Dutch extraction who emigrated from Russia in the 1870s and thereafter were exempted from military service by the famous Order in Council of 1873. In other words, to achieve postponement the *Kanadier* had only to prove membership in the Mennonite Church and continuous residency in Canada. All other Mennonites, the old Ontario groups as well as the new *Russlaender*, those twenty thousand who emigrated to the Prairies from the Soviet Union during the 1920s, had no guarantee of exemptions; they fell under the general category of 'conscientious objectors' and were required to articulate their religious objections to war individually. Consequently, the *Kanadier* Mennonites, relatively assured of postponements, initially opposed the idea of alternative service and their *Aeltestenkomitee*, or committee of elders, remained aloof from early pacifist lobbying in Ottawa. But the majority of Mennonites endorsed alternative service, even non-combatant duty in the case of the *Russlaender*, as perhaps the best way to ensure their official recognition as bona fide conscientious objectors.[10]

Among the *Russlaender*, moreover, alternative service was already a historical tradition and was viewed as an expression of faith rather than a compromise in principle. Their ancestors had performed such work in the forestry and medical corps in Russia under the tsar and they saw no reason not to make a similar contribution in Canada. Indeed, they actually hoped that by performing such service they would prove themselves patriotic to Canada and thereby dispel any lingering suspicions of German loyalty.[11] It was no surprise, therefore, when, in May 1939, at an inter-Mennonite conference held in Winkler, Manitoba, to consider the looming prospect of war, the *Russlaender* faction actively promoted the idea of alternative service as part of any Mennonite response. Their call for a united front was partly realized the following spring with the formation in Winnipeg of the Mennonite Central Relief Committee, the major organization representing the interests of western Mennonites during the war.[12]

Although they were much less enthusiastic, most Ontario Mennonites also accepted the general idea of alternative service – but, in contrast to the *Russlaender*, only if it did not include work directly related to the conduct of the war in, for example, the medical corps or a war industry.[13] Throughout the 1930s they had refrained from participating in what they termed the 'aggressive peace' movement, but by the end of the decade they recognized that some accommodation to the state and co-operation with non-sectarian pacifists might be appropriate in order to protect their religious beliefs and way of life. Thus, with the progressive *Russlaender* on the one end, willing to perform almost any type of alternative service, and the *Kanadier* and fundamentalist Mennonites on the other in staunch opposition, the more moderate Ontario peace churches, mainly the Mennonite Brethren in Christ and the Old Mennonites of Ontario, struck a compromise: acceptance of alternative service – but only of a civilian nature – as a means to secure the right to co status of all Mennonites. It was this position that came closest to that of Canada's non-sectarian pacifists.

Another and more serious restriction in the 1940 regulations was the clause requiring all conscientious objectors to belong to a religious denomination that prohibited, as a tenet of faith, the bearing of arms. Initially, therefore, men from major Protestant denominations, or any church other than the historic peace sects, were denied co status, and their plight became an important factor in the wider pacifist call for universal recognition of conscientious objectors in conjunction with alternative service. As early as August 1940, for instance, the chief registrar in Ottawa had received numerous letters from United Church pacifists; these were copies of a form letter devised and circulated by Lavell Smith urging the government to give all conscientious objectors the same privileges provided in Britain, including the opportunity to perform alternative national service.[14] More traditional pacifist groups, such as the Christadelphian Service Committee of Canada, made similar pleas but it was the Canadian Society of Friends that took the lead in organizing a pacifist front for alternative service in the interests of all prospective conscientious objectors.[15]

In reaffirming its peace testimony the Canadian Friends Service Committee assured all national political party leaders of the readiness on the part of Friends to serve in 'any constructive civilian capacity.'[16] The committee also circulated a questionnaire among its members to ascertain the exact types of humanitarian service Friends of military age would be willing to perform, and by mid-summer 1940 some specific recommendations were made.[17] In a letter to Prime Minister King the Service Committee's general secretary, Fred Haslam, outlined a program of alternative service work under civilian supervision consisting of any practical combination of forestry or agricultural work, road maintenance, social services in distressed areas, and perhaps even participation in post-war rehabilitation plans. The length of service in such work, he added, need not be limited to that of military training.[18]

Haslam emphasized that he was writing not only on behalf of Quakers but on behalf of all those with 'religious or moral objections to participation in war'. He also expressed the desire of Friends to join with other historic peace churches in representing the interests of all conscientious objectors in Ottawa, and with that goal in mind the Friends Service Committee communicated with the Mennonite and Brethren in Christ (Tunker) Churches in Ontario.[19]

The Ontario peace churches, already in the process of organizing a united response to the challenge of conscription, after 'due consideration' accepted 'in principle' the Quaker proposal for alternative service and invited the Society of Friends to join the newly formed Conference of Historic Peace Churches and its special subcommittee concerned with conscientious objectors, the Military Problems Committee.[20] The Friends accepted the invitation eagerly, and their association with the Conference of Historic Peace Churches throughout the war proved to be an important link between socially conscious liberal pacifists and those from the traditional religious sects.

By September 1940 the Military Problems Committee sent its first delegation to Ottawa on behalf of conscientious objectors. It included J.B. Martin, the committee chairman, Ernie J. Swalm, the chairman of the Conference of Historic Peace Churches, and Fred Haslam of the Society of Friends. In addition, David Toews represented western Mennonites, who were not officially members of the Ontario-based Conference of Historic Peace Churches. In a meeting with T.C. Davis, the associate deputy minister of national war services, the delegation reaffirmed its desire for the official recognition of all cos and presented specific proposals for alternative forms of 'constructive civilian service.'[21] Davis responded sympathetically and promised that his department would consider the recommendations, but he strongly suggested that in the meantime the peace churches should proceed with national registration and refrain from attracting publicity.

Although it was disappointed with this response, the Military Problems Committee agreed that its first priorities, in view of existing regulations, were to launch an immediate campaign to register its members and to safeguard their claims to conscientious objector status. Accordingly, a special registration card and application for postponement of military training were drafted and circulated among the various churches.[22] As for the Quakers, Haslam distributed the forms to monthly meeting clerks with instructions that all men of military age complete the registration questionnaire at once and send the application for postponement to the divisional registrar of their administrative district within twelve days of the call-up of their particular age group.[23]

Obviously, this procedure was of little use to prospective conscientious objectors from outside the peace sects since they were still completely barred from CO status by a strict interpretation of the 1940 regulations. Their dilemma finally became the focus of pacifist attention in November 1940 when the War Services Board in Saskatoon under the chairmanship of Mr Justice J.F.L. Embury refused the applications for postponement from military service of eight young men, most of them theological students at St Andrew's College at the University of Saskatchewan, on the ground that members of the United Church and the Church of England could not be considered conscientious objectors within the meaning of the regulations.[24] Although they had admitted that no tenet or article of faith in their church prohibited the bearing of arms or the undertaking of combatant service, the applicants argued that the United Church left the final decision on such matters to the individual consciences of its members. At one point the board 'tried very hard,' but in vain, to get the students to confess they were under the direct influence of Professor Carlyle King, popularly known by this time as a radical pacifist and socialist.[25]

Official reaction to the board's decision was completely favourable. For instance, the deputy adjutant-general of Division 'M,' Brig. George H. Cassels, actually boasted that it would 'do a lot to keep down applications for postponement or exemption on this ground' and suggested a copy of the decision be distributed to the chairmen of all other boards as a precedent.[26]

The response of pacifists, as well as of the churches directly affected by the decision, was one of alarm and protest. From his earlier discussions with officials in the Department of National War Services, Fred Haslam was under the impression that 'it was going to be the intention at Ottawa to judge conscientious objectors individually, regardless of and apart from church connections.' It was later suggested by a fellow pacifist, however, that perhaps the judgment of the Saskatchewan board could best be explained by the fact that 'the churches your committee represents have been pestering Ottawa and that the Anglican and United have made no representations on behalf of their members, except through the Christian Social Council, which has not kept at the job.'[27] Although this charge contained a certain amount of truth, it was not entirely accurate, especially since Haslam and the Canadian Friends Service

Committee had made every attempt to represent the interests of all pacifists regardless of church affiliation. As for the Christian Social Council of Canada, its executive passed a resolution asking the Canadian government to adopt the British procedure of basing co exemptions solely on individual conscientious convictions.[28] A similar resolution was passed and forwarded to the government by the ninth general council of the United Church.[29] None the less, the Saskatoon incident exposed the vulnerability of all young men claiming conscientious objection and thereby underlined the urgency of the situation at the very time that pacifists were preparing their major offensive on behalf of cos.

It was in an atmosphere of anxiety and tension, therefore, that the campaign for alternative service was again carried to Ottawa in November by a joint delegation composed of four representatives of western Mennonites and four eastern representatives from the Conference of Historic Peace Churches.[30] In a crucial series of meetings with the associate deputy ministers of national war services, T.C. Davis and Maj.-Gen. L.R. LaFlèche, the pacifists repeatedly argued for the introduction of civilian alternative service under civilian supervision. They had even drafted plans for a Canadian Fellowship Service that would co-ordinate a wide variety of pacifist public services under the direction of government welfare agencies.[31] Just as consistently, however, Davis and LaFlèche rejected their ideas as impractical and too costly. They urged the delegation to reconsider the goverment proposal for non-combatant service, possibly in civilian clothes but under military control.[32] The pacifists explained that the young men they represented would not agree to work in military camps regardless of whether uniforms would be worn. Finally, reiterating their demand for strictly civilian alternative service, the delegation forwarded specific recommendations, closely resembling Haslam's earlier proposals, in which alternative service work would be of an agricultural or forestry nature, including reforestation, land reclamation, and farm improvement, on government-owned land under the supervision of the Department of Agriculture and the Department of Mines and Resources. It was also suggested that first-aid courses be offered to prepare conscientious objectors to cope with epidemics or other wartime emergencies.[33] Although somewhat narrowed in scope, the delegation's recommendations were far in advance of government planning and served as a blueprint for the alternative service program that was ultimately established.

Throughout the various sessions the pacifists had tried to convey the essence of their peaceful and non-resistant faith – a faith that forbade participation in armed conflict and in any type of service temporarily allied with the military, but that permitted humanitarian relief work, regardless of the danger, as long as it was civilian in nature. The importance of this distinction was not grasped by government officials, and, while the negotiations were usually restrained in tone, there were a few times when tempers flared. At one point, for instance, after B.B. Janz, an Albertan, intimated to LaFlèche that the western *Russlaender* Mennonites would be willing to accept non-combatant medical service under the Red Cross, the other delegates angrily rejected the suggestion, insisting that the peace churches were united in their demand for nothing less than civilian service under civilian supervision.[34] When LaFlèche retorted, 'What'll you do if we shoot you?' Jacob H. Janzen of Waterloo exploded: 'Listen, Major-General, I want to tell you something. You can't scare us like that. I've looked down too many rifle-barrels in my time to be scared that way. This thing's in our blood for 400 years and you can't take it away from us like you'd crack a piece of kindling over your knee. I was before a firing squad twice. We believe in this. It's deep in our blood.'[35]

On this note the negotiations ended in a stalemate. Nevertheless, the pacifist delegates had made some significant advances. Most important, they had received a full hearing in Ottawa during which they exerted considerable influence upon government authorities, even if that influence was not completely visible until many of their specific recommendations for alternative service were later incorporated into government policy. Furthermore, a different type of pacifist alternative resulted from their suggestion to D.C. Clark, deputy minister of the Department of Finance. In order to allow the pacifist community to purchase war bonds without assisting the war effort, the government authorized a special series of non-interest bearing certificates, Series B, whose funds were earmarked for the relief of war victims.[36] Regardless of government decisions, however, the joint pacifist delegations sent to Ottawa in November 1940, as well as those who undertook subsequent visitations, came to symbolize pacifist unity. The various Mennonite groups in particular were encouraged to work together and overcome their differences, and the Conference of Historic Peace Churches represented the interests of all prospective conscientious objectors, including those outside the peace sects.

Along with pacifist demands to amend the War Service Regulations and allow for alternative service, government officials also faced increasing public resentment, especially in western Canada, over the whole question of exemptions. Prime Minister Mackenzie King raised the issue for consideration by the Department of National War Services in his reference to a letter in which George McDonald, a former Liberal member of the House from Souris, Manitoba, reported that many Manitobans were angered that Mennonites were escaping military training. McDonald complained that 'these young Mennonites are getting married and setting up homes for themselves. Many of our boys will have to take up arms, many will not return. While our sons are fighting these men will be building up good homes. It certainly isn't fair ... Our people here are going to be very bitter about this, and the government would be justified in compelling all our people to prepare themselves for at least home defence.'[37]

Such expressions of anger and suspicion were viewed in Ottawa as a matter for serious consideration, especially by the minister of national war services, James G. Gardner, who was from Saskatchewan. Consequently, public reaction came to play a part equal to if not greater than that of the pacifist influence in the formulation of plans for alternative service. Indeed, both military and government officials had agreed that the main reason to use cos in some type of non-combatant service was to 'placate the Westerners.'

Finally, under fire from all sides, and perhaps because he was particularly sensitive to western complaints, Gardner caved in and amended section 20 of the National War Services Regulations governing conscientious objectors.[39] By December 1940 an order in council deleted the requirement that cos belong to a recognized peace church, thus making the individual's conscientious beliefs the sole ground for exemption.[40] While the change certainly broadened the range of those who might claim the exemption, it also imposed specific responsibilities upon each prospective co. For instance, in addition to the usual letter of application for postponement, a co was now required to forward to his board a 'certificate' from the proper authority of his religious denomination verifying that he had 'sincere conscientious scruples against the bearing of arms.'[41] Most significant, however, was the clause requiring all cos found to be medically fit to perform one of three basic types of alternative service: non-combatant training in a military camp, non-combatant first-aid training in other than a military camp, or civilian labour service at other than a military camp. The period of such training or service and the rate of pay were to be identical to those in the military. A little over a year after Canada's entry into the war, Canadian authorities had officially recognized the right to conscientious objection of all individuals regardless of church affiliations and had begun to incorporate pacifist alternatives into the national war effort.

Whatever the major impetus behind this action, it was because of the persistence of the pacifists that the provision for civilian service under civilian supervision appeared as a possible form of alternative service. Most pacifist groups were pleased with the changes, with the exception of the Mennonite *Aeltestenkomitee*, the *Kanadier* bishops. Up to that point they had boycotted all negotiations with federal authorities; now, alarmed by the new provision for alternative service, the *Aeltestenkomitee* finally approached Ottawa and registered a desperate plea for the complete exemption of *Kanadier* youth from all types of service. But it was too late. In effect, the *Kanadier* had gambled that by remaining silent they would continue to enjoy the same type of exemption they had had during the First World War, and they had lost.[42] Thereafter the *Kanadier* Mennonites modified their absolutist stand and joined in the clamour for strictly civilian service under civilian supervision. Except for the continued stubborn resistance of Doukhobors and Jehovah's Witnesses to the authority of the state, the pacifists were united in support of alternative service. This marked the end of absolutism among conscientious objectors and the beginning of a new era of pacifist service in Canada.

II

Having won concessions on the question of conscientious objector status and the principle of alternative service, pacifists turned their attention to the exact nature of the work to be performed. Although it had been decided in principle that all persons exempted from military service would be required to render some form of alternative service, no definite plan was developed until the spring of 1941. Initially, the government favoured sending conscientious objectors to military camps for non-combatant training and service, especially since the original period of training was to be only thirty days. The military authorities, however, were against having cos in their camps 'under any condition,' and when the training period was lengthened to four months the Department of National War Services was finally swayed by the pacifist recommendation for a civilian-oriented program.

Once again the National War Service Regulations were amended. In accordance with plans outlined in May 1941 by the associate deputy ministers Davis and LaFlèche, conscientious objectors were now required to report to alternative service work camps where, for the duration of the war, they would be paid at the rate of fifty cents per day, with subsistence, including medical care.[43] Under the direct supervision of the Parks Board of the Federal Department of Mines and Resources, work camps were established in national parks across western Canada: Kootenay National Park, British Columbia; Banff and Jasper national parks, Alberta; Prince Albert National Park, Saskatchewan; and Riding Mountain National Park, Manitoba.[44] In addition, smaller camps were also created at two forest experimental stations: Kananaskis Camp in Seebe, Alberta, and Petawawa Camp in Chalk River, Ontario (see table 1 for a complete listing of alternative service work camps).

The conscientious objectors who first reported to the alternative service work camps in the national parks were mainly from western Canada and, as table 2 indicates, they represented a variety of religious, ethnic, and occupational backgrounds. It is possible, however, to construct a general profile of the typical alternative service worker in the national parks between 1942 and 1945. Predictably, he was single, a Mennonite of either Dutch or German extraction, had worked as a farmer or farm labourer, and was between twenty and twenty-five years old, the standard age of military call-up.

Although Mennonites and other conscientious objectors were directed to these camps as a matter of course, Doukhobors, 'so far as possible,' were segregated and assigned to separate road-building projects such as the construction of the Lac la Ronge Highway, a mining road in northern Saskatchewan. Unlike their Independent brothers in Saskatchewan, however, the Doukhobors in British Columbia, particularly the Sons of Freedom, were extremely hostile to the idea of alternative service and many even refused to report for medical examinations. Ironically, their pacifism was accompanied by a reputation for dramatic and sometimes violent resistance, from nude marches to bombings and burnings. As a result, the initial plan to employ them in the construction of a highway from Nelson, British Columbia, to the American border fell victim to the government's desire to avoid a potentially explosive confrontation.

In a cleverly worded rationalization, Davis and La Flèche actually recommended that Doukhobors in British Columbia not be asked 'to render any alternative service' since they were already subject to the penalty for failure to report for alternative service – disfranchisement at both the dominion and the provincial level. By using this criterion, they argued, the government was justified 'in doing nothing with the Douk-

TABLE 1
Alternative service work camps in Canada during the Second World War

NATIONAL PARKS	BRITISH COLUMBIA FOREST SERVICE		
Banff National Park	Location	Designation	Camps
Spray River Camp	Mainland	GT-1	Green Timbers
Healy Creek Camp		GT-2	Emory Creek
Castle Mountain Camp		GT-3	Vedder Crossing
		GT-4	Haney
Glacier National Park*		GT-5	Seymour Mountain
Jasper National Park		GT-6	Powell River
Maligne Road Camp	Vancouver	C-1	Hill 60
Kootenay National Park	Island	C-2	Cowichan
Mile 16 Camp		C-3	Koksilah
Mile 21 Camp		C-4	Langford
Banff-Windermere Highway Camp		C-5	Nanaimo
		C-6	Alberni
Prince Albert National Park		C-7	Timberlands
Waskesiu Camp			
		Q-1	Quinsam
Riding Mountain National Park		Q-2	Menzie's Bay
Wasagaming Camp		Q-3	Campbell River
		Q-4	Puntledge
Yoho National Park*		Q-5	Bowser
		Q-6	Horne Lake
FOREST EXPERIMENTAL STATIONS		Q-7	Loveland Lake
Kananaskis Camp (Seebe, Alberta)		Q-8	Kelsey Bay
Petawawa Camp (Chalk River, Ontario)			
	Non-specific	M	Mobile
SURVEY AND ENGINEERING PROJECTS			
Lac la Ronge Camp (northern Saskatchewan)*			
Montreal River Camp (northwestern Ontario)			

SOURCE: Public Archives of Canada, RG 14, D 2, vol. 451, no. 257; RG 27, vol 137, file 601.3-12
*Seasonal or short-lived

hobors in British Columbia and avoiding trouble there.'[45] Obviously, since all conscientious objectors were automatically disfranchised, they were proposing to treat Doukhobors differently from other groups. In time, the Cabinet War Committee agreed to their suggestion and issued a secret directive halting enforcement of the regulations against Doukhobors, since it was felt 'that to compel universal compliance in the communities in question would involve a very heavy undertaking and

TABLE 2
Statistical profile of alternative service workers in national parks: Religion, ethnicity, former occupation, and marital status by year*

Religion	1942	1943	1944	1945	1946
Anglican	6	1	2	1	—
Baptist	6	3	1	—	—
Christian	28	4	2	1	—
Christian Assembly	6	4	4	1	—
Christadelphian	—	20	7	—	—
Church of Christ	20	1	2	—	—
Church of God	2	4	1	—	—
Doukhobor	4	5	5	8	—
Free Methodist	3	3	—	—	—
Hutterite	39	37	101	44	—
Jehovah's Witnesses	13	17	226	283	128
Lutheran	7	6	3	1	—
Mennonite	663	348	206	100	7
Moravian	2	2	1	—	—
Pentacostal	10	3	1	—	—
Plymouth Brethren	27	35	5	—	—
Quaker	5	1	—	—	—
Roman Catholic	1	1	1	2	1
Seventh-Day Adventist	51	22	8	3	—
United Church of Canada	21	16	2	—	—
Other or unknown	99	32	17	12	3
Total	1013	565	595	450	139

Ethnicity	1942	1943	1944	1945	1946
Austrian	8	9	1	1	—
Belgian	—	—	2	2	2
Czechoslovakian	—	—	—	1	—
Danish	—	—	1	1	—
Dutch	597	256	250	135	11
English	88	72	102	93	44
Finnish	—	—	—	1	—
French	9	—	11	15	5
German	149	118	52	27	11
Greek	—	—	—	1	1
Hungarian	1	—	3	4	—
Icelandic	—	—	1	—	2
Irish	28	18	26	23	9
Italian	2	5	2	8	1
Macedonian	—	—	—	1	—
Norwegian	8	4	7	11	—
Polish	5	6	15	13	8
Rumanian	—	—	—	9	1

TABLE 2 – continued

Ethnicity	1942	1943	1944	1945	1946
Russian	42	33	20	7	3
Scottish	32	20	42	48	23
Spanish	1	1	—	—	—
Swedish	7	3	4	13	3
Swiss	17	11	31	13	—
Ukranian	12	7	18	23	10
Welsh	2	2	5	4	3
Unknown	5	—	2	2	2
Total	1013	565	595	456	139

Former occupation	1942	1943	1944	1945	1946
Carpenter	8	10	6	10	2
Clerk	28	10	7	14	12
Cook	—	2	—	3	—
Diesel engineer	—	2	1	1	1
Farmer	746	141	60	83	11
Farm labourer	22	249	322	176	27
Gas station operator	2	2	—	1	1
Labourer	—	5	23	20	8
Logger	—	5	1	11	2
Machinist	9	9	15	10	1
Mechanic	82	21	36	22	10
Millworker	12	4	—	4	—
Minister	—	—	11	19	18
Miner	—	—	—	4	3
Painter	1	1	1	4	—
Student	16	10	10	3	4
Teacher	8	12	7	1	—
Tractor operator	1	3	—	—	—
Truck driver	17	7	22	54	23
Miscellaneous or unknown	61	72	73	16	16
Total	1013	565	595	456	139

Marital Status	1942	1943	1944	1945	1946
Single	824	474	515	385	135
Married	189	91	80	71	4
Total	1013	565	595	456	139

SOURCE: Miscellaneous annual reports of the National Parks Branch, Department of Mines and Resources, Public Archives of Canada, RG 84, Vol. 213.
*All years April 1 to March 31 of following year, except April 1 to July 15 in 1946.

that no substantial effect could be anticipated from the Doukhobors so drafted for alternative service.'[46]

Despite the official adoption of this 'hands-off' policy, the government remained publicly committed to bringing all Doukhobors into alternative service.[47] In practice, however, the only serious attempt in that direction was the Lac la Ronge project. Although the project was later described by the authorities as having attained a 'considerable degree of success,' in reality it was a dismal failure. For example, while seventy Doukhobors put in an appearance at the camp, ninety-two others were imprisoned for refusing to report. After one season the experiment was abandoned.[48]

Another attempt at road-building was made at the Montreal River Camp, one of the earliest and largest alternative service work camps, located at an old logging site eighty miles northeast of Sault Ste-Marie, Ontario, at the mouth of the Montreal River. Unlike those in western Canada, this camp was under the direction of the Surveys and Engineering Branch of the Department of Mines and Resources; the work consisted almost exclusively of construction on the trans-Canada highway along the north shore of Lake Superior.[49] The first group of COs arrived there in July 1941, and for the next few years the Montreal River Camp became the main depot for conscientious objectors from eastern Canada. In effect, the Montreal River Camp was the mother of all other work camps. It was there that Canada's alternative service program was inaugurated. As the major CO reception centre, it housed men from a mixture of religious backgrounds in addition to the Mennonite majority. It was in the Montreal River Camp that conscientious objectors were first introduced to one another and to alternative service; the experience there served as the basis for later camp organization on the west coast.

The camp provided opportunities for a good deal of pacifist cross-fertilization. Life at Montreal River was hard, especially during the winter, and most of the young pacifists shared a common sense of isolation. The only way into the camp was by truck from the Soo, and, once there, the 'conchies' were almost completely cut off from the rest of society. Although they waited eagerly for letters and parcels from home, the camp post office was eighty miles away.[50] As a result, the COs spent much of their free time in group activities. Bible study and other religious functions were organized under the direction of the Reverend J. Harold Sherk, secretary of the Conference of Historic Peace Churches, who travelled to the camp about once a week. During the first few years at Montreal River, Sherk established the pattern for religious supervision later followed in other camps.[51]

The majority of cos in the camp were members of millennial sects or the Conference of Historic Peace Churches; consequently, they viewed alternative service simply as the price they had to pay to remain true to their faith. A smaller number of Quakers and liberal pacifists from the larger Protestant denominations viewed the work camps as experiments in Christian communal living and welcomed the opportunity to perform some 'disinterested service.' As one of these conscientious objectors wrote, '[we] are trying to take our position as cos seriously. We believe it lays responsibilities on us.'[52] Some were attracted to the War Resisters International in the belief that the effect of pacifism on their personal lives would produce some corresponding change in the structure of social institutions.[53]

The enthusiasm of the small group of activists was reflected in the birth at Montreal River of the first Canadian co publication, the *Northern Beacon*. Edited by Wes Brown, a co from Toronto with a United Church background, the mimeographed newsletter was intended to boost the morale of conscientious objectors in the various camps scattered across Canada and to publicize camp life to pacifists at home.[54] One of those in Toronto, James Finlay, commended the editor: 'You can well imagine that some of the lads who may succeed you were greatly interested to learn something of the situation.'[55]

Indeed, young pacifists such as Gordon Stewart, a student at McGill University, were so eager to learn about the work camps and other alternatives to military service and to help develop a pacifist network in Canada that they launched another newsletter, the *Canadian CO*.[56] This Montreal-based paper was designed to keep Canadian pacifists 'posted on what their isolated fellows and groups are doing' and in this way help dispel the 'almost inevitable' feeling of loneliness among conscientious objectors in the camps.[57] The paper also reserved space for contributions from women pacifists. Although women were not required to perform alternative service, it was felt that 'their pacifist stand can [be] and is being expressed conscientiously in many different ways.'[58] Above all, the main theme of the *Canadian CO* was 'pacifist action' in various fields of service at home and abroad.

By the spring of 1942 this call for the more useful deployment of conscientious objectors had become the major goal of liberal pacifists. Edis Fairbairn, for instance, reminded the 'campers' at Montreal River that 'beyond the work camp experience we still have to find some way of demonstrating our Christian citizenship by a sacrificial service comparable in risk and costliness to that service given, willingly or unwillingly, by the enlisted men.'[59] Fairbairn believed that conscientious objectors had to prove that alternative pacifist service was just as patriotic and useful as military service. As an example he cited the humanitarian work of British Quakers, and he suggested that the Conference of Historic Peace Churches might be able to arrange something similar in Canada.

The whole question of pacifist service had become a popular topic of speculation in the camp. There was a growing sense among conscientious objectors that the government had shipped them up to Montreal River merely to keep them out of the public eye. Their work, especially during the winter, seemed to be of minimal value, and some of them yearned to make a more useful contribution than swinging a pick and shovel. Even the work in the camps out west appeared more attractive; in the national parks alternative service personnel were responsible for the prevention and suppression of forest fires, and throughout the war years they formed the nucleus of fire-fighting crews. Silviculture and the control of insect infestation were other endeavours, and the alternative service men in the Banff and Kootenay parks were credited with saving large quantities of saw-timber and mine props.[60]

The demands from pacifist groups and the conscientious objectors themselves for more worthwhile work than that offered at Montreal River coincided with two other factors which, in combination, caused the government to expand the deployment of cos in forest areas. By April 1942 the authorities had come to recognize that the labour of conscientious objectors was to be a permanent and important resource for the duration of the war. At the same time there were warnings of forest fire emergencies on the west coast because of the danger of Japanese attacks with incendiary bombs. Consequently, the minister of national war services entered into an agreement with the province of British Columbia whereby up to one thousand conscientious objectors were to be made available to the British Columbia Forest Service for forest protection duties on Vancouver Island and the adjacent mainland.[61] For the next few years the west coast was the centre of activity for conscientious objectors in alternative service.

III

The work camps under the jurisdiction of the British Columbia Forest Service, which numbered fifteen to twenty at any given time, were established in three main project areas. The lower mainland camps were called 'GT' (green timber) camps, those on southern Vancouver Island were known as 'c' (Cowichan) camps and those north of Nanaimo were designated as 'Q' (Quinsam) camps (refer to table 1 for a complete list). Where possible, the alternative service camps utilized existing campsites and buildings, including those that had served as relief camps during the 1930s; in addition, new camps were hurriedly assembled with pre-fabricated huts and sometimes even tents, both of which added to the ability of the workers to meet fire emergencies.[62]

The main responsibility of the alternative service crews was fighting forest fires. The 'campers' in all three project areas were fully trained in fire-fighting measures, and during the summers of 1942 and 1943 they fought a total of 234 fires.[63] None of the fires, however, was caused by enemy action. Besides their actual fire-fighting work, the alternative service men accomplished valuable and essential forest protection and improvement work, such as snag-falling, truck-trail construction, and reforestation.

Most of the alternative service workers who first reported for these new duties in June 1942 were transferred from other camps, particularly from Montreal River. In fact, by the following month all but a few of the Montreal River 'campers' had been reassigned to the British Columbia Forest Service. The men from Montreal River exerted a great deal of leadership and influence in the new camps. Even the *Northern Beacon* resurfaced in British Columbia at Campbell River Camp under a new name, the *Beacon*, with the same editor, Wes Brown.[64]

Initially, conscientious objectors welcomed the idea of the British Columbia camps as a worthwhile and exciting adventure, especially since prior to the war many of them had never travelled more than a short distance from their homes. But it was not long before dissatisfaction set in. Faced with the prospect of life in the camps for the duration of the war, the Mennonites yearned to return to the work on their farms. The liberal activists, mainly young United Church idealists, complained that chopping wood and planting trees were not the types of wartime humanitarian service they had hoped to perform. Although they recognized the value of the work, they wondered if better use could be made of their skills.[65]

The issue came to a head when Wes Brown, circulated a questionnaire asking conscientious objects in the various British Columbia camps for their reaction to the idea of diversified alternative service in private industry and in such fields as agriculture, coal-mining, logging, and hospital and ambulance work.[66] The authors of the questionnaire suggested that an acute labour shortage in Canada would ultimately necesisitate the release of conscientous objectors from alternative service work camps for employment in more important fields of service.[67] As might have been expected, the authorities viewed the questionnaire as premature; they feared it would raise false expectations and create bitter discontent among a generally passive lot. The assistant chief forester in British Columbia reprimanded the authors for not having first obtained permission from the Forest Service to prepare the questionnaire, and he ordered the confiscation of the completed questionnaires.[68] As a result of his role in the fracas Wes Brown was forced to resign as editor of the *Beacon*.[69] Despite its overall failure, however, the questionnaire episode dramatized the intensified effort on the part of Canadian pacifists to persuade the government to provide conscientious objectors with legitimate alternatives within society rather than hiding them in the nation's forests.

As dissatisfaction grew among the interned conscientious objectors, the government authorities began to reassess their entire approach to the mobilization and utilization of manpower. By September 1942, for instance, the responsibility for the administration of the National War Service Regulations, including those governing alternative service, was transferred from the large, cumbersome Department of National War Services to the Department of Labour, and within a few months the regulations themselves were revoked and replaced by the National Selective Service Mobilization Regulations.[70] The nature of alternative service remained largely the same, but the transfer of responsibility to the new National Selective Service division of the Department of Labour meant that pacifists had to familiarize a whole new set of bureaucrats with their peculiar position. Pacifist spokesmen were quick to protest a few clauses within the new regulations. One was section 12, which stipulated that students in Canadian universities, colleges, or preparatory schools would no longer be recognized as conscientious objectors. On the contrary, all male students found to be physically fit were now required to enrol in a Canadian Officer Training Corps contingent at the educational institution or to report for military training.[71] Through its Military Problems Committee, the Conference of Historic Peace Churches charged that this regulation, as well as the requirement that all students for the ministry be willing to serve as military chaplains, was 'a discrimination on religious grounds' that was 'not in keeping with the general principle and practice of religious liberty in Canada.' If these restrictions were allowed to stand, the committee argued, it would be difficult, if not impossible, for the peace churches to recruit and properly train candidates for the ministry.[72] The pacifists requested that an alternative program be established within the universities 'which would be applicable to students in the same way that alternative service camps provide for non-students.' The Department of Labour insisted that implementing such a plan would be difficult because of public opinion and the relatively small number of students involved.[73] Needless to say, the pacifist suggestion was rejected and university students eventually reported to the work camps.

The debate over student deferments, however, as well as complaints from conscientious objectors in the camps, had sparked a broad pacifist critique of the entire alternative service program. Specifically, the Military Problems Committee objected to the power of the various mobilization boards whose decisions, it was argued, had caused serious inequities in the administration of the regulations which could be remedied only by allowing conscientious objectors to appeal the decisions of the boards.[74] (The most glaring example of this was the large number of *Russlaender* Mennonites denied co status by the Manitoba board.) Furthermore, the remuneration of alternative service workers at the basic rate of fifty cents a day with no allowance for clothing or dependants was criticized as insufficient, and it was suggested that provisions be made for the dependants of alternative service workers similar to that provided for the dependants of military personnel.

Concerning the alternative service program itself, the committee reiterated what was becoming a familiar call for more diversified forms of work, especially since a number of conscientious objectors were trained specialists – doctors, dentists, teachers, and engineers. Only a broader range of service, they argued, would 'enable each person to make the largest possible contribution to the good of Canada and of all mankind.' United Church pacifists echoed their demand. Lavell Smith, the chairman of the Canadian FOR, personally vouched for the ability of a number of cos 'to do work of much more urgent importance than snag-falling and road building,' and he urged the minister of labour to follow the British example and utilize them as hospital orderlies or as attendents in mental hospitals, both of which were in short supply in Canada.[75] Another United Church minister and pacifist spokesman, Harold Toye, complained that Canadian alternative service work camps were perceived as 'concentration or internment camps' rather than respectable alternatives to military service.[76] That impression would be changed only by employing conscientious objectors according to individual skills in more valuable jobs such as dental and medical services, education and farm work, and possibly in civilian ambulance service in war-devastated areas.

To a large extent the criticisms raised by pacifist spokesmen in Ottawa reflected the frustration they discovered during their personal tours of the work camps. In most of the eleven camps they visited, for instance, J.B. Martin and Ernie Swalm of the Military Problems Committee found 'a lot of anxiety' and reported that some of the men were so discouraged that a few were beginning to think that 'maybe after all the best way out would be to enlist in some corps of the military.'[77] Similarly, during his swing through the camps James Finlay met a number of conscientious objectors anxious to 'test' their pacifist convictions outside the camps. Although they felt it was probably easier psychologically to remain safely isolated in the work camps than to mingle in society, they yearned to be of more useful service.[78] It was this idea that they wished government officials to understand.

Finally, in response to the pacifist demands and as part of its overall effort to make efficient use of manpower, the Department of Labour began to reconsider completely the employment of conscientious objectors. By February 1943 the director of selective service, Deputy Labour Minister Arthur MacNamara, concluded that although work in the alternative service camps might be beneficial there was no question that the men in the camps 'could now be more usefully employed in agriculture or in essential industries where labour shortages exist.'[79] His superior, Labour Minister Humphrey Mitchell, agreed and approved a major reorganization of the alternative service program.

Basically, the action merely continued the movement already begun in the previous year with the transfer of alternative service responsibilities to the Department of Labour. The new directive further shifted it from the mobilization section of National Selective Service to the civilian section headed by a chief alternative service officer, L.E. Westman, with alternative service officers in each military district.[80] Most important, however, especially from the pacifist standpoint, was the broadening of alternative service by May 1943 to include essential work in agriculture and industry. This change was a turning-point in the struggle of pacifists for a meaningful role within Canadian society in wartime. Certainly, once conscientious objectors were allowed to perform a wide range of alternatives to military service, the pacifist alternative itself gained credibility as a legitimate and valuable part of the Canadian response to war.

IV

As a result of concerted pressure by pacifists and rethinking by government authorities, diversified pacifist service had finally become a reality. On the whole the broadening of alternative service was effected easily, although the initial news of the government's decision to employ conscientious objectors in work outside the camps was greeted by a barrage of protests, chiefly from lumbermen in British Columbia and government officials concerned with the prospect of losing their best source of low-paid labour for forest protection.[81] Other complaints, not surprisingly, came from irritated members of the Canadian Legion and the Imperial Order of the Daughters of the Empire.[82] There were also some favourable responses, particularly from the farm organizations, industries, and politicians such as John Diefenbaker, who had been lobbying for such a move for some time. For the most part, however, the government 'policy of silence' concerning the treatment of conscientious objectors meant that the general public was not even aware that they were employed outside the camps.[83]

Under the new arrangement, alternative service officers in each military district screened conscientious objectors and assigned them to jobs where their skills were most needed. Although a considerable number were assigned to laboratories, hospitals, and certain industries such as sawmills and food-processing plants, the majority, mostly Mennonites with farm experience, were directed to agricultural work. As table 3 illustrates, by the end of the war over one-half of all conscientious objectors in alternative service were employed in agriculture, and roughly one-quarter were working in a variety of industries and services.

The actual employment of conscientious objectors in agriculture and industry, however, was conditional upon their agreement to contribute part of their earnings to the Canadian Red Cross Society. Under the terms of a special contract with their employers, cos were paid at the 'prevailing wage rate' but received only twenty-five dollars per month. The remainder of their earnings, less taxes, was diverted to the Red Cross.[84] Those in agricultural work also received free board and lodging, and those in urban industries were paid an additional monthly allowance of thirty-eight dollars to cover living expenses.

Within a year, however, amid complaints from various pacifist groups that the financial reimbursement for alternative service was not only insufficient but totally unfair compared with that for military service, the government authorized additional allowances for dependants and

TABLE 3
Disposition of conscientious objectors under alternative service as of 31 December, 1945

6655	Employed in agriculture
1412	Employed in miscellaneous essential industries
542	Employed in sawmills, logging and timbering
469	Employed in packing plants and food-processing plants
269	Employed in construction
86	Employed in hospitals
63	Employed in coal mining
15	Employed in grain handling at the Head of the Lakes
170	Employed in alternative service work camps
14	Serving jail sentences
34	In hands of or being prepared for Enforcement Division
201	In hands of RCMP or other agencies to locate whereabouts
921	Cases under review
10,851	Total conscientious objectors under alternative service

SOURCE: J.F. Mackinnon, 'Historical Account of the Wartime Activities of the Alternative Service Branch,' Department of Labour Report, 11 April 1946, 20, Public Archives of Canada, RG 35, series 7, vol. 21.

for medical and dental services; thereafter the government continued to take steps to ease the financial burden on alternative service workers and their families.[85] Pacifist organizations such as the Canadian Friends Service Committee were instrumental in assisting the dependants of conscientious objectors and in finding jobs for the COs themselves, although the actual placement of men in specific jobs was made by the divisional alternative service officers through local employment offices.[86]

By the summer of 1943 the transfer of COs to the newly approved fields of service was in full swing. The number of men in the British Columbia Forest Service camps alone dropped from 750 to approximately 450.[87] Although this trend continued through the last two years of war, not all conscientious objectors agreed to perform the new jobs. Table 3 shows that by the war's end approximately one-eighth of conscientious objectors had been temporarily relieved of all forms of work, had refused outright to participate and therefore remained in the work camps, or had attempted to evade the alternative service requirement altogether. Apart from the newly postponed COs entering alternative service for the first time, those who remained in the camps were mainly those, such as Jehovah's Witnesses, who were unwilling to enter an employment contract or to allocate funds to the Red Cross because of its close association with the war machine.[88]

The Montreal River Camp, which had already lost most of its workers to the British Columbia camps the previous year, was closed in May 1943. The 196 men there at the time were either returned to farms in the Kitchener-Waterloo area or sent to work in the sugar-beet fields of southern Ontario near Chatham. An experiment using Jehovah's Witnesses in the sugar-beet work ended in failure because they regularly left the fields in order to spread the gospel in nearby towns. As a result, the offenders were sent to the Chalk River camp for the duration of the war, and thereafter Jehovah's Witnesses were denied employment outside the camps.

From the beginning Jehovah's Witnesses had resisted the principle of alternative service as part of their refusal to recognize the authority of the state. Consequently, of the 687 conscientious objectors prosecuted in Canada for failure to report for alternative service, 30 per cent were Jehovah's Witnesses. Following brief jail terms they were taken to work camps under police escort. Once in the camps they were the last to leave (see again the data for 1945 and 1946 in table 2). For all practical purposes they were prisoners rather than voluntary workers.[89] Perhaps for this reason Jehovah's Witnesses viewed the alternative service work camps as internment camps not far removed in principle from the camps at Buchenwald and Dachau.[90] The frustrated alternative service authorities, on the other hand, were 'quite definitely sure' that Jehovah's Witnesses were not conscientious objectors in the true sense of the term and concluded that 'they should not be so classified in the event of another war.'[91]

An even sterner recommendation was made regarding the Doukhobors who had also challenged the principle of alternative service but who, unlike the Jehovah's Witnesses, had largely escaped its enforcement thanks to the government's own ambiguous policy. In a letter to the deputy minister of labour, the chief alternative service officer proposed 'in all seriousness' a final solution to the Doukhobor problem on the west coast. His plan entailed negotiating with the governments of Mexico and other Central American countries an agreement whereby migrant Mexican labour would be allowed into British Columbia on a temporary basis to replace the Doukhobors who would be encouraged to resettle en masse in some country such as El Salvador, where they might be guaranteed full freedom from military service 'for a quite modest consideration.' 'If we had a place for them to go,' said Westman, 'it might be a good time to break the agreement about military service and start a very desirable exodus from British Columbia, especially of Sons of Freedom.'[92] Obviously, Doukhobors and Jehovah's Witnesses were viewed as obstructing an effective implementation of the diversified alternative service program.

By and large, however, the transition from camp life to the farms, factories, and hospitals was carried out smoothly and enthusiastically by the conscientious objectors affected. Nevertheless, the feeling persisted that the government had not gone far enough in offering cos real opportunities for humanitarian service in war zones. For instance, C.F. Klassen, secretary of the Mennonite Central Relief Committee in Winnipeg, reminded the labour minister that *Russlaender* Mennonites had always been willing to perform non-combatant medical work, and urged that a field ambulance corps be created as soon as possible.[93] Similarly, a small group of conscientious objectors at Banff proposed to form a civilian ambulance service 'to be used in whatever zone of war assigned by the authorities.' In a letter to J.W. Noseworthy, the ccf member of Parliament for York South, they reported that the five Toronto churches they represented were prepared to provide the necessary equipment for such a service, including a new ambulance. 'We are desirous to be of more valuable service to our country in this time of urgent need,' they wrote, 'than at our present occupation.'[94]

Despite the obvious willingness on the part of pacifists, government authorities remained hesitant to deploy conscientious objectors overseas in a non-combatant or humanitarian capacity. A precedent for such service, however, had been set the previous year with the inclusion of cos in the Civilian Corps of Canadian Firefighters sent to the United Kingdom.[95] Eventually twenty Canadian conscientious objectors, mainly Mennonites and United Churchmen, enlisted and served overseas as junior firemen of the same status as other untrained members.[96] Following some preliminary training, the Canadian fire-fighters assumed full responsibility for fire stations in Southampton, Portsmouth, Plymouth, Bristol, and London, where they not only extinguished fires but also carried on salvage and rescue operations. The young pacifists welcomed this opportunity to leave the work camps in Canada in order to help save life and property amid the destruction of war.[97] Nevertheless, some feared that perhaps a compromise had been made since the Firefighting Corps appeared to be in danger of becoming nothing more than a 'Fourth Arm' of the military.[98] Obviously, a thin line separated the concept of alternative service from indirect support of the war effort, but in the end most of the conscientious objectors concluded that service in the corps did not conflict with their consciences.[99]

The Firefighting Corps was an example of the type of relief work a growing number of young pacifists wished to perform, but the corps could only absorb a few COs. Most pacifists had to press for other possibilities, the most likely of which was the type of non-combatant medical service provided for conscientious objectors in Britain and the United States but initially opposed in Canada by the military.[100] By the spring of 1943, however, the authorities appeared to have a change of heart when the prime minister's personal assistant, J.W. Pickersgill, suggested that the government 'meet any group of conscientious objectors half-way so that they can participate in the national effort.'[101]

Finally, in September of that year an order in council authorized the enlistment of conscientious objectors for overseas service as non-combatants in the Royal Canadian Army Medical Corps and the Canadian Dental Corps.[102] Before the end of the war, over two hundred COs joined the non-combatant units, and many of them served overseas in various theatres of the European war. *Russlaender* Mennonites in particular were attracted to the new service, but others, especially the liberal Protestants, were less interested.

Although enlistment was voluntary and the service was to be strictly non-combatant, those who joined became subject to military law, and rumours soon circulated that, once overseas, only Mennonites and Seventh-Day Adventists were recognized as legitimate conscientious objectors, while others were ordered to undertake infantry training.[103] A number of COs also saw participation in the non-combatant units as constituting direct support for the war machine. What was needed, they insisted, was some type of relief and rehabilitation work conducted completely separately from the military.[104] The idea of a civilian ambulance unit overseas manned by conscientious objectors gained in popularity. More than any other proposal, it captured the imagination of pacifists seeking to translate the principle of non-violence into a realistic and meaningful response to the tragedy of world war.

The model for such an ambulance unit was the Friends Ambulance Unit (FAU) first organized by British Quakers during the Great War and revived by British and American Friends during the Second World War. The FAU was active in Europe, the Mideast, and North Africa, but it was the lure of the Far East, and of China in particular, that aroused the most enthusiasm among young conscientious objectors. Those in Canada were no exception, and since their first discussion of a possible ambulance unit pacifists had set their eyes on China as the field of service. The prospect of adventure as well as the opportunity to render humanitarian service aroused considerable excitement in the alternative service work camps, and numerous men expressed their willingness to volunteer.[105]

One of the leading spokesmen for the men in the camps was Gus Harris, a Toronto co attached to Spray River Camp No. 3 near Banff and the editor of the *Canadian Pacifist*, the newest co monthly. In a letter to Prime Minister Mackenzie King, Harris expressed the desire of conscientious objectors for 'more humanitarian work without avoiding danger.' He and his associates at Spray River had earlier volunteered to the Department of Pensions and National Health to serve as human guinea pigs for nutritional experiments in the clinical study of wartime and post-war illnesses, but their offer was rejected because of the lack of laboratory facilities. Now they were asking for permission to organize an ambulance unit in China.[106] J.W. Pickersgill dismissed their request as 'completely out of the question' in view of Canada's many other commitments.[107] Nevertheless, the prime minister's office informed Harris of a similar effort being undertaken by Canadian Friends.[108]

By the summer of 1943 the Canadian Friends Service Committee, through its general secretary, Fred Haslam, had begun preliminary negotiations for a Canadian contingent to join the FAU in China. The first major task was to secure government permission for Canadian cos to travel abroad, and the initial response from authorities was not encouraging. In reply to Haslam's inquiry, for instance, the chief alternative service officer, L.E. Westman, expressed doubt that conscientious objectors under alternative service could go to China simply because 'nothing within present regulations would seem to make this possible.' Rather, he suggested that interested cos join the newly created non-combatant units in the Royal Canadian Army Medical Corps and the Dental Corps. In his opinion, the only conscientious objectors who might be allowed to go to China would be those who had applied to a non-combatant unit but had been turned down for physical reasons. In any event, the question would have to be raised at several levels of authority, including the alternative service officers, the mobilization boards, the labour exit authorities, the Department of External Affairs, and the armed forces.[109]

Despite the obvious reluctance on the part of authorities, Haslam plodded ahead with plans for a Canadian contingent. During the winter of 1943–4 he, James Finlay, and several other pacifists formed a special personnel selection committee to process applications, interview candidates, and finally select those Canadians who would go to China. In keeping with the government policy of secrecy regarding conscientious objectors, the Friends Service Committee agreed to conduct its arrangements in a discreet 'personal way and not make a national issue out of it.'[110] Accordingly, the Chinese consulate was asked to submit an official request to the Department of External Affairs for the services of conscientious objectors.[111] The authorities also required that prospective unit members be recruited on an individual basis, thereby blocking the normal practice of simply posting notices at alternative service work camps.[112]

The momentum towards the formation of the unit was accelerated in the spring of 1944 by the visit to Canada of Dr Robert B. McClure, the Canadian missionary doctor who headed the FAU in China. McClure not only helped publicize the value of the FAU work but also assisted the Friends Service Committee in final negotiations with the Canadian government. Following a few meetings in Ottawa, McClure was assured that alternative service men would be granted exit permits. In the summer of 1944 twenty Canadian volunteers recommended by the selection committee were granted permission to travel to China as the Canadian contingent of the FAU.[113] The Canadian Red Cross agreed to furnish uniforms and equipment for the Canadians, and the Chinese War Relief Fund, a Canadian charitable organization, agreed to contribute approximately five hundred thousand dollars towards the support of the Canadian contingent and FAU medical work in China.[114]

In China the Canadians took their place alongside one hundred other FAU members from Britain, the United States, China, and New Zealand, and they performed various types of medical, mechanical, and administrative work. Some were stationed at hospitals and warehouses, while others hauled supplies. It was this task of distributing drugs and other medical supplies to the various mission hospitals scattered across inland China that earned the FAU 'China Convoy' its reputation as the lifeline of China during the war.[115] Canadian pacifists were especially proud of their role in this international relief effort, and the Canadian contingent to the China Convoy came to symbolize the rich possibilities of active pacifist service in assisting civilian populations in a time of war. Most of the Canadian volunteers returned home before the end of 1947 pleased that they had finally made an important contribution not only to humanitarian service in China but to the broadening of the humanitarian spirit in their own country.

During the last few years of the war there were quite a few options open to conscientious objectors. Besides working in alternative service work camps they could now assume diversified jobs on farms and in factories. There were also opportunities for humanitarian and relief work overseas in the non-combatant corps, the fire-fighters corps in England, and the Friends Ambulance Unit in China. This broad range of alternative service may have posed some new dilemmas for individual conscientious objectors, but on the whole the pacifists were pleased with the government's response to their demands for a meaningful role in the world crisis. Only the question of post-war demobilization still worried them.

Although the war officially ended with the Japanese surrender in August 1945, the men in alternative service were not completely demobilized until August of the following year.[116] The main reason for this delay appears to have been a reluctance on the part of the government and some pacifists to take an action that might arouse adverse public opinion. L.E. Westman had actually recommended the quick release of all alternative service men at the end of the war, but other influential individuals and groups warned that the Canadian public would resent the release of conscientious objectors before all military service personnel were home. The Conference of Historic Peace Churches agreed, and its spokesmen made a number of recommendations (later adopted by the authorities) for the gradual demobilization of alternative service men.

There was some displeasure among pacifists with this arrangement but the strongest protests came from Jehovah's Witnesses, who accounted for the majority of conscientious objectors kept in the work camps and in prison following the war.[117] Despite the Witnesses' cries of religious persecution, the government adhered to the policy of gradual demobilization while easing the restrictions on the men. In order to deal with those men who had refused diversified forms of alternative service, however, selected alternative service work camps remained open until July 1946, when all camps in the national parks were officially closed. In August, exactly one year after the end of the war, government control over conscientious objectors finally came to an end.[118]

v

During the Second World War well over 12,000 young Canadian men had been classified as conscientious objectors. As table 4 indicates, however, more than 700 of these had enlisted in the armed forces either as combatants or non-combatants, and another 548 had either died or had their co status revoked by mobilization boards, so that by January 1946 there were more than 10,000 conscientious objectors in Canada. While

TABLE 4
Number and disposition of conscientious objectors by province as of 31 December 1945

NUMBER OF COS	PEI	NS	NB	QUE	ONT	MAN	SASK	ALTA	BC	Total
Referrals from Registrars	6	33	2	41	3077	3400	2711	1318	2012	12,600
Subsequent changes in status										
Accepted enlistments (combat)	—	—	—	2	168	107	162	33	69	541
Accepted enlistments (non-combat)	—	2	—	3	55	31	49	27	60	227
Deaths	—	—	—	—	12	11	6	9	10	48
Revocations (other than enlistment)	—	2	—	5	91	183	110	25	84	500
Transfers to other divisions	3	1	—	3	122	55	77	50	122	433
Total changes in CO status	3	5	—	13	448	387	404	144	95	1,749
COS retaining status	3	28	2	28	2629	3013	2307	1174	1667	10,851

DISPOSITION OF COS	PEI	NS	NB	QUE	ONT	MAN	SASK	ALTA	BC	Total
Under Red Cross (in agriculture)	—	4	—	4	846	1446	1090	556	269	4,215
Under Red Cross (non-agriculture)	—	2	—	8	379	602	223	79	331	1,624
Relieved of Red Cross Agts. (physical or compassionate)	3	12	2	4	800	281	305	195	141	1,743
Relieved of Red Cross Agts. (1 June regulation changes)	—	3	—	2	442	507	529	123	270	1,876
In ASW Camps	—	5	—	9	83	13	67	36	28	241
Serving jail sentences	—	—	—	1	2	—	4	3	2	12
In hands of Enforcement Division	—	—	—	—	16	4	12	1	1	34
Can't locate/in hands of RCMP	—	2	—	—	15	12	61	15	112	217
Disposition pending/under review	—	—	—	—	46	148	16	168	513	889
Total COS	3	28	2	28	2629	3013	2307	1174	1667	10,851

Source: J.F. Mackinnon, 'Historical Account of the Wartime Activities of the Alternative Service Branch,' Department of Labour Report, 11 April 1946, 20, Public Archives of Canada, RG 35, Series 7, Vol 21.

approximately 250 men remained in the work camps or in prison for the duration of alternative service, almost 90 per cent accepted employment in agriculture and miscellaneous essential industries. By the time the alternative service program ground to a halt they had contributed $2,222,802.70 to the Canadian Red Cross Society.[119]

On the whole, therefore, Canada's first experiment in alternative service was considered a huge success, particularly by the pacifists who had helped shape it. They had achieved the right to refrain from military service on grounds of individual conscience, and they had contributed alternative services consistent with their religious beliefs and their growing social consciousness. Alternative service set an important precedent by allowing pacifists to assume an active role within wartime society, which in turn helped conscientious objection become recognized as a legitimate and constructive option in the Canadian response to war. Clearly, however, the state would see to it that it remained an option exercised by a tiny minority.

The most vocal demands for active non-violent service had come from the more socially radical Quakers and United Church members, but the staunch pacifist witness of the more traditional historic peace sects should not be underestimated. In numbers alone, for instance, Canada's Mennonites dominated pacifist resistance to military service in the Second World War as in the First. Although the more conservative Mennonites continued to refrain from social involvement, others, particularly the *Russlaender*, were more than willing to demonstrate their religious beliefs through social action. In Ottawa the Conference of Historic Peace Churches took the lead in negotiations on behalf of conscientious objectors. The Quaker representative, Fred Haslam, credited his Mennonite cohorts with much of their success: 'I cannot be too grateful for the way in which the Mennonites have stood firm on this matter of peace. It would have been difficult indeed to accomplish what has been done but for their gentle firmness in dealing with the Government.'[120]

Besides encouraging close co-operation between pacifists, the defence of conscientious objection through alternative service had a unifying effect upon the individual peace sects. Canadian Mennonites, for instance, reached a new level of understanding among themselves, and their pacifist witness helped forge a new spirit of unity and inter-Mennonite co-operation. For the Doukhobors, the wartime pressures enhanced the pacifistic as opposed to the nihilistic element in their philosophy; consequently, the bitterly divided factions of the previous decade began to consolidate and in 1945 they joined together to form the Union of Doukhobors of Canada. Nevertheless, this unity among Doukhobors, based as it was upon the necessity for a united response to the threat of conscription and to other outside hostilities, did not long outlast the war.[121] As for the Society of Friends, their unified response to conscription and other wartime problems through the Canadian Friends Service Committee resulted in the first joint meeting of all three Canadian branches in 1944 and in a Quaker presence in the Canadian ecumenical movement.[122]

Above all, the evolution of alternative service revealed that pacifists were anxious to undertake some real response to wartime circumstances – a personal witness that went beyond mere words. At the time, a diversified alternative service program for conscientious objectors appeared to be an answer to the eternal dilemma of the pacifist in wartime, and most pacifists, including many in the historic peace sects, were satisfied if not pleased with the arrangement.

In the long run, however, alternative service as prescribed in Canada failed to overcome the pacifists' moral problem of separating themselves from the war effort. Some conscientious objectors had recognized this new dilemma, but under immediate wartime pressures they could hardly resolve it. Most of them were relieved to be able to choose what they perceived as the least possible evil – performing some worthwhile service without actually taking up arms. Although the degree of their implication in the war effort varied according to the type of work performed, from the almost complete isolation of the alternative service work camps to the thinly disguised military function of the non-combatant corps, there was little doubt that most forms of alternative service work involved at least some indirect support for the war. This was especially the case once government authorities came to view conscientious objectors as an important and useful source of manpower and to utilize them in the national war effort. Despite their initial satisfaction in achieving a realistic alternative to military service, conscientious objectors failed to escape the total mobilization of society that modern war entailed. Rather than securing a pacifist option, therefore, alternative service could be seen as setting a powerful precedent either for the totally isolated internment of war resisters in any future war or for their complete assimilation in a diversified war effort.

Whatever effect the alternative service experience would have in the future, however, the state's recognition of an individual's right to conscientious objection regardless of church affiliation and the provision for alternative service under civilian supervision appeared to be appropriate concessions for the time and a tribute to the persistence of pacifist resistance to compulsory military service. It was a notable moral advance over the treatment of Canadian conscientious objectors during the First World War, but one that would always need defending. Meanwhile, military conscription was by no means the only threat to individual liberties facing pacifists during the war years. There were other concerns, such as the treatment of Japanese Canadians and the plight of refugees; in response to those issues, as in the case of conscientious objectors, pacifists searched for a realistic witness over and above moral indignation and dissent.

9

Relief and reconciliation

In the light of their own commitment to radical social change on the one hand and the challenge of Christian realism on the other, Canadian liberal pacifists were ever mindful of the necessity of confronting the reality of wartime circumstances if they were to exercise a meaningful role in reshaping society. Throughout the war they searched for ways in which to translate pacifism into practical action. Their response to conscription and their endorsement of alternative service for conscientious objectors were two examples: others were their co-operation with a variety of concerned Canadians in reconciling wartime tensions in society through the defence of civil liberties and in undertaking refugee and relief work.

I

The relief efforts of Canadian pacifists on behalf of refugees actually began in the mid-1930s. Both the Women's International League for Peace and Freedom and the Society of Friends, in conjunction with their counterparts throughout the world, had displayed an active interest in assisting primarily Jewish refugees fleeing Nazi persecution, but had received little support from Canadian authorities. Several countries, including Great Britain, the United States, Australia, France, Belgium, and Holland, had opened their doors to some of the refugees, but Canadian immigration regulations permitted the admission only of those Europeans who had immediate relatives residing in Canada or agriculturists with sufficient money to farm in Canada. These restrictions excluded the majority of the refugees.[1] In fact, the government explicitly restricted Jewish immigration and refused to allow into Canada ten thousand

Jewish refugees over a five-year period, even though the Canadian Jewish Congress had agreed to assume financial responsibility for the newcomers.[2]

Such a response, claimed the Canadian activists, was a national disgrace and demanded immediate counteraction. Accordingly, in 1938 a number of Canadians representing various church, liberal, and pacifist organizations formed the Canadian National Committee on Refugees and Victims of Political Persecution under the auspices of the League of Nations Society of Canada. The first task of the committee was to publicize the refugee problem in order to mount public pressure for a change in government policy, particularly with regard to the urgent question of Jewish refugees. Irving Abella and Harold Troper argue that the committee's efforts in that campaign 'proved too little too late' and ended in failure, partly because members of the refugee committee were 'elite non-conformists' without a base of popular support.[3] The fact that a good many of the members were suspect because of their pacifism tends to support that interpretation. Nevertheless, the committee succeeded in securing special immigration permits for individual refugees and in providing assistance throughout the war years in the readjustment and resettlement of those refugees who did make it to Canada.[4]

The Toronto-based National Committee on Refugees was directed by an executive composed of Senator Cairine R. Wilson, president of the League of Nations Society of Canada, as chairman, Constance Hayward as executive secretary, and Sir Robert Falconer and Sir Ellsworth Flavelle as honorary chairman and treasurer respectively.[5] From its beginning the committee contended that the admission of selected groups of refugees would constitute a sizeable contribution to the economic and cultural development of Canada, an argument later supported with specific examples. A promotional leaflet distributed in 1941, for instance, described the individual cases of several refugees who, with the help of the committee, had become productive residents of Canada. Although the committee admitted that it had become increasingly difficult for refugees to escape from German-dominated countries, it maintained that a few did trickle through, including engineers and experts valuable to Canada's war effort. Apart from the occasional patriotic reference, however, the committee usually emphasized the humanitarian side of the issue and argued that its major goal during the war and post-war years was to create a national awareness of 'the great problem of immigration.'

One of the committee's major efforts during the war concerned the 'friendly aliens,' particularly the refugee students, who had been interned in Great Britain and then transferred to internment camps in Canada. When British authorities began to reappraise the fate of these refugees, the refugee committee succeeded in enlisting the financial support and personal sponsors necessary for the release of the younger refugees from camps in order to continue their studies in Canada. To deal with this problem, the Canadian National Committee on Refugees, in conjunction with the United Jewish Refugee and War Relief Agencies, formed the Central Committee for Interned Refugees in November 1940.[6] The organization, based in Montreal benefited from the services of Cairine Wilson and Constance Hayward, chairman and secretary respectively, and of Stanley Goldner, liaison officer to the camps, and Charles Raphael, a co-ordinating officer representing the British refugee committees at Bloomsbury House, London, who had come to Canada to help refugees emigrate to the United States.

Of the Canadians who worked on behalf of the refugees interned in Canada, none were more involved than pacifists, particularly those in the Women's International League for Peace and Freedom and the Society of Friends. In effect, the problem of interned refugees offered pacifists another opportunity to perform a constructive humanitarian service at a time when outlets for pacifist action were limited. Largely because of its failure to attract younger women in the late 1930s, the WIL had gradually lost most of its base across the country.[7] In fact, outside of a few groups in Vancouver, Edmonton, and Winnipeg, the only office really active during the war was the league's national headquarters in Toronto. There the national president, Anna Sissons, and secretary, Laura Davis, continued to promote the organizations's humanitarian interests. Alice Loeb, another long-time WIL activist, became the national chairman of a special refugee committee representative of the group's general orientation during the war.

The concern with the refugee problem was shared by Canadian Quakers. As a result of their experiences in the First World War and because of their transition towards social activism, the Friends felt that their primary responsibility during war was not only to maintain their ancient peace testimony but also to help relieve the peresonal suffering and hardships caused by war. It was indeed possible, asserted the Canadian Friends Service Committee in 1940, for 'those who cannot condone war as a method, to be truly loyal to their country, and to help in the work of preservation and healing of the stricken peoples of the world.'[8] This line of thinking obviously strengthened the patriotic dimension of pacifism, thereby promoting the cause of humanitarian relief. Under the direction of its general secretary, Fred Haslam, the service committee successfully organized Quaker activity on behalf of conscientious objectors, and created a War Victims Relief Fund through which contributions were solicited for overseas relief projects conducted by British and American Friends. It was through the Friends in Britain that Canadian Quakers first learned of the plight of the refugees interned in Canada.

Canadian involvement in the internment operations began in the summer of 1940 when Britain, fearing a fifth-column danger at home, transferred thousands of interned and restricted enemy aliens to Canada and Australia for further detention. British tribunals had classified those aliens according to three categories: category A, dangerous aliens to be interned; category B, an intermediate group of doubtful risk; and category C, those presenting little or no risk. A further distinction, which cut across the categories, was made between political refugees and non-refugees. Aliens from all three categories were sent to Canada, including a number of 'Nazi sympathizers' as well as approximately twenty-four hundred German and Austrian males classified as 'refugees from Nazi oppression.' Among them were boys as young as seventeen, many of Jewish or partially Jewish ancestry.[9] After escaping from Germany and Austria many of these aliens had sought refuge in England with the hope of eventually emigrating to the United States. Suddenly, in the spring of 1940, they were interned and then transported across the sea together with regular prisoners of war.[10] Families were split up; there were reports of one brother going to Canada and another to Australia while the father or mother remained on the Isle of Man or in some other British camp. For its part the Canadian government agreed to take approximately sixty-seven hundred prisoners of war and internees from the United Kingdom for future internment in camps administered by the Internment Operations Branch of the Department of State.[11] Eventually eight such internment camps were established in Canada — one in New Brunswick, two in Ontario, and the rest in Quebec.[12]

The first ship of evacuated POWs and internees reached Quebec City on 1 July 1940. Upon their arrival they were immediately rushed 'through long lines of Canadian bayonets' to trains waiting to whisk them off to specially prepared camps which, the Canadian public was assured, were well guarded and situated 'far from civilization.'[13] A few days later another group of enemy aliens bound for Canada met disaster when their ship, the *Arandora Star*, was sunk by German torpedoes. While Canadian seamen managed to rescue over one thousand survivors, roughly six hundred German and Italian prisoners perished at sea.[14] Although the incident aroused little immediate sympathy in the British or Canadian press, the tragedy of the *Arandora Star* ultimately stirred public criticism in Britain of the whole internment operation,[15] especially when it was revealed that in addition to Nazis the victims also included anti-Nazis and German Jewish refugees.

Initially, the practice of mixing prisoners of war with the other interned enemy aliens was followed in Canada. All the internees who arrived in Canada, from the pro-Nazi aliens to the 'refugees from Nazi oppression,' were herded together into camps and treated as prisoners of war.[16] Despite a concerted effort by the Canadian Committee on Refugees to remedy the situation of 'friendly' aliens, they remained isolated as prisoners of war throughout the winter of 1940-1. Finally, under unremitting pressure from the Central Committee for Interned Refugees, the Canadian government separated the refugees from the dangerous aliens and bona fide POWs, and on 1 July 1941 an order in council removed the alien refugee camps from the prisoners-of-war administration and placed them under the control of a commissioner of refugee camps. The authorities selected two camp sites in Quebec to serve as major relocation centres for anti-Nazi internees: Camp N near Sherbrooke and Camp A at Farnham, approximately thirty miles from Montreal. The initial plan to reserve Camp N for Jews and Camp A for gentiles was foiled by the unwillingness of the refugees to be segregated along racial lines.[17]

The change in Canadian policy followed the relaxation of the internment policy in Britain, where a special tribunal had ordered the release of almost 95 per cent of the interned refugees, many of whom thereafter engaged in useful war work or joined the Pioneer Corps. While approximately 900 of those interned in Canada returned to England for release under this amnesty, 1,389 men remained in the Canadian camps, chiefly because of immigration technicalities.[18] As part of their new refugee policy, however, Canadian authorities did provide for the possible release of refugee students under twenty-one years of age so that they might continue their studies in Canada, provided that they received sufficient financial support from Canadian individuals or groups acting as sponsors.

It was at this point that the Canadian Friends Service Committee as well as the Women's International League and other pacifists became more directly involved. The Friends in particular received appeals from British and American Quakers to minister to the needs of the boys and help secure their release from the camps.[19] A substantial number of the young refugees had been registered with the Germany Emergency Committee of the Friends Service Council while in Britain. Once interned in Canada the refugees maintained communications with British Quakers, who then got in touch with Canadian Quakers on their behalf. By the summer of 1940 the Canadian Friends Service Committee also began to receive letters from the young internees sthemselves. Following the usual statements that the majority of the men in their camp were 'refugees from Nazi oppression' who had to leave Germany or Austria for 'racial, religious or political reasons,' the internees expressed their eagerness for release and pleaded for assistance. The letters from the camps also indicated that those who had associated with the Society of Friends in Britain desired to meet with Canadian Friends.[20] For instance, in a letter to Fred Haslam, Ernst-Ludwig Landsberg, a spokesman for a group in Camp N, wrote that he and his friends were anxious for Haslam or some other Canadian Friend to arrange a visit to the camp: 'This would enable us to discuss our problems with you, and I can assure you that your advice would be appreciated very much.'[21] Following similar requests from Friedrich Hoeniger and Ulrich Weil at Camp A, Haslam sought permission from the authorities to visit the refugee camps in Quebec.[22] The commissioner of refugee camps, Lt-Col. R.S.W. Fordham, replied that before such an aplication could be approved he would need to know the exact nature of Haslam's proposed visit. Since it was 'very easy to upset refugees,' he warned, it was necessary to ensure that anyone 'desiring to communicate with them [is] not engaged in missions that might prove upsetting to the Camp administrative system.'[23] Assured of the sincerity of Quaker intentions, Fordham agreed to Haslam's visits, subject to the agreement that only 'matters of welfare be discussed, but not questions relative to release.'[24]

Consequently, in October 1941, Haslam visited both the Farnham and Sherbrooke camps on behalf of the Canadian Friends Service Committee. He met the young men with whom he had corresponded, and at Sherbrooke he found a 'Society of Friends group' organized by thirty-five men who had been helped by the Germany Emergency Committee while in Britain.[25] In accordance with the ground rules for his visit, Haslam concentrated on the welfare and educational needs of the men in the camps, but he found the refugees most eager to talk about release, a topic he had agreed not to discuss. Although he was initially frustrated by the restriction he discovered that the authorities merely desired not to build up false hopes and thus avoid a possible repeat of the bitter disappointment experienced by the internees following the collapse of their efforts to emigrate to the United States. The large majority of those refugees had registered for American visas years before their internment. In fact, statistics on Camp N personnel showed that out of 422 prospective emigrants to the United States 60 per cent had registered in 1938 and 13 per cent in 1939.[26] When they became prisoners in Canada, however, they discovered they were no longer eligible. The Camp N survey also revealed that 45 per cent of the refugees were under the age of twenty-five, and 87 per cent under thirty; 94.3 per cent had been classified by British tribunals as 'refugees from Nazi oppression'; 34.6 per cent had been imprisoned in German concentration camps such as Dachau; and 32 per cent had lived in transit camps on the Continent and in England.

As a result of Haslam's tour of the camps, Canadians interested in assisting the refugees became better acquainted with their individual needs and better prepared to deal with specific problems in the future. Haslam was particularly hopeful that others, perhaps pacifists in Montreal, would undertake similar visits on a regular basis.[27] Among those who answered the call to visit the camps were John Hobart, a Montreal Quaker, and Clarence Halliday, the United Church pacifist minister who traded his church in Montreal for the unofficial duties of chaplain and welfare officer to the refugees. Visits were also made by Friends from outside Canada, including Mary M. Rogers from Philadelphia and Emma Cadbury from London.[28] The Canadian Friends Service Committee organized a nationwide drive for winter clothing and books for the camps, and in a few months donations arrived from as far away as Kootenay Bay, British Columbia.[29] Arrangements were made for Queen's University to offer correspondence courses to the refugees at reduced fees; the remaining fees, as well as textbooks, were subsidized by the Student Christian Movement.[30]

Meanwhile, Haslam had been co-operating with Constance Hayward, the secretary of the Committee for Interned Refugees, and Dr Jerome Davis, the Canadian director of the War Prisoners' Aid of the YMCA, in an attempt to secure the release of interned students. There were approximately three hundred such youths between the ages of seventeen and twenty-four who had been admitted to English schools and colleges prior to their internment and transfer to Canada. Since then a number of them had continued their studies in camp and a few had actually written matriculation examinations for entrance to Canadian universities.[31] According to government regulations, however, release of the students was contingent upon Canadian citizens acting as sponsors and accepting full responsibility for the cost of the student's education and maintenance for the duration of the war or until his education was completed. More specifically, sponsors were required to prove their ability to provide one thousand dollars in annual support for each student released.[32] This requirement, while viewed by authorities as a fair estimate of the annual costs of student support, made it exceedingly difficult for individuals to sponsor interned students without extra help. Consequently, various groups such as the Friends Service Committee, the WIL, and the National Council of Women pooled their resources to create a central sponsorship fund administered by the Central Committee for Interned Refugees. The Committee launched a national appeal on behalf of the refugee students. Families and organizations were urged either to sponsor refugees individually or to contribute to the committee's sponsorship fund.[33]

The Friends Service Committee was particularly interested in assisting two young men in Camp A, Friedrich David Hoeniger and Ulrich Weil, both of whom were well known to Friends in Britain.[34] (Hoeniger, for example, had attended a Quaker school in Ommen, Holland, and a Quaker camp in Cornwall, England, prior to internment.)[35] In order to secure Hoeninger's release, Haslam successfully sought the support of the WIL refugee committee.[36] In the final arrangement the Quakers made financial contributions to the Hoeniger fund, but it was the president of the WIL, Anna Sissons, who acted as Hoeniger's official sponsor.[37] In April 1942, nearly ten months after the initial move to secure his release, Hoeniger wrote Haslam that he was 'now happily sheltered' at Professor and Mrs Sissons's home in Toronto.[38] Although the gesture was not always a popular one, it was not unusual for pacifists to open their homes to the refugees; for instance, Arthur Dorland, chairman of the Friends Yearly Meeting, arranged for a young interned student to live at his home in London, Ontario, as did Lavell Smith when he was still living in Montreal.[39]

The Canadian Friends Service Committee and the Committee for Interned Refugees now shifted their attention to the prospect of securing the release of some of the older internees who had useful professions or trades. While visiting the camps Haslam had discovered that many of the men were skilled in medicine, research, engineering, and toolmaking.[40] The Committee for Interned Refugees exerted considerable pressure on their behalf, and the government gradually began to approve the release of men to work in essential war industries and agriculture. The first such men to be released were tool-makers such as Alexander Horak. Haslam immediately set out to find Horak a job with

Rogers Radio Tubes in Toronto.[41] In co-operation with Constance Hayward and Jerome Davis, Haslam also represented the interests of Alois Zockling, an engineer, and Hans Loewit, a former medical student at the University of Vienna. The release of skilled refugees progressed through the winter, and in the spring of 1942 arrangements were made with farmers to place some of the men in agricultural work. For instance, Reinhold Grischkat was offered a farm job in Burgessville, Ontario, upon his release from the Farnham camp.[42]

During the next few years Canadian pacifists, including Quakers, the WIL, and the FOR, continued to co-operate in a national effort to aid wartime refugees at home and abroad, but by the autumn of 1941 they also began to consider the prospect of post-war relief work overseas. Since most European refugees had been barred from entering Canada, pacifists claimed the best way Canadians could lend their support was to contribute to the Friends War Victims Relief Fund or a special fund collected by FOR chairman Lavell Smith for European relief work administered by War Resisters International.[43] Accordingly, pacifists began a program of relief work that continued well into the post-war era, and a number of Canadian Friends joined the relief teams. For instance, Barbara Walker, Haslam's one-time assistant in the Friends Service Committee office, was attached to a Friends Relief Service team in Germany; Naomi Jackson, a future McMaster University professor of fine arts, served in Finland, and Paul Zavitz of Sparta, Ontario, worked in Poland, both under the auspices of the American Friends Service Committee.[44] It was through relief work, both at home and abroad, that Canadian pacifists, and especially Quakers, found it possible to exercise some degree of influence during the war and early post-war years.

II

Perhaps because of their close association with Quakers and other pacifists during the war, particularly with respect to the problems of conscientious objectors, Canada's Mennonites also became involved in their own relief projects in China, India, and Poland. Unlike the Quakers, however, who had become social activists, the more traditional historic peace sects generally remained withdrawn from the mainstream of Canadian society. Although the issue of conscription during the two world wars and state regulations concerning education often forced them into confrontations with authorities, the sectarian pacifists, whether Mennonite, Hutterite or Doukhobor, strove to maintain their particular versions of Christian living independent of a hostile world. It was through this example of isolated communities that the peace sects had an increasing influence upon socially conscious Christian pacifists during the interwar period, an influence that resulted in the birth of Christian co-operative communities.

By the 1940s Canadian pacifists had become active in the movement for co-operative communities, largely through the efforts of Henri Lasserre and the Robert Owen Foundation. Lasserre and his pacifist associates were particularly enthusiastic about the experimental Cotswold Bruderhof in Britain founded by the Society of Brothers, a Christian pacifist communitarian group that emigrated from Germany and Austria during the 1930s. The Canadians were understandably frantic when they learned of the plight of the Society of Brothers during the war.

With the internment of German aliens in Britain in 1940 the Cotswold Bruderhof, largely composed of German and German-speaking members, came under direct attack from the local populace and was pressured to leave Britain. In July of that year the head of the Bruderhof, Eberhard C.H. Arnold, appealed to Lasserre and the Robert Owen Foundation to help persuade the Canadian government to allow the migration to Canada of the Bruderhof en masse.[45] Since exit permits from England had been secured and the Hutterian Brethren of Canada had offered the necessary financial guarantees, only the negative response of Canadian immigration officials blocked the way. Lasserre and pacifist allies in Canada made numerous appeals to Ottawa on behalf of the Bruderhof, but to no avail. Given the wartime atmosphere in Canada it was difficult, to say the least, for a handful of Canadians to plead the cause of a pacifist community like the Bruderhof. In the end, gravely disappointed by Canada's rebuff, the Cotswold Bruderhof emigrated to Paraguay.

For their part, Canadian pacifists remained attracted to the way of life proposed by the Society of Brothers and hoped to initiate similar community experiments in Canada. For instance, near the end of his long pilgrimage Fairbairn endorsed the movement for co-operative communities as the best way to bring in a new social order. Before Christian socialism could be successfully introduced on a large scale, he argued, people must first build model communities isolated from the prevailing world system.[46]

Although Lasserre was not an active pacifist during the war years, he associated with pacifists because socially minded pacifists and conscientious objectors were the most attracted to the idea and practice of

integral co-operative communities. Such a way of life appeared to promise the 'completest realization of ... their religious devotion to non-violence, simplicity and brotherly fellowship,' thus providing a living example
of a new social ethic for the future.[47]

In March 1943 a nucleus of pacifists, including Fred Haslam, George
Tatham, professor of geography at the University of Toronto, and several
conscientious objectors, including Leslie Johnson, Walter Alexander,
and Roy Clifton, joined with Henri and Madeline Lasserre in the formation of the Canadian Fellowship for Cooperative Community. The
new organization assumed the educational, research, and library functions of the Robert Owen Foundation, published a small newsletter and
pamphlets, and generally renewed Canadian interest in the movement
for co-operative communities. Its statement of principles explained the
need for such community:

The Fellowship believes that a cooperative democratic social order, freed from
competition greed and war, must sooner or later be brought about by the voluntary efforts of cooperatively-minded people, to replace [the] existing individ-
ualistic and acquisitive society or any totalitarian system which may follow the
present structure. There can be no durable peace until such a cooperative order
has been established. This order cannot be imposed by compulsion, but requires
for its establishment the free and general acceptance by the people of the new
human relationship implied. The Fellowship believes that the formation of
cooperative communities where these new relationships are experienced, practised and witnessed, is one of the factors required at the present stage of the
world's crisis for the preparation of this new social order.[48]

Idealistic and visionary, co-operative communities were seen as basic
building-blocks for a non-violent society. As with most utopian ventures,
however, the difficulty was how to realize those lofty goals.

One of the first actions of the Fellowship for Cooperative Community
was the creation of a land-based community on a farm at Aurora, Ontario.[49] Those associated with the Aurora experiment included the group's
leading members and several conscientious objectors as well as the poet
Wilson Macdonald. Although brief, the Aurora years were a valuable
introduction to co-operative living in Canada, and throughout the war
pacifists remained enthusiastic about the idea. The Fellowship of Reconciliation, for instance, developed a close relationship with both the
Canadian Fellowship for Cooperative Community and the Robert Owen

Foundation and promoted co-operative communities not only as a non-violent lifestyle but as the 'first cells ... of the social structure of the future.'[50]

III

Although the Women's International League and the Society of Friends assumed the lead in refugee work and the Canadian Fellowship for Cooperative Community provided an outlet for more idealistic experiments, the Fellowship of Reconciliation dominated wartime pacifist activities in Canada. Following its reorganization early in the war, the FOR attempted to broaden its membership base to extend beyond United Church pacifists. A small but important step in that direction was taken in December 1942, when two Toronto Anglicans, John Frank, the rector of Holy Trinity Church, and John F. Davidson of Upper Canada College, declared their support for the revived group. They expressed openly the hope that the presence of their names would encourage other Anglicans to do likewise.[51] But despite an intensive recruitment drive, the FOR membership of 350 remained overwhelmingly dominated by United Church pacifists.[52] Nevertheless, the fellowship quickly became the principal inter-pacifist organization in Canada and took the lead in advocating practical action in response to the serious issues confronting wartime society. Its executive believed their function was to comfort and consolidate fellow pacifists and, at the same time, to provide them with the direction and courage necessary to act upon their principles individually and in groups. Such unity of purpose, it was felt, would replace the individual's lonely consciousness of insufficiency with the strength and wisdom gleaned from co-operative action.[53]

With this task in mind the Canadian FOR embarked upon a simple but daring enterprise – the publication of its own magazine. Launched in October 1943, and usually published at least six times a year, *Reconciliation* was more than the official organ of the Canadian FOR. Its emergence marked a significant milestone in the development of the entire pacifist movement in Canada. Before *Reconciliation* was established, the expression of Canadian pacifist thought had been confined to several small mimeographed newsletters, usually issued monthly by the FOR national council and at irregular intervals by a few industrious individuals with regional interests. The new publication aimed at representing all pacifists in Canada.

The Canadian FOR chairman, Lavell Smith, claimed that the need for such a pacifist journal was greater in Canada than in either Britain or the United States since the Canadian pacifist population was smaller and the geographical distances greater. 'Many of us are unable to meet often with like-minded folk,' he explained, 'and the sense of isolation is often overpowering.'[54] Furthermore, although British and American pacifists had been more vocal and effective, their journals, such as the *Christian Pacifist*, *Peace News*, the *Conscientious Objector*, and the *Catholic Worker*, were not easily accessible to Canadians during the war. 'It is a strange commentary upon our Canadian conception of freedom of the press,' wrote Smith, 'that journals which circulate freely in Britain are frowned upon here.' The situation was aggravated by the fact that Canadian papers, both religious and secular, had 'failed almost completely to give space to pacifist writers or to allow their readers to judge for themselves the pacifist argument.'[55] Therefore, if the pacifist position was not to be left unstated in Canada, Canadian pacifists would have to publish their own journal. Smith boastfully predicted that the launching of *Reconciliation* would prove to be 'a more significant event than the launching of an aircraft carrier or the taking of Naples.' In any case, he added, it was the right of Canadian pacifists, as a resolute and law-abiding minority, to express their 'conscientious views and to circulate news nowhere else available.'

One of the first to congratulate the Canadians on their new pacifist magazine was the chairman of the International Fellowship of Reconciliation, John Nevin Sayre. Noting with satisfaction the witness of Canadian pacifists since the beginning of the war, Sayre praised the renewed commitment demonstrated with the publication of a magazine and added that it was 'not beginning a day too soon.' Furthermore, Sayre suggested that if *Reconciliation* succeeded in fusing Canadian pacifists into a 'beloved community' knowledgeable in the practice of non-violence it would have achieved a significant goal.[56]

Coincident with the birth of *Reconciliation* was the appointment of Albert 'Abe' Watson as the new executive secretary of the Canadian FOR and the managing editor of its new journal. Watson had been active in the United Church and the YMCA and had spent a year as a conscientious objector in an alternative service work camp in British Columbia prior to assuming his duties with the FOR. Working closely with Watson in the production of the journal was an editorial committee of several people, most notably Edith Fowke, Kathleen Green, and Roy Clifton, who were responsible for writing as well as layout and organizational work.[57] In addition to the material generated by the Toronto-based staff, the journal usually depended upon articles from various contributors scattered across the country, including Duckworth in Montreal, Fairbairn in Windermere, Ontario, King in Saskatoon, Huestis in Edmonton, and several conscientious objectors in alternative service work camps in British Columbia. In addition, the Canadian content was supplemented with original and reprinted articles by popular internationally known pacifists such as A.J. Muste and Richard B. Gregg, thus providing Canadian readers with a sampling of the world's leading pacifist thought.

Initially, the editors of *Reconciliation* featured articles on the general topics of pacifism and the Fellowship of Reconciliation along with regular news coverage of the peace movement in Canada. In the first issue, for instance, Lavell Smith, explained the pacifist tenets of the FOR. While granting full recognition and respect to pacifism reached by a logical, political, or historical approach, Smith emphasized that the FOR advocated a religious pacifism based upon the belief that warfare was 'contrary to the will of God, as revealed in Christ.'[58] Such a pacifist conviction, Smith argued, was not 'fanaticism,' since it was merely obedience to the word of God; nor was it 'passivism,' since it called for the application of Christ's message in all circumstances. The Canadian FOR obviously was now much more narrowly Christian than it had been in the 1930s.

Another regular feature of *Reconciliation* during its first few years was a column entitled 'Rev. R. Edis Fairbairn Says ...' in which the contentious pacifist wrote a series of articles on what he called 'The Elements of Sound Thinking.'[59] After the appearance of Fairbairn's fourth article, however, the editor of *Reconciliation* decided to stop publication of the series and ignored Fairbairn's numerous inquiries about the fate of his column.[60] Although the reason for this move is not clear, it appears to have reflected a growing opposition within the fellowship to the acidic tone of Fairbairn's criticisms.[61] Fairbairn, at first disappointed, appeared satisfied when an 'atheist-radical-pacifist editor in Scotland' promised to publish 'The Elements of Sound Thinking' in booklet form.[62] Nor was he particularly upset that he was no longer contributing to *Reconciliation*. Although he had agreed to support the new pacifist publication he did not do so at the expense of his own independent newsletter, as did other individuals. Instead, he turned his small publication into a monthly bulletin with an international readership.

Originally entitled 'To Maintain Courage by Sharing Conviction' but shortened in 1946 to 'To Share Conviction,' the bulletin was the product of a true one-man operation. From his home in Windermere Fairbairn wrote, typed, and mimeographed the bulletin, which usually ran to one or two pages in length, and then distributed several hundred copies at his own expense. He continued to publish regularly until his retirement in 1948 and then intermittently until November 1951. Fairbairn's reason for this undertaking was twofold. First, he was 'solidly convinced' of a fundamental need for radical pacifist journalism among Canada's conscientious objectors, as well as other pacifists, farmers, and 'ordinary religious people.'[63] His bulletin, he believed, would help them clarify and justify a pacifist stand they may have taken originally upon a 'blind but commanding impulse.'[64] Second, he was delighted with the prospect of complete freedom of expression, especially once other avenues for pacifist writing were largely closed.[65]

In his bulletin Fairbairn aimed to 'probe the implications of the antiwar stand from the Christian point of view.' He reiterated the same basic arguments he had used in the past, particularly in his 'Indictment' of the United Church, and which he later repeated in his book *Apostate Christendom*, published in 1948. Christendom, he claimed, had gone astray. The Church had 'compromised supreme loyalty to Christ with the State' and could not justify its existence 'until and unless it humbles itself, confesses its tragic forsaking of the way of Jesus, and sets out once again to do what Jesus asked it to do.'[66] The way of Jesus, wrote Fairbairn, was the way of the Cross, the alternative to messianic war; nevertheless, although Jesus died a pacifist, his insight went far beyond the mere repudiation of war: 'He did not so much repudiate war as affirm the reverse of it' and thus became the model for pacifists who placed their faith in the power of love to bring in a new era of social and economic justice.[67] But a peaceful and successful economic system was endangered, he warned, when the Church supported the war and therefore endorsed the essential use of violence.[68] As an example he cited the Fellowship for a Christian Social Order, a movement that exposed the 'economic wickedness of the world' and then 'wilted suddenly' when it committed itself to the war.[69] At the heart of Fairbairn's criticism was his frustration with the Church leadership, not only for abandoning the pacifism of Jesus, but also for supporting the war without producing a reasoned Christian ethic of war.

On the whole, the response to Fairbairn's bulletin was encouraging. Some readers, for instance, offered financial assistance to help Fairbairn fill the increasing number of subscriptions from across Canada and from Britain and the United States.[70] Fairbairn always sent a copy of the bulletin to the office of the American Fellowship of Reconciliation in

New York City, and A.J. Muste 'not infrequently' responded appreciatively. Furthermore, excerpts from certain of the bulletin's 'hotter issues' were used by similar American and British newsletters, and on several occasions Fairbairn was quoted in the 'English Community Broadsheet.'[71]

In the British Isles the bulletin was distributed to well over a hundred readers under the auspices of the Movement for a Pacifist Church or Pax Christi. This movement was a scheme promoted by the Reverend Albert D. Belden of England to remobilize the great churches of Christendom around a 'New Universal Christian Agreement' on pacifism. Hailed as the ultimate pacifist movement, the plan was to recruit all those Christians who felt they could take the pacifist stand only when supported by the authority of the Church.[72] It was Belden's hope that once thousands of Christians signified their willingness to refuse to participate in war the churches would be reborn on a pacifist basis and thereafter would save mankind from the worst of sins.

Initially, Fairbairn was keenly interested in the Pax Christi movement and publicized it as possibly the most 'practical way in which the present ineffective pacifist minority could become, if not a majority, at least a much more effective minority.'[73] In the final analysis, however, Fairbairn rejected the idea of a pacifist church as applying too narrowly the word and spirit of Jesus and for placing too optimistic a faith in the ordinary churches. 'Indeed,' he wrote, 'it looks increasingly dubious whether any church integrated in the capitalist economy can do other in a pinch than fire a radically Christian minister.'[74] If the hope of the future was not a pacifist church, he intimated, it might lie in the movement of religious co-operative communities.[75]

Belden was disappointed with Fairbairn's attitude, especially since he had hoped the outspoken Canadian pacifist would organize the Pax Christi movement in Canada.[76] After the war Belden personally toured Canada on behalf of the movement. Although he received a courteous reception, the Canadian FOR appears to have agreed with A.J. Muste's negative critique of Belden's scheme, and declined to give it a favourable endorsement.[77] Muste had rejected the Pax Christi on the ground that there was something 'basically wrong' with the suggestion that the individual Christian should not act on an issue of principle 'until a majority of his fellows are ready to do likewise.' Pacifism was not a matter of arithmetic.[78]

On the whole, the Canadian FOR adhered to A.J. Muste's philosophy that pacifism was the 'one adequate revolutionary movement in the world' since it was based upon the spiritual revolution of mankind as well as upon a non-violent social revolution.[79] In the pages of *Reconciliation* Muste reminded pacifists they had a 'positive responsibility to develop techniques of non-violence that can be used by mass organizations.' If pacifists failed in their revolutionary job, he warned, the masses would have no choice except 'to submit to injustice or to try to break their chains by the self-defeating method of violence.' Muste emphasized that the only alternative to total war in the future was total pacifism in the present.

In an attempt to translate this revolutionary pacifism into practical action, Canadian pacifists concentrated on what they considered the most important issue on the home front – the protection of civil liberties in wartime. Besides the threat of conscription, the issue that most strongly aroused pacifist emotions were the government's forced evacuation and relocation of Japanese Canadians from the west coast and their eventual dispersal throughout Canada.

IV

Shortly after the official entry of Japan into the war with the bombing of Pearl Harbor in December 1941, the Canadian government evicted twenty thousand Japanese Canadians from the British Columbia coast, confiscated their property, both real and personal, and herded them into 'relocation centres' hurriedly set up at old ghost towns in the British Columbia interior: Greenwood, Slocan City, Roseberry, New Denver, Sandon, Kaslo, Lemmon Creek, and Tashme.[80] Although it was ostensibly placed in 'protective custody,' all Japanese property was subsequently sold at prices far below its actual value. The Japanese Canadians themselves, most of whom were Canadian citizens, either lived out the remaining war years as refugees in the 'relocation camps' or were dispersed to other areas of Canada to work in sugar-beet camps, domestic service, steel plants, foundries, and chemical works. Approximately thirty-five hundred people were sent to the prairies; others were resettled in Ontario and Quebec.

The Japanese Canadians were subjected to restrictions not imposed upon Canadians of German, Italian, or other 'enemy' ancestry. They were forbidden, for example, to buy or rent property without the permission of the provincial minister of justice and attorney-general and were prohibited from crossing provincial boundaries without a special permit. In addition to being considered suspect because of their 'enemy' origin, it appears that Japanese Canadians were also victims of an official policy of racial discrimination. Later generations of Canadians would condemn the government's arbitrary action as one of the most glaring violations of civil rights in the nation's history, but at the time most Canadians, especially those in British Columbia, either remained silent or approved of the discriminatory measures. Pacifists claimed that the government's policy was a clear example of the kind of brutal, insensitive response of a society at war, similar but more vicious than the internment of enemy aliens during the first war.

By June 1943, a number of pacifists, representing the Fellowship of Reconciliation, the Women's International League for Peace and Freedom, and the Society of Friends joined with other concerned Canadians to found the Co-operative Committee on Japanese Canadians.[81] Although the committee was initially designed to help resettle the Japanese Canadians in Toronto and other parts of the country, it eventually became the instrument through which a number of conscientious citizens, working closely with the Japanese Canadians themselves, directly challenged the official discriminatory policies, particularly the government's post-war attempt to repatriate those of Japanese ancestry.

Since few ordinary citizens were aware of that plan, the first task of the committee was to publicize the plight of Japanese Canadians with the hope of arousing the national conscience. The committee also began to fight local hostility to the resettled Japanese Canadians and called upon the Canadian public to demonstrate tolerance. The editors of *Reconciliation* urged their readers to take the lead in working towards the community acceptance of Japanese Canadians and the achievement of practical goals such as finding them decent living accommodation and jobs, organizing English-language training classes, and relocating Japanese-Canadian students in schools and colleges.[82] Furthermore, pacifists were urged to register their opposition to repatriation with their members of Parliament.

It was the government's threat of deportation, or 'repatriation,' of Japanese Canadians, including those born in Canada, that infuriated some Canadians and led to increased support for the work of the committee. By June 1945 the committee had expanded into a federation of thirty-three groups and organizations interested in securing justice for Japanese Canadians.[83] Among the participating groups were the FOR, the WIL, the Society of Friends, the SCM, the National Council of Women, the Civil Liberties Association of Toronto, the Toronto Labour Council, the YMCA, the YWCA, and various churches. The task of co-ordinating the activities of these various groups into a unified front belonged to the committee executive: James Finlay, chairman, Donalda MacMillan, secretary, and Constance Chappell, treasurer.[84] As the pacifist pastor of Carlton Street United Church in Toronto and an executive member of the Fellowship of Reconciliation, Finlay personally ensured that the struggle on behalf of Japanese Canadians was a popular outlet for pacifist social activists. For instance, among the pacifists particularly active in the work of the committee were Albert Watson and Edith Fowke of the *Reconciliation* editorial staff.[85] A number of pacifists also worked directly with the Japanese Canadians in the relocation centres. Among these were Mildred Fahrni, Helen Lawson, Ella Lediard, and three conscientious objectors, Ernest Best, Donald Ewing, and John Rowe, all of whom taught at Japanese-Canadian schools in New Denver and Tashme.[86]

The work of the committee went into high gear in September 1945, when the Canadian government announced its plans to proceed with repatriation on the basis of its survey conducted earlier that year at the detention centres. At that time over 6,000 Japanese Canadians had agreed to the voluntary repatriation of what amounted to 10,347 people, mostly Canadian citizens, as an alternative to moving east of the Rockies. Since then, however, many of those who had approved of the scheme revealed that they had done so only because of direct threats of separation from their families or the loss of their livelihood.[87] The committee argued that the government survey merely indicated the dissatisfaction and frustration of a restricted people and was not a true measure of those who wanted to return to Japan.

In response to the imminent threat of deportation, the committee distributed 75,000 copies of a leaflet entitled 'From Citizens to Refugees – It's Happening Here!' The editors of *Reconciliation* had previously reprinted 1,000 copies of their issue on Japanese Canadians, of which 250 copies were sold before printing.[88] In addition, some individual groups, such as the Canadian Friends Service Committee, cabled Prime Minister Mackenzie King and selected members of Parliament urging the suspension of the repatriation scheme.[89] Despite such pleas, and despite personal visits to Ottawa by Finlay, Donalda MacMillan, and other committee members, the government proceeded with its plans, and in December 1945 tabled three orders in council providing for the deportation of all persons of Japanese ancestry and their families who had signed requests for repatriation and had not revoked their action prior to 1 September 1945.[90]

The Co-operative Committee on Japanese Canadians decided that its only recourse was to take legal action. Andrew Brewin, a Toronto lawyer who represented the Civil Liberties Association on the committee, was appointed as legal counsel and argued the committee's case before the Supreme Court of Canada when the ministry of justice agreed to test the legality of the orders in council. Popular support for the committee's effort to stop repatriation began to build, and donations came pouring in from across the country. In Toronto nearly a thousand people gathered to show their support and hear addresses by Senator Cairine Wilson, Senator Arthur Roebuck, Rabbi Abraham Feinberg, and Andrew Brewin. The meeting passed a resolution urging the prime minister to abandon plans for the expulsion of Japanese Canadians. Similar resolutions had already been passed at meetings in London, Brantford, Ottawa, Montreal, Winnipeg, and Vancouver.[91] National opposition to forced repatriation continued to mount after the Supreme Court ruled that the orders in council were legal simply because of the government's power to enact them under the War Measures Act.

In response the committee appealed the Supreme Court decision to the Privy Council; but, recognizing that the Privy Council's decision would deal only with the legal and constitutional questions involved, it also renewed its pressure on the government to suspend the policy of wholesale deportation. The committee distributed fifty thousand copies of a leaflet entitled 'Our Japanese-Canadians – Citizens, not Exiles' to help bolster support for their cause among the Canadian public. It appears that the committee anticipated the decision of the Privy Council, handed down on 2 December 1946, that the orders in council were indeed valid under the War Measures Act. Under increasing public pressure, however, the government finally backed down and on 24 January 1947 Prime Minister King announced that the orders in council providing for the repatriation of Japanese Canadians had been repealed.[92]

Overjoyed that its long campaign for social justice and civil liberties had succeeded at least in suspending repatriation, the Co-operative Committee on Japanese Canadians quickly turned its attention to other issues, such as compensation for property loss, and continued to function until 1951, when all restrictions on Japanese Canadians were finally removed and all their claims, except those for compensation, were settled.

In the end, pacifists came to view the practical achievements of the Co-operative Committee on Japanese Canadians as a clear example of pacifism in action. Together with sympathetic representatives of other sectors of society they successfully challenged wartime injustice as part of their overall effort to secure justice for all citizens. James Finlay, who had served as chairman of the co-operating groups for six years, later recalled that the plight of Japanese Canadians became the overriding concern of Canadian pacifists during the war and the immediate post-war years.[93] In effect, the issue became the 'battleground for peace and justice.'[94]

v

Members of the Fellowship of Reconciliation were investigating other avenues for countering the increasing insensitivity of Canadian society to the moral problems accompanying war. In January 1944, for instance, Lavell Smith questioned the morality of the Allied strategic bombing of German cities, which had come under considerable attack from pacifists and churchmen in Britain. Smith condemned Canada's churchmen for remaining silent.[95] He reminded the Church that during the days of the London blitz it had condemned the same type of indiscriminate bombing that it apparently tolerated when practised on German cities: 'Is it to be concluded that bombs dropped upon us are murderous and inhuman while bombs dropped by us are remedial or salutary?' The inconsistency of such a moral stand was aggravated as news dispatches revealed that more bombs were being dropped on Berlin in a single night than ever fell on London in a month. 'Our bombers are described as cutting swaths of utter destruction clear across a city. Our political leaders promise the enemy worse things to follow. Yet I listen in vain for the voice of the Canadian Church to condemn such indiscriminate bombing.'[96] The silence of the Church was indicative of the 'dulling of moral sensitivity' during wartime, and as a result pacifism in Canada was 'growing day by day.' In the long run, though, Canadian pacifists were never successful in arousing much opposition to strategic bombing, even though Vera Brittain, a leading spokeswoman for the Bombing Restriction Committee in Britain, lectured in Canada on several occasions at the invitation of the FOR.[97]

When over a hundred Fellowship of Reconciliation members gathered for their first annual conference in July 1944, it became evident that Canadian pacifists were concerned both with the immediate problems confronting Canadians directly affected by the war and with the larger economic issues underlying world peace. The conference delegates recommended that the national council set up a committee on race relations that would include members of the black, Japanese-Canadian, and Jewish communities of Canada. The committee would be primarily concerned with youth education and personal counselling and would also be responsible for publicizing cases of racial discrimination, providing speakers, and organizing a letter-writing campaign in keep the issue before the public.[98] The conference also endorsed several proposals for action in respect to economic problems, emphasizing that as Christian pacifists FOR members 'must be prepared to give courageous leadership in the field of social and economic reform.' The conference called for the socialization of the Canadian economy, and recommended that the FOR work with the Religion-Labor Foundation in the struggle for industrial democracy, promote closer co-operation between agricultural and industrial workers, encourage the establishment of credit unions and consumer and producer co-operatives, and advocate the immediate creation of public housing projects. In the international field the conference urged the creation of a co-operative world organization to guarantee fair distribution of the world's raw materials to all nations.

Overall, the Fellowship of Reconciliation conference reflected a renewed optimism among Canadian pacifists. In an effort to broaden its outreach, for instance, the FOR decided to affiliate with the War Resisters International and with the international FOR. The Canadians also began to develop closer co-operation with American pacifists. The previous year, for instance, John Nevin Sayre, chairman of both the American and the international FOR, visited Toronto for a two-day conference with the Canadian section.[99] In succeeding years the annual conferences usually featured internationally known pacifists such as A.J. Muste in 1945, John M. Swomley in 1946, Muriel Lester in 1947, and G.H.C. MacGregor in 1948.[100] This international exchange was balanced by Canadian representation at American conferences; Lavell Smith attended one FOR conference in New York City, and James Finlay addressed the national conference of the American FOR on the progress of the Canadian fellowship.[101]

As well as extending its international associations, the Canadian FOR underwent an internal reorganization at the war's end. The national council was expanded to include twenty-four members, twelve from Toronto and twelve from elsewhere in Canada; Albert Watson, who had served as executive secretary on a part-time basis the previous year, was reappointed on a full-time basis and given an annual operating budget of sixteen hundred dollars.[102] As the Canadian fellowship's first paid executive secretary, Watson devoted himself to promoting an effective program. He assumed related responsibilities as a member of a Toronto interracial committee and an adviser to the Japanese-Canadian credit union. Within a few years the Fellowship of Reconciliation successfully organized Canadian pacifist action on a wide variety of fronts.

Because the Fellowship of Reconciliation was centred in Toronto, it lacked an effective co-ordination of pacifists living in other parts of the country, and the difficulty of uniting a small minority of citizens scattered across a vast, sparsely populated country remained an intractable problem. In an attempt to minimize this handicap the executive decided to send Watson on a cross-country trip in the fall of 1945.[103] The initial plans had been made before the end of the war, and it was intended that one of Watson's primary goals would be to elicit the support of Canadians for the FOR's 'Campaign for a Constructive and Democratic Peace,' a version of the petition sponsored by the National Peace Council in England that called for a peace settlement built upon a radical reconstruction of society rather than upon national guilt, racial inferiority, or military power.[104] By the time Watson embarked on the trip, however, the war had ended and the attention of Canadian pacifists had shifted to the future of the Fellowship of Reconciliation in Canada and to postwar challenges such as the issue of peacetime conscription.

Watson's first stop was Quebec, where he helped reorganize a FOR unit in Montreal under the leadership of Jack Duckworth. In August he set out for the west coast. The journey had a fourfold purpose: to meet with as many FOR members and friends as possible; to organize new FOR units; to publicize the work of the FOR, particularly its 'Forerunner' program for teenage youth; and to promote the magazine *Reconciliation*.[105] Upon his return to Toronto, Watson expressed confidence that after addressing forty-six meetings and delivering several radio broadcasts he had succeeded in making valuable new contacts and in contributing to a greater sense of unity between western members and the national office in Toronto. He proudly reported that 'for the first time in its history' the Fellowship of Reconciliation was organized on a truly national basis, with groups active not only in Toronto, Hamilton, and Montreal but also in Winnipeg, Saskatoon, Regina, Edmonton, Medicine Hat, Calgary, and Vancouver. According to Watson, one of the highlights of his journey was his visit with the leaders of the co-operative Mennonite Community of Altoona, south of Winnipeg. He left convinced of the necessity to maintain and extend co-operation with Mennonites during the post-war years.

The value of Watson's personal diplomacy notwithstanding, *Reconciliation* remained the most valuable link between Canadian pacifists.

Within a year of its initial publication, the editorial staff modified the magazine's format to produce issues devoted to specific topics. From July 1944, approximately two-thirds of each issue was devoted to a single subject, such as anti-Semitism, Canadian immigration policy, Canadian unity, industrial relations, Japanese Canadians, conscientious objectors, refugees, and the movement for co-operative communities in Canada. The editors were able to focus attention on the various ways in which the pacifist ethic of non-violence was being breached within Canadian society and to reflect the primary concerns of Canadian pacifists in working towards practical solutions to controversial war-related problems.

VI

Throughout the war years pacifists in Canada strove to make a realistic response to actual wartime circumstances in such a way as to move society further towards their desired end. First and foremost they were concerned with liberty of conscience, and they endeavoured to implant the right of conscientious objection more deeply in Canadian soil. This was more than just a self-protective device, however, for they organized relief efforts to assist the victims of war overseas and worked on behalf of those groups in Canada who were victimized by internment. Moreover, using the communal lifestyle of the historic peace sects as an example, liberal pacifists began to take steps to build experimental co-operative communities which they hoped would serve as practical models for a co-operative and peaceful society. Another important action was taken when the Fellowship of Reconciliation began to publicize these issues through their own magazine, *Reconciliation*. In the context of topics ranging from race relations to industrial relations, its contributors explored the dynamic potential of non-violent action and humanitarian response. The Christian pacifist argument was also publicized in personal newsletters such as Fairbairn's bulletin. All in all, pacifists actively promoted a non-violent alternative social order, and by the end of the war they were confident they had successfully adapted their pacifism to the reality they faced.

But, in contrast to the Niebuhrian realism that rejected utopian ideals and demanded that Christians assume responsibility for the fight against the harsh realities of fascism, the realism of the pacifist response was confined within the limits of the pacifist ideal. Although prevented from sharing responsibility in the direct outcome of the war, pacifists considered their role a serious and important one. They attempted to make constructive contributions to wartime society, acting both as prophets, judging the war from the standpoint of believers in the Kingdom of God, and as reconcilers, enlarging the ground of civil liberties in Canadian society. Some pacifists were inclined to one role or the other; Fairbairn, for example, was clearly more prophetic judge than reconciling agent. But the perception of one role often depended upon the other; thus, Fairbairn could not envisage a reconciliation short of the total restructuring of society. Even the more withdrawn Mennonites emerged to help through their own relief organizations. In the end, the pacifist relief and reconciliation activities that had begun in response to the war continued well into the post-war era and served as a constant reminder of the non-violent alternative in a world conditioned by and to war.

Conclusion

The atomic bombing of Hiroshima and Nagasaki in August 1945 finally brought the Second World War to an end, but, in the light of the awesome new threat of mass nuclear destruction, peace and tranquillity were hardly secured. On the contrary, it was the beginning of an era of bewilderment, frustration, and increased international tension as a new armaments race began to escalate between the United States and the Soviet Union. A sense of impending doom was in the air. The imminent threat of atomic warfare imbued pacifism with an urgency that ultimately altered the character of the post-war peace movement in Canada.

I

In contrast to the initial feeling of hopelessness that greeted news of the atomic weapon, pacifists were encouraged to remain optimistic and continue the type of humanitarian activities they had begun during the war. Lavell Smith, for one, reminded his fellow members in the Fellowship of Reconciliation of pressing post-war social problems – millions of people faced cold and hunger in Europe, thousands of workers were on picket lines in North America, and racial minorities still suffered from systematic discrimination. 'In all these situations, as in others,' he wrote, 'the word of brotherhood and reconciliation needs to be spoken. It may even be that there are increasing numbers ready to hear it.'[1]

Not surprisingly, post-war relief and reconstruction continued to be one of the most popular areas of pacifist activity. The Canadian Quakers, in particular, launched a massive drive for refugee relief following the war, and, with the permission of the Canadian government, they issued their first public appeal for funds in February 1946.[2] As the donated funds became available, the Canadian Friends Service Committee purchased supplies and shipped them directly to the needy areas of central Europe and the Far East, where relief teams were organized by the American Friends Service Committee. From January to August 1947 the Friends War Victims Relief Fund raised over thirty-two thousand dollars, and by October fifty thousand dollars, worth of supplies had been sent overseas.[3] The shipments included bulk supplies of cod-liver oil and powdered milk as well as medical supplies, blankets, and clothing.[4]

The appeal of Canadian Friends for relief funds received the support of the entire pacifist community, and especially that of James Finlay, who used his weekly radio broadcast over Toronto station CFRB to publicize the Quaker cod-liver-oil program.[5] Such enthusiastic support for the Friends Relief Fund was typical of the co-operation between pacifists and the network of Canadian relief agencies, such as the Canadian Save the Children Fund, Canadian Church Relief Abroad, which represented the large Protestant denominations, and the Ontario Committee for Relief in Japan.[6] The Friends Service Committee would maintain its program of overseas relief into the 1950s and after.[7]

Following the war, pacifists also continued to display an active interest in experimental co-operative communities through the Canadian Fellowship for Cooperative Community. Although the death of Henri Lasserre in 1945 severely weakened the movement, both the Fellowship for Cooperative Community and the Robert Owen Foundation were kept alive by a small nucleus of pacifists. They continued to publish a newsletter and organized small experiments such as Dale House, a co-operative residence in Toronto.[8] Among those attracted to co-operative living were a number of conscientious objectors who had viewed life in alternative service work camps as an introduction to communal organization. Ultimately, several of these cos joined Bruderhofs in the United States.[9] The major (though still modest) Canadian experiment in co-operative pacifist living was the Winterbrook Community near Hornby, Ontario.

In addition to Christian pacifists, the Canadian Fellowship of Cooperative Community also encouraged co-operative farming experiments in the west, such as the co-operative farm for veterans at Matador, Saskatchewan. Still another venture was its support for the Jewish *chabitzim*, a group that maintained a communal residence in Toronto and a collective farm at Prescott, Ontario, as training for settlements in Palestine that were forerunners of the Israeli *kibbutzim*.[10] Thus, the Canadian Fellowship for Cooperative Community succeeded in uniting a wide range of Canadians – farmers, labourers, professionals, pacifists, Jews, and Gentiles – in a common quest for a new social order that would guarantee justice and peace.

Increasingly, however, the post-war pacifist response, such as support for co-operative communities, was viewed as irrelevant to the realities of the atomic age. In a *Reconciliation* article entitled 'Pacifism after Hiroshima' Dr J.J. Brown, the director of the Canadian Association of Physicists, claimed that the atomic bomb had placed pacifism in a serious dilemma.[11] Before Hiroshima, he argued, realistic pacifists had not expected to see much change in the common attitude towards war in their lifetime, although they believed their efforts would ultimately reach fruition. After 1945, however, the traditional pacifist approaches of moulding public opinion and building model communities were no longer relevant – the world had run out of time. Brown concluded that pacifism and its corollary, pacifist action, were in need of an urgent and 'thorough overhauling.'[12] Time was of the essence.

Brown clearly exposed the vulnerability of pacifism in the light of the new, inescapable nuclear dilemma, but some pacifists tried to argue that Christian pacifism remained unaffected by the possibility of imminent disaster because it was based upon religious conviction rather than rational political considerations. It soon became painfully obvious to most pacifists, however, that they had to meet the challenge posed by atomic warfare,[13] especially since Canada, as the leading supplier of the uranium used in the manufacture of the new bombs, bore much of the responsibility for unleashing nuclear power. Consequently, the Fellowship of Reconciliation appealed to the Canadian government to 'renounce war for all time,' to ban the atomic bomb, to work for a worldwide halt in the production of atomic weapons, and, most important, to place an immediate embargo on exports of uranium ore.[14] As a strategy for the nuclear era the FOR executive also proposed that pacifists take the lead in the various campaigns to stop the atomic arms race and achieve universal disarmament, to put an end to imperialism and promote understanding and friendship between Canada and the Soviet Union, to work for a more liberal immigration policy in Canada, and to abolish cadet training in Canadian high schools.[16] It was the last goal that attracted the most pacifist support in the immediate post-war years; the Fellowship of Reconciliation led the way, sidestepping the nuclear issue for the more familiar struggle against cadet training.

During the 1920s and 1930s the campaign against the cadet corps had actually succeeded in abolishing the programs in various school systems throughout the country; but in September 1944 cadet training was again made compulsory in the nation's secondary schools.[17] By the end of the war, however, the cadet corps was either placed on a voluntary basis (as in British Columbia, Saskatchewan, Quebec, and Prince Edward Island), or eliminated from the school program altogether (as in Manitoba). The glaring exception was Ontario where cadet training remained compulsory [18] In response, the FOR launched an all-out campaign to disband the Ontario cadet corps, labelling it 'Mr Drew's Army' after the premier of Ontario, George A. Drew. The FOR revealed that the Drew government required all boys in Ontario high schools to devote the majority of their physical and health education periods to cadet training and military drill.[19] In reference to the government's defence of the cadet system as valuable training in 'good citizenship,' the pacifist critic Albert Watson argued that the only way to train young people in good citizenship was 'to educate them from their childhood in Canadian ideals and privileges of democratic living ... It is not possible to train boys in democratic citizenship, by compelling them to submit to the authority of a military system.'[20] Instead of recruiting an army of boys, Drew was challenged to support alternative measures that would help achieve lasting peace, such as the improvement of race relations, jobs for all at adequate wages, decent labour legislation, and improved social services.[21]

As part of their campaign to abolish cadet training, the FOR distributed flyers presenting a point-by-point case against the cadet system and urging the people of Ontario to voice their opposition to cadet training in letters to the editors of local papers, to local school boards, to MLA's, and, to Premier Drew himself. 'ACT NOW,' it warned. 'THERE IS NO TIME TO LOSE!'[22]

In an angry reaction, Premier Drew charged that the Fellowship of Reconciliation was a 'crypto false front communist organization.'[23] The fellowship was also criticized by an old liberal ally, B.K. Sandwell, the editor of Saturday Night. In an editorial entitled 'Pacifism Again,' Sandwell accused the FOR of being inconsistent in supporting Canada's role in the United Nations, which included the supplying of military forces on the one hand while advocating the undermining of Canadian preparedness on the other.[24] Although he agreed that a good argument could be made for the exemption of students from compulsory cadet training for reasons of conscience, Sandwell was not prepared to share the logical conclusion to the pacifist line of thinking – the complete disarmament of Canada. Considering the inconsistency in the FOR's position, he wondered if pacifists really desired that end, implying that perhaps they wanted 'to be defended while doing nothing for defence.'[25] It was a stinging accusation that pacifists found difficult to refute, especially since the power of non-violence, as a realistic alternative to military force, was little appreciated outside their own community.

The FOR national council responded to Sandwell with an explanation of their campaign.[26] The heart of the issue, they argued, was that compulsory cadet training was not only an unwarranted form of conscription in itself but a prelude to national military conscription during peacetime. The solution was to nip it in the bud. Only by abolishing cadet training in the high schools could Canadians hope to put an end to militarism in Canada.[27]

After years of intensive campaigning by pacifists, the compulsory cadet-training system in Ontario was replaced by a new 'Citizenship Corps' training course. Although the solution was not completely satisfactory to pacifists, it was hailed as a 'vast improvement and a step in the right direction.'[28] In this instance the Fellowship of Reconciliation attained some limited success, but in the long run it was unable to escape the type of criticisms levelled by Sandwell and others that its brand of pacifism was unrealistic for the time.

By 1947 the FOR, like the entire Canadian peace movement, had reached a critical juncture. The movement was plagued by a lack of financial resources, a dwindling membership, and public apathy; the future of pacifism looked bleak, even though world peace was increasingly in need of defence. The previous summer, while attending the Alberta School of Religion, Scott Nearing, the American anti-war radical, had recognized the crisis and blamed it on the failure of Canadian pacifists and anti-war socialists to attract young converts. Few of those who came to meetings were under forty and most were over sixty. 'They are the stalwarts who learned to hold the torch on high before World War I,' he observed, but since then they had gained few loyal adherents, and death and disaffection had decimated their ranks. 'It is a rebel remnant, still rebellious, but thinning out with the years.'[29]

As a last resort, James Finlay, the post-war chairman of the Fellowship of Reconciliation, appealed to the American chapter for a grant of eleven or twelve hundred dollars a year for a two-year period.[30] Finlay proposed to use the funds for an office secretary, thus freeing Abe Watson, the executive secretary, for field-work in broadening and consolidating their membership across Canada.[31] But American financial assistance was not forthcoming. John Nevin Sayre replied that although he and A.J. Muste were solidly behind Abe Watson, the needs in Europe were far greater than in Canada. Accordingly, he suggested that Finlay begin with a less ambitious program for Watson, particularly since Canada might prove to be a 'financially arid country' for pacifist fund-raising.[32]

One of the first casualties of the financial crisis was the FOR publication, *Reconciliation*. The magazine was appearing less and less frequently, and but by October 1947 the national council was forced to suspend its publication permanently.[33] In its place the American journal *Fellowship* was distributed to Canadian subscribers. *Reconciliation* had been viewed not merely as a magazine but as a special bond between Christian pacifists in Canada. The breaking of the bond further weakened that part of the Canadian movement. Shortly after the demise of *Reconciliation* Abe Watson resigned as Canadian executive secretary and left to take up a new position with the American FOR.[34] He was succeeded by Mrs Mildred Fahrni, who eventually became one of the leading post-war figures in the Fellowship of Reconciliation, first as executive secretary and then as western secretary in Vancouver.

For the next decade the Fellowship of Reconciliation would continue to emphasize the theme of non-violent social action in such areas as race relations, labour disputes and penal reform. Above all, the FOR represented the last major vestige of a liberal Christian pacifism founded upon faith in a divine force working on its behalf. It was believed that in time religious pacifism would lead to a peaceful and just social order. The threat of atomic warfare, however, undermined the social hopes of liberal pacifism. Carlyle King, the first national chairman of the Fellowship of Reconciliation and the post-war president of the Saskatchewan CCF, was one of those who concluded that the pacifism of the FOR was outmoded by the realities of the atomic age.[35]

Indeed, during the 1950s the ranks of the peace movement swelled with a whole new group of adherents, known as nuclear pacifists or neo-pacifists, who were not willing to follow the lead of the FOR. Since the nuclear pacifists believed that it was the new dimension of atomic power which made war unthinkable, they were primarily concerned with removing the threat of atomic weapons and easing tensions between the Soviet Union and the West. The new wing of the peace movement was not strictly Christian in character; it hoped to forge a renewed alliance with the radical left, and it endorsed the Marxist ideal as the way out of the nuclear dilemma.

The move towards a radical post-war movement was accelerated with the founding of the Canadian Peace Congress in 1948. The initial stimulus for the congress came when Harry Ward of the Union Theological

College addressed a Toronto meeting that included a number of his former students, as well as A.A. MacLeod, the communist head of the League for Peace and Democracy before the war, and James Finlay and I.G. Perkins of the Fellowship of Reconciliation. Ward urged his audience to take some type of non-violent political action on behalf of peace. In response to his exhortation, a provisional committee was established to set up a peace congress in Canada.[36] To organize the congress on a national basis the committee enlisted Dr James G. Endicott, the radical United Church missionary who had resigned from his missionary post in China and from the ministry because of the church's disapproval of his outspoken support for the Chinese communists.[37] Endicott soon discovered that a number of like-minded peace councils had already been formed, such as the Vancouver Assembly for Peace founded by Norman Mackenzie, a student activist in the 1920s and later the president of the University of British Columbia, H.H. Stevens, leader of the Reconstruction party during the 1930s, and Watson Thompson. Within a year a national conference was called to co-ordinate the various peace councils, and the Canadian Peace Congress was officially launched.[38]

In the years to follow, Endicott and the Peace Congress would become embroiled in a concerted condemnation of u.s. foreign policy as part of a rather stormy campaign to halt the nuclear arms race and germ warfare. Much of the support for the congress came from former members of the now defunct communist-inspired League for Peace and Democracy, but it also came from other wings of the peace movement, including the Fellowship of Reconciliation, the Women's International League for Peace and Freedom, and the Student Christian Movement.[39] Endicott himself emphasized the ideal of openness in the congress, claiming that it 'did not exclude anyone, right, left or centre,' and many of those from the earlier days continued to exercise leading roles in the anti-nuclear campaign.[40]

Nevertheless, the emergence of the Canadian Peace Congress and its dominance throughout the early 1950s signalled a new stage in the evolution of the Canadian peace movement. In a desperate attempt to attain some semblance of harmony in a world threatened by nuclear destruction, the main activist force of pacifism moved onto more radical ground, carrying on a leftward transition that had begun before the Great War and that had received a major impetus from the depression. Reluctant liberal pacifists, the remnants of mainline Christian pacifism, and the historic peace sects were pushed to one side by the force of the new movement which actively sought to preserve world peace through public pressure for political solutions aimed at easing the tensions of the cold war and curbing the nuclear arms race. By the late 1950s and early 1960s a number of new groups, such as the Canadian Campaign for Nuclear Disarmament, the Voice of Women, and the Student Union for Peace Action, further broadened the new peace movement. The torch had been passed to a generation of peace activists who would build upon a Canadian pacifist tradition defined and defended during the first half of the century.

II

It has been the argument of this book that pacifism was an important force in the development of Canadian social values during the first half of the twentieth century. Pacifists were active in nearly all attempts to resolve human conflict, from labour-management mediation to international diplomacy, and through the example of sectarian communities and the initiative of social activists their influence was felt. Through the years Canadian attitudes to social violence and economic injustice, and particularly to war, came to be shaped in varying degrees by the pacifist ethic. This became especially evident during the 1920s and 1930s, when there was mounting public support for international co-operation, disarmament, and a neutral foreign policy as well as for radical solutions to the social and economic injustices that bred violence and war. While not quite the 'peaceable kingdom' it often purported to be, Canada emerged from the Second World War with an increased toleration for dissent, respect for the individual conscience, and commitment to social justice, in part because of the pacifist witness.

Although the pacifist phenomenon occurred throughout the English-speaking world, Canada had an especially rich and varied pacifist heritage, which, despite its later secular-socialist base of support, was rooted in two distinct but complementary traditions, both heavily religious in character. The first was the liberal Protestant and humanitarian tradition reflected in the peace movement. These mainstream 'integrational pacifists,' to use Peter Brock's classification, viewed pacifism as a way of reaching their social ideal, whether it was liberal or socialist in nature. The other tradition was the historic non-resistance of religious sects such as the Mennonites and Hutterites, which held pacifism as a social norm, a complete way of life. Since these 'separational pacifists' tried to remain aloof from war and society alike, they had little direct impact on the peace movement, but their steadfast refusal to submit to compulsory military service during the two world wars indirectly reinforced the principle of pacifist dissent, particularly that of conscientious objection, in Canadian society on the whole. Moreover, their peaceful co-operative communities served as living examples of the pacifist hope of building a new social order along communal lines.

Although the sectarian pacifists remained largely withdrawn from Canadian society, they also experienced a slight transition towards accommodation with the state. This adjustment was less evident among the Doukhobors and the eschatological groups such as the Jehovah's Witnesses, but on the whole the peace sects, especially some Mennonite groups, became more involved in society because of the need to defend their pacifist beliefs.

The valuable witness of the historic peace sects notwithstanding, the peace movement in Canada more directly reflected the liberal Christian tradition of pacifism. From their first appearance as part of the progressive reform movement in the late nineteenth century, liberal non-sectarian pacifists underwent a gradual movement towards the political left. Initially, the liberal-progressive peace movement reflected a complex set of Victorian social attitudes – forcefulness of character, imperialism, and hero worship – that made a real assertion of pacifism difficult, though not impossible. For a time the pacifist dimension of the liberal conscience found suitable expression in the maternal feminist campaigns for temperance and suffrage as well as in the Canadian Peace and Arbitration Society, the only secular peace organization active in Canada during the early years of the century.

By and large, the progressive pacifists hoped to maintain world peace by preserving rather than changing the social order. Amid the pressures of an escalating wartime crusade, however, this liberal pacifism proved to be utterly untenable. Those who wished to maintain their pacifist protest found it necessary to adopt a radical critique of the social and economic roots of war, and in doing so to abandon their liberal reformism for some variant of the socialist creed. For some, that too became a type of eschatological warfare against the established social order, not entirely unlike the struggle of their erstwhile colleagues who sought the reign of peace via 'the war to end war.' In conjunction with anti-war socialism a new socially radical pacifism emerged following the collapse of the progressive peace movement during the Great War.

Liberal pacifism re-emerged in the post-war years among such groups as the League of Nations Society, and again attracted a wide range of public support. In effect, the resurgent peace movement of the 1920s, representing a broad front of groups and activities, resembled an act of national repentance built upon revulsion against the Great War and the lingering belief that world peace could be ensured without radically restructuring the social and economic order. In one sense this resurgence of liberal pacifism served as a temporary diversion from the crisis confronting liberal reformism and from the task of developing a more profound Christian ethic of war.

The post-war movement was more than an expression of liberal pacifism, however; it was coloured by the socially radical pacifism the war had bred. This became increasingly evident during the depression years as socially radical pacifists allied with the political left in an effort to secure justice for all through radical reforms and social change. Pacifists assumed leading roles and helped formulate policy in such organizations as the Co-operative Commonwealth Federation, the League for Social Reconstruction, the Fellowship for a Christian Social Order, the Student Christian Movement, and the Women's International League for Peace and Freedom. Canadian feminists in the last group, for instance, were instrumental in transforming the resurgent peace movement of the 1920s into a dynamic campaign for social change. As feminists and pacifists they equated the material analysis of war with gender and class exploitation, thereby moving beyond the maternal, protective instinct to demand a complete reconstruction of society in line with the co-operative ideal, including sexual equality and economic justice.

For a time during the 1930s the quests for peace and social justice appeared to be compatible – even communists participated through MacLeod's League against War and Fascism – but pacifists were soon confronted with a dilemma when, in the light of increased fascist aggression, their pacifist rejection of the use of force came into direct conflict with the struggle for social justice. By mid-decade, particularly with the outbreak of the Civil War in Spain, social radicals began to abandon pacifism in favour of the fight against fascism. It was a process that continued well into the later 1930s and one that tended to rob pacifism, even a socially radical pacifism, of any sense of political realism.

Consequently, those who remained committed pacifists retreated behind the confines of a narrower Christian pacifism not entirely unlike that of the historic peace sects. Some among them assumed the role of the Christian prophet, engaging in social protests, such as the 'Witness against War' manifesto and conscientious objection to military service, and judging the war and its effects in the context of the Kingdom of God. Unlike their sectarian brothers, however, they could not escape the Niebuhrian challenge to reach a realistic response to the wartime situation. Thus, another role of the pacifist during the Second World War became one of reconciling the wartime tensions in Canadian society at large by exercising realistic pacifist alternatives, including alternative service for conscientious objectors, refugee and relief work, and the defence of civil liberties. In this way pacifists such as the Quakers sought to prove that they were not just idealists or politically irrelevant dreamers, but their sense of realism remained confined within the framework of the pacifist hope for the dawning of a new peaceful world – in contrast to Niebuhr's argument that that type of peace would never exist in history.

The wartime experience also had a unifying effect on the various pacifist groups and encouraged a new level of co-operation between the historic peace sects and the more socially active pacifists. In the end, pacifists of all stripes successfully maintained a witness against war, some merely by refusing as far as possible to co-operate with the state, others by exercising state-approved alternatives. Indeed, the pacifist witness was not effected without some accommodation to the state.

The most obvious example of this accommodation was the alternative service program that pacifists had hoped would secure their right to conscientious objection without compromising their rejection of war. In the end, despite its civilian nature, alternative service posed a new moral dilemma as pacifists found themselves mobilized and implicated in the national war effort. It was a problem most pacifists had not foreseen and one that young conscientious objectors under the pressures of the time tried to ignore. Moreover, in return for their exemption from military service, conscientious objectors forfeited not only basic civil liberties such as the franchise but also control of their own labour. They either worked for fifty cents per day in alternative service work camps or had the major portion of their wages diverted to the Red Cross. Thus, although the value of their labour was clearly recognized by government authorities, conscientious objectors were not allowed to reap its benefits. Pacifists could not escape the total wartime mobilization of Canadian society, and alternative service set a precedent either for the totally isolated internment of war resisters in any future war or for their complete assimiliation in a diversified war effort.

Despite the continued commitment of pacifists to a new social order, the disaffection of their radical colleagues before and during the war tended to undermine the radical social prophecy of Christian pacifism and left it unprepared to lead a more politicized peace campaign in response to the urgent threat of atomic weapons. Instead, the post-Second World War initiative was seized by the radical left, which forged a renewed alliance between the Marxist ideal and the pacifist search for harmony among all peoples of the world. Every stage of the peace movement in its leftward transition represented the religious quest to realize this ideal vision of an ordered, peaceful world. Pacifists who joined the Canadian Peace Congress in the 1950s believed they had reached the point where they had become part of the ultimate movement towards that kind of social order. They had gone beyond believing that liberalism was the best way to achieve their particular rendezvous with destiny.

But it was not an easy or a complete transition. Critics charged that the Canadian Peace Congress, like the League for Peace and Democracy before it, was largely an instrument of Soviet foreign policy, and, despite Endicott's insistence to the contrary, the reputation of the new peace movement was tarnished. Pacifists themselves criticized Endicott's inconsistency in working for peace while at the same time supporting the cause of the People's Liberation Army in China. It was all too similar to the pacifist dilemma of the 1930s, when the pursuit of social justice came into conflict with the pacifist commitment to non-violence; disappointment once again awaited pacifists as the Peace Congress broke apart over the conflicting international policies of the post-war communist states.

At mid-century, therefore, pacifism in Canada was represented by both the historic non-resistance of sectarian groups, somewhat accommodated to the state but still struggling to maintain their separate communities, and a radicalized peace movement that included both socialists and Christian idealists. Apart from the rural-oriented peace sects, those Canadians attracted to pacifism over the years represented a cross-section of Canadian society, especially once the business and community leaders who had dominated the early progressive peace movement gave way to a new alignment of pacifists from farm, labour, and professional backgrounds. Many were educated, and a few were intellectuals. Most were religious pacifists with roots in the social gospel, and much of the leadership in the Canadian peace movement was provided by clergymen. Although the pacifist movement's universal appeal blurred any sense of Canadian nationalism, the religious factor was characteristic of Canadian pacifists, and, despite a good deal of influence from the British and American movements, Canadian pacifism developed in its own distinctive way. Above all, the pacifists tended to be individuals of exceptional quality, and in nearly all areas of social concern they sought ideal solutions to harsh realities. Liberals and radicals alike were determined to help bring about a new peaceful order built upon a foundation of social and economic justice. That they were not entirely successful in this quest does not minimize the importance of their attempt to shape Canadian social attitudes.

In a larger sense, the study of pacifism raises serious questions about the relationship between church and state, particularly in wartime. Should the church, for instance, automatically endorse and defend the state at war? Or is its first priority to serve as a constant reminder of the moral basis of society, even if that runs counter to official policy? The Canadian experience reveals that not only were most churches reluctant to criticize the state's resort to war, they usually supported it with great vigour. This was particularly true during the first war, but even by 1939 the controversy within the United Church surrounding the 'Witness against War' manifesto proved that neither church nor state was comfortable with the idea of churchmen publicizing the pacifist alternative.

Another recurring theme in this book has been the pacifist attempt to identify pacifism with patriotism. Time and again, from the efforts of the Canadian Peace and Arbitration Society during the Great War to the campaign for alternative service during the Second World War, pacifists argued that they were as loyal and patriotic as those Canadians who marched off to war. They believed that their patriotic duty was to maintain the courage of their convictions and exercise the right of dissent, thereby keeping alive a free society. Pacifism was not always an easy response to make or to understand, but the pacifists were convinced that it was a patriotic one.

The fact remains, however, that throughout the first half of the twentieth century only a small number of Canadians became pacifists. At best, the peace movement enjoyed its widest popularity during times of peace, particularly in the early 1930s, when it embraced a broad range of individuals and groups, but true pacifists remained a small minority. The ranks of conscientious objectors in both wars were primarily filled by sectarian groups rather than adherents of the popular peace movement. The leading inter-pacifist organizations, such as the Women's International League for Peace and Freedom and the Fellowship of Reconciliation, never attracted a large number of members. Measured against the Hutterites, or against Canadian society at large, their communitarian ventures were pitifully small. But in the final analysis the pacifist phenomenon must be measured on some scale other than size.

Although pacifists formed a cultural island in the mainstream of society, as a moral minority they were influential beyond their numbers. Pacifism became an important ingredient in Canadian social thought, and for a time, especially during the depression, a pacifist-socialist alignment offered creative leadership. The gradual radicalization of pacifism to a political as well as a moral commitment resulted in a strengthened idealism and determination, which in turn inhibited the pacifist search for political relevancy. But more than offering a prophetic vision of an ideal, pacifism, in both the sectarian and liberal traditions, came to symbolize reconciliation and the priority of questions of conscience in a changing Canadian society. The mere survival of pacifism as a religious and social practice in the nuclear era is a tribute to those ideals of civil liberty and freedom of conscience for which earlier pacifists worked. Indeed, their preservation and advancement of enduring moral principles underlying Canadian culture remains the real legacy of the pacifist witness against war during the first half of the twentieth century.

Notes

INTRODUCTION

1 See C.J. Cadoux, *The Early Christian Attitude to War* (1919; reprint, London: Allen and Unwin, 1940). Other important works on New Testament pacifism are G.H.C. Macgregor, *The New Testament Basis of Pacifism* (New York: Fellowship Publications, 1954); Roland H. Bainton, *Christian Attitudes toward War and Peace* (Nashville: Vanderbilt University Press, 1960); and Jean Lasserre, *War and the Gospel* (1962). Lasserre is the son of the Canadian Henri Lasserre mentioned later in this book.

2 Peter Brock, *Pacifism in Europe to 1914* (Princeton: Princeton University Press, 1972), 4

3 Bainton, *Christian Attitudes*, 95

4 Peter Brock, *Twentieth-Century Pacifism* (New York: Van Nostrand Reinhold, 1970), 6; an exception was Tolstoy.

5 The standard British scholarship includes David Boulton, *Objection Overruled* (London: MacGibbon and Kee, 1967); John W. Graham, *Conscription and Conscience* (London: George Allen and Unwin, 1922); David A. Martin, *Pacifism: An Historical and Sociological Study* (London: Oxford University Press, 1970); Keith Robbins, *The Abolition of War: The 'Peace Movement' in Britain, 1914–1919* (Cardiff: University of Wales Press, 1976); and, most, recently, Martin Ceadel, *Pacifism in Britain, 1914–1945: The Defining of a Faith* (Oxford: Clarendon Press, 1980). A complete view of the American pacifist experience is provided in Peter Brock, *Pacifism in the United States: From the Colonial Era to the First World War* (Princeton: Princeton University Press, 1968); Charles Chatfield, *For Peace and Justice: Pacifism in America 1914–1941* (Knoxville: University of Tennessee Press, 1971); Lawrence S. Wittner, *Rebels against War: The American Peace Movement*

1941–1960 (New York: Columbia University Press, 1969); Charles De-Benedetti, *Origins of the Modern American Peace Movement, 1915–1929* (New York: KTO Press, 1978); and *The Peace Reform in American History* (Bloomington, Indiana: Indiana University Press, 1980).

6 One of the most important outbreaks of scholarship, for instance, occurred during and after the Vietnam war, with works appearing by writers such as Brock, DeBenedetti, Chatfield, and Wittner, as well as John K. Nelson, *The Peace Prophets: American Pacifist Thought, 1919–1941* (Chapel Hill: University of North Carolina Press, 1967), and Roland C. Marchand, *The American Peace Movement and Social Reform 1898–1918* (Princeton: Princeton University Press, 1972).

7 Ramsay Cook, *'The Regenerators: Religion and Reform in Late Victorian Canada* (Toronto: University of Toronto Press, 1985), and 'Francis Marion Beynon and the Crisis of Christian Reformism,' in *The West and the Nation*, edited by Carl Berger and Ramsay Cook (Toronto: McClelland and Stewart, 1976), and James Eayrs, *In Defence of Canada* 5 vols (Toronto: University of Toronto Press). Although John Herd Thompson made some recognition to pacifism in *The Harvests of War: The Prairie West, 1914–1918* (Toronto: McClelland and Stewart, 1978), his latest work almost completely ignores the impact of the interwar peace movement. See John Herd Thompson with Allan Seager, *Canada 1922–1939: Decades of Discord* (Toronto: McClelland and Stewart, 1985). The same is true of such standard works as H. Blair Neatby, *William Lyon Mackenzie King*, vol. III: *1932–39: The Prism of Unity* (1976), and Jack L. Granatstein, *Canada's War: The Politics of the Mackenzie King Government 1939–1945* (Toronto: Oxford University Press, 1975). Surprisingly, there also is little mention of pacifism in Gerald Friesen, *The Canadian Prairies: A History* (Toronto: University of Toronto Press, 1984).

8 Donald G. Creighton, *The Forked Road: Canada 1939–1957* (Toronto: McClelland and Stewart, 1976), 27

9 Frank H. Epp, *Mennonites in Canada, 1786–1920: The History of a Separate People* (Toronto: Macmillan, 1974), and *Mennonites in Canada, 1920–1940: A People's Struggle for Survival* (Toronto: Macmillan, 1982); M. James Penton, *Jehovah's Witnesses in Canada* (Toronto: Macmillan, 1976). Others include David Fransen, 'Canadian Mennonites and Conscientious Objection in World War II' (MA thesis, University of Waterloo, 1977); Victor Peters, *All Things Common: The Hutterian Way of Life* (Minneapolis: University of Minnesota Press, 1965); John W. Bennett, *Hutterian Brethren* (Stanford: Stanford University Press, 1967); George Woodcock and Ivan Avaku-

movic, *The Doukhobors* (Toronto: Oxford University Press, 1968); Arthur G. Dorland, *The Quakers in Canada: A History* (Toronto: Ryerson, 1968).

10 E.A. Christie, 'The Presbyterian Church in Canada and Its Official Attitude towards Public Affairs and Social Problems, 1875–1925' (MA thesis, University of Toronto, 1955); M.V. Royce, 'The Contribution of the Methodist Church to Social Welfare in Canada' (MA thesis, University of Toronto, 1940); J.M. Bliss, 'The Methodist Church and World War I,' *Canadian Historical Review*, XLIX (September 1968); David B. Marshall, 'Methodism Embattled: A Reconsideration of the Methodist Church and World War I,' *Canadian Historical Review*, LXVI (March 1985), 48–64

11 Donald Page, 'Canadians and the League of Nations before the Manchurian Crisis' (PH D dissertation, University of Toronto, 1972); Joan Sangster, 'Canadian Women in Radical Politics and Labour, 1920–50' (PH D dissertation, McMaster University, 1984)

12 Richard Allen, *The Social Passion* (Toronto: University of Toronto Press, 1973)

13 Roger Hutchinson, 'The Fellowship for a Christian Social Order: A Social Ethical Analysis of a Christian Socialist Movement' (PH D dissertation, Toronto School of Theology, 1975), and 'The Public Faith of a Democratic Socialist,' *Journal of Canadian Studies*, XXI (Summer 1986), 26–37

14 Michiel Horn, *The League for Social Reconstruction: Intellectual Origins of the Democratic Left in Canada 1930–1942* (Toronto: University of Toronto Press, 1980); Kenneth McNaught, *A Prophet in Politics* (Toronto: University of Toronto Press, 1959)

15 C.T. Sinclair-Faulkner, 'For Christian Civilization: The Churches and Canada's War Effort, 1939–1942' (PHD dissertation, University of Chicago, 1975)

16 Brock, *Pacifism in Europe*, pp. 474–5. Brock divides pacifists into six categories, the most important of which in the Canadian context are the separational and integrational pacifists and the 'eschatological pacifists' such as the Jehovah's Witnesses.

17 Peter Brock, *Twentieth-Century Pacifism*, 5

CHAPTER ONE: Early pacifist traditions in Canada

1 Peters, *All Things Common*, 9
2 Epp, *Mennonites in Canada*, 34
3 R.A. Knox, *Enthusiasm: A Chapter in the History of Religion* (Oxford: Clarendon Press, 1973), 169

4 Brock, *Twentieth-Century Pacifism*, 5; Knox, *Enthusiasm*, 147
5 Brock, *Twentieth-Century Pacifism*, 7
6 Epp, *Mennonites in Canada*, 51. 'This exemption, however, required service in other capacities such as extinguishing fires, suppressing the insurrections of slaves, caring for the wounded, and transporting food and information': ibid., 51.
7 Ibid., 100–1
8 Dorland, *The Quakers in Canada*, 317
9 Epp, *Mennonites in Canada*, 101. Especially noteworthy were the numerous Mennonite petitions: ibid., 102.
10 'Quakers Opposed War Preparations in Upper Canada,' *The Canadian Friend*, 1973, 10–11
11 Dorland, *The Quakers in Canada*, 109
12 31 Victoria, c. 40, s. 17 (1868), as quoted in Epp, *Mennonites in Canada*, 193
13 Ibid., 192–5, 315
14 Peters, *All Things Common*, 46–8
15 Bennett, *Hutterian Brethren*, 35. Both Mennonites and Hutterites share common Anabaptist roots in their faith and their withdrawn and separate lifestyles, but each reacted differently to the modern age. Whereas large numbers of Mennonites began to participate in society while eschewing modern technology, Hutterites accepted modern technology but remained isolated from society.
16 Woodcock and Avakumovic, *The Doukhobors*, 11
17 Ibid., 19, 49
18 The doctrine is common to other Christian groups, such as Quakers. The 'presence of Christ' refers to the external, expressive element of the Trinity, distinct from the man Jesus of Nazareth.
19 Woodcock and Avakumovic, *Doukhobors*, 20
20 Brock, *Pacifism in Europe*, 446
21 Woodcock and Avakumovic, *Doukhobors*, 95
22 Brock, *Pacifism in Europe*, 454. Tolstoy's pacifism is expressed in *The Kingdom of God Is within You.*
23 Brock, *Pacifism in Europe*, 456–61
24 Ibid., 454; George Woodcock, *Anarchism: A History of Libertarian Ideas and Movements* (London: Penguin, 1963), 18
25 Wookstock, *Anarchism*, 18, 207
26 Letter, Tolstoy to Doukhobors, 27 February 1900, as quoted in Woodcock and Avakumovic, *Doukhobors*, 167
27 Ibid., 112; Brock, *Pacifism in Europe*, 452

28 Brock, *Pacifism in Europe*, 464; Anarchist pacifists and neo-Tolstoyan communities did not surface until the Second World War: Woodcock, *Anarchism*, 218.

29 Allen, *The Social Passion*, 10

30 Brock, *Pacifism in Europe*, 461

31 The use of the term 'fundamentalist' refers to those groups within Protestantism that adhere to orthodox religious beliefs based on a literal interpretation of the Bible.

32 Brock, *Pacifism in Europe*, 401

33 Ibid., 403–5; other pacifist sects included the Disciples in Christ and various pentecostal groups.

34 Penton, *Jehovah's Witnesses in Canada*, 9; among his books were the six-volume *Millennial Dawn* series. At Russell's death in 1916, Joseph F. Rutherford became the new president of the Watch Tower Society: ibid., 10.

35 Ibid., 16; Russell's *The Divine Plan of the Ages* (1884) presents his view of history.

36 Ibid., 35–8

37 Donald Page, 'Canadians and the League of Nations before the Manchurian Crisis' (PHD dissertation, University of Toronto, 1972), 9–10; Merle Curti, *The American Peace Crusade* (New York, 1965), 36 and 118

38 R.S. Lambert, 'Forgotten Peace Prophet,' *Maclean's*, 1 March 1945, 18; another isolated example was that of the Reverend Nathaniel Paul, a black Baptist minister at Wilberforce Settlement for Fugitive Slaves in Upper Canada, who had converted to a completely pacifist position by 1835. See Peter Brock, *Radical Pacifists in Antebellum America* (Princeton: Princeton University Press, 1968), 28.

39 Monk's portrait by Holman Hunt hangs in the National Gallery in Ottawa.

40 Marchand, *The American Peace Movement*, x

41 Robert H. Wiebe, *The Search for Order, 1877–1920* (New York: Hill and Wang, 1967), 260–2

42 The three branches of Friends in Canada were the Genesee Yearly Meeting (Hicksite), the Canada Yearly Meeting (Conservative), and the Canada Yearly Meeting (Orthodox or Progressive). The three branches began to co-operate after the First World War and finally united in 1955.

43 Dorland, *The Quakers in Canada*, 133

44 Ibid., 327

45 Ibid., 326–7

46 Allen, *The Social Passion*, 5; 'The Social Gospel and the Reform Tradition in Canada, 1890–1920,' *Canadian Historical Review*, XLIX (December 1968), 384; see also Richard Allen, 'Background to the Social Gospel in Canada,' in *The Social Gospel in Canada*, edited by Richard Allen (Ottawa: National Museum of Man, 1975)

47 C.S. Eby, *God-Love*, The Word of the Kingdom Series, study I (Toronto, 1906), 7–8; C.S. Eby, *Christianity and Civilization*, Tokio Lectures I, 6 January 1883; *Canadian Men and Women of the Time: A Handbook of Canadian Biography of Living Characters* edited by Henry James Morgan (Toronto, 1912), 363

48 Morgan, *Canadian Men and Women*, 363; Charles S. Eby was born in Goderich, Ontario, in 1845 and spent his early boyhood in Elora. He received his BA from Victoria University of Coburg and attended the Theological University at Halle, Germany. He served as superintendent of the Methodist church's German Mission at Preston, Ontario, before leaving for Japan. After his return to Canada he served as the first secretary of the Canadian Anti-tuberculosis Association from 1900 to 1902: Charles S. Eby biography file, United Church Archives (hereinafter UCA).

49 C.S. Eby, *The World Problem and the Divine Solution* (Toronto, 1914), 27; Eby, *God-Love*; C.S. Eby, *Sermon on the Mount, the Charter of the Kingdom*, The Word of the Kingdom Series, study II (Toronto, 1907)

50 Eby, *The World Problem*, 24–5

51 Ibid., 29, 284, 314; Eby, *God-Love*, 53; Eby, *Sermon on the Mount*, 13

52 *Globe* (Toronto), 25 December 1899, 10

53 'Report of the Peace and Arbitration Department,' *Report of the Convention of the Dominion Woman's Christian Temperance Union* (1901), 67

54 Dorland, *The Quakers in Canada*, 327

55 Roland H. Bainton, *Pilgrim Parson: The Life of James Herbert Bainton (1867–1942)* (New York: Thomas Nelson and Sons, 1958), 61–2

56 Ibid., 66

57 Carman Miller, 'English-Canadian Opposition to the South African War as Seen through the Press,' *Canadian Historical Review*, LV (December, 1974), 432

58 Ibid., 432–3

59 Ross Harkness, *J.E. Atkinson of the Star* (Toronto: University of Toronto Press, 1963), 50

60 Miller, 'English-Canadian Opposition to the South African War,' 430–1; A. Ross McCormick, *Reformers, Rebels, and Revolutionaries: The Western Canadian Radical Movement 1899–1919* (Toronto: University of Toronto

Press, 1977), 16, 79, 86. Puttee's loss of credibility as a pacifist during the Boer War weakens McCormick's general characterization of him and other labour radicals as 'pacifists' during the Great War.

61 Prior to his position with *Citizen and Country*, Wrigley was the editor of *Canada Labor Council*, St Thomas, Ontario, *Canada Farmer's Sun*, Toronto, and *The Templar*, Hamilton.

62 *Citizen and Country*, 11 March 1899, 2

63 Ibid., 29 July 1899, 1

64 Ibid., 7 October 1899, 1

65 Ibid., 25 November 1899, 1; 29 July 1899, 1

66 Ibid., 7 October 1899, 1

67 Ibid., 12 August 1899, 1

68 Ibid., 9 December 1899, 4; Desmond Morton, *Mayor Howland: The Citizens' Candidate* (Toronto: Hakkert, 1973) 97–8. Thompson, a Bellamyite socialist and resident intellectual in the Toronto Theosophist group, supported North American continentalism, as did Goldwin Smith; but, unlike Smith, he based his conviction on working-class rather than racial solidarity. Although Thompson and Smith were poles apart in their analysis of and prescription for the crisis facing late nineteenth-century Canada, they both condemned involvement in imperialist wars. See Ramsay Cook, 'The Professor and the Prophet of Unrest,' paper presented at the Colloquium on Canadian Society in the Late Nineteenth Century, 17–18 January 1975, McGill University.

69 *Citizen and Country*, 4 November 1899, 4

70 Ibid., 22 July 1899, 1

71 Miller, 'English-Canadian Opposition to the South African War,' 424

72 Craig Brown, 'Goldwin Smith and Anti-Imperialism,' in *Imperial Relations in the Age of Laurier*, edited by Carl Berger (Toronto: University of Toronto Press, 1969), 13

73 Miller, 'English-Canadian Opposition to the South African War,' 424. The *Standard* (Regina) moderated its stand soon after the war began and refrained from criticizing the British cause.

74 Robert Craig Brown and Ramsay Cook, *Canada, 1896–1921: A Nation Transformed* (Toronto: McClelland and Stewart, 1974), 42

75 Miller, 'English-Canadian Opposition to the South African War,' 436

76 Marchand, *The American Peace Movement*, 19

77 Page, 'Canadians and the League of Nations,' 12

78 *Report of the Lake Mohonk Conference on International Arbitration* (Lake Mohonk: the Conference, 1907), 114

79 Page, 'Canadians and the League of Nations,' 44

80 *Report of the Lake Mohonk Conference*, 1903, 77
81 Ibid., 1906, 86; 1907, 113; Dorland, *The Quakers in Canada*, 328
82 W.L. Mackenzie King, 'The Bearing of Industrial Conciliation and Arbitration on International Peace,' *Report of the Lake Mohonk Conference*, 1910, 107
83 Dorland, *The Quakers in Canada*, 327; of particular assistance is Terry Crowley, 'Ada Mary Brown Courtice: Pacifist, Feminist and Educational Reformer in Early Twentieth-Century Canada,' *Studies in History and Political Science* (1980), 76–114. Crowley had access to the Brown-Courtice Family Papers, including a ledger of the Canadian Peace and Arbitration Society.
84 Crowley, 'Ada Mary Brown Courtice,' 87; Queen's University Archives (hereinafter QUA), Adam Shortt Papers, series I, box 2, folder 12, Andrew Courtice to Adam Shortt, 15 March 1907. Elias Rogers became the society's vice-president in 1912: Morgan, *Canadian Men and Women*, 962.
85 Ledger of the Canadian Peace and Arbitration Society, as quoted in Crowley, 'Ada Mary Brown Courtice,' 87
86 Shortt was often a member of boards of conciliation in industrial disputes: QUA, Adam Shortt Papers, series II, box 11, Adam Shortt Diaries, vol. I, 1907–10, 5
87 Ibid., series I, box 2, folder 12, Courtice to Shortt, 15 March 1907
88 *Report of the Lake Mohonk Conference*, 1907, 114–15
89 Page, 'Canadians and the League of Nations,' 45–6
90 Edward A. Christie, 'The Presbyterian Church in Canada and Its Official Attitude toward Public Affairs and Social Problems, 1875–1925' (MA thesis, University of Toronto, 1955), 101–3, 115–17
91 Ibid., 119
92 *Record*, December 1912
93 *Presbyterian* (Toronto), 19 February 1914, 127
94 *Christian Guardian*, 21 January 1914, 5; 28 January 1914, 7–8; 20 August 1922, 21
95 The Reverend William Sparling, 'Canadian Churches and Peace,' *Report of the Lake Mohonk Conference*, 1911, 163–5
96 Page, 'Canadians and the League of Nations,' 34–5
97 *Report of the Convention of the Dominion Woman's Christian Temperance Union*, 1896, 56–9
98 The department in Nova Scotia was established under the direction of Mrs Mary R. Chesley, the wife of Justice Samuel A. Chesley, vice-president of the Canadian Peace and Arbitration Society.
99 Crowley, 'Ada Mary Brown Courtice,' 89; Mrs Courtice opened a private

school in Toronto after the death of her husband, and as a member of the Toronto Board of Education she founded the home and school movement in 1914 that eventually spread throughout Canada: *Macmillan Dictionary of Canadian Biography*, 3 ed (Toronto: Macmillan, 1963), 157. As early as 1894 the Canadian National Council of Women had adopted a resolution approving the principle of international arbitration in the settlement of international disputes: *Report of the Lake Mohonk Conference*, 1895, 68.

100 V. Strong-Boag, *The Parliament of Women: The National Council of Women of Canada, 1893–1929* (Ottawa: National Museum of Man, 1976), 349.

101 Jill Conway, 'The Women's Peace Party and the First World War,' in *War and Society in North America*, edited by J.L. Granatstein and R.D. Cuff (Toronto: Thomas Nelson and Sons, 1971), 52

102 Flora Macdonald Denison, *War and Women* (Toronto: Canadian Suffrage Association, 1914), 6; for more on Denison, see Deborah Gorham, 'Flora Macdonald Denison: Canadian Feminist,' in *A Not Unreasonable Claim: Women and Reform in Canada 1880s-1920s*, edited by Linda Kealey (Toronto: The Women's Press, 1979), 47–70

103 Nellie McClung, *In Times Like These* (1915; reprint, Toronto: University of Toronto Press, 1972), 9–15

104 Byrne Hope Sanders, *Emily Murphy, Crusader* (Toronto: Macmillan, 1945), 345–7; Page, 'Canadians and the League of Nations,' 28

105 Hopkins, *Canadian Annual Review*, 1914, 134

106 Page, 'Canadians and the League of Nations,' 13

107 McClung, *In Times Like These*, 15

108 Crowley, 'Ada Mary Brown Courtice,' 89

109 Robert M. Stamp, 'Empire Day in the Schools of Ontario: The Training of Young Imperialists,' *Journal of Canadian Studies*, VIII (August 1973), 32–9

110 Page, 'Canadians and the League of Nations,' 29

111 Hopkins, *Canadian Annual Review*, 1914, 134

112 John H. Thompson, *The Harvest of War: The Prairie West, 1914–1918* (Toronto: McClelland and Stewart, 1978), 19

113 Page, 'Canadians and the League of Nations,' 22–3

114 Ibid., 24–5

115 Martin Robin, 'Registration, Conscription and Independent Labour Politics, 1916–1917,' in *Conscription 1917*, edited by Carl Berger (Toronto: University of Toronto Press, 1969), 60–1; Hopkins, *Canadian Annual Review*, 1914, 135

116 Arthur G. Dorland, 'Militarism in Canada,' *The Canadian Friend*, (July,

1913), 14–15; Arthur G. Dorland was born in Wellington, Ontario, in 1887. After receiving a BA from Queen's University in 1910, an MA from Yale in 1911, and a PHD from the University of Toronto in 1927, he made a career of university teaching, first at Queen's and then at the University of Western Ontario. During the first half of the twentieth century he was one of the most prominent members of the Society of Friends in Canada.

117 Ibid., 16

118 'Memorial of the Religious Society of Friends to the Government and People of Canada,' *Minutes of the Canada Yearly Meeting of Friends* (Toronto: Society of Friends, 1913), 23–5; Orthodox Friends created a special committee on Canadian military and naval propaganda.

119 Ibid., 28

120 Lewis E. Horning, 'England and Germany,' *Addresses Delivered before the Canadian Club of Hamilton, 1913–1914* (Toronto: Canadian Club, 1914), 112–14

121 Lewis E. Horning, 'Some Aspects of the Questions of World Peace,' *Christian Guardian*, 13 May 1914, 8–9

122 Victoria University Archives (hereinafter VUA), Lewis Emerson Horning Papers, vault 9, J

123 Macdonald was the editor of two Presbyterian newspapers, *Presbyterian* and *The Westminster* before becoming editor-in-chief of the *Globe* in 1913, succeeding J.S. Willison: *Presbyterian*, 10 January 1913, 37.

124 Marchand, *The American Peace Movement*, 112; James A. Macdonald, *The North American Idea* (Toronto: Fleming H. Revell, 1917), 93

125 *Globe* (Toronto), 11 November 1912, 6

126 The executive committee of the Canadian Peace Centenary Association consisted of Sir Edmund Walker, the Honourable Senator Raoul Dandurand, Traver Lewis, and C.A. Magrath: *Canadian Peace Centenary Association Circular*, no. 5, 2–3.

127 *Canadian Peace Centenary Association Circular*, no. 3, 8

128 Page, 'Canadians and the League of Nations,' 52; *Canadian Peace Centenary Association Circular*, no. 5, 3

129 *Canadian Place Centenary Association Circular*, no. 7, 1.

130 Bennett, *Hutterian Brethren*, 40

131 Brock, *Twentieth-Century Pacifism*, 267

132 Dorland, 'Militarism in Canada,' 14

133 J.M. Bliss, 'The Methodist Church and World War I,' in *Conscription 1917*, edited by Carl Berger (Toronto: University of Toronto Press, 1969), 42

CHAPTER TWO: The collapse of liberal pacifism

1 J.C. Hopkins, *Canadian Annual Review*, 1914, 132–3
2 Norman Angell, 'Canada's Best Service for British Ideals,' *Addresses Delivered before the Canadian Club of Toronto, 1913–1914* (Toronto: Canadian Club, 1914); in *The Great Illusion* (1910) Angell made a critical analysis of war and economics concluding that the popular belief that a successful war brings material gain was an optical illusion.
3 Lt-Col. J.T. Fotheringham, quoted in Hopkins, *Canadian Annual Review*, 1914, 135
4 *Globe* (Toronto), 3 August 1914, 4
5 Ibid., 21 August 1914, 4
6 Hopkins, *Canadian Annual Review*, 1914, 136
7 Macdonald, *North American Idea*, 240
8 J.E. Atkinson, 'The Aftermath of the War,' *Addresses Delivered before the Canadian Club of Toronto, 1915–1916* (Toronto: Canadian Club, 1916), 60–1
9 *Minutes of the Genesee Yearly Meeting of Friends, 1915*, 25
10 VUA, Lewis E. Horning Papers, Lewis E. Horning, 'The Two Ideals,' *Acta Victoriana* (October 1915), 2
11 Ibid., Lewis E. Horning, 'The New Citizenship,' unpublished manuscript
12 UCA, Methodist Church of Canada, General Conference Office, general correspondence, 1914, box 3, file 59, Lewis E. Horning to T.A. Moore, 26 September 1914, 2
13 Ibid.
14 Ibid.
15 Hopkins, *Canadian Annual Review*, 1915, 350
16 VUA, Horning Papers, vault, 12 E.W566TP
17 Denison, *War and Women*, 6
18 Sanders, *Emily Murphy*, 286
19 Hopkins, *Canadian Annual Review*, 1915, 334–5
20 John H. Thompson, 'The Beginning of Our Regeneration: The Great War and Western Canadian Reform Movements,' *Historical Papers* (Toronto: Canadian Historical Association, 1972), 238–9
21 Christie, 'The Presbyterian Church in Canada,' 124
22 Ibid.; see also Colm Brannigan, 'The Anglican Church in Canada and the Great War' (Paper prepared for Department of History, McMaster University, 1978) and Steven R. Ramlochan, 'The Baptists of Ontario and World War I, 1914–1918' (Paper prepared for Department of History, McMaster University, 1973).
23 Christie, 'The Presbyterian Church in Canada,' 122; *Presbyterian*, 13 August 1914; 20 August 1914, 148

24 *Presbyterian*, 26 November 1914, 496

25 *Christian Guardian*, 19 August 1914, 5; W.B. Creighton was born in Dorchester, Ontario, in 1864 and graduated from Victoria University in Coburg. He served as associate editor of the *Christian Guardian* from 1901 to 1907 and as editor until church union in 1925, when he became editor of the *New Outlook*. He retired in 1937 and died in 1946: UCA, W.B. Creighton biography file.

26 *Christian Guardian*, 26 August 1914, 5

27 Ibid., 16 September 1914, 5

28 Albert Marrin, *The Last Crusade: The Church of England in the First World War* (Durham: Duke University Press, 1974), 124–5

29 McClung, *In Times Like These*, 15–17

30 Ibid., 18

31 Thompson, 'The Beginning of Our Regeneration'

32 *Christian Guardian*, 25 December 1914, 8

33 *Presbyterian Record*, October 1914, 433; the same connection between the war effort and temperance was made by *Presbyterian*, 12 November 1914, 436.

34 *Christian Guardian*, 1 November 1916, 5

35 Ibid., 3 April 1918, 1

36 Ibid., 1 May 1918, 5

37 *Presbyterian Record*, June 1918, 161

38 Marrin, *The Last Crusade*, 253, 131

39 Bliss, 'Methodist Church and War,' 57

40 *Presbyterian Record*, June 1916

41 *Minutes of the Genesee Yearly Meeting of Friends*, 1915, 24–33

42 *Minutes of the Canada Yearly Meeting of Friends*, 1917, 23–4. During the First World War Dorland was a graduate student at Yale University in the United States and a lecturer in history at Queen's University. Although he was ready to take his stand as a conscientious objector, the war ended before his classification group was called up: Arthur G. Dorland, *Former Days and Quaker Ways* (Picton, Ont.: The Picton Gazette Publishing Company, Ltd, 1965), 178–91; interview with Arthur G. Dorland, 29 January 1976.

43 *Minutes of the Canada Yearly Meeting of Friends*, 1917, 23–4

44 Ibid., 1918, 23; *Minutes of the Genesee Yearly Meeting of Friends*, 1916, 44. Pickering College was used by the government as a military hospital until July 1920: *Minutes of the Canada Yearly Meeting of Friends*, 1920.

45 *Minutes of the Genesee Yearly Meeting of Friends*, 1915, 41

46 Chatfield, *For Peace and Justice*, 54

47 *Minutes of the Genesee Yearly Meeting of Friends*, 1915, 33; 1917, 59

48 Saskatchewan Archives Board, Saskatoon (hereinafter SABS), S.V. Haight
   Papers, file A5.8, Elsie Charlton and Laura Hughes to S.V. Haight,
   n.d.; Zoe Haight and Violet McNaughton were the first women in Saskatchewan to be interested in the Women's International League for Peace
   and Freedom (WIL). Other WIL members in Toronto included Flora
   Macdonald Denison, Harriet Dunlop Prenter, Christine Barker, and
   Dr Margaret Gordon. See Carol Lee Bacchi, *Liberation Deferred? The Ideas of
   the Canadian Suffragists, 1877–1918* (Toronto: University of Toronto Press,
   1983), 122–3

49 Barbara Roberts, 'Why Do Women Do Nothing to End the War?' Canadian
   Feminist-Pacifists and the Great War, CRIAW Papers (Ottawa: Canadian
   Research Institute for the Advancement of Women, 1985), 4

50 *Mail and Empire* (Toronto), 23 April 1915, 9

51 Hopkins, *Canadian Annual Review*, 1915, 334

52 Jill Conway, 'The Women's Peace Party and the First World War,' in *War
   and Society in North America*, edited by J.L. Granatstein and R.D. Cuff
   (Toronto: Thomas Nelson and Sons, 1971), 58; Walter I. Trattner, 'Julia
   Grace Wales and the Wisconsin Plan for Peace,' *Wisconsin Magazine of
   History*, XLIV (1961). Julia Grace Wales was born in Bury, Quebec, graduated from McGill University in 1903, and taught English and Shakespear-
   ean literature at the University of Wisconsin from 1905 to 1919. She
   returned to Canada in 1946 and died in 1957.

53 Page, 'Canadians and the League of Nations,' 30. The Canadian Women's
   Peace Party was also briefly named the Women's Peace Organization
   and the Canadian League for International Reconstruction before it
   became affiliated with the WIL: ibid., 59; SABS, Haight Papers, file A5.8,
   Charlton and Hughes to Haight, n.d.

54 Martin Robin, 'Registration, Conscription, and Independent Labour
   Politics, 1916–1917,' in *Conscription 1917*, edited by Carl Berger (Toronto:
   University of Toronto Press, 1968), 72–3

55 Roberts, 'Canadian Feminist-Pacifists and the Great War,' 4

56 Alice Chown, *The Stairway* (Boston: The Cornhill Company, 1921), 81.
   Autobiographical in content, this book is the main source for the information on Chown that follows.

57 Ibid., 294

58 Ibid., 296.

59 Ibid., 261

60 UCA, S.D. Chown Papers, box 10, file 214, Alice Chown to S.D. Chown,
   17 December 1918

CHAPTER THREE: Conscience and conscience

1 McCormick, *Reformers, Rebels and Revolutionaries*, 118
2 The Military Service Act 1917, 7–8 Geo. V, c. 19.
3 Elizabeth Armstrong, *The Crisis of Quebec, 1914–1918* (New York: Columbia University Press, 1937; reprinted Toronto: McClelland and Stewart, 1974), 226–30; Brown and Cook, *A Nation Transformed*, 306
4 Armstrong, *Crisis of Quebec*, 226–7
5 Ibid., 250
6 Christie, 'The Presbyterian Church in Canada,' 133
7 Bliss, 'Methodist Church and War,' 44
8 UCA, The Methodist Church of Canada, Army and Navy Board, 1915–19, box 2, file 17
9 *Christian Guardian*, 20 June 1917, 5
10 *Presbyterian and Westminster*, 6 September 1917, 230
11 *Presbyterian Record*, March 1917, 65
12 *Christian Guardian*, 29 March 1916, 1
13 Robin, 'Registration, Conscription, and Independent Labour Politics,' 64–5; McCormick, *Reformers, Rebels and Revolutionaries*, 124–7, 138
14 Robin, 'Registration, Conscription and Independent Labour Politics,' 70
15 Thompson claims that historians such as Charles Lipton and Martin Robin have overdrawn their generalizations concerning the anti-war sentiment of the trade union movement, and argues instead that anti-conscriptionists were unable to create 'a working class based opposition to conscription within the West.' See Thompson, *The Harvests of the West*, 117.
16 Robin, 'Registration, Conscription, and Independent Labour Politics,' 64–5, 71, 76. Labour had long adopted the radical critique. Prior to the war Keir Hardie toured Canada denouncing war as a capitalist device to check democracy: Hopkins, *Canadian Annual Review*, 1912, 163.
17 Robin, 'Registration, Conscription and Independent Labour Politics,' 71, 76; McCormick, *Reformers, Rebels and Revolutionaries*, 131–2. Following the 1917 TLC convention it was apparent that the Canadian labour movement was split between the eastern establishment and western radicalism.
18 As an example of violent protests McCormick cites the strike of Vancouver dockworkers that occurred when a stevedore was challenged for not carrying his registration papers, and the riot of loggers at Big River, Saskatchewan, when military authorities tried to collect draftees.
19 McCormick, *Reformers, Rebels, and Revolutionaries*, 138–9

20 Ibid., 129
21 W.R. Young, 'Conscription, Rural Depopulation, and the Farmers of
  Ontario, 1917–19,' *Canadian Historical Review*, LIII (September 1972)
22 *Presbyterian and Westminster*, 13 September 1917
23 Thompson, *The Harvests of War*, 151–156
24 As quoted in Roy St George Stubbs, *Prairie Portraits* (Toronto: McClelland
  and Stewart 1954), 99
25 *Manitoba Free Press*, 19 January 1917, 1
26 David J. Bercuson, *Confrontation at Winnipeg: Labour, Industrial Relations,
  and the General Strike* (Montreal: McGill-Queen's University Press, 1974), 42
27 *The Voice*, 10 November 1916, 1; 19 January 1917, 13; 13 July 1917, 5;
  Western Labor News, 9 August 1918, 5. One pacifist later praised *The Voice*
  for its priceless wartime service of providing an open forum for the
  'bludgeoned minority.'
28 Cook, 'Francis Marion Beynon.' Lillian Beynon Thomas was the founder
  and first president of the Winnipeg Political Equality League as well
  as chairman of the speakers' bureau: C.L. Cleverdon, *The Woman Suffrage
  Movement in Canada* (Toronto: University of Toronto Press, 1950), 55–6.
29 Public Archives of Canada (hereinafter PAC), MG 27, Woodsworth Papers,
  correspondence, A.V. Thomas to Woodsworth, 18 June 1918
30 Ibid., and Thomas to Woodsworth, 24 April 1918
31 Ibid., Thomas to Woodsworth, 18 June 1918
32 Ibid., and Thomas to Woodsworth, 24 April 1918
33 Ibid., Thomas to Woodsworth, 18 June 1918
34 Ibid., Thomas to Woodsworth, 16 January 1919
35 Cook, 'Francis Marion Beynon,' 197–9
36 *Grain Growers' Guide*, 24 November 1915, 10
37 Ibid., 3 March 1915, 10
38 Ibid., 7 March 1917, 10
39 Ibid., 2 July 1917, 9
40 Ibid., 13 June 1917, 10
41 Ibid., 27 July 1917, 10; Cook, 'Francis Marion Beynon,' 200. In New York,
  Francis Beynon worked with her sister Lillian at the Seamen's Church
  Institute and wrote the novel *Aleta Day*, a fictionalized autobiography. The
  novel, set in wartime Winnipeg, reveals the various currents of thought
  prevalent among reformers, especially with regard to militarism, Christianity and socialism. In the book Beynon argued that traditional Christianity, or 'Churchianity,' had failed. Rather than advocating the
  abandonment of religion, however, Beynon proposed a new radicalized

Christianity as the best hope for the future: Francis Marion Beynon, *Aleta Day* (London: W.C. Daniel, 1919).

42 *Grain Growers' Guide*, 6 June 1917
43 *Western Labor News*, 29 November 1918, 2
44 Cook, 'Francis Marion Beynon,' 203
45 Allen, *The Social Passion*, 61
46 Eby, *The World Problem*, 394–6
47 Kenneth McNaught, *A Prophet in Politics: A Biography of J.S. Woodsworth* (Toronto: University of Toronto Press, 1959), 67
48 J.S. Woodsworth, 'My Convictions about War,' *Vox* (December 1939), 4
49 *Studies in Rural Citizenship*, edited by J.S. Woodsworth (Winnipeg: The Canadian Welfare League and the Canadian Council of Agriculture, 1914), 87
50 Woodsworth, 'Convictions about War,' 5
51 McNaught, *A Prophet in Politics*, 75
52 *Manitoba Free Press*, 28 December 1916
53 J.S. Woodsworth, *Following the Gleam* (Ottawa, 1926), 4
54 Allen, *The Social Passion*, 47–8
55 Woodsworth, *Following the Gleam*, 9
56 Ibid.
57 Ibid.
58 Ibid., 10
59 Allen, *The Social Passion*, 50–1
60 PAC, Woodsworth Papers, correspondence, vol. 2; Thomas to Woodsworth, 24 April 1918
61 Ibid., Thomas to Woodsworth, 18 June 1918
62 Ibid., Thomas to Woodsworth, 24 April 1918
63 The *Western Labor News* was established by the Winnipeg trades council as part of its joint campaign with the Socialist party of Canada to break the power of Arthur Puttee, editor of *The Voice*, whom they now considered too moderate and therefore dangerous to their cause: McCormick, *Reformers, Rebels and Revolutionaries*, 146.
64 *Western Labor News*, 9 August 1918, 5
65 McCormick, *Reformers, Rebels and Revolutionaries*, 153
66 J.S. Woodsworth, *The First Story of the Labor Church and Some Things for Which It Stands*, (Winnipeg, 1920), 7–13
67 Two other representatives of the social gospel left wing, William Irvine and Salem Bland, were also dismissed from their posts during the war. Although neither was a pacifist, Irvine's problems did stem from his

criticism of the war effort. Bland supported the successful prosecution of the war effort as being harmonious with his radical reform objectives. But he may have been a little too radical for the Board of Directors of Wesley College. See Allen, *The Social Passion*, 46–56.

68 *Minutes of the Genesee Yearly Meeting of Friends*, 1917, 54; *The Canadian Friend*, October 1917, 6–7

69 *Canadian Friend*, October 1917, 7

70 *Minutes of the Canada Yearly Meeting of Friends*, 1917, 24

71 *Minutes of the Genesee Yearly Meeting of Friends*, 1918, 55

72 *Who's Who and Why, 1919–1920* (Toronto: International Press), 759

73 Interview with Arthur G. Dorland, 29 January 1976. The FAU was organized by Phillip Noel Baker, British Quaker and son of the former Canadian Quaker Joseph Allen Baker: ibid.

74 *Canadian Friend*, November 1917, 10–11

75 (1917) 7–8 Geo. V, c. 19, s. 11(8)(f)

76 Ibid.

77 Epp, *Mennonites in Canada*, 378

78 Canada, Department of National Defence (hereinafter DND), vol. 5953, HQ 1064-30-67-3; 'Petition Presented to the Honourable the House of Commons of Canada, in Parliament Assembled, 1917,' ibid., vol. 2029, HQ 1064-30-67, 'Declaration by the Seventh-Day Adventists of the Dominion of Canada and the United States Concerning Bearing Arms'

79 PAC, DND, RG 24, vol. 4498, MD4–60–1–2, Canadian Expeditionary Force Routine Order, 22 July 1918

80 Epp, *Mennonites in Canada*, 381–2

81 Ibid., 384–5

82 Allen Teichroew, 'World War I and the Mennonite Migration to Canada to Avoid the Draft,' *Mennonite Quarterly Review* (July 1971), 230

83 *I Would Like to Dodge the Draft-Dodgers but …*, edited by Frank H. Epp (Waterloo: Conrad Press, 1970), 13

84 Teichroew, 'Mennonite Migration,' 244

85 Epp, *Mennonites in Canada*, 385

86 Ibid., 337, 371

87 1918, 7–8 George V, c. 19, sections 4–8

88 Brown and Cook, *A Nation Transformed*, 221

89 PAC, DND, RG 24, vol. 5953, HQ 1064–67–3, judge advocate-general, memorandum: 'Treatment of Conscientious Objectors in Canada'

90 Ibid.; generally, most of the longer sentences were mitigated to ten years' imprisonment.

91 Ibid., vol. 2029, HQ 1064–30–67, memorandum, chief of the general staff to Militia Council, August, 1918

92 Ibid., vol. 5953, HQ 1064–30–67–3, Judge advocate-general, memorandum, 'Treatment of Conscientious Objectors in Canada'

93 Ibid., vol. 2029, HQ 1064–30–67, deputy minister, Department of Militia and Defence, to deputy minister, Department of Naval Service, 11 July 1918; deputy minister, Department of Militia and Defence, to deputy minister, Department of Naval Service, 9 August 1918

94 Ibid., vol. 2029, HQ 1064–30–95, Capt. O.S. Tyndale, secretary, Military Service Sub-committee, 28 August 1918

95 Ibid., vol. 2028, HQ 1064–30–67, C.F. McVagh, president, Western Canada Union Conference of Seventh-Day Adventists, to T.M. Tweedie, House of Commons, 12 May 1918; J.L. Wilson, president, Maritime Conference of Seventh-Day Adventists, to Sir Robert Borden, prime minister, 23 May 1918

96 Ibid., adjutant-general to GOC Military District no. 6, 4 June 1918

97 Ibid., the Reverent Fred F. Prior, St Boswells, Saskatchewan, to minister of militia, 8 June 1918

98 Ibid., central appeal judge to Capt. O.S. Tyndale, secretary, Military Service Sub-committee, 20 May 1918

99 Ibid., vol. 5953, HQ 1064–30–67–3, L. Clark, Ildeston, Ontario, to minister of militia, (n.d.)

100 Ibid., vol. 4498, MD4–60–1–2, Louis Friedenberg, Montreal, to Maj.-Gen. E.W. Wilson, GOC Military District No. 4, 27 September 1917

101 Ibid, RG 24, D2, vol. 36, file 105, Sessional Papers No. 105, 'Report of the Military Service Council on the Administration of the Military Service Act, 1917,' 1918

102 Ibid., RG 24, vol. 4498, MD4–60–1–1, 'Report on the Administration of the Military Service Act in Military District No. 4,' Montreal, 16 December 1918

103 Ibid., vol. 4498, MD4–60–1–2, Cyril Heath to Brig.-Gen. E.W. Wilson, March 1916

104 Ibid., Brig.-Gen. E.W. Wilson to H.J. Ross, 6 March 1916

105 Ibid., H.J. Ross to Brig.-Gen. E.W. Wilson, 4 March 1916

106 *Winnipeg Evening Tribune*, 24 January 1918

107 PAC, RG 24, vol. 2028, HQ 1064–30–67, 'Proceedings of a Regimental Court of Enquiry Assembled at Winnipeg, Manitoba, 24, January 1918,' 35

108 *Winnipeg Evening Tribune*, 24 January 1918

109 Ibid.

110 PAC, DND, RG 24, vol. 2028, HQ 1064–30–67, T.A. Crerar, minister of agriculture, to Maj.-Gen. S.C. Mewburn, minister of militia and defence, 28 January 1918

111 *Manitoba Free Press*, 25 January 1918. For the British experience, see John Rae, *Conscience and Politics*.

112 PAC, DND, RG 24, vol. 2028, HQ 1064–30–67, John Livesey, secretary-treasurer, Manitoba Grain Growers' Association, Swain River, Manitoba, to minister of militia and defence, 21 February 1918

113 Sir Robert L. Borden Papers, RLB 2309, Borden to Mewburn, 8 February 1918

114 Penton, *Jehovah's Witnesses in Canada*, 59

115 Borden Papers, RLB 2309, Mewburn to Borden, 9 February 1918

116 PAC, DND, RG 24, vol. 2028, HQ 1064–30–67, GOC Winnipeg to judge advocate-general, 8 April 1918

117 PAC, Borden Papers, RLB 2309, William Ivens to T.A. Crerar, 25 February 1918

118 Ibid., RLB 2309, Justice Department Memorandum, 25 March 1918; Penton, *Jehovah's Witnesses in Canada*, 61

119 Ibid., RLB 2309, E. Robinson, secretary, Winnipeg Trades and Labor Council to Borden, 8 April 1918

120 PAC, DND, RG 24, vol. 2028, HQ 1064–30–67, GOC Winnipeg to judge advocate-general, 8 April 1918

121 Ibid., ADCANEF, London to Militia, Ottawa, 4 May 1918

122 Ibid., vol. 2029, HQ 1064–30–67, ADCANEF, London to Militia, Ottawa, 22 August 1918

123 *Golden Age*, 29 September 1920, 710

124 Ibid.

125 PAC, DND, RG 24, vol. 2028, HQ 1064–30–67, F. Heap, Winnipeg, to Department of Militia, 4 May 1918; ibid., vol. 5953, HQ 1064–30–67–3, ADCANEF, London, to ACONTICONE, Ottawa, 11 September 1918

126 Ibid., vol. 4498, MD4–60–1–2, Canadian Expeditionary Force Routine Order 471, 22 April 1918

127 Ibid., vol. 2028, HQ1064–30–67, judge advocate-general to ADCANEF London, 10 May 1918

128 Penton, *Jehovah's Witnesses in Canada*, 62

129 PAC, DND, RG 24, vol.5953, HQ 1064–30–67–3, deputy minister of militia to deputy minister of justice, 7 December 1918

130 Canada, *Debates of the House of Commons*, 1919, vol. 1, 781

131 PAC, DND, RG 24, vol. 5953, HQ 1064–30–67–3, CB St George, Parry Sound, Ontario, to Minister of militia, 15 February 1919

132 Canada, *Debates of the House of Commons*, 1919, vol. 1, 781

133 Ibid., 782–4

134 Among those publications prohibited in Canada were the *New World*, a

radical Christian pacifist magazine from New York later retitled the *World Tomorrow*; Jehovah's Witness books and Watch Tower Society tracts; and *Christlicher Bundesbote*, the weekly organ of the General Conference Mennonites: Penton, *Jehovah's Witnesses in Canada*, 63; Joseph A. Boudreau, 'The Enemy Alien Problem in Canada, 1914–1921' PHD dissertation, University of California at Los Angeles, 1965), 42.

135 Hopkins, *Canadian Annual Review*, 1915, 354
136 PAC, Woodsworth Papers, correspondence, vol. 2, Thomas to Woodsworth, 24 April 1918
137 *Globe* (Toronto), 14 June 1916, 4
138 More than 8,500 men of enemy alien origin were interned in 23 prison camps across Canada: see Boudreau, 'Enemy Alien Problem,' 34, and Desmond Morton, 'Sir William Otter and Internment Operations in Canada during the First World War,' *Canadian Historical Review*, LV (March 1974), 32
139 Christie, 'The Presbyterian Church in Canada,' 137. Canadian theological colleges had not yet expanded or liberalized their curriculums to include a serious examination of war in the light of the Christian conscience, even though courses in the study of Christian ethics, moral philosophy, and social problems had been added a decade earlier. Such courses, which might have encompassed international problems and the issue of war, were centred instead on rural and urban problems: Charles M. Johnston, *McMaster University*, vol. 1: *The Toronto Years* (Toronto: University of Toronto Press, 1976), 123–4, 133, 141–4; McMaster University, *Calendar*, 1888–94, 1899–1917; *Vox Wesleyan*, Wesley College, Winnipeg, 1899–1909; Wesleyan Theological College, Montreal, *Calendar*, 1894–5, 1899–1919; the Methodist Church of Canada, *The Doctrine and Discipline of the Methodist Church in Canada*, 1910, 1914.
140 *Western Labor News*, 5 September 1919, 6
141 'Report of the Peace and Arbitration Committee,' *Minutes of the Genesee Yearly Meeting of Friends*, 1919, 21

CHAPTER FOUR: A resurgent peace movement

1 *Minutes of the Genesee Yearly Meeting of Friends*, 1919, 21
2 Brock, *Twentieth-Century Pacifism*, 122
3 Norman Penner, *The Canadian Left: A Critical Analysis* (Scarborough, Ont.: Prentice-Hall, 1977), 181
4 Allen, *The Social Passion*, 313–30
5 Brock, *Twentieth-Century Pacifism*, 109

6 For a full account of post-war agrarian politics, see W.L. Morton, *The Progressive Party in Canada* (Toronto: University of Toronto Press, 1960), and L.D. Courville, 'The Conservatism of the Saskatchewan Progressives,' *CHA Historical Papers*, 1974, 183–212.

7 W.R. Young, 'Conscription, Rural Depopulation, and the Farmers of Ontario, 1917–19,' *Canadian Historical Review*, LIII (September 1972), 289–320. Throughout the war farm journals criticized the cost of the war and the treatment of conscientious objectors, and repeatedly denounced militarists and armed preparedness: see Page, 'Canadians and the League of Nations,' 373.

8 Thomas P. Socknat, 'Canada, Imperial Foreign Policy and the Abrogation of the Anglo-Japanese Alliance, 1921' (MA thesis, University of Nebraska, Omaha, 1967)

9 Page, 'Canadians and the League of Nations,' 374

10 *The Canadian Friend*, January 1919, 10

11 An exception was S.D. Chown's effort to promote the league in local congregations of the Methodist church.

12 Page, 'Canadians and the League of Nations,' 185, 430

13 Ibid., 261

14 Allen, *The Social Passion*, 314–15

15 Page, 'Canadians and the League of Nations,' 368; Allen, *The Social Passion*, 196, 313

16 Allen, *The Social Passion*, 313

17 *Christian Guardian*, 4 October 1922, 12

18 *Globe* (Toronto), 4 July 1923

19 Page, 'Canadians and the League of Nations,' 366

20 *Christian Guardian*, 11 October 1922, 6

21 Ibid., 20 February 1924, 1

22 Ibid., 2 April 1924, 13

23 Ibid., 9 April 1924, 4–5

24 Ibid., 11 October 1922, 6

25 Allen, *The Social Passion*, 319–20

26 Ibid., 322–3. Kirby Page was the secretary of the Fellowship for a Christian Social Order in the United States, a socialist-pacifist organization.

27 Allen, *The Social Passion*, 323–4; *Christian Guardian*, 4 June 1924, 4

28 *Christian Guardian*, 28 May 1924, 5; 4 June 1924, 6; 18 June 1924, 7

29 Ibid., 16 June 1924, 7

30 Ibid., 23 July 1924

31 Ibid., 28 May 1924, 14

32 Ibid., 3 September 1924, 4, 7

33 Ibid., 7 January 1925, 4
34 Ibid., 23 July 1924, 4; Allen, *The Social Passion*, 324
35 R. Edis Fairbairn, *Apostate Christendom* (London: Ken-Pax, 1948)
36 UCA, Army and Navy Board, box 24, file 507
37 Ibid., The Reverend J.H. Bateson, secretary, Wesleyan Army and Navy Board, to the Reverend T.A. Moore, secretary, Army and Navy Board of the Methodist Church of Canada, 27 May 1916
38 Ibid., Fairbairn to Moore, 17 June 1916
39 Ibid., Moore to Fairbairn, 1 August 1916
40 *Christian Guardian*, 23 July 1924, 5, 23; 24 September 1924, 5
41 Ibid., 7 January 1925, 6
42 Ibid., 25 March 1925, 5
43 Ibid., 3 December 1924, 5
44 Ibid., 20 May 1925, 11
45 Ibid., 24 September 1924, 6; Allen, *The Social Passion*, 326
46 During the interwar years Fairbairn wrote over sixty-five articles for the *Christian Guardian* and its successors, the *New Outlook* and the *United Church Observer*.
47 Richard Roberts, 'How the Fellowship Began,' *Fellowship*, IX (January 1943), 4
48 Ibid., 5; UCA, Richard Roberts Papers, file 31, Gwen R.P. Norman, 'Richard Roberts,' unpublished manuscript, 1966
49 Norman, 'Richard Roberts,' 73, 82
50 UCA, Richard Roberts Papers, box 2, file 39, M.A. Coffey, U.S Attorney, to Roberts, 13 December 1917
51 Ibid., Hodgkin to Roberts, 9 November 1917
52 Ibid., Roberts to Brokway, 19 September 1916
53 Richard Roberts, 'The Problem of Conscience,' *International Journal of Ethics* (April 1919), 337
54 Ibid., 338
55 Norman, 'Richard Roberts,' 91
56 W.A. Gifford et al., *The Christian and War* (Toronto, 1926), 18
57 Ibid., 90–6
58 Ibid., 221
59 Allen, *The Social Passion*, 330
60 Among those pacifists who endorsed *The Christian and War* were Arthur Dorland in the *Canadian Friend*, R. Edis Fairbairn in *The New Outlook*, and Violet McNaughton in the *Western Producer*.
61 Gifford et al., *The Christian and War*, 207
62 *Christian Guardian*, 9 April 1924, 5

63 Ernest A. Dale, *Twenty-one Years A-building: A Short History of the Student Christian Movement of Canada, 1920–1941* (Toronto: SCM n.d.), 5

64 Ibid., 21. An exception was J. Davidson Ketchum, a returned war veteran who had been a German prisoner of war. Ketchum remained prominent in the SCM leadership.

65 Margaret Beattie, *A Brief History of the Student Christian Movement in Canada* (Toronto: SCM, 1975), 16

66 Ibid. The Student Volunteer Movement was a parent organization of the SCM devoted to the study of foreign missions for the purpose of encouraging students to become missionaries.

67 *Canadian Student*, February 1924, 151. N.A. Mackenzie later became a Canadian authority on international law.

68 *Varsity*, 11 January 1924, special supplement

69 Beattie, *The SCM in Canada*, 19

70 Page, 'Canadians and the League of Nations,' 380

71 SABS, Violet McNaughton Papers A1.E95(2), Laura Jamieson, WIL circular letter, 26 March 1931; PAC, Woodsworth Papers, MG27, III, C7, vol. 2, J.S. Woodsworth to Hattie, 25 August 1921

72 SABS, McNaughton Papers, A1.H.32(1), Women's International League for Peace and Freedom, Vancouver branch, pamphlet, n.d.

73 Donald M. Page, 'The Development of a Western Canadian Peace Movement,' *The Twenties in Western Canada*, edited by S.M. Trofimenkoff (Ottawa: National Museum of Man, 1972), 90

74 SABS, McNaughton Papers, A1.H.32(1), Women's International League for Peace and Freedom, Vancouver branch, pamphlet, n.d.

75 Page, 'Western Canadian Peace Movement,' 89–90

76 SABS, McNaughton Papers, A1.E.95(1), McNaughton to Jane Addams, 4 October 1927

77 Page, 'Western Canadian Peace Movement,' 89–90

78 SABS, McNaughton Papers, A1.E.52, Laura Jamieson to McNaughton, 20 October 1924

79 Ibid.; Gertrude Bussey and Margaret Tims, *Women's International League for Peace and Freedom, 1915–1965* (London: George Allen and Unwin, 1965), 39

80 Ibid., 49

81 *Christian Guardian*, 18 June 1924, 11, 22

82 Ibid., 21 May 1924, 3; Bussey and Tims, *Women's International League*, 49

83 *Evening Telegram* (Toronto), 6 June 1924, 15; Page, 'Canadians and the League of Nations,' 103

84 Margaret Stewart and Doris French, *Ask No Quarter* (Toronto: Longmans, Green, 1959), 140–1

85 *Canadian Friend*, July 1924, 7
86 *Minutes of the Genesee Yearly Meeting of Friends*, 1924, 25
87 *Canadian Friend*, August 1926, 17. The participation of young people in peace work continued during the following years, and in 1928 ten young delegates with varied religious backgrounds represented Canada at the World Youth Congress of Peace in Holland: ibid., April 1928, 15.
88 SABS, McNaughton Papers, A1.E.52, Women's International League for Peace and Freedom, Vancouver branch, pamphlet, n.d.
89 Ibid., A1.E.95(1), McNaughton to Jane Addams, 26 October 1927
90 Ibid., A1.E.52(2), Laura Jamieson, 'How Did the Peace Conference Turn Out?' *The Church Review*, n.d., 8
91 Ibid., A1.E.51(1), 'Addresses Given at the Peace Conference held on June 28th 1929,' and 'Resolutions Passed at the Farm Women's University Week'
92 Ibid., A1.E.52(2), Jamieson, 'How Did the Peace Conference Turn Out?' 8
93 Page, 'Western Canadian Peace Movement,' 100; SABS, McNaughton Papers, A1.E.95(1), Agnes Macphail to McNaughton, 1 March 1929; ibid., Jamieson, WIL newsletter, 7 September 1929
94 Despite their anti-war and anti-imperialist prejudices, French Canadians were not receptive to pacifism, probably because of their conservative Catholicism. On the other hand, there is no clear explanation for the general lack of support for the peace movement in the Maritimes; perhaps it is related to a conservative pro-imperial spirit.
95 SABS, McNaughton Papers, A1.H.32(1), Women's International League for Peace and Freedom, Canadian section, pamphlet. Beatrice Brigden was to become an influential exponent of social radicalism as well as pacifism in the interwar era. For more on her, see Beatrice Bridgen, 'One Woman's Campaign for Social Purity and Social Reform' in *The Social Gospel in Canada*, edited by Richard Allen, 1975, 36–62.
96 SABS, McNaughton Papers, A1.H.32(2), Women's International League for Peace and Freedom, Canadian section, pamphlet
97 Ibid.
98 Ibid., A1.D.69, J.S. Woodsworth to McNaughton, 4 March 1924
99 Page, 'Canadians and the League of Nations,' 393; *Minutes of the Canada Yearly Meeting of Friends*, 1921, 22; ibid., 1926, 12
100 Isa M. Byers, *Report of the Canadian School History Textbook Survey Committee* (Toronto: Women's International League for Peace and Freedom, Toronto branch, 1931)
101 Ibid.; Page, 'Western Canadian Peace Movement,' 93
102 James Willis Howard, 'A Study of Cadet Training in the Dominion of Canada' (PHD dissertation, Cornell University, 1936)

103 *Military Training in Canadian Schools and Colleges* (Toronto: Women's International League for Peace and Freedom, Toronto branch, 1927)

104 As quoted in Stewart and French, *Ask No Quarter*, 88

105 SABS, McNaughton Papers, A1.E.95(1), Alice Loeb to McNaughton, 6 May 1925

106 Howard, 'A Study of Cadet Training,' abstract

107 *Military Training in Canadian Schools and Colleges*

108 Ibid.

109 *Canadian Friend*, May 1929, 1

110 *Minutes of the Genesee Yearly Meeting of Friends*, 1920, 23

111 Ibid., 1924, 11

112 *Canadian Friend*, September 1928, 12

113 Ibid., May 1929, 1

114 *Military Training in Canadian Schools and Colleges*

115 *Canadian Friend*, September 1928, 12

116 *Military Training in Canadian Schools and Colleges*

117 Page, 'Western Canadian Peace Movement,' 95

118 *New Outlook*, 3 January 1926, 11

119 Ibid., 4

120 Ibid., 17 October 1928, 4

121 Nelson, *Peace Prophets*, 8–10

122 Albert S. Rogers, 'The London Conference,' *Canadian Friend*, October 1920, 19

123 Ibid.

124 Mahatma Gandhi, 'Non-Violence – The Greatest Force,' *Canadian Friend*, November 1926, 7

125 *Minutes of the Canada Yearly Meeting of Friends*, 1920, 22

126 Ibid., 1921, 7

127 Ibid., 1920, 21

128 *Minutes of the Canada Yearly Meeting of Friends*, 1922, 8; *Canadian Friend*, March 1922, 11; Fred Haslam, *1921–1967: A Record of Experience with Canadian Friends (Quakers) and the Canadian Ecumenical Movement* (Toronto: Society of Friends, 1970), 12–13

129 *Minutes of the Canada Yearly Meeting of Friends*, 1921, 22

130 Interview with Arthur G. Dorland, 29 January 1976; Arthur G. Dorland, *Former Days and Quaker Ways: A Canadian Retrospective* (Picton, Ont.: Picton Gazette, 1965)

131 Page, 'Canadians and the League of Nations,' 364

132 Ibid., 364–5

133 *Canadian Friend*, August 1923, 8

134 Page, 'Canadians and the League of Nations,' 365–6
135 Ibid., 367
136 *Canadian Friend*, December 1923, 8
137 *Minutes of the Canada Yearly Meeting of Friends*, 1920
138 *Minutes of the Canadian and Genesee Yearly Meetings*, 1930
139 *Canadian Friend*, January 1927, 11; July 1927, 21
140 Ibid., September 1928, 12
141 Frank H. Epp, *Mennonite Exodus* (Altona, Man.: D.W. Friesen and Sons 1962), 139, 146
142 Woodcock and Avakumovic, *The Doukhobors*, 253
143 Ibid., 255–7
144 Allen, *The Social Passion*, 339
145 PAC, Woodsworth Papers, MG 27, III, correspondence, vol. 2, J.S. Woodsworth to E.D. Morel, 12 May 1924
146 Nelson, *The Peace Prophets*, 122. Nelson claims this became the typical approach of British and North American pacifists in the 1920s.
147 Brock, *Twentieth-Century Pacifism*, 128. Brock notes that this general upsurge in pacifist feeling throughout the English-speaking world at the end of the 1920s was illustrated in a whole spate of popular anti-war novels, plays, and memoirs which appeared in the years 1928–30. One such Canadian novel was Charles Yale Harrison, *Generals Die in Bed* (London, 1930, reprint, Hamilton, Ont.: Potlatch Publications, 1975).
148 The idea of framing the Peace Pact and displaying it in schools seems to have been originated by the Reverend Harold T. Allen, a United Church minister in British Columbia. The practice gained the support of the dominion government through the effort of Dr Hugh Dobson, the western field secretary of the United Church Department of Evangelism and Social Service: Hugh Dobson Papers (in personal file of A.R. Allen), William Deans to Dr Hugh Dobson, 19 August 1929; Dobson to W.L. Mackenzie King, 23 December 1929; interview with Harold Allen, 18 May 1976, Hamilton, Ontario. For more on Harold Allen, see Harold T. Allen, 'A View from the Manse: The Social Gospel and Social Crisis in British Columbia, 1929–1945,' *The Social Gospel in Canada*, edited by Richard Allen 154–85.
149 *The New Outlook*, 19 September 1928, 2

CHAPTER FIVE: In search of peace and social justice

1 *Canadian Friend*, December 1930, 8
2 Maurice N. Eisendrath, *Can Faith Survive?* (New York: McGraw-Hill,

1964), 75; see also 'Can Human Nature Be Changed?' and 'Why I Am Not an Atheist,' *Holy Blossom Pulpit*, vol. 1, series 1931–2: Toronto Jewish Congress/Canadian Jewish Congress Ontario Region Archives, Toronto.

3 SABS, McNaughton Papers, E 52 (1), 'All Day Peace Conference,' poster (reproduced elsewhere in this book); *Canadian Friend*, December 1930, 8; *Globe* (Toronto), 11 November 1930, 17.

4 Wilson Macdonald, 'War,' in *A Flagon of Beauty* (Toronto: Peace Tree Publishing Co., 1931), 137. Eisendrath quoted this poem in one of his sermons the following month. Edis Fairbairn was also a particular fan and friend of Macdonald.

5 *Canadian Friend*, December 1930, 8

6 *Canadian Forum*, December 1930, 85

7 SABS, McNaughton Papers, H 32 (1), Women's International League for Peace and Freedom, Toronto branch, 'Newsletter,' April 1931

8 Those organizations included the Federated Women's Institutes of Toronto, the Board of the Women's Missionary Societies of the United Church, the Women's Baptist Foreign Missionary Society of Western Ontario, Eastern Ontario, and Quebec, the National Women's Missionary committee of the Church of Christ (Disciples), the Women's Auxilary to the Missionary Society of the Church of England in Canada, the National WCTU, and the National Council of the YWCA: ibid.

9 Ibid., E 95 (2), Women's International League for Peace and Freedom, Canadian section, 'Newsletter,' 19 January 1931

10 Ibid., Women's International League for Peace and Freedom, 'Preliminary Programme of an Institute on The Economic Basis of Peace'

11 PAC, National Council of Women Papers, Manuscript Group 28, I 25, vol. 69, Lady Aberdeen to Presidents of National Women's Organizations, 24 July 1931

12 Ibid., Lady Aberdeen to Mrs Bundy, 17 August 1931

13 Ibid., 'Resolution of the Toronto Local Council of Women,' proposed by Mrs J.A. Maitland

14 Ibid., M. Winnifred Kydd to All Peoples Association, London, 27 October 1931

15 Ibid., Lady Aberdeen to M. Winnifred Kydd, 14 January 1932

16 Ibid., M. Winnifred Kydd, 'Broadcast from Geneva,' 28 February 1932

17 Ibid., statement by the Disarmament Committee of the Women's International Organizations

18 SABS, McNaughton Papers, H 32(1); *New Outlook*, 10 February 1932, 1

19 *New Outlook*, 12 October 1932, 940

20 UCA, Richard Roberts Papers, box 2, file 47, Roberts to Prime Minister

R.B. Bennett, 12 December 1933; both J.S. Woodsworth and W.L. Grant charged that Canada had helped to undermine the success of the World Disarmament Conference by sending professional militarists such as the general staff officers Gen. A.G.L. McNaughton and Col. H.D.G. Crerar to Geneva as technical advisors to the Canadian delegation. See James Eayrs, *In Defence of Canada*, vol. 1: *From the Great War to the Great Depression* (Toronto: University of Toronto Press, 1964), 118–19.

21 UCA, Richard Roberts Papers, box 2, file 47, Roberts to R.B. Bennett, 12 December 1933

22 SABS, McNaughton Papers, E 95 (2), Women's International League for Peace and Freedom, Canadian section, 'Newsletter,' 19 January 1931

23 Interview with Ida Siegel, Toronto, 5 February 1976

24 PAC, C.B. Sissons Papers, MG27, III, F3, vol. 5, Women's International League for Peace and Freedom, Toronto branch, 'Newsletter,' 1 November 1935

25 SABS, McNaughton Papers, E 95 (4), Women's International League for Peace and Freedom, Toronto branch, 'Newsletter,' July 1936

26 Ibid., July 1936

27 Ibid., McNaughton to Anna Sissons, 13 November 1934

28 Ibid., Blake to McNaughton, 20 September 1936

29 Ibid., M. Cousineau to McNaughton, 15 October 1934

30 Ibid., McNaughton to Sissons, 13 November 1934

31 Ibid., D 34, Jamieson to McNaughton, 3 July 1932

32 Ibid., McNaughton to Jamieson, 6 July 1932

33 Ibid., E 95 (4), Women's International League for Peace and Freedom, Toronto Branch, 'Newsletter,' July 1936

34 A well-known socialist, Rose Henderson had also been on the executive of the Ontario Labour Party in the early 1930s. See John Manley, 'Women and the Left in the 1930s: The Case of the Toronto CCF Women's Joint Committee,' *Atlantis*, V (Spring 1980), 100–17.

35 *Canadian Forum*, February 1931, 167–8

36 Ibid., 168; Judge Coatsworth claimed that this conclusion was based on an article sympathetic to Russia written by Rabbi Eisendrath, president of the FOR.

37 UCA, Richard Roberts Papers, box 2, file 45, Roberts to General Draper, 8 January 1931 (letter mistakenly dated 1930)

38 *Canadian Forum*, February 1931, 168. Sixty-eight professors from the University of Toronto signed a public letter protesting the police commission's action limiting the right of free speech of the socially concerned pacifists in the Fellowship of Reconciliation only to be followed by an

outburst of indignation from those whom the *Canadian Forum* sarcastically called the 'good people' of Toronto: *Canadian Forum*, March 1931, 210–12

39 Maurice N. Eisendrath, 'In Defence of Freedom,' *Holy Blossom Pulpit*, vol.1, series 1931–2, and 'What's Wrong with Violence?' *Holy Blossom Pulpit*, vol. 2, series 1931–2, TJC/CJC Ontario Region Archives

40 The Research Committee of the League for Social Reconstruction, *Social Planning for Canada* (Toronto: Thomas Nelson and Sons, 1935; reprint, Toronto: University of Toronto Press, 1975), vi and ix

41 Ibid., xxiii. Government and business leaders were still very suspicious and even antagonistic towards the idea of socialism.

42 A Belgian refugee in England during the Great War, Grube served as an interpreter with the British army. He received a master's degree in classics from Cambridge University, and after moving to Canada in 1928 he became well known for his scholarly works on classical Greek and Roman philosophy. During the 1930s and 1940s Grube played an active role in the development of democratic socialism through the LSR, the CCF, and the *Canadian Forum*: QUA, G.M.A. Grube Papers

43 G.M.A. Grube, 'Pacifism: The Only Solution,' *Canadian Forum*, June 1936, 9

44 Ibid., G.M.A. Grube, 'Pacifism and Human Nature,' *Canadian Forum*, July 1936, 14

45 *Canadian Forum*, October 1936, 9; also see, Maurice N. Eisendrath, 'The Greatest Man in the World Today: Who Is He?' *Holy Blossom Pulpit*, vol. 1, series 1931–32, TJC/CJC Ontario Region Archives

46 Grube, 'Pacifism: The Only Solution,' 10

47 F.R. Scott et al. *Social Planning for Canada*, xiii

48 Michiel Horn, 'Frank Underhill's Early Drafts of the Regina Manifesto 1933,' *Canadian Historical Review*, LIV (December 1973), 416; see also Thomas P. Socknat, 'The Pacifist Background of the Early CCF,' in *Building the Co-operative Commonwealth*, edited by J. William Brennan (Regina: Canadian Plains Research Centre, 1985).

49 Interview with Carlyle A. King, Regina, 29 September 1977

50 Michiel Horn, 'The League for Social Reconstruction: Socialism and Nationalism in Canada, 1932–1945' (PH D dissertation, University of Toronto, 1969), 517

51 Tim Buck, *Thirty Years* (Toronto: Progress Publishing Co., 1952)

52 Michiel Horn, 'The League for Social Reconstruction and the Development of a Canadian Socialism, 1932–1936,' *Journal of Canadian Studies*, VII (November 1972), 11

53 Walter Young, *The Anatomy of a Party: The National CCF 1932–61* (Toronto: University of Toronto Press, 1969), 39

54 Horn, 'The League for Social Reconstruction and the Development of a Canadian Socialism,' 11. The FCSO had no connection to the former American organization of the same name.

55 Roger Hutchinson, 'The Fellowship for a Christian Social Order: A Social Ethical Analysis of a Christian Socialist Movement' (PHD dissertation, Toronto School of Theology, 1975, 23

56 Interview with R.B.Y. Scott, Toronto, 9 November 1976

57 Ibid.; *The New Outlook*, 27 January 1932, 81

58 J. Russel Harris to H.T. Allen, 11 February 1932, FCSO file in possession of Prof. Richard Allen; Harold T. Allen, 'A View from the Manse: The Social Gospel and the Social Crisis in British Columbia, 1929–1945' in *The Social Gospel in Canada*, edited by Richard Allen (Ottawa: National Museums of Canada, 1975), 162

59 *Christian Social Action*, 11 (March 1940): 1

60 Ibid.

61 *The Handbook of the Christian Commonwealth Youth Movement*, edited by Norman A. Colley (Calgary: National Council of the CCYM, 1932)

62 Ibid., 21

63 Ibid., 22

64 Hutchinson, 'The Fellowship for a Christian Social Order,' 24

65 Ibid., appendix 1, 'The Fellowship for a Christian Social Order, Basis of Agreement and Constitution, 1935,' 273

66 Ibid., 275

67 Minutes of the Western Institute on Social and Economic Affairs, 1–10 July 1973, summarized version in possession of Prof. Richard Allen

68 J. King Gordon, 'A Christian Socialist in the 1930s,' in *The Social Gospel in Canada*, edited by Richard Allen, 125

69 For example, see J. King Gordon, 'Capitalism – A Played Out Creed,' *The Echo*, 4 (Winter 1932), 15, McGill University Archives, Montreal

70 Gordon, 'A Christian Socialist in the 1930s,' 140–3

71 UCA, Richard Roberts Papers, box 2, file 47, Roberts to A.O. Dawson, 30 November 1933

72 Interview with J. Stanley Allen, Hamilton, 4 August 1976

73 *Towards the Christian Revolution*, edited by R.B.Y. Scott and Gregory Vlastos (New York, Willett, Clark, 1936)

74 Ibid., 139

75 Ibid., 164

76 Ibid., 182
77 In *The Industrial Struggle and Protestant Ethics in Canada* (Toronto: Ryerson Press, 1961), 90, Stewart Crysdale cites Havelock's contribution as proof that the entire FCSO leadership gave a 'renewed Christian sanction' to the liberal idea of inevitable progress. A careful study of the book, however, reveals that the authors did not speak with one mind. A fairer analysis made by Roger Hutchinson in 'The Fellowship for a Christian Social Order,' is presented here.
78 *New Outlook*, 19 February 1937
79 John Strachey, 'The Churches Speak at Last,' *Left News*, May 1937, 369
80 *Radical Religion*, Spring 1937, 42–4
81 By 1937 the FCSO included at least 265 active and associate members, many of whom were of pacifist persuasion, and FCSO study groups were organized in every province of Canada and Newfoundland: Gordon, 'A Christian Socialist in the 1930s,' 139.
82 Saskatchewan Archives Board, Regina (hereinafter SABR), H.M. Horricks Papers, I 2, Mrs H.M. Horricks to Richard Allen, 22 June 1963
83 Ibid., interview with Carlyle King
84 SABR, Horricks Papers, I 2, Alberta School of Religion, program of annual sessions, 1928–1946
85 Ibid., Mrs H.M. Horricks to Richard Allen, 22 June 1963; T. Kagawa to Horricks, 4 September 1931; R. Niebuhr to Horricks, 16 September 1929
86 Ibid.
87 Ibid., 'The Horricks Fellowship Pledge'
88 Watson Thomson, *Pioneer in Community: Henri Lasserre's Contribution to the Fully Cooperative Society* (Toronto: Ryerson Press, 1949), 9–15
89 Ibid., 2
90 Ibid., 42–3
91 Ibid., 59; Ian MacPherson, *Each for All: A History of the Co-operative Movement in English Canada, 1900–1945* (Toronto: Macmillan, 1979), 144–5
92 The same attitude was shared by pacifists in Britain and the United States and even in Japan by the followers of the Christian pacifist and evangelist Toyohiko Kagawa. Kagawa was also extremely popular in North America, and in the early 1930s the Kagawa Co-operating Committee, an interdenominational group of Canadian churchmen, was formed in Toronto under the direction of Richard Roberts: UCA, Roberts Papers, box 2, file 47, Roberts to Kagawa, 13.
93 Thomas Sinclair-Faulkner, 'For Christian Civilization: The Churches and Canada's War Effort, 1939–1942' (PH D dissertation, University of Chicago, 1975), 24–26; Allen, *The Social Passion*, 301

94 Sinclair-Faulkner, 'For Christian Civilization,' 27
95 Interview with John F. Davidson, Toronto, 26 October 1976
96 UCA, Roberts Papers, box 3, file 74, Richard Roberts, 'Radical Religion Forty Years Ago'
97 Norman, 'Richard Roberts,' 163, *Globe* (Toronto), 25 April 1936, 1; *Mail and Empire* (Toronto), 26 April 1936, 1
98 *Globe* (Toronto), 24 September 1936, 2
99 Sinclair-Faulkner, ' " For Christian Civilization," ' 28
100 The United Church of Canada, *On Peace and War*, statements of the sixth and seventh general councils held at Kingston 1934 and Ottawa 1936 (Toronto: Board of Evangelism and Social Service, United Church of Canada, 1936), 2
101 Ernest Thomas, 'General Council of War and Peace,' *New Outlook*, 9 (January 1935), 30
102 Ibid.
103 United Church of Canada, *On Peace and War*, 3
104 W.A. Gifford, 'May We Hope in the General Council?' *New Outlook*, 23 (September 1936), 871
105 United Church of Canada, *On Peace and War*, 1
106 *New Outlook*, 17 February 1939, 158
107 Ibid.
108 Allen, *The Social Passion*, 343
109 Ernest Thomas, 'Should the United Church Condemn War?' *New Outlook*, 12 August 1925, 5
110 Ernest Thomas, *The Quest for Peace* (Toronto: Board of Evangelism and Social Service, United Church of Canada, n.d.), UCA.
111 Ibid., 32
112 Allen, *The Social Passion*, 343–6
113 *New Outlook*, 26 December 1934, 1165
114 Ibid.
115 Ibid., 4 March 1936, 204; 28 October 1936
116 Ibid., 21 November 1934, 1030–46
117 Ibid., 16 May 1934, 352
118 Ibid., 23 August 1933, 612
119 Ibid., 21 November 1934, 1028
120 Lavell Smith, one of the leading figures in Montreal's pacifist circle, had served in the army during the First World War with the army of occupation on the Rhine. Upon his return to Canada, Smith completed his university training at Victoria College. During the 1920s he attended Union Theological Seminary in New York and there, under the influence

of Harry Emerson Fosdick and other pacifist theologians, he embraced pacifism: interview with Mrs J. Lavell Smith, Toronto, 23 November 1976.

121 *New Outlook*, 21 November 1934, 1033

122 Ibid.

123 Ibid., 12 December 1934

124 Ibid

125 *McMaster Silhouette* , 20 November 1934, 3

126 Ibid.

127 Ibid.; Eayrs, *In Defence of Canada*, vol. 1: *From the Great War to the Great Depression*, 110

128 *McGill Daily*, 20 November 1934

129 *McMaster Silhouette*, 4 December 1934

130 *Queen's Journal*, 29 January 1934, 1, 7

131 Ibid., 7 December 1934, 1; the peace issue was often raised at Queen's by Winnifred Kydd, a peace activist in the National Council of Women who became dean of women at Queen's University in 1934.

132 Margaret Beattie, *A Brief History of the Student Christian Movement in Canada* (Toronto: SCM, 1975) 19

133 Ibid., 21

134 *New Outlook*, 2 July 1930, 632

135 Besides his role in the peace caravan, Copithorne was secretary of the Toronto branch of the League of Nations Society and contributed a monthly column to *Canadian Friend* entitled 'Peace Parade.'

136 *Canadian Friend*, August 1934, 7

137 *New Outlook*, 2 July 1930, 632

138 As late as 1938 a young Canadian from Saskatchewan was caravanning for peace: *Minutes of the Canada and Genesee Yearly Meeting*, 1938, 57.

139 Beattie, *The SCM in Canada*, 21

140 *Echo*, Winter 1932, 17–18

141 *Canadian Friend*, November 1931, 7; Haslam, *Canadian Friends*, 49

142 Haslam, *Canadian Friends*, 49; *Minutes of the Canada and Genesee Yearly Meetings*, 1932, 59

143 *Canadian Friend*, March 1938, 5

144 Haslam, *Canadian Friends*, 50; *Minutes of the Canada and Genesee Yearly Meetings*, 1935, 9

145 *Canadian Friend*, May 1939, 7

146 Haslam, *Canadian Friends*, 50; *Minutes of the Canada and Genesee Yearly Meetings*, 1936, 56

147 *Minutes of the Canada and Genessee Yearly Meetings*, 1938, 58

148 Ibid., 1934, 7
149 Ibid., 1935, 9
150 Ibid., 1933, 46
151 *Canadian Friend*, July 1934, 4
152 Ibid., May 1937, 8–9

CHAPTER SIX: Crisis and consolidation

1 Woodsworth, however, wanted oil sanctions to be accompanied by a demand for disarmament. See Agnes Jean Groome, 'M.J. Coldwell and CCF Foreign Policy 1932–1950,' (MA thesis, University of Saskatchewan, 1967), 17–20.
2 The Canadian government withdrew its support for the proposal for oil sanctions against Italy initiated by the Canadian advisory officer in Geneva, Walter Riddell. For a full discussion of this incident see: Eayrs, *In Defence of Canada*, vol. II: *Appeasement and Rearmament*, 12–27; Robert Bothwell and John English, 'Dirty Work at the Cross-Roads: New Perspectives on the Riddell Incident,' CHA *Historical Papers*, 1972, 263–86.
3 Brock, *Twentieth-Century Pacifism*, 130
4 Interview with Mrs A.A. MacLeod, Toronto, 30 March 1976
5 *World Tomorrow*, 1931–4
6 Ibid., 25 January 1933
7 Chatfield, *For Peace and Justice*, 178
8 Interview with Mrs A.A. MacLeod
9 Avakumovic, *The Communist Party in Canada*, 128
10 A.A. MacLeod Papers (in possession of Mrs A.A. MacLeod, Toronto)
11 Ibid.
12 Avakumovic, *The Communist Party in Canada*, 127–8
13 McMaster University, Special Collections (hereinafter MU) Canadian Youth Congress (CYC) Papers, Box 1, File 2, Minutes of the Canadian Youth Congress, Toronto, 24 July 1935
14 MacLeod Papers, League for Peace and Democracy, agenda of events
15 SABS, McNaughton Papers, E 95 (4), Report of the Canadian Women's International League for Peace and Freedom National Convention, June 1937
16 MacLeod Papers
17 For a full account of these activities see Victor Hoar, *The Mackenzie-Papineau Battalion* (Toronto: Copp Clark, 1969).
18 MU, CYC Papers, box 1, file 1, Continuing Committee of the Canadian

Youth Congress and the Toronto Youth Council, *Why a Canadian Youth Congress?* (Toronto: April 1938); Memorandum on the Canadian Youth Congress Movement, n.d.

19 Ibid., Memorandum on the Canadian Youth Congress Movement

20 Ibid., box 1, file 2, minutes of the Canadian Youth Congress, Toronto, 5 June 1935, 10 July 1935 and 24 July 1935

21 Ibid., box 12, file 3, CYC 1935 Questionnaire file. The quote is taken from Woodsworth's completed questionnaire.

22 Ibid., box 1, file 1, Memorandum on the Canadian Youth Congress Movement

23 Ibid.; *The Silhouette* (McMaster University), 1 October 1936, 1

24 Wilfred Cantwell Smith, 'The Canadian Youth Congress,' *Canadian Forum*, July 1936, 16

25 Ibid.

26 MU, CYC Papers, box 1, file 1, Canadian Youth Congress, 'Declaration of Rights of Canadian Youth' (Ottawa: May 1936), 7

27 Ivan Avakumovic, *The Communist Party in Canada* (Toronto: McClelland and Stewart, 1975), 125

28 Kenneth Woodsworth, 'The World Youth Congress,' *The New Outlook*, 14 October 1936

29 MU, CYC Papers, box 1, file 1, memorandum on the Canadian Youth Congress Movement

30 Woodsworth, 'The World Youth Congress'

31 Ibid.

32 MU, CYC Papers, box 1, file 1, Memorandum on the Canadian Youth Congress Movement; box 12, file 1, Youth Peace Day file. In November 1937 the CYC received numerous messages of support and encouragement for their work on behalf of Youth Peace Day from members of Parliament, senators, principals of universities, church officials, and the governor-general, Lord Tweedsmuir.

33 Ibid., box 1, file 3, minutes of the national committee meeting, Kingston, November 1938

34 Ibid., minutes of the national committee meeting, Montreal, 25 September 1938; Toronto, 5 February 1939; *Canadian Congress Journal* (June 1938), 10

35 MU, CYC Papers, box 3, file 6, Ken Woodsworth to local councils, 16 November 1938

36 The CYC also endorsed the 'Vassar Peace Pact' adopted by the Second World Youth Congress meeting at Vassar College in New York State in August 1938, and was in regular contact with the British Youth Assembly and the American Youth Congress.

37 For much of this information I am indebted to Groome, 'M.J. Coldwell and ccf Foreign Policy.'

38 This is also related in McNaught, *A Prophet in Politics*, 286.

39 Reinhold Niebuhr, 'Why I Leave the for,' *Christian Century*, 3 January 1934, 17–18

40 Nelson, *The Peace Prophets*, 95

41 Reinhold Niebuhr, *Moral Man and Immoral Society* (New York: Scribners, 1932)

42 For Richard Roberts's response to Niebuhr, see chapter 7.

43 Arthur G. Dorland, 'Some Dilemmas of Christian Living and of Pacifism Today,' *Canadian Friend*, May 1937, 6

44 Ibid., 7

45 Ibid., 8

46 Ibid., 7

47 Ibid., 8

48 John Oliver, *The Church and Social Order: Social Thought in the Church of England, 1918–1939* (London: A.R. Mowbray, 1968), 190

49 uca, Roberts Papers, box 2, file 49, Roberts to Sayre, 27 May 1937

50 Norman, 'Richard Roberts,' 176–7

51 Sinclair-Faulkner, 'For Christian Civilization,' 28

52 Norman, 'Richard Roberts,' 177–8; *Globe and Mail* (Toronto), 20 September 1937

53 Ibid., 21 September 1937

54 *Christian Advance*, 15 November 1937, 15

55 Ibid., 13

56 uca, Roberts Papers, box 2, file 49, Sisco to Roberts, 22 September 1937

57 *Minutes of the Canada and Genesee Yearly Meetings of the Society of Friends*, 1938, 57

58 Ibid.

59 Haslam, *Canadian Friends*, 64–5

60 *Canadian Friend*, June 1933, 11; December 1935, 13

61 Ibid., March 1936, 6

62 Ibid., December, 1938, 6; sabs, McNaughton Papers, e 95 (5). According to Violet McNaughton's contact in New York, Katherine Blake, one-third of the refugees were Christians.

63 sabs, McNaughton Press, e 95 (5), Women's International League for Peace and Freedom, Toronto branch, 'Newsletter,' 1936

64 Ibid., e 95 (4); the wil petitioned Prime Minister King for an embargo on Japan.

65 Ibid., Anna Sissons to McNaughton, telegram, 16 February 1937

66 Ibid., Lila Phelps to McNaughton, 9 April 1936
67 Ibid.; McNaughton to Phelps, 22 April 1936
68 Ibid., Minutes of the Organization Conference, Women's International League for Peace and Freedom, Canadian Section, Winnipeg, 1–2 June 1937
69 Ibid.
70 Ibid., McNaughton to Jamieson, 27 April 1937
71 Gordon K. Stewart to Thomas P. Socknat, 7 March 1978; interview with J. Stanley Allen
72 Interview with Harold T. Allen, Hamilton, 18 May 1976
73 SABS, McNaughton Papers, E 95 (4), Interim Statements of Aims of the Saskatoon Peace Group
74 Interview with Carlyle King
75 SABS,Carlyle King Papers, 27:152, Carlyle King to J.M.C. Duckworth, 31 January 1938
76 King to Mildred Fahrni, 1 November 1961, copy enclosed in King to Thomas P. Socknat, 29 November 1976
77 SABS, Carlyle King Papers, 27: 151, John Nevin Sayre to Carlyle King, 29 November 1938
78 Ibid., Sayre to J.M.C. Duckworth, 29 October 1937; Sayre to J. Lavell Smith, 23 November 1937.
79 Ibid.
80 Ibid., Sayre to Duckworth, 29 October 1937
81 Ibid., 27: 153, Fellowship of Reconciliation, Montreal unit, 'A Protest,' leaflet, 30 July 1938
82 Ibid., Cleo Mowers to R. Edis Fairbairn, 20 April 1939
83 Ibid., minutes of the FOR Meeting Held in the Diet Kitchen, Toronto, 27 September 1938
84 Ibid.
85 Ibid., 27: 151, Mowers to P.G. Makaroff, 29 August 1938; Mowers to R. Edis Fairbairn, 20 April 1939; King to Farhni, 1 November 1961
86 Ibid., 27: 152, Lavell Smith to King, 4 November 1938
87 Ibid., King to members of the national council, Canadian FOR, 28 November 1938
88 Ibid., King to Lavell Smith, 27 December 1938; Fellowship of Reconciliation, Canadian section, 'Basis and Aims,' leaflet, 1939
89 Ibid., Lavell Smith to King, 20 January 1939
90 Ibid., Mowers to Fairbairn, 20 April 1939
91 Ibid., Lavell Smith to King, 4 November 1938
92 Ibid., 27: 153, King to Fred Young, 14 May 1937

93 Fellowship for a Christian Social Order, Toronto branch, 'Our Battle for Peace' (Toronto: FCSO, 1939). The leaflet also recommended a bibliography of popular pacifist books, pamphlets, and periodicals.

94 SABS, Carlyle King Papers, 27:152, Mowers to Fairbairn, 20 April 1939

95 Ibid., C. Clare Oke to King, 16 May 1939

96 Ibid., Stanley Knowles to King, 17 February 1939

97 Ibid., Joseph Round to King, 17 February 1939

98 Ibid., Mowers to Fairbairn, 20 April 1939

99 Ibid., Mowers to Tillman, 21 November 1938; Duckworth to King, 3 January 1939

100 Ibid., 27: 151, Harold E. Fey to Duckworth, 22 November 1938

101 Ibid., Sayre to King, 29 November 1938

102 Ibid., King to Sayre, 27 December 1938; Oke to King, 14 February 1939

103 Ibid., Fellowship of Reconciliation, Canadian section, 'Basis and Aims,' leaflet, 1939

104 SABS, Carlyle King Papers, 27:151, King to Sayre, 27 December 1938

105 Ibid., Sayre to King, 23 January 1939

106 Ibid

107 Ibid., King to Booth, Duckworth, Halliday, Oke, and Smith, 6 February 1939

108 Ibid., Duckworth to Sayre, 15 February 1939

109 Ibid., Sayre to Duckworth, 24 February 1939

110 Ibid., Booth to King, 15 February 1939; King to Oke, 21 May 1939

111 This statement referred to Communists and the FOR's confrontation with the Toronto Police Commission over the issue of free speech in the early 1930s.

112 SABS, Carlyle King Papers, 27:151, Booth to King, 15 February 1939

113 Ibid., Sayre to King, 11 May 1939

114 Ibid., 27:152, Oke to King, 16 May 1939

115 Ibid.; ibid., Halliday to King, 31 March 1939

116 Ibid., 27:151, King to Percy Bartlett, 18 May 1939

117 Ibid., Bartlett to King, 26 June 1939

118 Ibid., 27: 152, Sayre to King, 6 July 1939

119 Ibid., Lavell Smith to King, 30 August 1939

120 Ibid.

121 Ibid., 27:154, King to Fairbairn, 25 June 1941

122 Ibid., 27:151, R. Tillman to King, 24 August 1939

123 United Church Observer, 15 July 1939, 11

124 Trinity College Archives, G.M.A. Grube Papers, MS 98, Box 15

125 United Church Observer, 15 July 1939, 11

126 Ibid., 1 April 1939, 18; 15 August 1939, 19; 15 September 1939, 19
127 Ibid., 15 May 1939, 21
128 Ibid., 15 July 1939, 16

CHAPTER SEVEN: The courage of conviction

1 *Historical Documents of Canada*, vol. v: *The Arts of War and Peace 1914–1945*, edited by C.P. Stacey (New York: St Martin's Press, 1972), 601–2. Although the War Measures Act was immediately reinstated, it was not until 10 September that Canada officially declared war on Germany. The delay, which allowed time for the country and the government to consider the ramifications of the action, was no doubt caused primarily by the post-war upsurge of Canadian nationalism that had held Canada aloof from British foreign policy in the 1920s and continued to colour Canadian external policy throughout the 1930s.
2 Donald Creighton, *The Forked Road: Canada 1939–1957* (Toronto: McClelland and Stewart, 1976), 28
3 J.L. Granatstein, *Canada's War: The Politics of the Mackenzie King Government, 1939–1945* (Toronto: Oxford University Press, 1975), 20
4 Unlike Grube and a few others in the LSR, Underhill had never endorsed outright pacifism.
5 Frank H. Underhill, 'Keep Canada Out of War,' in *In Search of Canadian Liberalism*, edited by Frank H. Underhill (Toronto: Macmillan, 1960), 184
6 Horn, 'The League for Social Reconstruction: Socialism and Nationalism in Canada,' 108
7 McNaught, *A Prophet in Politics*, 286
8 Williams was perturbed by the pacifism within the CCF and was extremely vocal in his opposition to an isolationist or neutralist foreign policy, which he believed could only hurt the CCF in Saskatchewan. On the whole his provincial party was much cooler to pacifism than the federal CCF. See Friedrich Steininger, 'George H. Williams: Agrarian Socialist' (MA thesis, University of Regina, 1976), 353–6.
9 Canada, *Debates of the House of Commons*, special session, 1939, 42–3
10 Ibid.
11 McNaught, *Prophet in Politics*, 298
12 Canada, *Debates of the House of Commons*, special session, 1939, 45–6
13 Ibid., 47
14 Ibid.
15 McNaught, *Prophet in Politics*, 313–14

16 Canada, *Debates of the House of Commons*, Special Session, 1939, 42
17 McNaught, *Prophet in Politics*, 313
18 PAC, J.S. Woodsworth Papers, correspondence 7, vol. 3, C.C. Annett to J.S. Woodsworth, 16 September 1939
19 Ibid., Escot Reid to Woodsworth, 13 September 1939
20 Ibid., Howard Patton to Woodsworth, 16 September 1939
21 Ibid., H.G.L. Strange to Woodsworth, 13 September 1939
22 Sinclair-Faulkner, 'For Christian Civilization,' 30
23 *United Church Observer*, 15 January 1940, 1
24 Sinclair-Faulkner, 'For Christian Civilization,' 28–40
25 Ibid., 42–3
26 Ibid., 44–5
27 Woodside to United Church clergy, 8 September 1939, as quoted in ibid., 46. The moderator's letter was chiefly the work of J.R.P. Schater and R.B.Y. Scott.
28 Norman, 'Richard Roberts,' 184
29 David R. Rothwell, 'United Church Pacifism, October, 1939,' *Bulletin* (United Church of Canada), xx (1973), 37
30 *United Church Observer*, 15 October 1939, 21
31 Ibid., 15 November 1939, 25; while the manifesto revealed a rift within the United Church on the issue of pacifism, the fact remains that the signatories represented a small minority within the total of approximately 3,497 United Church ministers in Canada in 1939: the United Church of Canada, *Yearbook*, 1939, 148–9.
32 *United Church Observer*, 15 October 1939, 21
33 Ibid.
34 Ibid.
35 Rothwell, 'United Church Pacifism,' 38
36 Ibid., 39
37 Ibid., 40
38 *Globe and Mail* (Toronto) 21 October 1939, 4
39 Rothwell, 'United Church Pacifism,' 47–9. Rothwell quotes freely from all three Toronto dailies.
40 Ibid., 50
41 Ibid., 51
42 Sinclair-Faulkner, 'For Christian Civilization,' 54
43 *United Church Observer*, 1 November 1939, 4
44 Sinclair-Faulkner, 'For Christian Civilization,' 46
45 *United Church Observer*, 15 November 1939, 17

46 Norman, 'Richard Roberts,' 185
47 UCA, Richard Roberts Papers, box 2, file 51, Fairbairn to Roberts, 27 March 1940
48 Ibid., box 2, file 50, Roberts to Lavell Smith, 27 October 1939
49 Ibid., box 3, file 64, Roberts to Margaret P. MacVicar, 28 October 1939
50 Ibid., box 2, file 50, Roberts to Lavell Smith, 27 October 1939
51 Ibid., box 3, file 64, Roberts to MacVicar, 28 October 1939
52 Ibid., Roberts to MacVicar, 20 November 1939
53 Ibid., box 2, file 50, Lavell Smith to Roberts, 27 October 1939
54 *United Church Observer*, 15 October 1939, 2
55 United Church of Canada, War Services Committee file, minutes of meetings of 31 October 1939 and 29 November 1939
56 Ibid., 29 November 1939
57 Sinclair-Faulkner, 'For Christian Civilization,' 83
58 Interview with Mrs J. Lavell Smith, 23 November 1976
59 *United Church Observer*, 15 September 1939, 18
60 Interview with Mrs J. Lavell Smith; *Reconciliation* 1 October 1943, 12
61 Ibid.
62 *United Church Observer*, 15 May 1942, 24
63 Interview with Mrs J. Lavell Smith
64 *Reconciliation*, 1 October 1943, 12. In explaining his position to a leading member of the congregation Smith wrote: 'On the positive side: I have given my blessing to the Red Cross and Refugee work. I have communicated both to the Chief Chaplain and the Commanding Officers of two military units my readiness to have their troops attend Divine Service in our Church. I have expressed no single doubt as to the sincerity of purpose of young men donning the uniform. My attitude to any who have consulted me has been that their going or remaining at home must be a matter of their own individual conscience. It is not for me to determine pro or con. I have communicated with every enlisted man belonging to the congregation, so far as known to me, and with others who have had only the loosest sort of connection. I have had replies from several of these men and quite a number of them have made it a point to see me before leaving. I am now in process of sending out "Commendation Cards" to these men to be used by them as an introduction to churches or chaplains wherever they may be going': UCA, Lavell Smith biography file, Smith to H.S. Cheesbrough, 5 January 1940
65 Telephone conversation with Mr Beverly Bailey, Montreal, 12 November 1976; interview with Muriel Duckworth, Toronto, 7 November 1976
66 Telephone conversation with Mr Beverly Bailey

67 Sinclair-Faulkner's assertion that 'R. Edis Fairbairn and Harold Toye parted company with the United Church during ww ii' is not correct. Fairbairn remained in the parish ministry, and Toye entered industrial evangelism. Both remained in the church.

68 Fairbairn relates his experience in *Apostate Christendom* (London: Ken-Pax, 1948).

69 Ibid., 35

70 United Church Archives, Harold Toye Papers, box 1, file 6, miscellaneous papers.

71 Ibid., Rothwell, 'United Church Pacifism,' 52. Rothwell based his information on an interview with Toye.

72 uca, Toye Papers, box 1, file 6, 'The Religion-Labor Foundation,' micellaneous papers

73 E. Harold Toye, *Trifling with Destiny* (Toronto: Religion-Labor Foundation, 1948), 18

74 Ibid., 17

75 Ibid., 67

76 uca, Toye Papers 'The Religion-Labor Foundation,' Miscellaneous Papers,

77 Rothwell, 'United Church Pacifism,' 52

78 Sinclair-Faulkner, 'For Christian Civilization,' 57

79 Interview with Ernest Nix, Toronto, 9 November 1978. Another signatory, Nelson T. Chappel of Westminster Church, Saskatoon, changed his mind and became a chaplain in the rcaf.

80 *Toronto Daily Star*, 18 June 1940

81 Ibid.; interview with James M. Finlay, Toronto, 21 October 1976

82 *Toronto Daily Star*, 18 June 1940

83 Ibid.

84 Interview with James M. Finlay

85 Ibid.

86 *United Church Observer*, 15 April 1939

87 Fairbairn, *Apostate Christendom*, 31

88 R. Edis Fairbairn, 'Indictment,' *United Church Observer*, 1 February 1941, 11

89 Ibid.

90 *United Church Observer*, 15 March 1941, 16

91 Ibid.

92 Ibid., 17

93 Interview with R.B.Y. Scott. According to Scott, all fcso members were anti-militarists.

94 *Christian Social Action*, December 1939, 1

95 Ibid., 2
96 Interview with James M. Finlay. The FCSO 'more or less broke up' following its annual convention at Toronto's Carlton Street United Church in 1942. One of the main causes for the discord was that the newer breed of Christian leftists, newly arrived from Britain, aligned with the communists: interview with R.B.Y. Scott.
97 Interview with Stanley Allen
98 Interview with James M. Finlay
99 SABS, Carlyle King Papers, 27:153, King to Miss Marguerite Corner, Gypsenville, Manitoba, 24 September 1939
100 Ibid. King specifically suggested that FOR units communicate with Mennonites, Quakers, Doukhobors, Latter Day Saints, Jehovah's Witnesses, Ministerial Associations, trades and labour councils, the CCF, the CCYM, the SCM, the FCSO, the WIL, the WCTU, and the Canadian Civil Liberties Union: SABS, Carlyle King Papers, 27:153, King to Mrs N.A. Fraser, Winnipeg, 15 October 1939
101 Ibid.
102 Ibid., King to Miss Corner, 24 September 1939
103 Star-Phoenix (Saskatoon), 29 March 1938, 1
104 Ibid., 9 April 1938, 1; 3 October 1938, 4
105 Ibid., 2 April 1938
106 Regina Daily Star, 30 March 1938, 4
107 Star-Phoenix (Saskatoon), 9 April 1938, 1
108 Ibid.
109 Ibid., 30 April 1938, 4
110 Ibid., 11 April 1938, 1
111 Leader-Post (Regina), 11 April 1938, 4
112 Star-Phoenix (Saskatoon), 29 September 1938, 1
113 University of Saskatchewan Archives, Saskatoon, C.A. King Papers, III, 3, rough draft of letter
114 SABS, Carlyle King Papers, 27:152, King to Canadian FOR national council, 3 January 1940
115 Ibid., Lavell Smith to King, 11 January 1940
116 Ibid., 27:154, King to Fairbairn, 25 June 1941
117 Ibid., 27:152, Ted Mann to King, 3 April 1940
118 Ibid., Mann to King, 10 September 1939; 27:153, Mann to King, 12 December 1939
119 Interview with Kay (Yearsley) Pearce, Kingston, March 1985
120 SABS, Carlyle King Papers, 27:154, King to Fairbairn, 25 June 1941.
121 Ibid., King to Fairbairn, 27 July 1941. Despite Fairbairn's apparent interest

in reviving the FOR, he failed to take an active role in the reorganization and although he remained a member of the FOR throughout the war years he preferred to carry on his pacifist pursuits free of the confines of any organization.

122 UCA, FOR, box 1, file 3, Lavell Smith to 'Canadian Lovers of Peace', 3 January 1942
123 Ibid.
124 Ibid., box 2, file 24, Finlay circular letter to Friends of Peace, April 1942
125 Ibid., box 1, file 3, Newbery to Canadian FOR members, 7 September 1942
126 UCA, FOR papers, box 1, file 1, Fellowship of Reconciliation, Canadian section, 'Statement of Purpose,' leaflet, post-1943
127 King to Mildred Fahrni, 1 November 1961
128 UCA, Richard Roberts Papers, box 3, file 64, Roberts to Margaret P. MacVicar, 1 June 1940
129 Norman, 'Richard Roberts,' 188
130 UCA, Richard Roberts Papers, box 3, file 91, Roberts to Niebuhr, n.d.
131 Ibid.
132 Ibid.
133 Ibid., Niebuhr to Roberts, n.d.

CHAPTER EIGHT: Alternative pacifist service

1 Canada, *House of Commons Debates*, 30 March 1939
2 Ibid., 8 September 1939
3 J.L. Granatstein, *Conscription in the Second World War 1939–1945* (Toronto: McGraw Hill-Ryerson, 1967), 39ff
4 See André Laurendeau, *Witness for Quebec*, edited by Philip Stratford (Toronto: Macmillan, 1973).
5 The vote in the country at large was 2,945,514 to 1,643,006 in favour of release; the Quebec vote was 993,663 to 376,188 against release: *Historical Documents of Canada*, vol. V: *The Arts of War and Peace 1914–1945*, edited by C.P. Stacey (New York: St. Martin's Press, 1972), 631. Outside Quebec the constituencies voting 'no' were populated by French Canadians, Ukrainians, Germans, Mennonites and other ethnic groups. For plebiscite results see *Canada Gazette*, 23 June 1942.
6 For a thorough discussion of conscription debates during the Second World War, see Granatstein, *Canada's War*, and J.L. Granatstein and J.M. Hitsman, *Broken Promises, a History of Conscription in Canada* (Toronto: Oxford University Press, 1977).
7 Two Privy Council Orders (PC 3086, 9 July, and PC 3156, 12 July) called

for national registration to begin in August: Granatstein and Hitsman, *Broken Promises*, 144–5

8 The National War Services Regulations, 1940 (Recruits) were issued shortly after the creation of the Department of National War Services in July 1940: (1940) Geo. VI, c.22.

9 Frank H. Epp, *Mennonites in Canada 1920–1940*, vol. II: *A People's Struggle for Survival* (Toronto: Macmillan, 1982), 18–27; 565

10 The complex differences between the *Kanadier* and *Russlaender* Mennonites is explained in Epp, *Mennonites in Canada*, vol. II; for a fuller discussion of Mennonites and alternative service, see David Warren Fransen, 'Canadian Mennonites and Conscientious Objection in World War II' (MA thesis, University of Waterloo, 1977).

11 Epp, *Mennonites in Canada*, vol. II, 572–4

12 Fransen, 'Canadian Mennonites,' 25–37

13 Epp, *Mennonites in Canada*, vol. II, 573

14 PAC, Labour, RG 27, vol. 624, file 35–6–9–7–5, J. Lavell Smith to Chief Registrar, 17 August 1940

15 PAC, DND, RG 24, vol. 5953, HQ 1064–3267, vol. 3, H.W. Smallwood, chairman, the Christadelphian Service Committee, to Ernest Lapoint, minister of justice, 6 January 1937

16 PAC, Privy Council, RG 2, 18, vol. 5, D-27, Fred Haslam to Prime Minister King, 31 July 1940

17 CQA, CFSC Papers, CO file, Voluntary Peace Registration Form

18 Ibid., Haslam to King, 31 July 1940; PAC, Privy Council, RG2, 18, vol.5, D-27, J.W. Pickersgill to Haslam, 3 August 1940; in order to ensure that the prime minister thoroughly understood their position, the CFSC also sent him a copy of Arthur Dorland's history of the Society of Friends in Canada.

19 *Minutes of the Canada and Genesee Yearly Meetings,*1941, *Tenth Report of the Canadian Friends Service Committee*, 57; Fransen, 'Canadian Mennonites,' 45

20 Ibid.

21 CQA, CFSC Papers, CO file, Haslam to monthly meeting clerks, 11 September 1940; Fransen, 'Canadian Mennonites,' 46–7

22 Ibid., Haslam to monthly meeting clerks, 11 September 1940

23 Ibid.; a copy of each completed registration questionnaire was filed with the Military Problems Committee, since questions concerning occupational skills and training were included specifically in order to assist the committee in negotiating the question of alternative service.

24 PAC, DND, RG 24, vol. 6573 HQ 1161–3–4, Report of J.L. Embury, chairman NWS Board, division 'M.' The other members of the board included

George Bickerton, president of the Saskatchewan section of the United Farmers of Canada and Carl Stewart, MLA for Yorkton: *Star-Phoenix* (Saskatoon), 14 November 1940, p. 3. The young men in question included Ian Kenilo, O.A. Olsen, Harvey Moats, W. Vernon Barker, J. Douglas McMurtry, and Keith and Clyde Woollard, all members of the United Church, as well as a lone Anglican, John M. Marshall. Marshall was the nephew of Saskatoon Doukhobor pacifist Peter Makaroff. His grandfather, John Marshall, had left Queen's University during the Boer War over the same issue. Once these men were recognized as cos, Moats and Keith Woollard joined the Canadian Firefighter Unit in Britain, and McMurtry joined a Canadian contingent of the Friends Ambulance Unit in China.

25 Interview with Carlyle King

26 PAC, DND, RG 24, vol. 6573, HQ 1161-3-4, G.H. Cassels, deputy adjutant general, division 'M,' to Maj.-Gen. L.R. LeFlèche, associate deputy minister of national war services, 21 November 1940

27 CQA, CFSC Papers, CO file, Frank Wadge to Haslam, 21 November 1940

28 *Minutes of the Canada and Genesee Yearly Meetings*, 1940, 61

29 PAC, Privy Council, RG 2, 18, vol. 5, D-27, James G. Gardner, minister of national war services, press release, 6 December 1940

30 Mennonite Archives of Canada, Conference of Historic Peace Churches Papers, XV, 11.6.1

31 Ibid., IV, 11.1.1; Fransen, 'Canadian Mennonites,' 48

32 Fransen, 'Canadian Mennonites,' 95

33 J.A. Toews, *Alternative Service in Canada During World War II* (Winnipeg: Christian Press, 1959), 35–6

34 Fransen, 'Canadian Mennonites,' 100–1

35 Quoted in ibid., 102

36 Ibid., 105–6

37 PAC, Privy Council, RG 2, 18, vol. 5, D-27, extract from letter from George McDonald, n.d.

38 PAC, DND, RG 24, vol. 6573, HQ 1161-3-4, G.H. Cassels to adjutant-general, 7 October 1940

39 PAC, Privy Council, RG 2, 18, vol. 5, D-27, Gardner, press release, 6 December 1940

40 Order in Council PC 7215

41 Gardner, press release, 6 December 1940. The application for postponement is reproduced elsewhere in this book.

42 Fransen, 'Canadian Mennonites,' 110–11

43 PAC, Privy Council, RG 2, 18, vol. 5 D-27-(1941), Davis and La Flèche,

memorandum to Cabinet War Committee, 19 May 1941; PAC, RG 14, D2, vol. 435, no. 228a

44 PAC, *Privy Council*, RG 2, 18, vol. 5, D-27 (1941), Davis and LaFlèche memorandum; the initial proposal also called for an ASW camp in Cape Breton Park for COS from the Maritimes and for one in Gatineau Park for those from Quebec and Ontario, but this plan was later rejected.

45 Ibid.

46 PAC, Privy Council, RG 2, 18, vol. 16 M-5–6, P. Heeney to H. Mitchell, 7 February 1944

47 PAC, interdepartmental committees, RG 35, series 7, vol. 21, J.F. Mackinnon, 'Historical Account of the Wartime Activities of the Alternative Service Branch,' Department of Labour, unpublished, 11 April 1946, 26

48 Woodcock and Avakumovic, *The Doukhobors*, 320–1

49 Toews, *Alternative Service in Canada*, 76

50 Paul L. Storms, 'Life at Montreal River Camp,' *Canadian Friend*, 33 (April 1942): 11–12

51 Ibid.; Toews, *Alternative Service in Canada*, 76

52 Roy Clifton Papers, Clifton to Sid, 16 January 1943 (in possession of Roy Clifton, Richmond Hill, Ontario).

53 Ibid., Clifton to H. Runham Brown, secretary, War Resisters International, 26 December 1942

54 John L. Fretz, 'An History,' *Beacon*, 1 March 1945, 1

55 *Northern Beacon*, 4 April 1942, 5

56 Ibid., 30 May 1942, 5

57 *Canadian CO*, August 1942, 2–5

58 Ibid.

59 *Northern Beacon*, 9 May 1942, 1

60 Toews, *Alternative Service in Canada*, 78

61 MacKinnon, 'Alternative Service Branch,' 9

62 Toews, *Alternative Service in Canada*, 83–4

63 Ibid., 86

64 Ibid., 101; *Beacon*, 1 March 1945, 1

65 UCA, FOR Papers, box 2, file 24, 'Implications of the Use of Force Today,' notes of a conference at ASW camp Q6 with James M. Finlay, n.d.

66 CQA, CFSC Papers, CO file, 'Questionnaire on Alternative Service'

67 Ibid., Questionnaire Committee to fellow COS in British Columbia Forest Service camps, n.d.

68 Ibid., Military Problems Committee file, G.P. Melrose, assistant chief forester, to Wes Brown, 18 March 1943

69 Toews, *Alternative Service in Canada*, 101; in a letter to the Conference of

Historic Peace Churches Brown reported that the 'Questionnaire Committee had in mind only good purposes' and asked for their help in securing releases from the camps: CQA, CFSC Papers, Military Problems Committee file, Brown to CHPC, 28 March 1943.

70 MacKinnon, 'Alternative Service Branch,' 1; these changes were effected through order in council PC 8800, 26 September 1942 and order in council PC 10924, 1 November 1942.

71 National Selective Service Mobilization Regulations, PC 10924; CQA, CFSC Papers, co file, student conscientious objector memo

72 CQA, CFSC Papers, Military Problems Committee file, memorandum to Ottawa, n.d.

73 Ibid., co file, student conscientious objector memo

74 Ibid., Military Problems Committee file, memorandum to Ottawa

75 PAC, Department of Labour, RG 27, vol. 131, 601.3–6 vol. 2, Lavell Smith to Humphrey Mitchell, 20 March 1943

76 Ibid., Harold Toye to Mitchell, 13 April 1943

77 CQA, CFSC Papers, co file, J.B. Martin and E. Swalm, 'Report of Alternative Service Workers in BC and Alberta'

78 UCA, FOR Papers, box 2, file 24, 'Implications of the Use of Force Today,' notes of a conference with James M. Finlay at British Columbia Forest Service ASW camp Q6

79 PAC, DND, RG 24, vol.6473, HQ 1161–3–4, A. MacNamara, director of selective service, to H. Mitchell, minister of labour, February 1943

80 MacKinnon, 'Alternative Service Branch,' 2–3; under authority of order in council PC 2821, 1 May 1943

81 PAC, RG 27 vol. 131, 601.3–6, vol. 1, W.H. McLallen, President, Canadian Forestry Association to Mitchell, 24 February 1943; G.S. Raphael, Consolidated Red Cedar Shingle Association of British Columbia to Mitchell, 25 February 1943; L.R. Andrews, BC Lumber and Shingle Manufacturers Association to Mitchell, 25 February 1943; Robert McKee, BC Loggers Association, to Mitchell, 23 February 1943; W.C. Mainwaring, Provincial Civilian Protection Committee, to Ian Mackenzie, minister of pensions and national health, 22 February 1943; A. Wells Gray, British Columbia minister of lands, to LaFlèche, 29 January 1943

82 Toews, *Alternative Service in Canada*, 59–60

83 MacKinnon, 'Alternative Service Branch,' 13a

84 Ibid., 14–17. This also applied to cos allowed to return to their own farms.

85 Ibid., 4; PAC, RG 27, vol. 131, 601.3–6, vol. 2, T.C. Douglas to Mitchell, 26 May 1943. On 1 June 1945 the maximum monthly payment to the Red

Cross was reduced to five dollars for those in agriculture and fifteen dollars for those in industry. All married cos over thirty years of age were exempted entirely from Red Cross payments but remained under the jurisdiction of the alternative service officers.

86 CQA, CFSC Papers, McNinch file, Haslam to A.S. McNinch, divisional alternative service officer, 29 July 1944; UCA, FOR Papers, box 1, file 3, James Finlay to MacKinnon, 29 September 1943.

87 Toews, *Alternative Service in Canada*, 87

88 Penton, *Jehovah's Witnesses in Canada*, 169

89 MacKinnon, 'Alternative Service Branch,' 8–9, 25, 28; Penton, *Jehovah's Witnesses in Canada*, 164–71. The authorities steadfastly refused to recognize the main argument of Jehovah's Witnesses that all baptized Witnesses were ministers entitled to exemption from military service and alternative service.

90 PAC, DND, RG 24, vol. 6573, HQ 1161–3–4, G.J. Hill to Prime Minister King, 3 July 1945

91 MacKinnon, 'Alternative Service Branch,' 25–6

92 PAC, RG 27, vol. 1514, 60–34, L.E. Westman to A. MacNamara, 2 June 1944

93 PAC, RG 27, vol. 131, 601.3–4 vol. 1, C.F. Klassen to Mitchell, 2 February 1943

94 Ibid., Allen Rayner Reesor, ASW Camp, Banff, to J.W. Noseworthy, July 1943

95 PAC, RG 35, 7, vol. 27, 'History of the Corps of (Civilian) Canadian Firefighters,' 16

96 Ibid. Among those were Keith Woollard and Harvey Moats, two of the Saskatoon men originally denied co status because they were members of the United Church and Gordon Stewart, a former McGill student and editor of the *Canadian CO*. A breakdown of the cos according to denomination follows: seven Mennonites, eight United Churchmen, one Presbyterian, one Roman Catholic, one Brethren, one Brethren in Christ and one Church of Christ.

97 *Canadian CO*, August 1942, 1

98 Ibid., December 1942, 3

99 Ibid.; interview with Keith Woollard, Toronto, 25 March 1976; recorded letter, Gordon K. Stewart to author, received 7 March 1976. The co fire-fighters served overseas until the corps was demobilized in 1945. At the time most Canadians returned home but some of the cos entered relief work in Europe. Keith Woollard remained in England in order to assist Donald Soper in the London Mission.

100 *Canadian CO*, December 1942, 1, 6

101 PAC, RG 24, vol. 6573, HQ 1167-3-4, J.W. Pickersgill to Maj.-Gen. H.F.G. Letson, adjutant-general, 4 May 1943

102 order in council, PC 7251

103 FOR Papers, box 1, file 3, James Finlay to L.E. Westman, 26 July 1944; RG 24, 6573, HQ 1161-3-4, Manley J. Edwards MP to Prime Minister King, 16 February 1943. Edwards charged that even Seventh-Day Adventists were forced to undertake basic training.

104 *Reconciliation*, December 1943, 7–8

105 For a more in-depth discussion of this topic see Thomas P. Socknat, 'The Canadian Contribution to the China Convoy,' *Quaker History* (Autumn 1980).

106 PAC, DND RG 24, vol. 6573, HQ 1161-3-4, Harris to Prime Minister King, 23 April 1943

107 Ibid., J.W. Pickersgill to Letson, 4 May 1943

108 Ibid., H.R.L. Henry, private secretary to the prime minister, to Harris, 9 June 1943

109 CQA, CFSC Papers, Westman file, Westman to Haslam, 11 November 1943

110 Ibid., Tennant file, Gordon Keith to Peter Tennant, 13 January 1944 (excerpt)

111 Ibid., McClure file, McClure to Dr Liu Shih Shun, 6 April 1944

112 Ibid., Tennant file, P. Tennant to FAU Headquarters, 24 February 1944, 3

113 Organized in Toronto by the Canadian Friends Service Committee, the Canadian contingent was composed of volunteers from almost every section of Canada and represented various denominations: six United Churchmen, five Anglicans, five Friends, one Presbyterian, one Disciple of Christ, and two with no religious affiliation. Members included Ed Abbott, Walter Alexander, Joe Awmack, Russell Beck, Wes Brown, Al Dobson, Jack Dodds, Albert Dorland, Terry Dorland, Delf Fransham, Elmer Hobbs, Wilf Howarth, Russell McArthur, Vernon Mjolsness, Stan Outhouse and Francis Starr, as well as United Church ministers Doug McMurtry and George Wright, and two women, Harriet Brown and Kathleen Green.

114 CQA, CFSC Papers, G. Pifher files, D.H. Clark, executive secretary, Chinese War Relief Fund, to G. Pifher, Department of National War Services, 18 May 1944

115 Socknat, 'The Canadian Contribution to the China Convoy'

116 Toews, *Alternative Service in Canada*, 70

117 Penton, *Jehovah's Witnesses in Canada*, 178–9

118 Toews, *Alternative Service in Canada*, 73; PAC, National Parks Branch, RG

84, vol. 218, U-165–2–8, J.D.B. MacFarlane, 'Operation of ASW Camps in National Parks, Report, July 1946'

119 MacKinnon, 'Alternative Service Branch,' 23

120 CQA, CFSC Papers, CO file, Haslam to Andrew Petrie, 24 September 1943

121 Woodcock and Avakumovic, *The Doukhobors*, 320

122 Haslam, *Canadian Friends* 24

CHAPTER NINE: Relief and reconciliation

1 Constance Hayward, 'The Canadian National Committee on Refugees,' *Reconciliation*, November 1944, 7

2 Irving Abella and Harold Troper, 'The Line must be Drawn Somewhere: Canada and Jewish Refugees, 1933–9,' *Canadian Historical Review*, LX (June 1979), 207, for a full account of Canada's response to the Jewish refugee problem before the war see Irving Abella and Harold Troper, *None Is Too Many* (Toronto: Lester and Orpen Dennys, 1983).

3 Abella and Troper, *None Is Too Many*, 65, 284

4 For instance, A.A. MacLeod, who was active in the committee throughout the war years, was instrumental in the emigration of Czech intellectuals to Canada following the Munich crisis: interview with Mrs A.A. MacLeod 30 March 1976.

5 Canadian National Committee on Refugees, 'New Homes for Old', leaflet, 1941; J.R. Mutchmor, secretary of the United Church's Board of Evangelism and Social Service represented the United Church on the CNCR, and Raymond Booth of the Society of Friends served as secretary of the CNCR's promotion campaign: United Church of Canada, *Yearbook*, 1939, 34.

6 PAC, National Council of Women (NCW) Papers, 1:25, vol.80, Canadian National Committee on Refugees, bulletin no. 14, 8 April 1941

7 Interview with Ida Siegel

8 *Minutes of the Canada and Genesee Yearly Meetings of the Society of Friends*, 1941, 55

9 CQA, Canadian Friends Service Committee (CFSC) Papers, Internees File, 'Refugee Students;' For a full account of the refugees interned in Canada see Eric Koch, *Deemed Suspect* (Toronto: Methuen, 1980), and Paula Draper, 'The Accidental Immigrants: Canada and Interned Refugees' (PHD dissertation, University of Toronto, 1983).

10 C.E. Silcox, 'Young Refugees Interned in Canada,' *Canadian Friend*, January 1942, 8–9

11 *Globe* (Toronto), 11 July 1940, 1

12 The Canadian internment camps for enemy aliens were as follows (Koch,

Deemed Suspect, 263):
Camp Location
- L Quebec City, Quebec
- Q Monteith, Ontario
- T Trois Rivières, Quebec
- B Little River, New Brunswick
- I Ile aux Noix, Quebec
- N Sherbrooke, Quebec
- A Farnham, Quebec
- R Red Rock, Ontario (category A aliens only)

13 *Globe* (Toronto), 2 July 1940, 1–2
14 Ibid., 4 July 1940, 1; Koch, *Deemed Suspect*, 262
15 *Globe* (Toronto), 5 July 1940, 1; Austin Stevens, *The Dispossessed: German Refugees in Britain* (London: Barrie and Jenkins, 1975), 202–4
16 Interview with Ida Siegel, 5 February 1976, Silcox, 'Young Refugees Interned in Canada,' 9
17 Koch, *Deemed Suspect*, 126
18 CQA, CFSC Papers, Internees File, 'Refugee Students'
19 Ibid., Mary S. Milligan, London, to Barbara Walker, Toronto, 25 October 1940; Sara Bright Skilling, Winnipeg, to Haslam, 4 February 1941; Haslam to Horace G. Alexander, Birmingham, England, 22 October 1941; Raymond Booth to Haslam, 16 June 1941; and other letters
20 For many such letters see CQA, CFSC Papers, internees file
21 Ibid., E.L. Landsberg to Haslam, 26 September 1941
22 Ibid., Haslam to Horace G. Alexander, 22 October 1941; Haslam to Lt-Col. R.S.W. Fordham, 6 October 1941; U. Weil to Haslam, 11 August 1941
23 Ibid., Fordham to Haslam, 3 October 1941
24 Ibid., Fordham to Haslam, 7 October 1941
25 Ibid., Haslam to Mrs J.M. Garner, 22 October 1941; Haslam to Mrs C.B. Sissons, 23 October 1941
26 NCW Papers, I:25, vol. 80, C. Raphael, 'Report on Emigration of Interned Refugees,' 24 June 1941
27 CQA, CFSC Papers, internees file, Haslam to Fred J. Tritton, Friends Service Council, 22 October 1941
28 Ibid., Haslam to John H. Hobart, 17 December 1941
29 Ibid., H. Graham Brown, Kootenay Bay, to Haslam, 24 January 1942
30 Ibid., Haslam to Mrs J.M. Garner, 22 October 1941
31 Ibid., 'Refugee Students.' For example, Ulrich Weil had taken the matriculation exam for McGill: Weil to R. Booth, 31 July 1941.
32 PAC, NCW Papers, I:25, vol. 80, Constance Hayward to Mrs E.D. Hardy,

4 July 1941; CFSC Papers, internees file, Haslam to Mrs J.M. Garner, 5 August 1941; Jerome Davis to Haslam, 25 July 1941

33 Ibid., Hayward to Mrs E.D. Hardy, 4 July 1941

34 Ibid., Haslam to Jerome Davis, 1 August 1941

35 Ibid., Hoeniger to Haslam, 23 July 1941

36 Ibid., Haslam to Mrs C.B. Sissons, 13 August 1941; Haslam to Mrs J.M. Garner, 5 August 1941

37 Ibid., Mrs C.B. Sissons to Haslam, 3 September 1941; Laura Davis, WIL treasurer, to Haslam, 7 March 1942

38 Ibid., Hoeniger to Haslam, 12 April 1942

39 Interview with Arthur G. Dorland; interview with Mrs J. Lavell Smith; interview with Ida Siegel. Another who was interested in sponsoring a refugee student was the FCSO spokesman Gregory Vlastos: George J. Hoeniger, Chicago, to Haslam, 1 July 1941, internees file, CFSC Papers.

40 Fred Haslam, 'Refugee Camps,' *Canadian Friend*, 38 (December 1941): 9; CFSC Papers, internees file, Haslam to John H. Hobart, 17 December 1941

41 CQA, CFSC Papers, internee file, Haslam to Kathleen A. Bell, Victoria, 15 August 1941; Haslam to F.J. Cluett, Rogers Radio Tubes Ltd, Toronto, 15 August 1941

42 Ibid., Haslam to C. Hayward, 6 May 1942; Haslam to J. Davis, 7 October 1942

43 *Reconciliation*, September 1944, 4

44 Haslam, *A Record of Experience with Canadian Friends*, 66. A group of Canadian conscientious objectors, including Friends, also served in the Friends Ambulance unit in China. A discussion of this Unit appears in chapter 8.

45 Thomson, *Pioneer in Community*, 91

46 UCA, FOR Papers, Fairbairn, 'To Maintain Courage by Sharing Conviction,' bulletin no. 4; In 1946 Fairbairn confided to a friend: 'I wish very much that the Fellowship for Cooperative Community could see its way to initiate something in Canada like the Bruderhof. In another two years I would be superannuated and free, perhaps, to participate from the woodcraft end!' ibid., box 1, file 12, Fairbairn to Howey, 20 April 1946. For expressions of the interest of other pacifists, see *Reconciliation*, May 1944, 13.

47 Thomson, *Pioneer in Community*, 91

48 'Statement of Principles of the Canadian Fellowship for Cooperative Community,' quoted in Thomson, *Pioneer in Community*, 115

49 Interview with George Tatham, Toronto, 12 February 1976

50 *Reconciliation*, May 1944, 13.

51 UCA, FOR Papers, box 1, file 3, John Frank and John F. Davidson to Canadian FOR members, 16 December 1942. A one-time member of the national executive of both the FCSO and the SCM, Davidson advocated what he called a 'socially conscious pacifism': interview with John F. Davidson, Toronto, 26 October 1976

52 UCA, FOR Papers, box 1, file 3, Fellowship of Reconciliation, Canadian section, newsletter, May 1943. In May 1943 the Canadian FOR membership list included 111 members, mainly United Church, but not all exhibited a lively interest: ibid. By October 1943 Canadian membership was 250: J. Lavell Smith, 'We Launch Our New Magazine,' *Reconciliation*, October 1943, 1.

53 UCA, FOR Papers, box 1, file 3, Fellowship of Reconciliation, Canadian section, leaflet, n.d.

54 Smith, 'We Launch Our New Magazine,' 1

55 Ibid., 11

56 Ibid., 9

57 Others on the editorial committee included Isabel Alexander, Edna Barnett, Peter Gorrie, Gus Harris, and Frank McPhee, the first business manager.

59 *Reconciliation*, May 1944, 10.

60 UCA, FOR Papers, box 1, file 12, Fairbairn to Harvey Howey, 1 May 1945

61 Ibid., Fairbairn to J.M. Finlay, 10 March 1948; Fairbairn to Howey, 3 May 1948

62 Ibid., Fairbairn to Howey, 1 May 1946. It is not known if the booklet was ever published.

63 Ibid., Fairbairn to Howey, 20 April 1946; R. Edis Fairbairn, 'To Maintain Courage by Sharing Conviction,' bulletin, 19 January 1943

64 Fairbairn, bulletin no. 37, 20 February 1946. Although the bulletins were numbered consecutively, Fairbairn was inconsistent in this practice. Some issues were both dated and numbered, while others included only a number or a date.

65 In addition, Fairbairn apparently attributed a kind of divine importance to his bulletin, arguing that 'God still needs a human voice to utter to men His indignation,' and over the years he eventually came to think of himself as a 'modern day prophet' with an obligation to preach the unwelcome truth: Fairbairn, bulletin, 12 February 1944; 20 June 1948.

66 Ibid., no. 45, 20 October 1946

67 Ibid., no. 6, 22 July 1943; no. 20, 20 March 1945

68 Ibid., no. 9, 29 October 1943

69 Ibid., 1 March 1943

70 Ibid., no. 8, 24 September 1943
71 UCA, FOR Papers, box 1, file 12, Fairbairn to Howey, 6 March 1944
72 Albert D. Belden, *Pax Christi*, 2d ed. (Wallinton: Corwal Publications, 1944), 34–46
73 *Reconciliation*, October 1943, 8.
74 Fairbairn, bulletin, no.29, 20 June 1945
75 UCA, FOR Papers, box 1, file 12, Fairbairn to Howey, 30 April 1946
76 Ibid., box 1, file 3, Belden to Howey, 17 February 1944
77 Ibid., box 1, file 4, Fairbairn to Finlay, 11 October 1946; FOR notice, 24 October 1946
78 Ibid., A.J. Muste to executive committee and staff, 8 February 1946
79 *Reconciliation*, September 1944, 7.
80 Edith Fowke, *They Made Democracy Work: The Story of the Co-operative Committee on Japanese Canadians* (Toronto: Garden City Press, n.d.), 3
81 Ibid., 4–5
82 *Reconciliation*, March 1944, 13.
83 Fowke, *They Made Democracy Work*, 11
84 In 1946 Donalda MacMillan was succeeded as secretary by her husband Hugh, a former missionary in Japan.
85 While a student at the University of Saskatchewan, Fowke was attracted to the FOR by Professor Carlyle King, but she did not completely agree with the group's Christian bias. Nevertheless, once in Toronto during the war she maintained her membership in the FOR, helped edit *Reconciliation*, and became deeply involved in the effort to aid Japanese Canadians.
86 *Reconciliation*, March 1944, 15.
87 Fowke, *They Made Democracy Work*, 10–16
88 *Reconciliation*, September 1944, 6.
89 CQA, CFSC Papers, Japanese-Canadian file, Fred Haslam to Mackenzie King, John Bracken, and M.J. Coldwell, telegram, 15 October 1945
90 The orders in council were PC 7355, 7356, and 7357. Fowke, *They Made Democracy Work*, 18.
91 Ibid., 20
92 Ibid., 24
93 Interview with James M. Finlay, Toronto, 21 October 1976
94 UCA, FOR Papers, box 1, file 4, The Co-operative Committee on Japanese Canadians, Bulletin no. 7, 14 September 1946
95 *The United Church Observer*, 1 January 1944, 17
96 Ibid.
97 Brittain made Canadian appearances in 1937, 1940, and 1946.

Reconciliation, December 1943, 10; *Canadian Friend*, November 1946, 13; McMaster University Special Collections, Vera Brittain Papers, lecture contracts. For more on Vera Brittain and the Bombing Restriction Committee, see Yvonne Bennett, 'Vera Brittain and the British Pacifist Movement, 1939–1945,' (PH D dissertation, McMaster University, 1984).

98 *Reconciliation*, September 1944, 11–14
99 UCA, FOR Papers, box 1, file 3, Fellowship of Reconciliation, Canadian section, newsletter, April 1943
100 Ibid., suggested program for two-day seminar, 16–17 August 1945; ibid., box 1, file 4, program for annual conference, February 1946; box 1, file 1, program for annual conference, June 1947; FOR meeting agenda, 2 April 1948
101 Ibid., box 1, file 3, Fellowship of Reconciliation, Canadian section, 'Newsletter,' May, 1943; box 1, file 4, A.J. Muste to Finlay, 19 July 1946
102 *Reconciliation*, September 1944, 6.
103 UCA, FOR Papers, box 1, file 3, Lavell Smith to FOR national council, 18 January 1945.
104 Ibid.; National Peace Council, London, England, 'National Petition for a Constructive Peace,' August 1944
105 *Reconciliation*, April 1945, 2–5

CONCLUSION

1 J. Lavell Smith, 'Whither the FOR?' *Reconciliation*, December 1945, 14
2 Haslam, *A Record of Experience with Canadian Friends*, 65–6
3 *Minutes of the Canada and Genesee Yearly Meetings*, 1948, 20–1; CQA, CFSC Papers, war victims relief file, 'Canadian Friends and War Victims,' newspaper clipping
4 CQA, CFSC Papers, war victims relief file, newspaper clipping
5 Haslam, *A Record of Experience with Canadian Friends*, 66
6 Ibid., 67; *Reconciliation*, September 1944, 2
7 Haslam, *A Record of Experience with Canadian Friends*, 67; CQA, CFSC Papers, war victims relief file
8 CQA, CFSC Papers, Alexander file, Barbara Walker to Walter Alexander, 5 January 1946
9 UCA, FOR Papers, box 1, file 2, minutes of the FOR national council meeting, March 1951
10 Thomson, *Pioneer in Community*, 92–3
11 J.J. Brown, 'Pacifism after Hiroshima,' *Reconciliation*, July 1946, 1

12 Ibid.

13 Clare Oke, 'Pacifism Unaffected by the Possibility of Imminent Disaster,' *Reconciliation*, July 1946, 12

14 UCA, FOR Papers, box 1, file 1, Canadian Fellowship of Reconciliation, *'The Atom Bomb Demands that War Be Abolished,'* n.d.

15 Ibid., Canadian Fellowship of Reconciliation, 'Pacifist Strategy and Program in the Atomic Era'

16 Ibid.

17 Ibid., 'Memo on Cadet Training'; children of Friends and other pacifist sects were excused from cadet training in Ontario, *Minutes of the Canada and Genesee Yearly Meetings*, 1945, 42

18 'Memo on Cadet Training'

19 A.G. Watson, 'Mr Drew's Army Must Be Disbanded,' *Reconciliation*, February-March 1947, 10

20 Ibid., 11

21 Ibid.

22 SABS, Carlyle King Papers, 27:154, FOR flyer, 'Abolish Cadet Training'

23 UCA, FOR Papers, box 1, file 1, minutes of FOR national council meeting, 9 May 1947

24 B.K. Sandwell, 'Pacifism Again,' *Saturday Night*, 3 May 1947, 5. Apparently, Sandwell wrote the editorial in response to a request by Watson that *Saturday Night* present an argument against the compulsory nature of cadet training in Ontario. UCA, FOR Papers, box 1, file 1, minutes of FOR national council meeting, 9 May 1947

25 Sandwell, 'Pacifism Again'

26 UCA, FOR Papers, box 1, file 1, minutes of FOR national council meeting, 9 May 1947

27 Ibid., Fellowship of Reconciliation, Canadian section, 'Militarism Must End in Canada,' n.d.

28 Ibid., box 1, file 5, draft of a letter on behalf of the FOR to the chairman of the Chatham Board of Education, Chatham, Ontario, n.d.

29 Scott Nearing, *World Events*, September 1946, 6. Although pacifism failed to attract much support, the question of world peace itself had become a dominant issue of public concern, and even the theme of the Roman Catholic congress of cardinals in Ottawa in June 1947. Henry Somerville, 'Congress Takes Theme of Prayers for Peace,' *Saturday Night*, 7 June 1947, 16

30 UCA, FOR Papers, box 1, file 5, James Finlay to John Nevin Sayre, 19 July 1947

31 Ibid.

32 Ibid., Sayre to Finlay, 28 July 1947
33 Ibid., box 1, file 1, minutes of FOR national council meeting, 3 October 1947
34 Interview with Albert Watson
35 Interview with Carlyle King
36 Stephen Endicott, *James G. Endicott: Rebel Out of China* (Toronto: University of Toronto Press, 1980), 262
37 Ibid., 262–3
38 Ibid., 264
39 In June 1947 Charles Huestis, a FOR activist and an original member of the Alberta School of Religion, had already begun to argue that Canada should declare herself a neutral nation, refuse to allow U.S. military bases on Canadian soil, and develop lines of friendship with the Soviet Union: *Saturday Night*, 21 June 1947, 4.
40 Endicott, *Rebel Out of China*, 264

Index